Xmas 2004

To Dave,

With fond memories
of the wonder Saint Louis
in the boulangerie and all
those "baguettes traditionnes"
that became my daily bread
last summer.

Bon appetit!
Bonne lecture,

[signature]

Meine Bread

Praise for the French edition of *Good Bread Is Back*:

"It is thanks to a celebrated American historian, impassioned by French bread, that the consumer dormant in all of us has finally awakened. . . . Steven Kaplan conducts an investigation into the realm of the bakery and confirms the renaissance of the baguette. A best-seller to savor slice by slice."
    —*Madame Figaro*

"This impassioned and tasty book is also a plea for a French-style art of living, of which our American in Paris casts himself as the defender with still more fervor than the natives themselves."
    —*Quinzaine littéraire*

"In asking the question: 'What is good bread?' [Steven Kaplan] brilliantly blends history, technology, and the gustatory approach to the legend of bread, and draws evocative portraits of the principal actors of the renaissance of the bakery."
    —Jean-Claude Ribaut, food critic of *Le Monde*

"It is to an American citizen that we owe the most masterly work ever published on the genius of French bread. Its mastery lies in the immensity of the undertaking, the rigor of the research, and the incredible erudition amassed in this voyage to the heart of our national bakery."
    —Perico Lagasse, food and wine critic for *Marianne*

GOOD BREAD IS BACK

GOOD BREAD
IS BACK

A contemporary history of French bread,

the way it is made, and the people who make it

STEVEN LAURENCE KAPLAN

Translated by Catherine Porter

Duke University Press *Durham & London* 2006

© 2006 Duke University Press
Originally published as *Le retour du
bon pain: une histoire contemporaine
du pain, de ses techniques et de ses
hommes.* © Perrin, 2002.
Printed in the United States of
America on acid-free paper ∞
Designed by Amy Ruth Buchanan
Typeset in Dante by Tseng
Information Systems, Inc.
Library of Congress Cataloging-in-
Publication Data appear on the last
printed page of this book.

*Duke University Press gratefully
acknowledges the support of* THE
FLORENCE GOULD FOUNDATION,
*which provided funds toward the
translation, production, and marketing
of this book.*

*We also gratefully acknowledge the
support of* THE FRENCH MINISTRY OF
CULTURE/NATIONAL BOOK CENTER.
Ouvrage publié avec le concours du
MINISTÈRE FRANÇAIS CHARGÉ DE LA
CULTURE — CENTRE NATIONAL DU
LIVRE.

For Marie-Christine

Contents

Introduction

A LAMENT OF LONG STANDING WAS THE STARTING point for this book. As early as the mid-1970s, I began to notice that French bread, which I loved with a passion, was unmistakably deteriorating in quality. I had a history with bread that probably made me more alert than ordinary consumers and more apt to notice change. As a young historian, I had worked on bread; I had touched crumbs from loaves made in the eighteenth century that were still hiding in the seams of account books kept by bakers (and even more often by their wives[1]) — holy relics that scorched my fingers. Above and beyond this archaizing mystical adoration, I also had a modicum of practical experience: I had worked dough with my own hands in two Paris bakeries during internships lasting several weeks each. For years afterward, I dropped in on bakers who were willing to have me. On July 11, 1969, I almost missed my son's birth because I spent the whole afternoon with Pierre Poilâne. More recently famous for his large sourdough loaves, Master Poilâne was then still making glorious golden-brown *bâtards* whose dense *mie* (crumb) exploded with aromas evocative of harvests and dried fruit. On weekends in Paris I used to taste and rate baguettes and *bâtards* from five or six bakeries. I was rarely satisfied; I often found the bread inedible, and threw it away. No doubt about it, I was a pain in the ass. I would ask the baker's wife to tell me how her husband made his bread; frequently, she had only the vaguest notion. Worse still, fascinated by the epidemic of underweight bread that occurred in the eighteenth century, I would ask her to weigh the bread she was selling me: this almost always triggered an angry invitation to leave the premises at once.

These experiments, repeated many times over, were the source of twin disappointments, both hedonistic and moral. I was enraptured and exalted by good bread. It excited all my senses; it spurred dreams. Delighting body and spirit alike, it inscribed deep traces of beauty and joy, Proustian moments that immobilized time. Good bread was sufficient unto itself, at any hour of the day; it needed no accompaniment, not even butter. It jealously satisfied all desires: *vox panis, vox dei.* And yet the pleasure of finding it and eating it was now becoming rare. I felt this abandonment of quality to be a betrayal of a certain idea of France that I cherished. I was as indignant as I was disappointed. France did not have the right to do this to me, I felt. How could it allow a decline in the quality of this literally divine delicacy, this precious element of its patrimony, this somewhat hackneyed but historically accurate metaphor for Frenchness?

Prudently, I said little about my despairing, negative judgment of bread. I was afraid of being perceived as the stereotypical "ugly American": arrogant, critical, a know-it-all. Perhaps I was wrong to idealize my subject. Most people close to the world of breadmaking, not to mention the popular press, proved quite reticent about the decline in the quality of bread when the subject came up around 1970. It was almost a crime against the motherland to address the issue frankly. Unsurprisingly, one of the most vehement denunciations of the "modern" decline in bread quality — a double-edged consolation, for me — was offered by an American journalist, Meg Bortin, writing in the now-defunct weekly *Paris Métro.* If daily per capita consumption went down from 750 grams[2] (some say 900) at the end of the nineteenth century to under 150 grams in Paris at the end of the twentieth, it was not only because an improvement in the standard of living had made a more diversified diet possible. "One thing is certain," Bortin wrote, "the quality of the bread here is going downhill . . . *le pain n'a plus de goût* [bread no longer has any taste]." Might it be that taste no longer mattered to the consuming public? With unmistakable, though wounded, disdain, Meg Bortin noted that "despite what seems to be overwhelming acceptance of this miserable situation on the part of the French, excellent bread is still to be found in Paris."[3]

During this time, in the small world of breadmaking professionals, Raymond Calvel and a handful of other experts made bold to express their dismay at "the dramatic decline of the gustatory qualities of bread, starting in the period 1957–1969." I became aware of this specialized literature only in the early 1990s, when I was working on a history of Paris bakeries in the eighteenth century. Its title, *Le meilleur pain du monde* (The Best Bread in the World), underscored my distress and disenchantment over the degradation of this noble product (noble because eminently popular). Much more important for the mobilization of public opinion—and very reassuring for me—was the publication of Jean-Pierre Coffe's *Au secours le goût* (Taste Needs Help) in 1992. On the French side, no one denounced "the degeneration of the quality of bread" more passionately than Coffe, as if to atone for the delay in the national reaction. I shared his horror at eating insipid baguettes "without joy, without feeling, without appetite."[4] Still, just when Coffe was having his say, a few signs surfacing here and there suggested that breadmaking might be about to undergo a renewal. These encouraging hints led me to look more closely into the reasons for such a profound crisis and at the efforts to overcome it that were converging from various horizons.

It has been thirty-five years since, as a young doctoral student wildly enthusiastic about France, I first tackled bread. Not that I confused France with "Monsieur Rougeaud," a stout red-faced fellow with a beret on his head, a Gauloise in his mouth, and a baguette under his arm. (Even so, I am more strongly convinced than ever that the historical trajectory of the "panivore" played a considerable role in the construction of French identity.) I focused on bread because I was looking for a way to get straight to the heart (and thus to the stomach) of the major concerns of French people under the Old Regime: the have-nots and the haves, subjects and princes. Social life depended on cereals in myriad critical ways. Grain dominated the economy: in addition to its determining role in the agricultural sector, it influenced the development of commerce and industry, directly and indirectly; it regulated employment and constituted a major source of revenue for the state, the church, the nobility, and a large fraction of the third estate. Subsistence needs account amply for this dependence. The vast majority of people drew the bulk of their calories—their survival ration—from grains. Yet nothing was more uncertain than crops, and even an apparently abundant harvest was not enough to stave off anxiety, for the modalities of distribution were complicated by a host of risks, both natural and artificial—that is, human. The disquieting precariousness of life did as much as actual privation and chronic penury to set the tone.

The compelling need to secure food supplies marked the social organization, the administration, and the ideology of pre-Revolutionary France in a decisive way. Daily life was tied to the necessity of getting bread. Most peasants bought grain instead of selling it; it would be wrong to suppose that the distribution of food was a concern only for towns and urban areas. Fear of famine tormented the authorities as much as the consumer population, and it wove strange bonds of solidarity among these protagonists. As the harvest was an affair of state, provisioning was a political problem: no question had greater mobilizing and destabilizing force than penury — or the fear of want. For its scale and its implacable predictability, nothing could compare with the massive daily gatherings over which the police presided more or less discreetly. In Paris, tens of thousands of people visited the shops every day and the markets twice a week, routinely creating a peaceful commotion that spared no street and perhaps no building in the city. Consumers were as much clients of the police as clientele of the bakers. Their demands were simple and unchanging: they wanted bread of good quality, in sufficient quantity, and at a reasonable price. Mediating between buyers and sellers, the police orchestrated from on high a triangular relation of reciprocity and suspicion, hope and anguish, submission and rebellion.

The maintenance of order on a daily basis ultimately relied on what I have called the social contract. In this solemn exchange, which defined and structured the relations between state and society under the Old Regime, consumers were subject to taxation, conscription, and other forms of extraction; they acquiesced in a more generalized form of submission and docility, as long as they could be confident that they would not be allowed to starve to death. As a nurturing prince, the embodiment of the state, the king became not the provider of everyday foodstuffs (although he oversaw the mechanisms that served the purpose) but the baker of last resort. The women who marched to Versailles in October 1789 understood the king's role and its meaning perfectly: insisting that the contract be respected, they forced the royal family — "the baker, the baker's wife, and the baker's boy" — to return to Paris.[5]

While the imperative of subsistence held society hostage, vulnerability to shortages still did not mean that people ate more or less anything they could get. For eighteenth-century Parisians, bad bread was an intolerable insult and a threat. As surely as a rise in prices, a lowering in bread quality was a sign of disarray. Various reports refer to consumers who brandished frightful "black breads" in the central market area, the Halles, during the May 1775 riots: their bread had become a toxic substance that was infecting the belly of Paris. It was so unusual to see such disgusting and offensive bread in the capital, even in the midst of a crisis, that some police officials suspected that it had not been made in the city but had been imported from outside. Friends of Turgot, the minister who attempted to deregulate the grain and flour trades even as he brutally repressed the uprising, contributed to the rumors; they attributed the obscene bread to evil conspirators determined to discredit Turgot's liberal policies.

It is hardly surprising that Jacques Necker (in certain respects an anti-Turgot, Necker had the same responsibilities as his liberal predecessor on the eve of the Revolution) was so intent on tracking down sources of good quality supplies, anywhere in the kingdom. To be sure, he could have gotten hold of Polish wheat mixed with rye; it could — just barely — have produced a strange-looking and strange-tasting dark bread. But he was afraid that "the inhabitants of Paris would be of one mind as they discovered how it differed from the bread they were used to." The political impact of this physiological and cultural alienation could have proved worse than shortages. A vivid memory of bread that had been both better and cheaper was a leitmotif of pamphlets that circulated in 1789. In 1793, nothing marked the limits of the Revolution and of counter-revolutionary subversion more powerfully than the fact that "for some time [people] have been eating grayish bread of poor quality that smells dusty and gives most people a stomach-ache."[6] Concern with quality was a matter of ordinary dignity, not a question of luxury or displaced envy. At all events, the tyranny of bread was as much symbolic as material. To borrow images from Pascal, if "the cords of necessity" held consumers to the yoke, "the cords of imagination" bound them just as tightly.

Bread is located at the crossroads between the material and the symbolic, between economics and culture. Under the Old Regime, the population did not live on bread alone, even if bread was a major factor in keeping it alive. Bread was at the heart of pressing material preoccupations, but at the same time it bore an immense symbolic charge. It conveyed a host of significations that ultimately distinguished it from all other goods, including absolute "essentials."

Even if other foodstuffs were available, as the *Encyclopédie méthodique* noted in 1789, "most people believe[d] they [would] die of hunger if there [were] no bread."[7] Attached exclusively to bread by the "cords of the imagination," the French of today, too, have trouble imagining a real meal without bread. Bread was not simply a matter of calories and nutritious ingredients for the consumers of yesteryear: the same thing can be said today. Crystallizing collective identity as well as individual destiny, bread forges complex links between the sacred and the profane, hope and anguish, whole and part, mother and child, prince and subject, producer and consumer, seller and buyer, justice and injustice.

Bread bears the indelible and ineffable mark of the sacred, apart from any denominational associations — even if the Eucharist endows it with the most spectacularly effective property, for the vast majority of believers. Commonly associated with the human body as well as with the divine, bread is a hyphen between life and death, linking the here and now to the hereafter. As "Living Bread," among many other things, Jesus was "a nurturing God who addressed a population suffering from a chronic dearth of food." "This is my body," Christ said of bread when he instituted the Eucharist. Nothing in Christian worship is more moving than the moment of communion, when believers and their God become one through the intermediary of bread and wine. The model of the Eucharist undoubtedly reinforces the conviction that bread alone can perpetuate life in its deepest sense: that food only acquires providential force and status when it takes the form of bread.[8]

Quasi-liturgical practices became widespread in the daily routine of breaking bread. The most familiar example is the custom of tracing the sign of the cross over bread with the point of a knife. To avoid any reversals of fortune, believers went to great pains not to turn a loaf of bread upside down, as if to do so would have been a gesture of profanation. It was sacrilegious to waste bread, not to use all the leftovers in soup or in some other dish, unless the excess was given away as alms. The gesture of offering consecrated bread stressed the link between material and spiritual concerns, highlighting the sanctification of bread along with the social obligations it imposed. This sacrificial ritual had a redistributive function, although its detractors claimed that most of the consecrated bread never got to the needy folk for whom it was intended.

In the eighteenth century, someone's well-earned disgrace could be referred to as "blessed bread," "a godsend." Apart from its sacred meta-phorical vocation, bread left its mark on everyone's thinking, conveying all sorts of notions: health, fortune, intelligence, hearth, family, love, work, joy, relative value, and so on. For the eighteenth-century scientist Dr. Paul-Jacques Malouin, who relied on Greek and Hebrew as well as current usage, life and bread were "synonymous terms." In the same spirit, Voltaire said of a Jesuit opponent that he "did me the honor of printing in Lyon two volumes against me to earn some bread (I do not believe it was white bread)."

When he was asked why he was carrying a hammer, a master locksmith who had been arrested by the police in May 1775 explained: "It's my bread." In 1739, about a day laborer who had fled, it was said that he was "neither at his bread nor at his wages." With the Enlightenment, the *Babillard* observed, "the art of thinking and writing has become a way of earning one's bread," a livelihood. After World War II, the expression *gagne-bifteck* (steak-earner) came into fashion in place of *gagne-pain* (bread-earner) as a way of describing someone's job; the shift from bread to steak marks the considerable socioeconomic distance traversed in two centuries (well before the age of mad cows and a new set of fears about food, the eclipse of bread in favor of steak signified providential progress).

A person who is gravely ill has lost "the taste for bread." A man who is well along in years "has baked more than half his bread." A guileless person is "as good as bread." A marvelous individual is "better than good bread." A taciturn, doleful person "has lost his bread in the oven." A young woman who is pregnant out of wedlock "has borrowed a loaf from the batch." (In Alsace, in the nineteenth century, couples in a hurry "took loaves from the batch," but some men learned at their own expense that "the one who heats the oven isn't always the one who bites into hot bread.")

Tropes like these evolved imperceptibly into a host of proverbs characterizing a wide range of behaviors. To "eat your white bread first" is to have an easy life before running into difficulties. To "eat one's bread right out of the bag" is to demonstrate a deplorable degree of selfishness. To say that one is tired of an experience, one can say that "it's as long as a day without bread." Someone who raises vain hopes "promises more butter than bread." To indicate the right to help himself to a neighbor's bread, some-one may say that "cut bread has no master"—a whole political program in one sentence!⁹

Another adage: "If you put it in the oven the wrong way round, you'll get bread with horns": in other words, it is hard to fix something that has gotten off to a bad start. Here is a lesson that artisanal bakers might have done well to contemplate as they were failing to raise the low level of bread quality during the last few decades of the twentieth century. Still, even in this stricken landscape we must not forget that a certain number of artisans managed to resist the slump. In Paris, these included the Poilânes, Ganachauds, Poujaurans, and others of their ilk. I say very little about them in this book precisely because they never stopped making good bread. Proud, creative, and exacting, they knew how to give priority to tastes and smells, to the pleasure and confidence associated with a legendary past. The exemplary case—but at the same time an exceptional case, given his breadmaking and marketing strategies—is that of the late Lionel Poilâne, probably the most prestigious baker of his time.

Lionel Poilâne deserves a book all to himself. His father Pierre, intuitive and offbeat, had founded a thriving business. But Lionel's career did not begin on a blissful note: he *had* to be a baker. Without ever putting it in so many words, his father had not given him a choice. Lionel felt "trapped, at a dead end," until he thought of a way to "bring the world into the trade" and then to transform some aspects of the trade in light of his views about the world. These youthful "illuminations" were enriched by an authentic philosophy inspired by the notion of bread-as-civilization. In their technological dimension, they led to the idea of "retro-innovation," which allowed Poilâne to reconcile artisanal practices (long sourdough fermentation, baking in wood ovens, and so on) with production on a quasi-industrial scale. In their commercial dimension, Poilâne's ideas led to an astonishingly simple and effective concept: large, brownish loaves leavened with sourdough culture according to a traditional recipe that was very specific but that left his bakers, trained in artisanal "good sense," the leeway to compensate as necessary for the different variables. Fleshy, tender, with a taste that lingers in the mouth, bursting with odors of spices and hazelnut, Poilâne's *miche* (round loaf) is known throughout the world. In addition to his two shops in the sixth and fifteenth arrondissements in Paris, his bread is found in countless supermarkets, in hundreds of bistros, and in all the countries of the planet, transported by plane (special delivery) within forty-eight hours of baking.

Lionel Poilâne attributed the collapse and disgrace of French bread to unfavorable (but not insurmountable) circumstances and to faltering actors (with some exceptions). World War II constituted an "unimaginable" break. In its aftermath, "peoples' heads were elsewhere." Once reconstruction was under way, as they encountered a consumer society and a proliferation of items on offer, bread eaters "lost their bearings." Bread was no longer a secondary but a "tertiary" commodity, and it no longer commanded the same "vigilance." Instead of reacting by asserting their values and skills, most bakers took the easy way out: they managed to earn a living with increasingly risky methods, but they sold their artisanal heritage off cheaply. In a pastiche of a passage by the poet Charles Baudelaire, Lionel Poilâne described such bakers as "reverse alchemists" who transformed gold into mud. Poilâne identified more with the idea of the artisan baker than with the actual trajectories of the artisanal bakers who were his contemporaries. He had little affinity with their "baguettocentrism" (he reproached them with "memory loss") or with professional organizations (the bakers' association "had not wanted anything to do with [him]" when he had approached it earlier, and the experience hurt). Despite his reservations about the *return* of good bread—"you never go backward"—he was quite prepared to recognize that there were many signs of a renewal in breadmaking, especially "the new approach by way of quality."[10]

A handful of artisans could not lift up an entire profession. The crisis into which artisanal baking plunged starting in the 1970s had been long in the making. The principal sign, a crude measure (for it did not take social and demographic differences into account, and the data on which it was based were often of doubtful origin), was the average consumption of bread per person per day. At the end of the eighteenth century, estimates varied enormously, given the extreme variability of the population in question and the imprecision of the available measuring tools. The figures ranged, *grosso modo*, between one and three pounds, the latter corresponding more or less to the dosage needed to support hard labor.[11] Taking all bread eaters taken together, I very much doubt that per-person consumption averaged more than 900 grams a day on the eve of the Revolution—and this is precisely the figure often given for the end of the nineteenth century. If this estimate is more or less reliable, it means that the process of social and alimentary modernization, which necessarily includes the desacralization of bread, began in France only quite late. Whatever the case, what interests us more immediately here is the continued decline that can be observed from the turn of the twentieth century to the end of the 1990s, when daily per capita consumption had fallen below 150 grams.

While this book retraces the age-old story of a fall and a resurrection, the trajectory is not a linear one, nor does it entail a struggle between the forces of Good and the axis of Evil. Our story begins with an interpretation of this uninterrupted decline, which is one of the principal markers and (intermediary) causes of the crisis in artisanal breadmaking (chapter 2). First of all, structural factors were inscribed in the development of many western European countries, such as a considerable reduction in the need for calories, major improvements in the conditions of everyday comfort, social ascension, and dietary diversification. In addition, bread was increasingly marginalized owing to the anathema cast on it by a large part of the medical establishment, especially in its white version. Finally (and this last point remains the most controversial and the most difficult to demonstrate conclusively), many consumers evinced a conspicuous loss of interest in bread. This rejection, spurred by the loss of quality, owes little to a desire on the part of consumers to assert their adherence to socio-economic modernity by cutting "the cords of necessity" through a gesture of symbolic violence. A handful of bakers in western France came up with the post-war "solution," probably a myopic one but logical enough nonetheless: bread that was whiter than white, voluminous and beautiful, the exact opposite of the miserable wartime loaf. But this "Western" tale (chapter 3) ends badly: it traps artisanal breadmaking in the vicious circle of mechanization, one of the forms of exaggerated modernization that all of France embraced, thinking it had found a way to guarantee a glorious future.

Disenchantment set in gradually among the artisans. This "progress" did nothing to stop the decline in consumption; worse still, it gave rise to rival forces—industrial production and large-scale supermarket distribution of bread—that stole market shares from the artisans, whose numbers began to decline. The same modernization that allowed their new competitors to flourish ensnared the bakers, who had believed they would find their bliss by following the same path. Never having had to confront competition on such a scale and with such a level of efficiency, the artisanal bakers succumbed to confusion and depression (chapter 4). To combat its unexpected new enemies, the profession appealed to its hereditary enemy.

Historically subject to control by the state, the artisan bakers believed for a long time that their salvation lay in their emancipation from regulations, especially price-fixing, not only in order to save their trade, but in the name of a sort of French sociocultural exception in which their role went beyond that of simple commodity producers (chapter 5). Even before the resurgence of the bakers' association and the state's entry into the lists, other actors intervened, millers in particular. They too were extremely concerned about the steady decline in consumption; persuaded that the historic immobility of the artisanal sector would prevent it from coming to grips, the millers decided to take the renewal in hand. If the "Banetti-zation" of breadmaking was a profound transformation but also a translation of the perpetually strained relations between millers and bakers, many artisans found the relation of servitude humiliating (chapter 6). In another sign of a renaissance, a corps of mavericks emerged, young bakers who practiced "quality" along the lines laid out by their great predecessors (chapter 7).

But before we begin to study this dense saga, we must take a look at bread itself (chapter 1). To clarify my analysis and to take advantage of my background as a historian, in this book I shall frequently shift between past and present, between the Old Regime and the contemporary world. These juxtapositions and comparisons turn out to be particularly useful in the discussion of how bread is made. For more and more often, in our day, artisanal bakers invoke "ancestral" or "old-style" practices. After examining the techniques of yesteryear, I shall trace the evolution of breadmaking: modifications, innovations, betrayals, expiations. If we are to appreciate bread as fully as possible, it seems to me that we need to equip ourselves with ways of talking about it more coherently and more boldly. Despite all the risks that this implies, it is probably time to create an authentic taxonomy for bread tasting, with a more or less standardized vocabulary for differentiation and evaluation. I shall thus propose a flexible grid whose only purpose is to help consumers better express their preferences or to broaden their palette of flavors and aromas. I ask indulgence in advance for a few lyrical flights in my descriptions of bread, where I let myself get carried away by love for my subject.

chapter one

Good Bread:
Practices and Discourses

L ET US GO INTO THE NARROW, OPPRESSIVE SPACE OF an eighteenth-century baking room. In Paris, this probably means heading down into an ill-ventilated basement, lit by the few candles grudgingly granted by the owner's wife, who kept the accounts. Even though the conditions may have already been less difficult in her day, George Sand did not find the expression "dark dungeon" too strong. The work was hard and often mind-numbing. Someone had to prepare wood for the fire, then light it, draw water, handle bags of flour weighing nearly 150 kilos, then knead 100 kilos or more with his hands and sometimes his feet. The baker's boy responsible for the kneading was called *le geindre*, the groaner, because of the sounds he made while he worked: "A kind of painful cry," Sand called it, "you'd think you were witnessing the final scene of a murder." From the worker's standpoint, this "forced labor" came under the heading of criminal behavior: "Night, a time of rest, is a time of torture for us," bakers' "boys"—journeymen—complained in 1715, and the refrain was echoed throughout the nineteenth century by others protesting this "nocturnal slavery," this morally and physically destructive "captivity."[1]

In the mid-eighteenth century, bakers' assistants working for Mistress Lapareillé began their day at 11:30 P.M.; those working for Masters Marreux and Barré started at midnight. Another master worked with his *compagnons*, or journeymen, almost without interruption from 8:00 P.M. to 7:00 A.M. Constantly on the job, obliged to stop the breadmaking process and start it up again, tormented by a powerful need to rest that they could satisfy only sporadically, the assistants usually slept in the bakeries, as did journeyman Martin Macadrez, who went to bed at 7:00 A.M. "above the oven." This was the hellish rhythm of a society that lived on bread, that could not get along without it for a moment.

The air in the bakery was heavy, sometimes thick with flour dust and sometimes suffocatingly humid. When the oven was in use, the heat was overwhelming. Apprentices worked in rough underclothing (often made of old flour sacks) and dripped with sweat, enriching (or infecting) the dough. Before baking began, especially in winter, the bakery was damp and freezing cold. The environment was as unhealthy as the work was exhausting. Louis-Sébastien Mercier, a chronicler of eighteenth-century Parisian ways, was struck by the contrast between butchers' boys, who were sturdy, ruddy fellows, and bakers' boys, who could be seen in shop doorways looking wretched, haggard, and pale, like flour-drenched scare-crows. The baking room was usually cluttered with tools, work surfaces, and supplies. There was just enough room to maneuver and carry out the simplest operations. Sometimes the workers could barely stand upright.

Let us visit the bakery of Master Briquelot, on Rue Saint-Martin, around 1730, in a house he rented for the tidy sum of 850 pounds per year.[2] This was a tiny, dilapidated, windowless room made smaller still by ad hoc re-pairs. The ceiling had had to be reinforced by an improvised trellis made of planks and poles: "As the plank is very low," a police officer noted, "it is very hard to work without bumping one's head; the workers have to limit their movements and bend over in order to knead."[3]

Today, a baker's work is only rarely a "prison," and bakers do not die as Master Philibert Rouget did in the middle of the night, "worn out" at the age of forty. Still, while it is no longer "hell," now as then the bakery is located behind the shop or in the basement, although a growing num-ber of enterprising craftsmen have installed part of their workspace in the shop itself in order to create both a sense of transparency and a theatri-cal atmosphere. But many bakers still remain flour-coated cave dwellers, working in the sort of underground baking room that Antoine-Augustin Parmentier deplored at the end of the eighteenth century, a space so nar-row that you can hardly manipulate the paddle, so hot that the dough melts as it rises, so dark that you can't see much of anything, so suffo-cating that you can hardly breathe. Room for storing flour is still a problem, although today's bakers no longer need a place to bolt and mix, for these tasks are now done by millers. Certain eighteenth-century master bakers already practiced some of the sophisticated channeling systems in use today for stocking flour and bringing it to the kneading trough. No baker can get along without a kneading trough and an oven. Today's versions are mechanized and modernized, but they remain recognizable as kneading troughs and ovens. The dividing machines, shaping machines, resting compartments, and refrigeration units would be more astonishing to workers of the Old Regime. But paddles, wicker trays, canvas carpets, spatulas, pastry cutters, knives, and brushes belong to bakeries of all eras.[4]

Definitions

Defining bread is a concern for modern specialists, not for consumers, who let themselves be guided by their practical sense of things. In the eighteenth century, even for experts, the problem was not how to define bread but how to make it properly. Foreign travelers and local commentators all praised Parisian bread as the best in the world. But the scientists who were beginning to be interested in this staple asserted, to the great displeasure of bakers, that "their art [was] still in the cradle." While a self-taught but imaginative practitioner such as César Bucquet instinctively felt that "a Baker would have to be really inept if he couldn't make good bread with good ingredients," Parmentier, as a laboratory scientist, deplored the cruel want of an "enlightened work force," which counted for "infinitely more than the quality of the raw materials used." It fell to men of science to teach bakers to make bread. "Making bread from wheat is a chemical operation that has to be explained by chemists; blind routines denature the process," Mercier notes. The "popular errors" and "blind routines" that Parmentier and Cadet de Vaux, his collaborator in the creation of a school for bakers, intended to stamp out were no less than "trade secrets passed along from father to son," the basis of the wisdom of the profession.[5]

At the dawn of the twentieth century, French people generally had faith in bakers and their way of working. But to protect the public and codify breadmaking practices for the benefit of the profession, the experts proposed a quasi-legal definition of bread during the International Congress for the Suppression of Fraud (1908–1909): "The word *bread*, without any other qualifier, is exclusively reserved for the product resulting from cooking dough made with a mixture of wheat flour, sourdough culture or yeast (made from beer or grain), drinking water, and salt."

Half a century later, under the aegis of the French National Center for Coordination of Studies and Research on Food and Nutrition (CNERNA), one of the largest groups of experts ever gathered together to talk about bread took another look at this definition. This time, the goal was less to suppress fraud than to take stock of technological innovations in milling and baking and to reassure consumers, who had been shaken as much by the shadow of doubt that various critics had cast over bread's healthfulness and quality as by their own experience of the very bad bread available during World War II. Torn between science and public relations, participants worried, for example, about the growing rumor that bread was contaminated and adulterated by toxic or even cancer-causing substances, in particular so-called chemical yeast, which was either demonized in itself or confused with baking powder. "People shouldn't think that when we put a package of yeast in the kneading trough we are adding something forbidden," a participant warned, "whereas if we just put in a 'natural' leavening agent the operation is legal." Speakers suggested referring to a "fermenting agent" (sourdough culture and/or yeast) in the revised definition, although another expert feared that for an uninformed public the idea of "fermentation" might be "very dangerous." Someone else suggested using the term "living yeast" rather than evoking an anxiety-producing fermentation process.[6]

CNERNA's work continued almost to the end of the 1970s. According to *Le recueil des usages concernant les pains en France*, a code of customs surrounding bread that was included in the proceedings of a 1977 colloquium,

> the word "bread" without any other qualifier is reserved for the product that results from cooking the dough obtained by kneading a mixture of wheat flours intended for breadmaking, and corresponding to an officially defined type; drinking water; cooking salt; and a fermenting agent. This mixture may include certain adjuvants and/or additives of which limited use is authorized in the fabrication of bread for ordinary consumption.

While the Direction générale de la concurrence, de la consommation et de la répression des fraudes (a government agency dealing with competition, consumption, and the suppression of fraud) has added clarifications here and there, this definition is still the standard one today.[7]

From Defining to Producing: Fermentation Is the Key

Like the definition of bread, the process of breadmaking itself has not evolved very much in its fundamentals. Even if they have modified working procedures, altered methods, and introduced mechanical equipment, good bakers today can relate to the environment in which bread was made in the past and to the principal steps in the process. Michel Perrier, a virtuoso baker in Dordogne, used to maintain that "the baker's real skill lies in the way he manages fermentation." Parmentier spoke of this much earlier as "the soul of breadmaking." In other words, the quality of the bread produced depends in large part on the fermentation process. Fermentation offers ongoing proof that bread is literally a living thing, impossible to reproduce exactly, difficult to master without demonstrated knowledge and skill. While the great French microbiologist Louis Pasteur discovered the micro-organisms that induce fermentation, we know about fermentation of bread in allegorical terms in particular through the story of the ancient Hebrews, who discovered by accident that a bit of dough left behind in a container had produced a light bread that tasted good. Dough that remains exposed to the air is transformed: it swells up and becomes somewhat sour, like milk that takes on flavor when it is left to age, or crushed grape juice, which tastes sweet and sour at the same time. The same process of fermentation lies behind a large number of foodstuffs: certain cheeses, yogurt, wine, beer, cider, and vinegar. These organic bodies all contain carbon, which mixes with oxygen during fermentation and forms carbon dioxide, a particularly crucial factor in the fermentation of bread dough.[8]

The bread of the Hebrews began to ferment because the flour contained an enzyme—a biochemical catalyst of protein origin—called amylase, which acts on the starch in the flour and transforms it into a sugar called maltose. In the breadmaking we know, about 5 percent of the starch granules are damaged in the grinding process; these tend to decompose rapidly and are then converted into sugar. The fermentation that takes place in the bakery occurs when the maltose and other sugars naturally present in flour break down and are converted into carbon dioxide and alcohol. The action of the micro-organisms called yeasts—yeast being one kind of fermenting agent—can accelerate this natural transformation, which is rather slow, either wild yeasts (which are found in air, soil, grain, and flour) or yeasts developed from beer (the eighteenth-century approach), grains (nineteenth century), or molasses (twentieth century). The sugars already in the flour (no more than 1 to 2 percent of its weight) are transformed by enzymes contained in the yeasts, especially zymase, which quickly breaks down all the simple sugars at the same time that the starch in the flour is being converted into simple sugars, a fairly complex chain reaction initiated by the amylases when they are activated by contact with water in the kneading trough. The nature of the flour (which is highly variable in its enzymatic strength), the temperature, the quantity of water, and the length of fermentation all condition the work of the amylases. The fermenting agents—the yeasts—can only create the carbon dioxide that causes the dough to rise when they are nourished by the simple sugars (glucose, for example) produced by these multiple decompositions.

During fermentation, the dough swells (puffs up) and develops. Along with the kneading that precedes and the baking that follows, fermentation gives the dough its characteristic physical structure, owing to the release of carbon dioxide, in the form of a supple alveolate crumb surrounded by crust. During kneading, carbon dioxide seeks to escape but is held back by gluten, an elastic substance in the protein family. Ordinary breadmaking flour contains 8 to 14 percent gluten; an astute baker tries to get a flour that has good gluten content and thus adequate gas-retaining power. During fermentation, the physical qualities of the dough evolve. The glutinous mesh formed during kneading undergoes modifications. The baker tries to find the right balance between the dough's elasticity (its capacity to expand enough to retain and store carbon dioxide)—which is gradually diminishing—and its tenacity (its resistance to deformation, the property that keeps the dough from tearing under the pressure of the gas)—which is gradually increasing. The baker tries to maintain both suppleness and body, good resistance in the dough and good tolerance: the dough should be able to withstand all the accidents and manipulations (by machines and hands alike) that occur in this extremely delicate process. The baker wants fermentation to produce the right volume of carbon dioxide to generate a strong gaseous impulse (spring) when the bread first starts to bake. During baking, the gluten will coagulate, imprisoning the air and the carbon dioxide, and the grains of starch will swell up, burst, and harden, forming a starchy substance (the crumb). By rising at the same time that it takes shape as a solid, the dough, transmuted into bread, will definitively maintain the alveolated structure—marked by uneven cavities engraved into the crumb, the memory sites of fermentation—that it was given by pressure from the expanding carbon dioxide within. Beautiful to the eye, well developed and properly baked, bread should also be able to boast of its goodness, for when fermentation takes place as it should, it generates organic acids that inscribe aromas in the dough, enriching its taste and even determining its flavor.[9]

Working Methods: Using Sourdough Culture (*Levain*)

Fermentation may be handled in a number of different ways. The baker's choice determines the recipe, or, more broadly speaking, the procedure, the way in which the work is organized. The *direct* method, a relatively recent approach, is the one most commonly used today. It is the simplest of the fermentation techniques, requiring no advance preparation. The baker seeds the dough *directly* with a suitable amount of industrial yeast (known as baker's yeast), equivalent to 1–3 percent of the weight of the flour. The time needed for fermentation is governed both by the amount of yeast used and the temperature of the dough. The chief advantage of the direct method is that each batch can be handled independently; this offers considerable flexibility for the organization of tasks in the baking room. Associated with the modernization of the breadmaking industry, the direct method is implicitly defined in opposition to the canonical approach to breadmaking—the only legitimate one in the eyes of someone like Parmentier—in which the procedure is based on a sourdough culture and each batch depends intimately on an earlier one.[10]

Sourdough is dough that does not require the injection of baker's yeast in order to begin the fermentation process. Fermentation takes place owing to the presence of wild yeasts and bacteria in the raw materials used or in the baking room environment. The sourdough is perpetuated by systematic and successive refreshments (or enrichments) that ensure the selection and reproduction of the flora, which are essentially constituted by a symbiotic association of sourdough's acidifying bacteria (lactic and acetic) and its own yeasts. The dough rises less than a dough made with baker's yeast and also more slowly. Its crust is thicker. It keeps significantly longer. It has greater nutritional value, partly because it is richer in certain vitamins and enzymes that are by-products of lactic fermentation, and it contains less phytic acid, which blocks mineral absorption. Sourdough bread tastes robust, rustic, slightly but agreeably acidic, sometimes with an aftertaste—depending on the baker's technique—hinting at the fruit that triggered the fermentation process.

Today, the baker who wants to begin producing sourdough bread has to create a starter culture (*levain chef*); in a batch of dough mixed from flour and water alone, fermentation originates from bacteria in the flour or in the baking room. The baker renews this matrix over a period of several days, kneading part of the sourdough with flour and water each time. Bakers do this only when a new starter has to be made from scratch. In practice, the *chef* is usually taken from an existing batch of dough that has been seeded in the same way from an earlier batch, and so on. Beyond the burden of the work itself, the sourdough method imposes an extremely heavy constraint: since each batch depends on a previous one, any defects in the dough are inevitably reproduced.[11]

If we follow Parmentier, we shall be tempted to conclude that the history of French breadmaking since the late eighteenth century is nothing but a long, undramatic apostasy. Normally, eighteenth-century Parisian bakers refreshed their *chef* three or four times during the kneading process. The operation included incorporating water and flour into the sourdough in order to multiply the fermenting agents, develop acidity, and give the mixture more strength. The sourdough *chef* required from twelve to fifteen hours to ripen. The stage called the first leaven followed; after six to seven hours, it could be added to a batch for the second leaven, which required four or five hours—although even in the mid-eighteenth century it is unlikely that most bakers found the time to respect such draconian standards. A final leavening stage (*toutpoint*) rarely took more than an hour.

The chief disadvantage of fermentation based on sourdough was the exorbitant amount of time it required. Parmentier was a fierce partisan of this method, but even he deplored the "painful enslavement" that it imposed on bakers, who could never rest for more than three hours straight. Parmentier came up with a method based on a single batch of sourdough, but he did not spell out the technique in a convincing fashion. The only alternative was to use brewer's yeast. Widely practiced by Paris bakers (those who claim that it was introduced by the Viennese in the nineteenth century are mistaken), this method was seductive because it speeded up fermentation and made the dough much easier to work with.[12]

Although he was by no means a partisan of brewer's yeast, Dr. Paul-Jacques Malouin, another great scholar of breadmaking, conceded that when it was used properly it produced a "lighter and better-tasting" bread than sourdough. But he warned that it had to be used skillfully, for any mistake in fermentation with brewer's yeast was much more detrimental to bread quality than a mistake in sourdough preparation. When bread made with brewer's yeast turned out badly, it was at once sour, bitter, and sticky. In order to exploit each of these techniques to the greatest advantage, Malouin recommended a yeast and sourdough synthesis that was apparently already in widespread use.[13]

Parmentier, who did not have Malouin's pragmatic reservations, launched a virtual crusade against the use of brewer's yeast. He drew on his own long-standing skepticism, going back to the great debate of the 1660s and 1670s over what was known as *pain mollet*, a light and tender luxury (specialty) bread that was prized by the upper classes and that had led a contingent of doctors from the Faculty of Medicine to argue that brewer's yeast was unfit for human consumption. In the eighteenth century, some people continued to see it as an adulterant. In his dictionary of arts and trades, Macquer raises questions about its impact on consumers' health. A large number of doctors, echoed by moralists, were convinced that bread made with yeast had the same perverse effects as beer itself on the nerves, the urinary tract, the skin, and the mind.

The breadmaking recipe based on sourdough imposed hard labor, Parmentier acknowledges, but the "remedy" of brewer's yeast is "worse than the disease." To produce good bread, the dough has to ferment gradually and evenly. Whereas the sourdough *chef* acts gently, the yeast and sourdough blend provokes a violent disturbance in the dough and forces fermentation before the dough's components are ready to form "a perfect, homogeneous whole." According to Parmentier, when dough is kneaded with brewer's yeast, a baker can never be sure of success. At best, he will get a loaf that is acceptable the first day, but whose taste will deteriorate afterward and whose crust will break down rapidly. At worst, the dough will soften suddenly because the fermentation was too abrupt: in this case the bread will be tasteless, unless it collapses in the oven and ends up tasting bitter.[14]

An examination of the documents reveals a certain disaffection with sourdough as early as the eighteenth century; while it was recognized as the authentic matrix for good bread, sourdough was deemed extremely demanding to work with, in Paris and undoubtedly in other large cities. Starting in the 1830s, many bakers used yeast to make their *pâtes bâtardes* (medium-density dough), according to a manual from the period, "more to shorten the work than to improve the quality of the bread." While the technique of using sourdough and yeast together continued to gain ground in urban areas throughout the nineteenth century, the so-called direct approach became increasingly popular in the aftermath of World War I. Truncated or degraded versions of the sourdough procedure, and especially its marriage with baker's yeast—a mismatch in the eyes of the traditionalists or fundamentalists—tolled the death knell for the old method.

Émile Dufour, the author of *Traité pratique de panification française et parisienne* (Practical Treatise on French and Parisian Breadmaking), published in 1937, recounts his youth as a worker: "In 1912, as *brigadier* [chief assistant, or head baker's boy], I did day work in the 18th [*arrondissement*]; the owner did not prepare sourdough for French bread, but he kept dough from the previous batch as a leavening agent. When you went into the baking room, you were struck by an acidic odor; the bread had already turned sour." "French bread" was the term used for bread made with sourdough, with or without yeast; the synthesis (or the compromise?) was already consecrated. Yet as of the 1930s, according to Dufour, "this bread [was] gradually disappearing. In the first place, it is more difficult to make, and it takes longer, especially for the first batch." People were already worrying about the drop in consumption. "While today, perhaps more than yesterday, bread leaves something to be desired, we must not conclude that it would increase consumption if we went back to sourdough," warned the former baker who had become a specialist. First, most bakers in the Paris region would not be capable of going "back to sourdough." Second, as Dufour explains, "French bread often smells of sourdough, and has a slightly sour taste. The consumer no longer tolerates this taste. He used to be habituated to it; now, he does not want it any longer. He will stick with his preference for Viennese bread [made with yeast], which is sweeter."[15]

On the eve of World War II, Raymond Geoffroy, who was to become one of the leading specialists in bread and flour, considered the matter settled: "The more or less general replacement of sourdough by yeast" is an accomplished fact. Sourdough is a dead letter; its time is up; it is of no further use except in museums: "Sourdough bread, our fathers' bread, quite wrongly called 'the good bread of yesteryear,' will no longer appear on our tables; this is the consequence of social progress in breadmaking." Nostalgia was a reactionary attitude, for bakers—and especially bakery workers—were not about to regret a law that established an eight-hour workday and did away (in theory) with night work. Like other observers with firsthand knowledge of baking rooms, Geoffroy remarked that "the right way to make [bread] is increasingly being forgotten, and bakers who still know how to prepare it are rare!" He himself had no regrets, for he was convinced that "fresh yeast . . . must make the consumer happy," so long as the baker avoids the two mistakes that are still denounced in our day: using too much yeast and not allowing enough time for fermentation. These practices alter "the characteristics of bread, especially its flavor, its good taste."[16]

Still, the classic sourdough process was not extinct. It was still practiced here and there, in its canonical form, in the countryside; Raoul Lemaire built his organic empire on fermentation by means of sourdough, and sourdough bread found secure refuge in Pierre Poilâne's baking room, while awaiting its dramatic revenge in the skillful hands (and head) of Pierre's son Lionel, who boldly positioned himself between the eighteenth century and the twenty-first. Seeking to profit from a market that had been increasingly energized by so-called specialty breads, in the early 1980s a number of suppliers opened up a semi-industrial path leading back toward natural sourdough. The Philibert Company sold stabilized liquid yeasts, apparently with "growing success." To overcome the constraint of launching the complex process of fermentation by means of sourdough, in 1984 the Catherine Company put out a product called Caty levain, a powder made from freeze-dried yeast that made it possible to finish a sourdough in forty-eight hours. The Lesaffre Company—currently the largest manufacturer in the world of fermenting agents for bread—seduced a number of bakers with its "yeast starter," which promised to "give aroma and taste to your bread in less than twenty-four hours."[17]

For sourdough partisans, the decisive advance was probably the development and marketing of a fermenting machine: the old dream of a handful of mavericks in the late nineteenth century had finally come true. In fact, the technology was not truly innovative; it took a mechanism long used by Germans (although rarely on the artisanal level) and adapted it to French tastes. Since the early 1990s, several manufacturers in France have been producing a fermenter that solves two of the biggest problems in sourdough preparation: start-up and stabilization. Devised so as to ensure a homogeneous mixture of sourdough, the machine has a system for heating and cooling that allows for precise temperature control. The baker extracts the quantity needed through a hatch, up to some fifty kilograms a day.[18]

A liquid leavening agent brings to mind another indirect method, a somewhat distant cousin of sourdough, the *poolish* or *pouliche*, among other spellings. (According to Dufour, "a yeast-based sourdough, very tender and soft, is called a *pouliche*.") Probably created and spread by Polish bakers, later improved by Viennese bakers during the second half of the nineteenth century, this method was quite common before World War I. It consisted of a culture of ferments developed prior to kneading; it was ordinarily made up of equal parts flour and water seeded with a sufficient dose of baker's yeast to support fermentation. Very liquid in consistency, "more like a cream than a dough," as Roland Guinet says, the *poolish* ferments in a moderately warm spot for three to eight hours. When it is slightly hollowed out in the center, the baker adds the rest of the raw material and subjects it to thorough kneading. This method has many advantages: it takes relatively little yeast; it makes the organization of the work easier, as it allows the baker to put off the moment of fabrication; it favors fine streaks (the incisions that the baker makes in the dough to allow carbon dioxide to escape during cooking); and it produces a bread with a long crumb that is nicely alveolated in a highly irregular fashion; it keeps well and is highly flavorful, without too much acidity. According to the pope of the *poolish*, Bernard Ganachaud, the baker most closely associated today with the revival of this fermentation technique, this is "the method best suited to the crumb-crust relation of out-of-the-ordinary bread [*pains de fantaisie*, or specialty breads]."[19]

The Direct Method

For the last three quarters of a century, the most widely used approach to fermentation has been the direct method. The simplest and most practical procedure, it calls for the incorporation of baker's yeast (sometimes known as industrial or, more euphemistically, organic yeast) all at once into the entire batch of flour and water, and it requires no preparation—no preliminary fermentation—before kneading. "Many baking rooms have reached the point of kneading the first batch during the night without using sourdough," a specialist noted around 1920; fermentation is achieved by the addition of a carefully calibrated quantity of brewer's yeast, so that by the next morning the batch will have fermented normally. This work is called "direct," the expert added; "it saves a great deal of time." In the very early days of the Popular Front, when a reduction in working hours was one of the movement's primary social objectives, the *Bulletin de l'Association des anciens élèves de l'École de boulangerie des Grands Moulins de Paris* (Alumni Bulletin of the Bakery School of the Great Mills of Paris [GMP]) announced "the triumph of the direct method in breadmaking."[20]

Energetically spread by the school and its mill, this method achieved "such success" because "the breadmaking business was in a turmoil over the new social laws" (anticipating Léon Blum's program for suppressing night work and eight-hour days). The direct method seemed to reconcile social requirements and the technical conditions that were indispensable for making good quality bread, because "faster work that nevertheless made warm bread available to the clientele in the morning" was required and because at least part of the medical establishment preferred the purity, cleanliness, and efficiency of yeast to the unpredictability of sourdough, which was kept under poor conditions in hot weather and became too acidic. But the *Bulletin* concluded that it was especially "the ease with which one could obtain consistent bread, of fine quality, that [made] it successful." The legitimate desire to free bakery workers from long hours of tedious labor, the gradual decline in the number of bakers skilled in the French method (as opposed to the Viennese method of working with yeast), and above all the labor shortage following World War I undoubtedly contributed to the spread of the direct method.[21]

During the same period, Émile Dufour confirmed the triumph of bread "made without sourdough, without *pouliche*, made exclusively with yeast, [which] tends to replace all the others." But in 1937 he was already warning against abuses of the direct method, long-lived abuses still subject to severe criticism today. The radical shortening of preparation time would inevitably be held against the trade (although it took more than fifty years before most bakers understood this). "I have seen kneading take place at 2 P.M. and the bread in the shop at 4 P.M.," Dufour observed. "This is a shame to the profession, and the baker who allows these procedures is working against himself by alienating the consumer." Dufour explained that "what is required above all in the direct method is the first fermentation (*pointage*). The greatest harm that can be done to bread is not to let it rise sufficiently, to rush it in the kneading process and in the oven."[22]

The *pointage* (less commonly called *piquage*) is the first period of fermentation, a very active rest period that begins just after the kneading machine or mixer has stopped turning, and it lasts until it is time for shaping (*tournage*). The best results are obtained when the entire mass of dough undergoes *pointage* in the vat. To compensate for the absence of any prior fermentation (to ensure the mechanical and physiochemical transformation of the dough under the best possible conditions, and in particular to ensure the production of aromas that will influence the taste), the *pointage* needs to be fairly lengthy; however, this principle was violated by many bakers from the start. Dufour said it should take four to six hours; the GMP bakery school advocated at least four hours. An advertisement for the GMP in the 1930s stresses the many advantages of the direct method: a better yield, less waste in the oven, a sturdier and more voluminous bread, a finer crust, and a better aroma. We may suppose that these good results are obtained by the choice of good flours ("for example, those of the Grands Moulins de Paris") and by a *pointage* lasting more than four hours. As breadmaking procedures were modernized after World War II, with the artificial stimulation of intensive kneading (we shall come back to this subject), *pointage* nearly disappeared. Today, virtually everyone in the profession agrees on the need to "go back" to a long *pointage*, to the almost mythical process that was never universally respected by the practitioners of the direct method.[23]

Despite the risks and some slipups, the definitive triumph of the direct method in the 1930s inaugurated what Raymond Calvel calls "the great period of French bread. . . . The fame of French bread throughout the world dates in particular from this period." Thanks to the intelligent use of "fresh industrial yeast," "the bread produced is beautiful, lighter than bread obtained from sourdough; its texture is lovely, creamy, more alive to the eye; its taste and aroma are more seductive, less acidic." Calvel insists, however, on the need for four hours of *pointage*; this much time is required for the development and enrichment of the complex perfumes that will make the bread stand out. The temptation to add additional yeast must be resisted: increasing the dose makes it possible to reduce the *pointage* time, but at the price of lessening the dough's tolerance and penalizing the quality of the bread ("a short and friable crumb, a pronounced taste of yeast, less flavor, a tendency to grow stale more quickly").[24]

Alongside all these accolades, yeast was criticized by other commentators as a chemical agent and thus potentially dangerous. At the end of the nineteenth century, even after the introduction of a new, more stable yeast by the Springer Company, a certain number of practitioners complained that the yeast was "extremely changeable." The most virulent attack came from the proto-ecologist and naturalist milieu. In the 1950s, for example, Georges Barbarin denounced "the chemification of bread." The so-called chemical yeasts were said to contain sulfuric acid and other substances that could be harmful to health. Starting in this period, CNERNA was concerned about the impact of such ideas on French bread consumption, which was already in decline. A 1962 study showed that 20 percent of the population believed that baker's yeast was a "chemical product," without being able to explain exactly what that meant.[25]

From Chemical Products to Additives

Bakers suffered a great deal from accusations — often but not always calumnious — that they were putting chemicals in their bread. As early as the eighteenth century, alum and other powders were used to whiten flour. In the nineteenth century, flour from fava beans (protein-rich seeds) was added; this unquestionably natural ingredient was associated with adulterating agents used to spur fermentation and boost volume. Before World War I, various "improving powders" circulated under the counter. The occasional application of authorized chemicals to compensate for a shortage of protein-rich wheat or to "correct" certain deficiencies in flour triggered an outpouring of indignation among some doctors and consumers. The passage of stringent legislation that dealt specifically with the use of chemical products in food did not appease everyone. Indeed, not everyone approved: in 1969, an article in *France-Soir* denounced the rigidity of the government, which was refusing to follow Brussels on the use of certain natural adjuvants, thereby handicapping the French breadmaking industry in relation to its foreign competition. The list of elements that could legitimately be added to bread was quite long, and it continued to arouse concern, even when the products involved were guaranteed to be "natural" or "harmless," or were rarely used by artisanal bakers: substances for treating flour, emulsifiers, enzymes, preservatives, antioxidants, and acidifying agents.[26]

The rumors about chemical pollution in breadmaking worried the experts on CNERNA's Commission on Bread: their task was to reassure the public, and they sought to inform and educate consumers while preserving the artisans' freedom to use certain ameliorating techniques deemed harmless and necessary or useful. The commission's president wondered in 1958 whether it might not be necessary to provide a new definition of bread asserting that it was "made without any chemicals." When the agronomist Jean Buré declared that it was absolutely essential to leave bakers a little leeway, Raymond Geoffroy, also an agronomist, responded with a warning: "But be careful, because you'll be accused of making chemical bread."[27]

The debate among commission members over the addition of ascorbic acid (vitamin c) — which was widely used to improve bread's tenacity, tolerance, resistance, and volume — brings out the dilemma quite clearly. Once again, Geoffroy warned that the public would see this as chemical tampering. "On the contrary," Buré declared, with a touch of irony, "we'll say that it's 'vitaminized' bread." Roland Guinet, a teacher of breadmaking, succumbed to a somewhat naive positivism and maintained that ascorbic acid, like malt, was not a "chemical ameliorant; the term can't be pejorative to clients' ears, quite the contrary." Much more cynically, another researcher, A. Bourdet, asserted that "the client doesn't need to know this."[28]

The use of additives in food production has a very long history. People have always sought ways to improve quality and/or yield, to embellish, preserve, and enrich products, and to facilitate their handling and correct their effects. We find traces of coloring, stabilizing, and emulsifying agents dating back to earliest antiquity; there is later evidence of spices and aromatic substances. Speaking of additives, Guinet quite rightly mentions yeast, used in association with sourdough culture to regulate fermentation; he describes it as "one of the earliest corrective means used in breadmaking," the functional equivalent of an additive. Additives are natural or synthetic substances added to the ingredients during breadmaking to facilitate the process (in modern breadmaking, for example, certain additives are used to improve the machinability of the dough, its capacity to tolerate the brutalizing mechanical operations of division and shaping), to reinforce or preserve certain qualities of the dough or the bread (physiochemical or sensorial, for example), or to improve the bread's appearance or extend its shelf life. Euphemistically, or perhaps as a gesture toward a distinction that has never been clearly made, people also speak of adjuvants and technological auxiliaries. From time immemorial, the success of an additive has been calculated in terms of the cost-benefit ratio, in the broadest sense (with reference to quality as well as expense). The problem is that the benefits for some quickly mutate into costs for others.[29]

After an interlude of relative calm, public anxiety about chemicals has recently been revived in reaction to the introduction of American hormones, genetically modified organisms, various scandals involving contamination of food products, and the obsession with traceability crystallized by mad cow disease. One outcome has been a spectacular renewal of interest in organic production, a sector that has itself been shaken by seriously fraudulent representations concerning the origin of raw materials. The same factors led to a series of attempts on the part of the Confédération nationale de la boulangerie (National Bakery Confederation) to reassure the public, reminding people that France alone was resisting an increase in the number of permissible additives. In February 1995, Brussels had authorized some one hundred additives in bread. ("It's no longer bread," according to the association newsletter, "it's a whole sandwich.")[30]

Today, malt and gluten (which is added to increase protein value) are still used with discretion; fava flour is used less and less; and Dominique Saibron, one of the brilliant young men in the profession, is almost alone in condemning out of hand the use of any fungal amylase. But it is much harder to wean bakers from their dependence on ascorbic acid, the magic lozenge that is added, twice if necessary, when the dough seems recalcitrant. Thus "bread in the French tradition" — which is infinitely better than the standard baguette, but harder to make, in large part because bakers are obliged, if they are law-abiding and self-respecting, not to add any ascorbic acid — is making a laboriously slow start. Raymond Calvel, one of the great masters of modern breadmaking, has never rejected ascorbic acid. Implicitly siding with the artisans who were afraid they would not be able to make the new bread without the lozenge, Calvel looks at this additive as a precious auxiliary that is completely harmless and leaves no trace in bread; vitamin c reinforces the dough's tenacity and tolerance and even protects its taste by diminishing the risk of overoxidation. Today, the professor's soothing verdict bears the hallmark of an earlier era in breadmaking.[31]

Deferred Fermentation

In the eighteenth century, the idea of progress came into its own to a spectacular degree: thanks to critical reason and the scientific method, one could look forward to more or less everything. In the breadmaking business, even the most confident experts remained humble before the process of fermentation, for this operation was governed by an often haughty and capricious nature. At best, human beings might attenuate its fluctuations, reduce its vagaries somewhat, but they could never fully comprehend or master it. The increasingly widespread recourse to yeast, systematized in the direct method, was evidence that the process could be simplified and speeded up; these were important steps, to be sure, but they did not signify the conquest of fermentation. Even with the direct method, many bakers still had to work at night in order to sell their bread early in the morning. And bread that was fresh in the morning could easily turn limp or stale, depending on conditions, in the course of the day. In the twentieth century, as early as World War I in some places but especially during the "Thirty Glorious Years" following World War II, more and more consumers demanded fresh bread at all hours. When bakers finally achieved a degree of control over the fermentation process through the use of refrigeration, they freed themselves from some heavy constraints even as they responded to public demand.[32]

Generally christened deferred fermentation (the action of the fermenting agents was actually slowed down or blocked), several techniques using cold temperatures allowed bakers to introduce a more rational organization that limited or even eliminated night work and enabled them to spread the baking process throughout the day. Modern experts seem to agree that, in order to implement the use of cold temperatures successfully, bakers have to be even more attentive than usual to the basic rules, and they need to select suitable raw materials: protein-rich flour with good staying power, very active fresh yeast, and vitamin c (alone or in a cocktail called, for example, a "special controlled growth" ameliorant); according to the authors of breadmaking manuals, the latter is an "indispensable" ingredient, but this position had—and has—numerous challengers.[33]

While commercial distribution of refrigeration units, vehicles for the practice of deferred fermentation, did not get off the ground until the 1960s, the idea and even the construction of several prototypes go back much further. In the mid-1930s, an article in the Alumni Bulletin of the GMP bakery school declared that "nothing . . . seems to stand in the way of the penetration of the baking room by the refrigeration industry." This development was seen as a way of reconciling social legislation, which had been attempting for some time to eliminate night work, with "the legitimate requirements of the public." To encourage the use of dough chambers, Springer, a major yeast manufacturer, put an especially slow liquid yeast on the market.[34]

At almost the same time, the Frigidaire Company proposed a "revolution" to liberate bakers from their painful subjection to the yoke of fermentation, in particular the obligation to begin work around midnight, tyrannical toil that imposed its rhythm without regard for the human costs. "Stop being a slave to dough; be its master instead," urged an advertisement. "Modernize. The 'Frigidaire' process gives you the means." Under the new work procedure, late afternoon rather than midnight is the time for kneading. When the dough has been turned, or shaped, the baker entrusts his *pâtons* (unbaked loaves) to the Frigidaire, where fermentation takes place in slow motion in a damp, cold environment. "The next morning, you find your dough just the way you want it. You put part of it in the oven at the most convenient time." This took care of everything; if Frigidaire did not succeed, it was no doubt partly because its refrigeration units were not efficient enough, but chiefly because craftsmen viewed the system as a serious transgression with respect to tradition, a deviation that was also quite costly.[35]

The first commercial successes involving refrigeration were associated with the inventors, manufacturers, and promoters from western France who played a crucial role in the renewal of breadmaking methods starting in the late 1950s; for example, Michel Bouton, a former baker, worked with the refrigerator manufacturer Briquet on the construction of a chamber for slow rising. Ten years later, in Niort, today a nerve center of innovative breadmaking, refrigeration specialist Norbert Cosmao perfected a sophisticated device that ensured a much slower controlled rising under good conditions (no crusting on the dough); it was programmed to stop the rising process and then restart it a few hours later, thanks to an automatic warming system. Later, the chamber was enlarged and outfitted with carts, first for the purpose of cold storage and later to facilitate automatic transfer to the oven (innovative transfer mechanisms were developed around the same time).[36] We do not have the figures, but it is clear that more and more bakers were acquiring refrigeration equipment. Even if they could handle the cost, however, some had trouble accommodating bulky refrigeration units in bakeries that were often quite small. Many who used refrigeration continued to operate their ovens at night: the new method offered infinitely more flexibility, but did not necessarily draw the profession out of the world of "bats," as people used to say. The debate over the need for ameliorants to ensure the success of deferred fermentation is still going on today. Few practitioners have taken as forceful a position as Hervé Malineau: one of the most creative members of the new generation, Malineau rejects refrigeration as the midwife of fermentation. For his Pain Paulette baguette, he will accept no substitutes for a genuine, prolonged (fifteen-hour) pointage with a rabat (punching down) every two hours. But how many bakers can afford to devote such constant attention to their production?[37]

The Principal Stages in Breadmaking:
From Kneading to Shaping

Once the raw materials have been selected and the (decisive) choice of fermentation method has been made, the first major operation is kneading, the process of mixing the ingredients together to form the dough. Some bakers, such as Philippe Gosselin, a laureate in the competition for the best baguette in Paris, stress the need to be rigorous: "Every day I weigh my flour, my yeast, and my salt just as a pastry chef would. My results are more predictable." The baker wants the flour to be well hydrated; he wants the gluten particles to absorb water and swell up so that they will stick together. In this way, they form a sufficiently resistant network to retain the carbon dioxide that will be produced by fermentation. The amount of water added has to be very carefully calculated to make sure that the final consistency of the dough will be satisfactory. During the second round of kneading, air is incorporated into the dough, which is being structured by the development of a glutinous mesh. Experts warn that mistakes committed during kneading are "difficult if not impossible to correct later on." At the end of the kneading process, the dough should detach easily from the sides of the trough. "Whether he is the owner, a worker, or an apprentice," Émile Dufour claims in his 1937 *Traité pratique de la panification*, "if a baker is not capable of *reading* his dough, he will never be sure of his work and will never be anything but a mediocre craftsman." For Gosselin, when kneading is over the dough will snap. "The baker recognizes wellkneaded dough by ear." For others, what counts is the feel, the look, or sometimes the smell.[38]

In the eighteenth century, as we have seen, kneading was done by hand; it was an extremely difficult task. The baker poured a sourdough culture resulting from the final stage of fermentation into water and added flour; this step was called *délayage* (dilution; dissolving the sourdough was also called discharging). The copious leavening culture had to impregnate the rest of the dough. The baker mixed, pressed, and divided so vigorously that all the lumps (or "chestnuts") gave way. Then he introduced still more flour and gradually thickened the dough with rapid gestures. He had to act quickly enough to prevent the dough from "languishing," but gently enough to prevent it from "burning." The *frase* that resulted formed a supple, elastic body that the baker worked lightly. Then came the *contrefrase*: the baker worked the dough with a quick hand, blending it into a single large mass before breaking it into pieces and heaving them forcefully to one side and then the other in the trough. He drew the dough out and worked it with his fingers in such a way that every part of the dough felt the pressure. In the fourth phase, the *bassinage*, the baker prepared the dough for the most critical operation by adding water in order to dilute the flour particles that might somehow have managed to avoid incorporation until then (today, *frasage* is the initial mixing of the ingredients, *contrefrasage* is the addition of flour, and *bassinage* the addition of water).

Refreshed, the dough was then subjected to *battage*, or beating. The baker plunged into the mass, pounded, pulled, turned, stretched, slapped, and sliced it, and threw ten- to twenty-pound pieces all around the kneading trough. He had barely three quarters of an hour to knead up to two hundred pounds; if he took longer, the dough would be weakened, for the fermentation would go beyond the point of optimum intensity. The *battage* stage made the dough "long" and "equal," resistant to separation. Toward the end of the operation, the baker had to tone down his aggressive approach. If he continued to pound the dough instead of turning it and folding it toward the center, he risked making it resistant, hard to manipulate. The baker knew that it was ready when it no longer stuck to his hands.

The work was exhausting and discouraging, so much so that workers and even some master bakers were increasingly reluctant to make the necessary investment. They compensated for their reduced efforts by using a higher dose of yeast, a compromise that saved energy but kept the dough from achieving maximum cohesion and robbed the bread of some of its pure whiteness and its taste. For reasons that will become clear later on, the bakers held out against mechanization for a long time, although the first mechanical devices became available in the late eighteenth century. The French baking industry did not shift to mechanical kneading on a large scale until after World War I, in part because of consumer distaste for what was derisively called mechanical bread. (It is revealing that, in 1995, certain wistful French consumers still thought that "kneading by hand" was the most appropriate emblem for artisanal breadmaking.) Today, 75 percent of the bakeries in France are equipped with oblique mixers, 20 percent have spiral mixers, and a small number have vertical spindle mixers. The choice of machine is of real importance, but for the past thirty years or so the only question that has spurred debate among breadmaking professionals has had to do with the length and intensity of kneading (we shall come back to this issue). The speed and duration of kneading have a direct and sometimes decisive influence on the quality of the dough and thus of the bread produced. Bakers have moved from a slow process (fifteen minutes at low speed) to intensive or accentuated kneading (four to six minutes at low speed, then eighteen to twenty at medium speed). Many bakers, noting the disadvantages of the intensive method, have opted for a compromise approach, "improved kneading," in which the first phase is maintained at fifteen minutes, but the second phase is reduced to ten or twelve minutes total. The best artisans deplore the way intensive kneading "massacres" the dough; they interpret this retrospectively as an unfortunate step backward, modernization gone awry, and many are returning to moderate or even slow kneading.[39]

The first fermentation, or *pointage*, follows kneading; this is the key moment for developing the dough's physical properties and the aromas that powerfully condition the taste of the resulting bread. *Pointage* was virtually eliminated by the overwhelming predominance of the direct method, but it is currently regaining its sacred status; bakers commonly allow it two, three, or even four hours at room temperature and even longer in cold chambers.

Form and weight are closely linked, because the contours of the bread help to determine how much supplementary dough ("bonus") has to be added to compensate for weight loss in cooking. This was the chief concern of eighteenth-century bakers, for short weight was an extremely common but serious infraction, sanctioned by the confiscation of all the bread from the batch and by fines — or worse, in the case of repeat offenders (bread was sold by the piece, and it was not weighed in front of the client). Around 1750, elongated loaves surpassed round loaves in popularity for breads weighing six pounds or less, especially white and middling (*bis-blancs*) breads. The round form was associated with firm dough, a compact crumb, and as little crust as possible. Soft dough required a flatter form with more crust, hence its elongated form. The change in fashion was not in the bakers' economic interest, for the round loaves rose more rapidly and took up one-third less space in the oven for the same weight; they kept better and, most important, lost markedly less weight in the oven because they contained less water and offered a smaller surface to evaporation.

For the final *apprêt*, the baker put the small loaves on *couches*, wooden shelves lined with damp flour sacking in summer, woolen cloth in winter. The long loaves went into *pannetons* (called *bannetons* today), wicker baskets designed to maintain the shape of the loaves, contain fermentation, and protect against humidity and dust.[40]

Today, dividing and weighing are done automatically, wholly or in part. Bakers gain in speed and consistency, but not without a trade-off: the automatic divider, for instance, which separates by volume or weight, cannot be used to divide dough that has benefited from a long *pointage*, and its rough handling of gluten harms the quality of the resulting bread. After division comes *boulage*, or preshaping, an intermediate step between weighing and shaping. The baker works the *pâtons* to ready them for the next step; bread well formed is half shaped, as artisans say. *Boulage* is done by hand or by machine. The machines (*bouleuses*) are frequently paired with a resting chamber where the *pâtons* relax and continue their fermentation for fifteen to twenty minutes, regaining their strength in preparation for the ordeal of shaping. The *pâton* has to regain its suppleness—it must be quite relaxed and endowed with good elasticity—to keep from being excessively crushed by the shaping machine.[41]

Tourner sa fournée, turning one's batch, was the time-honored expression for hand shaping until fairly recently. Today, in the vast majority of bakeries, machines have replaced the skillful *tourne*. In hand shaping, the baker works the dough one last time and gives it its definitive form. This process, which is not easy to master, has three stages: flattening, folding, and lengthening. The artisan takes up each *pâton* in turn and squeezes it according to the degree of fermentation and the consistency of the dough. The experts say that even to bring off a good mechanical turn, "you first have to sense how the dough reacts to manual shaping." The shaping machine mimics the phases of the manual turn: sheeting (where the rollers are placed closer together or farther apart depending on the dough's physical state, its quantity, and the baker's procedure), rolling, and lengthening.[42]

A recent publication by the Institut national de la boulangerie-pâtisserie (National Bread and Pastry Institute [INBP]) advocates an at least partial return to hand shaping. The last truly manual gesture linking modern breadmaking to ancestral practices, the manual turn contributes important cultural capital. On the practical level, it gives the baker much more freedom to vary the form of the loaf and to inflect its interior structure, personalizing production in a way that will please the clientele. "If we always shape mechanically," notes Jean-Claude Mislanghe, an INBP faculty member, "we forget the gestures and the feel of the dough." He adds that bakers who shape by hand set themselves apart from industrial breadmaking and mass distribution in their clients' eyes, for identical, standardized breads have less and less appeal.[43]

After shaping, the baker deposits the formed *pâtons* for their second fermentation or *apprêt* on cloth-covered shelves, in traditional wicker baskets, or, in a more ostentatiously modern way, on baking sheets or molds or even on conveyor belts. The *pâtons* are laid out in a so-called Parisian cupboard or are placed in a chamber for deferred fermentation. While the *pointage* produces the bread's aromas as it improves or corrects the dough's strength, the *apprêt* gives the bread its volume. With a strong retentive capacity ensured by high-quality gluten, the *pâtons* can stock a maximum amount of the carbon dioxide produced as the starchy sugars break down. As always, time plays a crucial role. If the *pâtons* are weakened by an overlong *apprêt*, they may well collapse as they bake. Generally speaking, the more time is reserved for the *pointage*, the less is needed for the *apprêt*.[44]

Just before putting the loaves in the oven, the baker "signs" them by slashing the surface. This moment is at once exalting and full of uncertainty. The bread is made, without being entirely finished. Called scoring, scarifying, or slashing, the gesture demands great dexterity. It is a rite of passage, and it also has practical, aesthetic, and physical dimensions. The incisions allow the carbon dioxide to exit by following a path traced by the baker, to borrow from the limpid pedagogy of the INBP manual. If the artisan did not make the cuts, the carbon dioxide would still escape, but it would do so by bursting the bread open. Well-made slashes ensure that the bread will look attractive and develop harmoniously.[45]

Baking

If the dough did not begin to bake "at the peak of its exaltation," as they put it in the eighteenth century, the bread could not achieve optimal quality. Here was the baker's moment of truth. As he hurried to prepare the oven, it was not uncommon to hear him curse "amid the smoke that surrounded him, . . . throw down his tools, accuse his comrades, because his vigilance had been taken by surprise and the dough, owing to an unexpected change in the weather, had reached a point where it could wait no longer."[46]

A baker viewed his oven as his most important tool. A well-built and well-maintained oven increased his chances of producing excellent bread, and it helped limit the expenditure of energy. Ovens were generally installed in the basement or in the back of the shop, although they were also set up in courtyards, probably just for use during hot weather. Sometimes bakers were prevented from setting up their ovens under their shops by landlords or other tenants in the building who coveted the basement space or were afraid of fire; they had to have their ovens in other buildings, sometimes several hundred meters away. (A baker in that situation today does not have the right to call his shop a *boulangerie*, because he does not bake on the premises where he sells to the consumer.)[47]

In the eighteenth century, it was hardly profitable to bake just one or two batches a day, because the extra energy needed to bake five or six more was relatively insignificant; still, only a minority of bakers were able to maintain the optimal rhythm. The oven had to be heated for forty-five minutes to an hour before the remaining embers could be removed and the *pâtons* put in to bake. An oven measuring 2.0 to 2.7 meters could accommodate about three hundred pounds of large loaves, but no more than two hundred pounds of small ones. The process of putting loaves in the oven took about half an hour. Master bakers assigned the head journeyman to this task, for it took very little to "break" or "tire" the *pâtons* if the paddle was handled clumsily. There was not yet any system for misting, but sometimes the worker gilded the *pâtons* with honey, egg yolk, or milk to add color just before putting them in the oven.[48]

Of all the transformations that food must undergo, Parmentier observed, the cooking process is the most treacherous. The baker cannot remove the bread to see how it is doing. He has to *know* just when to take it out, because once he has done so he cannot put it back in the oven without doing serious damage to its color and to the quality of the crumb and the crust. Baking times vary according to the type of flour and dough, the shape of the loaves, and the weather. As a general rule, a four-pound long loaf requires an hour, an eight-pound round loaf two hours, and a twelve-pound loaf three hours! Just as much care is required to take the bread out of the oven as to put it in. Bread that cools slowly will stay fresh longer: that is why the baker puts the loaves close together to keep them warm. If they are a bit overcooked, he covers them in order to retain steam and humidify them. As soon as they have cooled, the loaves are sprinkled with flour, covered again, and stored in a dry place.

"Properly baked bread is always good," as an age-old aphorism has it. For the eighteenth-century baker, as for his counterpart today, good bread gave an impression of proud plenitude. Golden yellow in color, neither too pale nor too bright, the crust had a uniform thickness and a smooth surface, with no cracks. The crumb could not be doughy, ashy, sticky, dry, or brittle. Elasticity was the proof of a "good blending which [was] the result of a good mixing through kneading and fermentation." Well fermented, the crumb gave off a slight odor of wine and presented hundreds of little "eyes" that attested to vigorous kneading and good aeration. This even texture (which is rejected today, but in the context of a different method of breadmaking) had to be accompanied by a creamy color and a velvety, more or less delicate and silky crumb, which came apart readily in layers.[49]

Just as wheat takes a year and flour takes a month, Malouin declares, bread requires a day of rest after cooking to reach perfection. Like the American Sylvester Graham, a nutritional reformer and Protestant minister in the 1930s, a certain number of doctors warned against bread that was too fresh; it would cause gas, bloating, and colic. Still, the protective hard crust that formed after a day repelled certain consumers. Moreover, bread with a soft crust clearly tasted better the first day, and stale bread aggravated "melancholy humors." As the eighteenth century advanced, more and more Parisians of all conditions came to expect fresh bread on a daily basis, foreshadowing habits that we think of as contemporary.[50]

The oven remains the key element in baking rooms today. Modern equipment includes the use of sheet metal ovens in place of masonry constructions, bringing a noticeable reduction in bulk as well as weight; the use of indirect instead of direct heat (a more and more common practice in the past half-century); and the use of conveyor belts and other automatic or semiautomatic devices instead of paddles to move bread in and out of the oven.[51]

Nostalgia makes baking in a wood-fired oven commercially attractive. Although the method is not particularly convenient, wood-burning ovens embody a tradition of authenticity in the minds of some bakers and many consumers; they remain the object of an ongoing debate. The realists — who include almost all breadmaking experts — refer to CNERNA studies according to which wood, or rather the odors released when wood is burned, cannot contribute to the taste of bread (although the slow cooking provided seems clearly advantageous for the quality of large loaves in particular). Even though he criticizes wood as a mediocre fuel that is hard to handle, Roland Guinet readily acknowledges the commercial justification of its use "if the oven is well built and well managed."[52]

The choice of fuel is not viewed as a determining factor in bread; in contrast, the baking method used is crucial. Bread baking takes place by conduction: heat is transmitted largely via the hearth. This age-old practice, known as *sur pavé* (on a stone), makes the dough "explode," in the final magical rising or "oven spring" that accentuates the bread's development and announces its definitive constitution. Thanks to the hearthstone, each side of the bread offers a different crust. This method produces high water loss and thus reduces the risk of later softening. The method of cooking in molds, often in rotating rack ovens, was very popular starting in the late 1960s, for it was closely identified with the modernization of France (a movement from which bakers did not want to be excluded), and it promised significant economies: it offered less manipulation, more rapid transfer to the oven, and significantly increased productivity. This method gives a fine, regular crust. There is less water loss and greater susceptibility to variations in climate, so the risks of softening or drying out are correspondingly greater.[53]

For proper baking, the oven has to be prepared in advance; it has to reach 250° C (482° F) at the right moment. Using a built-in device, the baker projects water vapor (or mist) into the oven before putting in the loaves. By surrounding the *pâtons* with a thin film of water, he makes the dough more supple; this facilitates the release of carbon dioxide and thus helps the *pâtons* develop properly. The slight softening of the dough improves the regularity and appearance of the slash marks, which form fine streaks (the bread is also said to "spit"). Serving as a protective screen, the thin layer of water limits evaporation and delays drying out, thus increasing the yield of the flour and ensuring the delicacy of the crust. Finally, the mist that saturates the atmosphere during caramelization gives the bread a lovely golden color, a subtle sheen.[54]

The way loaves are put in the oven depends on the type of oven used. The process is very simple with rack ovens, where the racks themselves are inserted. More skill is required with the hearthstone oven, whether the work is done manually or mechanically. When the *pâtons* are put in by hand with a paddle, the process requires deftness, dexterity, and speed to ensure the transfer and placement of the *pâtons* under good conditions. Even when a conveyor belt is used, the *pâtons* have to be placed on the moving canvas very carefully to keep them from collapsing; they must not be too close together, and the regularity of their form must be respected (or corrected before it is too late).[55]

The dough is transformed into bread in several stages. As it heats up rapidly from 25° to 50° C (77° to 122° F), the dough undergoes a final, very intense fermentation that ceases abruptly with the destruction of the fermenting agents. Under the effect of the heat, which rises from 50° to 80° C (122° to 176° F) inside the dough, increasing pressure from the expanding carbon dioxide amplifies the bread's development as the loaf increases in volume. The alveoli that structure the crumb are formed at this stage. At around 60° C (140° F), the starches swell up with water and form a viscous mass, which Gérard Brochoire, head of the INBP, compares to béchamel sauce. At around 70° C (158° F), the gluten coagulates like egg whites, and the bread's development is complete. When the temperature in the heart of the dough reaches 100° C (212° F), some of the water in the bread evaporates, building a resistant crust and a nonsticky crumb. The heat caramelizes the sugars on the surface. The phenomenon of coloring is reinforced by what is called the Maillard reaction: browning takes place when a protein-sugar mix is heated, creating aromas and deepening the colors of the crust.[56]

When the bread comes out of the oven, it is not yet ready: it has to undergo what bakers call resweating. This entails a cooling-off period during which the bread releases water vapor and carbon dioxide. The bread loses up to 2 percent of its weight, and its crust flakes slightly, an effect of the harsh disparity in temperatures between the oven and the baking room. While we are obliged to acknowledge that even the best bread will eventually grow stale, good bread should not begin to lose its freshness, its crustiness, or its aroma for at least twelve hours.[57]

How to Recognize Good Bread

Quality, for bread as for many other products, edible or not, can be assessed by objective studies, at least on certain points. This is not to deny that subjectivity plays an important role in the consumer's judgment, even though we know that taste in the broadest sense of the term is itself the product of various influences, including social, ideological, moral, material, and even chemical and biochemical factors. Consumers rule: they have the right to like whatever they please, just as they have the right to make mistakes. It is not for specialists to lay down the law or to play the role of gastronomy police. However, a specialist does have the right and perhaps even the obligation to practice a nonsectarian pedagogy by offering analytical criteria or an open and flexible reading grid that may help consumers better articulate the reasons for their preferences and aversions.[58]

Writing in 1977 on the occasion of a CNERNA-sponsored colloquium on bread, one expert proposed four rubrics for evaluation, not all readily accessible to the consumer. First, nutritional qualities, which are often concealed, neglected, or consigned to the realm of medical expertise. Second, health-related qualities; these are sometimes difficult to separate from the first group, and they are frequently just as hard to grasp, even for attentive consumers. Third, economic qualities, in particular the price and utility of a product that buyers ordinarily appreciate in terms of their own means, needs, and desires. Fourth, the organoleptic field entailing the qualities perceived by the sense organs, qualities that consumers are in theory (and, with some effort, in practice) capable of grasping directly. Consumers apprehend the qualities of a loaf of bread with all five senses: by looking at it, listening to it, touching it with fingers and mouth, breathing it, smelling it, and tasting it; these latter operations are intimately interconnected, as they involve both nose and mouth. To these four rubrics we may add others—for instance, bread's keeping capacity—that find no place in this classification system. In attempting to describe good bread, I shall emphasize the fourth category and focus on organoleptic or sensory criteria.[59]

Although bread "as it used to be" remains a sort of mythical gold standard, we have to note that the good bread of yesteryear had very little in common with today's good bread, and even the latter has evolved rather spectacularly over the past several decades. While scattered exceptions persist (rustic, regional, and organic breads, for example), the current typology of good bread is much less diversified and less stratified than it was in earlier eras. Flour varieties, fermentation methods, kneading practices, shaping techniques, cooking surfaces, hand work—all these have undergone modification. In the eighteenth century, city people ate wheat bread except in times of crisis (Parisians rejected rye, barley, and buckwheat even during stretches of serious dearth); this bread was often on the white side even for the working class. Parisians ate little dark bread (*pain bis*); the very common middling bread (*bis-blanc*) sometimes called *bourgeois* probably was something like a cross between Poilâne's grayish round loaf and Jean-Luc Poujauran's slightly lighter *demi-gros* (medium-size) loaf. The white bread of the day, in four-pound long loaves or six-pound rounds, would strike us as rather dark, according to the ethereal criteria of the 1960s and 1970s.

After a brief transition period of moral abnegation with regard to food during the Revolution, the process of democratization in the direction of white bread and emulation of one's social superiors resumed in the nineteenth century. "People of all classes want to eat the same bread," an 1859 study reveals, but beyond the color, more or less white according to the criteria of the period, we cannot specify any particular sensory characteristics.[60]

"In bread of good quality, the crust is rounded, thin, smooth, without bubbles or cracks; the crumb is spongy, light, elastic, and it adheres to the crust," writes Léon Boutroux in his 1897 treatise on breadmaking, highlighting many of the qualities that we praise today. But when he evokes organoleptic qualities involving taste, he becomes peculiarly nebulous: "The odor of bread is an excellent indicator of its quality; this can best be judged if the bread is cut while it is still warm, when it comes out of the oven. The color is best appreciated when the bread has fully cooled. Its taste, the pleasure one takes in eating it, are indicators of prime importance, but these do not need to be described." On the contrary! Several years later, the volume of the *Encyclopédie Roret* dealing with bread offered a similar, somewhat less laconic definition that placed even stronger emphasis on volume and unequivocal whiteness: "Well-made bread must be light, well risen, and very puffy. Its color must be a precise shade of yellow with hints of brown; it must be sonorous when struck; its surface must be smooth, its interior full of cavities or large crevasses; its crumb white, very spongy and very elastic." Between the two World Wars, Émile Dufour lauded a bread that is completely out of fashion today, in which the crumb—"the soul of bread"—eclipsed the crust.[61]

Giving absolute primacy to sensory or organoleptic analysis does not protect the taster from certain pitfalls. First, one must resist certain biases, a priori assumptions, or internalized rules that condition one's appreciation of the product. For example, once we know that bread baked on a rack is considered inferior to bread cooked on a hearthstone, we may be hard put to taste it innocently, without inadvertent preconceptions. Similarly, we should not underestimate the role of filtering and association played by memory, that powerful subterranean force mobilized by both Proust and Pavlov to quite different ends. Roger Drapron reminds us that "the organoleptic quality of a traditional food such as bread stems more from pleasures repeated and committed to memory in the past than from the intensity of the immediate sensations."[62]

To the problems of symbolic, normative, or personalized mediations, Daniel Richard-Molard adds a warning about the gap between the thing itself and the idea one constructs of it, between reality and its experiential representation — a call for caution that might be taken for the perfidious appeal of a postmodern siren if it did not come out of a laboratory. Richard-Molard distinguishes clearly between consumers' tastes, the way these tastes are constructed and explained, and the taste of different breads, composed of intrinsic chemical characteristics. "Aroma, taste, and color will be considered simply as resulting from the presence of specific molecules in greater or lesser quantities," he writes, "and not as the effect or the impression that these molecules may produce on the taster." And he hammers home the imperative of philosophico-scientific humility: "Causal relations between these molecules and the taster's perception of flavor are still far from being established with rigor. . . . The consumer, for his part, will make his choice according to physiological sensations and sensory impressions that remain for the time being connected in a very subjective way to the physiochemist's molecules." Tasters are thus left at once quite free and somewhat disoriented in their undertaking.[63]

Appearance

The first sensory contact with bread comes through sight. We look at a loaf on the baker's shelf and again, more closely, when we buy it. An attractive appearance announces first of all an appetizing bread, one that inspires not simply aesthetic admiration but a sort of lust, an eagerness to begin eating. It arouses desire, a rudimentary but energizing and promising desire. Like good wine, good bread has structure. This is both an architectural and a gustatory phenomenon: a baguette, for example, stands up nicely, straight and regular in form. This bread has a smooth golden yellow crust with no visible defects; it is not puffy or puckered, as the craftsman would say. The duller bottom surface must not be either dirty or burned. The canonical test of the craftsman's dexterity, the design engraved in the bread — the famous slashing—also serves as an index of organoleptic quality. These scarifications are of equal length, each one tracing a well-defined fishbone, called an ear, on the upper part of the loaf. A good opening and good spacing prefigure good flavor.[64]

"Good-looking bread is not always good bread," Bernard Ganachaud has observed, expressing a feeling more commonly shared by the best bakers—those who manage to achieve both a good appearance and good taste simultaneously—than by those who try to mask deficient quality behind a fine appearance. This is an old debate, both in the baking room and in life: essence in relation to appearance. We must not neglect the image that consumers form of the product, an image that influences their taste. As Claude Lévi-Strauss noted in an entirely different context, the product has to be "good to think" before it is good to eat. A manifestly ugly bread engenders mistrust. But in the 1960s and 1970s, the profession wagered virtually everything on the external appearance of bread: first and foremost volume, which consumers associated with abundance and a certain voluptuousness, but also the color of the crumb, where extreme whiteness was identified with purity and well-being. Certain critics decried bread of this sort as being obtained "at the expense of aroma and taste"; others pointed out "the progressive disappearance of taste." From his professorial vantage point at the École française de meunerie (millers' school), Raymond Calvel reminded bakers that "clothes don't make the man," urging them not to "mistake the habit for the monk." In the bakery version of a Marxist analysis, Calvel distinguished what was superficial and contingent—bread's external appearance and size—from the "deeper and truer reality of its smell, its taste, and its consistency—that is, its flavor." Today, while people often speak of bread as well developed, few would cite volume as a sign of excellence.[65]

Proper baking, which is rarely defined with rigor, is a quality often tied to the appearance of the loaf, although it brings additional criteria into play as well. A study done in 1962 revealed that the public was not satisfied with the way its bread was baked (or with its keeping qualities, moreover). Bread was found to be baked either too long or not long enough. Professionals, for their part, deplored consumer infatuation with underdone bread. Some critics held bakers responsible for this tendency: they were under pressure to work too fast. In the late 1950s, Gringoire, the president of the National Bakers' Confederation, was already expressing the hope

"that bread would be baked longer," for in his view this was one of the principal guarantees of organoleptic excellence. The *Recueil des usages* adopted
a very diplomatic position by warning "certain consumers who confuse
the color of the crust with the degree of baking and who, in order to avoid
having a highly colored bread, ask for a loaf that is 'not too cooked.' A
deeply-colored crust does not necessarily mean that the bread has been
baked too long; conversely, a pale crust does not necessarily signify insufficient cooking time."[66]

Crust and Crumb, or How to Make Opposites that Attract

Given the primordial role played by the crust in the contemporary definition of French bread, we need to linger over it for a moment. If today's
bread can be characterized by a single word, at least on the demand side,
it is crusty. It is this crust, thin and crunchy rather than thick, hard, or
breakable, that the consumer covets, in seeming indifference at times to
the quality and even to the very substance of the crumb. The hegemony of
the crust worries some bakers, who militate for a better balance between
outside and inside. The crust's sonority constitutes one more test of its success. As soon as bread comes out of the oven, bakers say that it "sings," as a
result of the cracking produced in the crust during the cooling process. In
the customer's hands, under light pressure, the crust must crack slightly.
When the bottom of a loaf is tapped with a finger, the crust must resonate,
according to some, "like a drum." In combination with auditory cues, tactile sensitivity holds a particularly important place in bread tasting. Bread
is one of the rare foods that is not picked up with a fork but with the fingers, as Drapron stresses. By touching, breaking, and feeling bread, the
fingers participate in assessing the quality of its crust and crumb; by apply-
ing pressure to expel the air trapped in the alveoli, the fingers help to put
the bread's aromas into play. Tactile sensitivity also operates in the mouth,
where lips and tongue judge temperature and consistency while the jaw
cuts and pulverizes. The jawbones transmit the vibrations of chewing to
the sound receptors in the ears, conveying the highly prized impression
of crustiness.[67]

The chemical phenomena that produce the crust, and in particular its
golden yellow color, also give rise to volatile compounds translated by aro-

mas that confer on crust a specific taste complementing the taste of the crumb. The optimal aromas, according to Calvel, produce a subtle amalgam of grilling, hazelnut, and frying. Calvel reminds us that the quality of the crust also depends on a variety of factors going back to the beginning of the breadmaking process: the degree to which the flour is rich in proteins and sugars, the composition of the dough, the development of the *pâtons*, the type and temperature of the oven, the presence or absence of water vapor, and the duration of baking. Good coloration, going beyond golden yellow to reach the orangish tint discreetly associated with light brown, is intimately connected with the release of flavor.[68]

Crushed, as it were, by the crust, the crumb resists; it has recently been revitalized by the widespread return of long *pointages* that bring out its aromas, which are "more significant than those of the crust," according to Calvel. Calvel maintains that between a good loaf of bread and a bad one, the crumb in particular makes the difference, on the level of smell and taste. Like the quality of the crust, that of the crumb depends on several factors: the type of flour selected, the way the dough is "seeded," the techniques involved in kneading and shaping, the kind of oven used. The crumb is judged by its structure, its plastic qualities, and its color. The "eyes"—the cavities or alveolage constituting the internal structure of a loaf—should not "be distributed equally or have the same dimensions throughout," as Paul Nottin put it in his 1940 manual. Today's best crumb is long, with irregularly shaped and spaced alveoli that have delicate, pearly surfaces, varying in dimension according to geographical region. A superwhite crumb is no longer viewed as a mark of excellence or a seal of distinction, although this criterion, too, yields to some regional variations. The crumb of the twenty-first century artisan is creamy in color with a certain disposition toward yellow, unless it is the product of sourdough fermentation, which produces a tint tending toward gray. Well aerated in texture, adhering well to the crust, neither sticky nor dry, the crumb must demonstrate elasticity after it is compressed or stretched. When the dough is made with sourdough or *poolish*, the crumb is denser and slightly less elastic: it is prouder, more sure of itself. Proof of a successful crumb comes with prompt salivation and an easy first bite introducing a pleasant, nonsticky experience in the mouth punctuated by a taste that increases in intensity during chewing.[69]

Odor and Aroma, Taste and Flavor

Under Anglo-Saxon influence, people have been using the term *flaveur*, flavor, for some time in French breadmaking circles. This term offers a useful condensation of two complex notions that are difficult to separate, chemically and subjectively: smell and taste. The experts define flavor as "the set of sensations perceived by the olfactory organ, the taste buds, and the oral cavity." Associating maturations, oxidations, hydrolyses, phenomena deriving from fermentation, and reactions to heat, the formation of flavor in bread manifests much more complex "technological origins" than those of wine and cheese. This complexity probably explains why it is harder to talk about bread than wine in terms of its gustatory and olfactory properties. Indeed, studies devoted to the organoleptic qualities of French breads are "very rare," according to one of the authoritative French specialists, Daniel Richard-Molard.[70]

In order to speak of tastes, smells, and aromas, we need to evoke on the one hand a multitude of molecules, bearers of stimulation, and on the other a variety of mechanisms and sites of reception and interpretation. We know that gustatory impressions and olfactory perceptions are almost inseparable, but we do not understand very well how this complicity works. Some studies have led to the conclusion that taste depends largely on smell; recent research concludes that "taste influences the perception of odor." Olfactory impressions consist in two distinct parts: what can be perceived directly by the nose when one approaches food, and what will be sensed retronasally through the mouth as the food is chewed. It is this communication between the back of the mouth and the nose that makes the two senses inseparable. The retronasal passage allows volatile odorific substances, ingested through the mouth, to spread and quickly reach the sensory receptors of the olfactory mucus membranes. Information transmitted by the olfactory system enters more or less directly into the cerebral cortex, where it is incorporated into the sensation of flavor. The data registered by taste buds on the tongue, the palate, and the inside walls of the mouth make several stops before reaching the same point. People do not all have the same capacity to taste. A significant recent study distinguishes between supertasters, average tasters, and nontasters. The systematic study of flavor allows human beings to optimize their search for food items that are both essential for survival and enjoyable in terms of well-being. At the most basic level, taste determines what is edible; smell detects, identifies, and archives the various foods, recording them in memory, which plays a crucial role in the recognition of flavor.[71]

When we seek to move beyond the general mechanisms for producing and receiving tastes and smells — many of whose mysteries remain to be solved — to the specific phenomena involved in the formation of flavor in bread, we venture onto a terrain that is even less clearly mapped out. Studies on aromas in bread have shown that they are constituted by some two hundred volatile compounds generated primarily during the process of fermentation — a geyser of flavor. While some twenty of these compounds play a preponderant role in perfuming the crumb in French bread (imparting the aroma of hazelnut or rose, for example), scientists assert than no single one of the isolated volatile constituents can be viewed as the "key substance" of an aroma. As for taste, "specific experimental works on the taste of bread are more or less nonexistent," according to Richard-Molard. Until recently, researchers have settled for comparisons focusing on the more or less acidic character of the crumb (for example, the impact of acetic acid, which varies according to the method of fermentation) and the more or less salty taste, which depends directly on the amount of sodium chloride used.[72]

We know more about the question of flavor — taste and aroma — on the practical level than on the theoretical level. Very summarily defined as the "total sensory impression . . . in the mouth," taking into account smell, taste, and mouthfeel in particular, flavor as characterized by Raymond Calvel in The Taste of Bread is an implicitly quantitative notion (consisting of x grams of taste plus y grams of aromas, produced by making a particular gesture with particular ingredients), for on the qualitative level it is hardly differentiated and articulated at all. Calvel describes flavor in excessively general (although generous) terms to which is it impossible to give a precise content or weight (bread is "pleasant" or "appetizing" or "agreeable when eaten" or "seductive in the mouth") or he describes it quite simply in terms of its intensity: the taste is "decided," "delicate," or "subtle," or it is "weak" or of "moderate" flavor. In Calvel's writing, the entire negative register seems easier to manipulate and is in the end more telling discursively: the taste of bread may be "denatured" or "unpleasant"; it may be "insipid," "mediocre," or definitively "bad."

Despite his unparalleled expertise in the field, the breadmaking professor has trouble finding a descriptive language that is at once concrete, precise, and clear. He evokes "the flavor inherited from wheat"; the term is imagistic and rings of authenticity, but it is not necessarily very edifying for the urban consumer. Speaking of the use of sourdough culture, he brings into play one of the fundamental sensations, acidity, which is easy for most consumers to taste. The taste of bread made with yeast is not very acidic; it leaves room for "the aromas contributed by wheat flour" in association with the "alcoholic fermentation" of the dough and with "the baking process itself." Decidedly complicated and not very transparent, this formulation does not tell us just what flavor(s) may be involved. In the following passage, Calvel comes closer to specificity, which might reassure a consumer, but in a context that remains vague overall and even hermetic, "an original smell and taste which are the subtle amalgam of the odor of wheat flour and the oil of the germ with the slight hazelnut perfume it conveys, associated with the odor of the alcoholic fermentation of the dough and with the odor that results from the caramelization and baking of the crust, an odor that we find again, in a discreet form, in the crumb."[73]

Thus we observe how immensely difficult it is to develop a descriptive and analytic taxonomy of the sensory qualities of bread. It may well be impossible to go further. Nor have the best contemporary practitioners succeeded in forging tools for discrimination and appreciation that the consumer can readily use. Some speak of the "development of the aroma" as if there were but one, a sort of magical perfume that everyone can recognize because it unmistakably sounds the bell of quality. Others treat taste in the same involuntarily cavalier manner. There is such a thing as good taste, it is obvious, it evokes pleasure; these are sybaritic but sibylline appreciations. Rejecting the primacy of appearances, still others nevertheless end up speaking of virtually nothing else ("Sight: we do not eat with it, but . . ."). It is not surprising that consumers cannot say what good bread is when bakers themselves, including some of the most gifted practitioners, feel it only by instinct or habit and do not manage to articulate their criteria. How, then, can one speak about (good) bread? The remarks that follow do not purport to solve the problem; they aim primarily to relaunch and enrich the debate.

Tasting

From the perspective of professional bakers and consumers alike, it would seem interesting to develop the practice of tasting. Far too little attention is paid to this practice—and when it is discussed, for want of even a minimal formal apparatus (categories, vocabulary, and so on), the result is cacophony rather than reasoned and coherent debate. People are not necessarily talking about the same things when they evaluate a loaf of bread. In order to name, designate, compare, or measure (even in approximate terms), in order to advance both in improving the product and educating the consumer, a cognitive structure is a prerequisite. This need not be a procrustean bed where a single outlook would be born. On the contrary: given a prudent system of codification, we could accommodate the various sensibilities and subjectivities and take into account all the regional and local differences while making them more intelligible. A flexible protocol for tasting would give consumers more autonomy and more confidence; it might even make them more demanding. Consumers would be able to make informed choices. As they acquired additional sophistication, some would learn to vary their criteria for different types of bread and would associate certain types of food with certain breads. And all consumers, better informed and, I would hope, more enthusiastic, would have a tendency to eat more bread—although not just any bread.

The obvious model here is wine. However, the model must be used with considerable caution. A higher species in the gastronomic eucharist, wine has always been more aristocratic, more snobbish. Its solemn tasting can be a theatrical ritual, an aestheticized science, an art constructed in scholarly fashion. In relation to wine stewards or other confirmed connoisseurs able to detect a bouquet of animality at the first contact with a particular Bordeaux, a whiff of banana tempered by certain flowers in a Beaujolais, or an aromatic hint of truffle in aged red wines of superior quality, the rest of us feel organoleptically disadvantaged. While wine tasting at its most elaborate can appear to be over-the-top, pretentious ceremony, it nevertheless has the great merit of ensuring that wine is talked about, everywhere in the world, according to a system of codification that is essentially French. Discourse about wine has a coherent, common core, even if many tasters take shortcuts, simplifying some aspects of the protocol and adapting them for their own convenience. Moreover, professionals in the wine business encourage the democratization of tasting, offering increasing reassurances to customers who might be put off by the esotericism if not the preciousness of some aspects of the canonical high-level tasting practices.

Although the haughtiness of certain oenophiles can send shudders through bread lovers, who are more humble by nature, the latter should not fail to note the liberation from constraints that a touch of vanity can bring about. While bread tasters, positivist in their outlook, await the instructions of science before venturing forth into the sensory field, wine lovers do not hesitate to assert, concerning aromas, for example, that "the nose is often a much more sensitive detector than laboratory equipment, which explains the primacy of tasting where wine is concerned."[74]

So let us base our tasting system on a good blend of humility and cheek. Our goal is as much to raise awareness, or to arouse a passion, as to provide a useful framework for evaluation. Useful, in the case in point, means several things at once: accessible and relatively easy to handle; flexible enough to lend itself to both fairly simple and unabashedly refined assessments; anchored in the everyday reality of observations and sensations (working backward from certain indicators to facts that they make more or less probable), but without ruling out the possibility of speculative inference, thoughtful conjecture, or even fantasy (in moderate but bracing doses).[75]

To avoid becoming too disoriented, we shall return to familiar categories in our grid, although we shall endow them with a differentiated and more elaborate content in certain respects: appearance, crust, crumb, mouthfeel, odors and aromas, tastes and flavors, and harmony.[76] Let us add a final, personalized category to be called bread intuition.

Appearance
At first sight, good bread stimulates a desire to eat it. Of a deep golden yellow hue, it has a good structure, and its skin is more or less smooth and regular. It manifests confident scarification and attests to sufficient, well-managed baking.

Crust
Coming out of the oven, it sings, the result of cracks that form during cooling. A little later, when struck by a finger, it resounds like a drum and cracks

slightly under pressure. Its principal quality, for most French people today, is its crispness — its crustiness. Thin and crackly, the crust gives off particular smells evocative of grilling, caramel, and perhaps hazelnut, among others.

Crumb

Pearly in color rather than white, with a recent tendency toward a yellowish hue, the crumb reveals a highly elastic texture, neither gluey nor fluffy. It is naturally plump and often creamy. Its structure is the principal sign of its quality; its alveoli are irregularly shaped and spaced. Smooth to the touch, engaging in the mouth, the crumb nevertheless resonates, like the crust, when it is tapped. Between a good and a bad loaf, where aroma and flavor are concerned, the crumb rather than the crust makes the difference.

Mouthfeel

The first impression in the mouth is a pleasant sensation, an initial contact that is not an attack. Good bread is tender; it offers no resistance in the mouth (except for sourdough loaves, to a certain degree). The texture is not sticky; the bread is easy to taste. It stands up to chewing; it does not melt in the mouth right away, and it reveals the force of its taste only gradually.

Odors and Aromas

The oral (retronasal) phase of olfactory perception is generally conflated with what is perceived directly through the nose. In both cases, the active agents are volatile molecules that have to reach the olfactory epithelium that lines the inner walls of the nose.

If bread has a soul, as Baudelaire said of wine, it is surely to be sought in the constitution of its odors. A well-made bread will inexorably give off aromas. The first ones arise from the crust, but if the stronger and more differentiated aromas from the crumb are to be liberated, a baguette has to be sliced open vertically. In an initial phase, the taster will concentrate on the most obvious factor: the *overall intensity* of the aromas, going from zero to very strong. This factor might be rated according to a numerical scale, for example, from 1 to 5. Then the taster will move from intensity to the *form* of the aroma, in binary terms: it is either simple (a single odor, let us say, or one odor that predominates strongly) or complex (several distinct components can be identified).

The taster finally comes to the last rubric in this category, the *identification* of aromas and odors. This third rubric, for bread as for wine, applies only to great vintages, products of high quality, the fruit of in-depth research on the part of a small minority of bakers who are true creators, constantly renewing their production. Exceptional bread remains the prerogative of an elite. We may hope that the bakers who experiment endlessly with smells and tastes will bring their colleagues with them along the path to excellence. Thus, after characterizing the strength and form of the aromas or odors present, the taster tries to pin them down by *identifying* their properties. But here the distinctions are much more subtle and can easily escape us. Initially, to express identity, we might turn to a sort of scale of intensity, this time using words; for example, an aroma may be pale and weak as opposed to sparkling and lively, or, in a different register, it might be interesting or monotonous. Then we can try to express our impressions more precisely. The most obvious odors are probably those of grilling (some prefer to speak of an aroma of roasting, related to the caramelization of the crust), flour (but this odor is most readily detected by bakers, who are intimately familiar with the referent), yeast (a somewhat disagreeable odor, also more naturally detected by an artisan), or fermentation (an odor that may be pleasant, and should be accessible to the consumer). Many consumers would be able to identify the aroma of hot cereal. Some speak of the scent of harvest, but, to be operative, this metaphor has to have a basis in memory. It is perhaps tied to the strong sensation of freshness projected by a good loaf. Evocative for those who have a basis for familiarity is the aroma evoking a specific geographical and cultural location (*terroir*), a notion that is no longer the private preserve of wine since the great upheaval of restaurant chefs that took place some years ago. A loaf of sourdough bread often gives off the aroma—or the taste—of spices and honey (or gingerbread).

The quest to identify may lead tasters to venture into the riskier but not uninteresting realm of analogies with flowers, fruit (fresh, dried, or preserved), aromatic substances, and perhaps vegetables (in specific or generic terms). Without specificity, one hesitates to continue. Still, virtuosi such as Dominique Saibron and Éric Kayser invite us to feel and think

in terms of subtle tastes and smells, difficult to define, delicate in character, perhaps fleeting, but rich and interesting, sensations that envelop us
and call out to us simultaneously. Describing his *tourte* (made with stone-
ground flour and a natural sourdough culture), Kayser has said that "its
odor recalls honey and dried yellow flowers. It is an airy, balanced bread
that reveals its subtle floral aromas little by little during tasting." His rye
bread offers us an even more exotic sensory itinerary, with "its odor of
warm oriental spices, honey, pine sap, licorice, even anise." Kayser is ambitious, determined to convince us that his breads not only have disparate
perfumes but a true bouquet, aromatic characteristics that constitute a
cohesive whole. The baker does not ask us to take his word for it; he wants
us to try his bread, breathe it in, taste it, and then discover and identify
for ourselves the aromas that strike us. Our evaluation will not necessarily
correspond to the baker's somewhat idealized portrait. But by encouraging us to undertake the analysis, he will have provoked, enriched, perhaps
disoriented, and quite probably seduced us. Still, let us remain lucid so far
as our analytic grid is concerned: here we are flying high.

Tastes and Flavors
Let us recall that it is very difficult to distinguish between smells and tastes,
given the extent to which the two sensations are intermingled in production and reception alike. For many craftsmen, taste is, as it were, the summary of all the qualities of the bread, the last word. This complicates the
task of isolating taste(s), of measuring taste(s) in some way, of appreciat-
ing the taste or tastes of a particular bread. I propose to follow the same
approach as for the sister qualities, aromas and odors. First, we shall assess
the strength or overall intensity of the taste or tastes, influenced in particular by the first contact in the mouth. Then we can proceed to a binary
decoding of the form: simple (a single taste) or complex (several, in competition or in synergy). But before moving on to identification, I propose
two new headings, which do not necessarily presuppose great vintages:
the structure of the flavor (the impression of its morphology in the mouth
rather than of its specific gustatory characteristics) and the persistence of
the taste or tastes in the mouth.

Several terms allow us to give concrete form to the notion of gustatory structure in the mouth. In good bread, this structure is round rather
than angular. It fills the mouth well, amply but without heaviness. It

gives off the impression of creamy softness, a certain unctuousness. Well-structured bread has substance; it is not thin, weak, or fleshless. One feels that it has good balance. Structure without personality and without generosity is neutral at best, hollow if softness yields to weakness. The idea of gustatory persistence is easier to grasp. Another descriptive term borrowed from wine, this one refers to the impression of lingering presence that bread leaves after it is eaten. This criterion is of course linked to the overall intensity of flavors. Measured immediately in seconds, and measured again over time by its short-term and long-term inscription in memory, the duration of persistence—the length of time the taste lingers in the mouth—correlates with bread quality.

The identification of taste(s) poses all the problems already discussed in connection with smells. As long as we remain with the four elementary sensations, almost everyone can navigate more or less comfortably, with breads of highly variable quality. A good bread might hint of saltiness; some bakers count too much on salt to perk up the taste of their products. For Bernard Leblanc, who trains bakers at the GMP bakery school in Paris, a good loaf almost tastes of sugar "without being cloying"; this taste of sweetness is extremely familiar and carries a positive, reassuring connotation. Rarely bitter, bread may have an acidic taste, especially if it is made with sourdough. For me, Lionel Poilâne's entire genius is summed up in the note of acidity that marks his fine round loaves; others find them a little sour. Dominique Saibron and Éric Kayser, each in his own way, the first with solid sourdough culture and the second with a liquid version, have succeeded in greatly attenuating the acidity of their bread without sacrificing all the organoleptic advantages of sourdough. Frédéric Lalos develops the lactic action of fermentation to cultivate a sweet taste in opposition to the piquant note produced by an acetic fermentation.

The challenge of identification comes into play when one leaves the four elementary sensations behind for a more rarefied gustatory ambiance. On a still modest register, we are all familiar with the tastes of grilling and caramel produced by the crust and sometimes penetrating the crumb, analogous to the aromas discussed earlier. In certain delicious breads, I detect a pronounced taste of hazelnut, somewhat the way one can in a good Chardonnay, occasionally associated with an aromatic hint of butter. But can we go further? And, if so, by what methods? The system of analogies adopted for aromas sometimes lends itself to tastes. Thus, Éric Kayser describes the way his Paline bread tastes of dried fruit and almonds, with a blend of wheat and buckwheat. In practice, one ends up speaking not of taste but of flavor, as we have already seen—of the inextricable combination of taste and aroma that more faithfully reflects the sensory impression experienced by most people.

Harmony

To sum up our overall organoleptic evaluation, we can fall back on the notion of harmony. This is the idea of a more or less profound concord, on the sensory level, among all the components of a loaf of bread. When these relations, grasped by the senses, are cordial or balanced, they augur good quality.

Bread Intuition

This is a sort of right to extraterritoriality that invites consumers to give their imagination free rein in evaluating bread. This is where consumers can make their slash marks, inscribe their signatures, personalize their appreciations, through intuitions that do not enter into the categories of our grid: a sudden affection for a particular baker or product, a moment of irritation with the service in the bakery, a reaction that has no direct relation to the sensory qualities of the bread but that deserves critical notice nonetheless. Memory, which intervenes insidiously and often without our awareness, in the practice of our judgment, conditions all our choices, especially in the realm of food, and it may act openly here. In my own bread intuition, I express myself without worrying about the reality principle or about providing a rational justification for my opinion. This is where I can say without embarrassment that in every other loaf of Jean-Luc Poujauran's *demi-gros* I discover a slight taste of chocolate.

A Scoring System

A scoring system, like any theory, is reductive. This stems from its very nature and is the source of its potential usefulness. Using the categories developed above, I shall propose a weighting system that can of course be modified according to the consumer's own values and knowledge. Above the maximum official score of twenty points, the consumer may award up to one bonus point for an overall impression of coherence and effective-

Table 1. Evaluation of a Loaf of Bread

Criterion	Best possible score (in points)
Appearance	3
Crust	3
Crumb	3
Mouthfeel	1
Odors and aromas	5
Tastes and flavors	5
Harmony	1 [a]
Bread intuition	1 [a]
Total	20

[a] These are possible bonus points that do not count toward the total.

ness and a second point in order to correct or otherwise inflect the result in accordance with his own ideas.[77]

Warm Bread at Any Time of Day

One last question, a very current one, deserves our attention. It has to do with the association of good bread with warm bread. The identification of high quality with freshness, an extremely powerful one today, actually has a long history, although the notion of freshness has evolved considerably. In the nineteenth century, for example, fresh bread was first of all bread baked the previous day, before it became associated with the heat of cooking, despite the warnings of experts such as J. de Brévans saying that "it is good to let [bread] cool completely and grow partially stale." At the beginning of the twentieth century, in the face of a growing demand for an ultrafresh product, a breadmaking manual warned consumers against the dangers that loomed were they to eat warm bread: "Its crumb is still soft, heavy, and somewhat glutinous; this is why, in this state, this food produces serious indigestion and even leads to recurrent, intermittent fevers." This verdict could not have surprised the naturalists, from Sylvester Graham to Georges Barbarin, who asserted that "good bread, natural bread, is made to be eaten stale; the first day it is indigestible." Not to mention the first hour![78]

"Consumers are increasingly demanding that their bread be steaming hot," Émile Dufour complained in his treatise on the baking industry, published just before World War II. If there was a decline in quality and in the care that went into breadmaking, Dufour held customers partly responsible. Although other factors — social, legal, and professional — contributed to the modification of breadmaking techniques, Dufour was not entirely wrong to claim that Paris bakers "have been obliged to abandon the use of sourdough in breadmaking in order to satisfy the requirements of their clients, who want hot bread at any time of day." In addition to the storefront plaques reading "hot bread at all hours," in 1964 the trade press cited other evidence that many bakers baked "without respite." A few years later, Roland Guinet noted that clients identified fresh bread with warm bread. In 1990, a SOFRES (Société française d'études par sondages — a French survey institute) survey showed that the vast majority of customers preferred their bread very fresh, without specifying whether or not that meant hot. The same year, faced with increasingly brutal competition from industrial outlets (called terminals) and supermarket chains, the bakers' association in Paris advised its members to try "to offer warm bread at all hours, even late in the evening; your clientele will be grateful."[79]

Thanks to the use of refrigeration and delayed fermentation, warm bread can now be produced throughout the day without excessive expense. Since this is what consumers want, it is perfectly legitimate to conclude that warm bread is a good thing; Kayser thus assures us that "warm bread is offered to clients all day long."[80] In our day, no one worries about recurrent fevers or even indigestion, but there is concern about the effect of heat on flavor. Warm bread is extremely unstable. During a normal sweating followed by a gentle cooling-off period, the crust is rehumidified at the expense of the crumb. While the loaf is losing 1 to 2 percent of its weight through evaporation, an exchange of volatile compounds takes place between crumb and crust. In other words, the tastes and smells are still in the process of establishing themselves. The consumer who eats her bread warm is quite probably preventing the flavor from reaching its peak development. Still more seriously, heat itself has a tendency to mask smells and tastes, whatever their degree of maturity and specificity. Served very warm, in a friendly, sociable atmosphere, a quite mediocre bread could pass for a decent one. In the long run, the current leaning toward warm bread may threaten organoleptic quality as much as the earlier leaning toward "not too well-done" bread.

The Secrets of Good Bread

At the end of the long itinerary that has taken us through baking rooms past and present, how can we sum up the mystery of good breadmaking? Lionel Poilâne's profession of faith strikes me as pertinent: "One only makes good bread if one truly loves bread." But while this affective ferment may be absolutely necessary, it is not sufficient. Virtually everyone agrees that there is not just one single recipe. Still, this wholesale relativism has to be nuanced. Raymond Calvel has never tired of repeating that good bread "is a bread made with respect for the nature of things." Abstract and somewhat incantational, this formula appears luminous to its adherents and perfectly opaque to everyone else. We see what he is getting at more clearly when he evokes "the rules of the art, attached to the trade," practices and standards whose evolution we have followed over several centuries. Or when he says that good bread "is nature first of all, and then men." Nature and culture: the two poles that structure a large part of social life. But what role is to be attributed to each? Henri Nuret, a major specialist in wheat and flour who welcomed the young Calvel in 1936 as a baker in the École française de meunerie, stressed "the absolutely primordial importance of breadmaking technique for bread quality." Without being able to attribute precise coefficients to all the factors that have to be faced from one end of the chain to the other (and supposing the absence of significant anomalies), Nuret attributed 70 to 75 percent of the responsibility to the baker, 15 to 20 percent to the wheat, and 5 to 10 percent to the miller.[81]

Since Nuret was not a baker, we might have expected an overvaluation of the contribution made in the initial stages by farmers and millers. Hardly inclined to underestimate their contribution to the fabrication of good bread, the young masters of today, direct descendents of Dr. Malouin and Professor Calvel, place more stress on the fact that their results depend in large part on putting to work a good flour, drawn, a fortiori, from a wheat known for its breadmaking qualities. "Just as the cépage has a great influence on wine," Éric Kayser maintains, "so the taste of bread is to a large extent determined by the flours used." A Jansenist baker (a character trait befitting an artisan whose baking room is located a few steps away from the old Saint-Médard cemetery), Dominique Saibron, to safeguard the purity of his aromas and tastes, imposes a draconian set of requirements on his miller, excluding any sort of additive, adjuvant, or technological aid, even the fungal amylases that are omnipresent in flour. Patrick Castagna, a professor at the National Bread and Pastry Institute, postulates for his part a direct link between the quality of the flours used (the best ones being those that "let themselves go") and the originality of the taste, celebrating stone-ground flour in particular (here he is going against the Calvel doctrine, as Calvel turns out to be an apologist for the contemporary milling industry; he maintains that metallic cylinders give the same results as millstones).[82]

And yet at the start of the third millennium, the precise causes that lie behind the production of good bread remain obscure. We simply know that various factors come into play: the quality of the flour, the way the dough is kneaded, the dosage of the fermenting agent, the duration of fermentation, and the mode of baking—to the point that we have trouble determining whether a change in the fabrication procedure clearly modifies the quality of the taste or the aroma. Looking to the future, certain millers envisage a kind of flavor engineering that would allow artisanal bakers to achieve more or less precisely the tastes and odors promised by the breadmaking procedure they adopt. Thanks to a better knowledge of the wheat genome—one of the most complex there is—and to the mastery of techniques of traceability, millers are projecting a significant expansion in the "interactions between farmland [and] the farming method on the one hand, and the taste and quality of the bread produced on the other." They count on being able to create flours corresponding to "various sensory profiles," made-to-measure taste for an increasingly segmented market. For certain bakers, the prospect amounts to an organoleptic Eldorado; for others, it smacks rather of Huxley's brave new world.[83]

The fact remains that with the best raw materials in the world, an ill-trained or insufficiently motivated baker cannot make good bread. This is why Nuret attached so much weight to the competence of the artisan. And it is why we have paid so much attention to breadmaking techniques from the eighteenth century on. I have stressed fermentation as the key to breadmaking. In a way, the story of sourdough eclipsed by yeast sums up the entire history of modern breadmaking. (The discreet return of sourdough today, often in the context of deferred fermentation facilitated by refrigeration, is probably mapping out one possible scenario for the future.) But we have also seen the enormous influence on bread quality of the other stages, especially kneading, shaping, and baking. Each of these phases is extremely delicate and complex, and each sums up the chronic tension between past and future, tradition and innovation, social progress and artisanal nostalgia, hands and machines, slowness and speed, quality and productivity, fidelity and apostasy. We shall examine certain of these tensions more closely in the chapters that follow, and this will help make it clear how bread came to fall so low, and why it is coming back to life.

chapter two

Bread: The Double Crisis

D URING THE EIGHTEENTH CENTURY, IN A CONTEXT
of chronic penury and recurrent food shortages, virtually the entire French population drew most of its
calories from bread, and the authorities dreamed of reducing consumption. In the late twentieth century, when bread no longer had
society bound up by the "cords of necessity," the utopian dream
of the guardians of the bakery trade was of increasing consumption. One
of the most telling statistics in the past three centuries of French history
is precisely that of bread consumption per capita per day. Social, political,
and economic modernization took place in parallel with the desacralization of bread. Before it was a pleasure, bread was a matter of (material)
survival and (spiritual) salvation, a symbol in daily life more of misery and
dependence than of well-being and transcendence. The tyranny of bread
was articulated with other forms of oppression suffered by subjects, who
were not yet citizens. One of the paradoxes of the Old Regime was that
the power structure did not escape this tyranny any more than the populace did, for the stability and legitimacy of those in power depended to a
large extent on the way they managed the problem of the food supply, the
greatest *political* question of the time. Freeing itself from the ever-heavier
and often brutal domination of bread was a great relief to the state as
well as to society; this shift was perceived by all sides as real progress. The
emancipation in question came about in the course of several sociopolitical and cultural revolutions, some spectacular technological mutations, an
uneven and nonlinear but in the long run continuous economic growth,
and the gradual spread of an improved standard of living. In the wake of

the democratization of access to white wheat bread (long seen as the best and most prestigious of breads)—a necessary reparation of timeless injustices—the decline in bread consumption among all social strata could only be interpreted as a favorable indicator.

The Crisis and Its Causes

This uninterrupted decrease in bread consumption seemed to sound the death knell of traditional French breadmaking. For in the logic of its stubborn persistence it appeared to signal not only the massive material adjustment required by modernization but a supplementary rejection, even a true sanction, disaffection rather than mere diversification in social and nutritional habits. Despite certain polemical or mythico-sentimental exaggerations, the statistics cannot be challenged, not so much in the rigor of their details (for if we go back to 1750 we are unable to come up with a reliable picture of bread consumption in terms of age, sex, type of work and socioeconomic status, place, and so on) but in their general, overall tendency. Toward the end of the eighteenth century, when an active farmer ate up to a kilo of bread a day (more at harvest time) and an urban worker ate a good three-quarters of a kilo, the average estimates vary between 550 and 700 grams per day (these figures may well be low). Per capita consumption went up in the nineteenth century: almost 700 grams at mid-century; around 800 at century's end according to one source, between 500 and 600 according to another. Around 1920, estimates range from 628 to 424 grams. In 1930, estimates fall just below 400 grams; 373 in 1940, a somewhat contestable figure; 500 in 1946, doubtless an overoptimistic calculation; 324 in 1950, perhaps a bit low; 290 in 1975; between 267 and 300 in 1960 (the sources differ); then the collapse becomes clear: from 236 grams in 1965, there is a shift to 182 in 1975, then 150 in 1993, before a slight improvement at the end of the twentieth century, when the average may have reached 165 grams.

How did consumption fall so far? Some observers began to raise that question as early as World War I. It became a real obsession in the trade during the Thirty Glorious Years, the period of economic prosperity following World War II. The notion of underconsumption, the standard term for discussing the phenomenon, betrays a normative judgment as well as a category of evaluation.

Turning to the question in a rather similar way despite very different trajectories and formal interests, scholars and professionals have quickly gotten into the habit of distinguishing between legitimate causes (legitimate because they are inscribed in the evolution of humanity and thus inevitable because they are reasonable) and illegitimate factors (illegitimate because they are based on erroneous principles or because they are unjust). The curiously reassuring consensus—for it involves effects beyond anyone's control—is that the first great cause of the decline in bread consumption was simply progress in all directions. This was one of the major conclusions of the national center for study and research in applied nutrition (CNERNA), which began holding scientific colloquia devoted to bread in 1948. Technological innovations, social advances, legislative interventions, and psychocultural metamorphoses all flowed into a society in which people were expending much less energy than before. The mechanization of agricultural and factory work, transportation, and household tasks, along with improvements in heating systems, considerably reduced energy needs, especially the need for carbohydrates, the main constituents of cereals. How could we not congratulate ourselves over this reduction in the sometimes exhausting efforts to which people had been subjected?

A less mechanical but hardly less important factor was the rise of the least privileged social classes toward increased well-being. Cereals were supplanted by foods long considered the prerogative of the well-to-do classes: fresh vegetables, fruit, cheese, fish, and especially meat. This second cause seems equally justified: it results from a "legitimate desire" on the part of individuals to enjoy all the edible goods produced, to replace nutritional monotony and the excessive preponderance of one particular food, and to increase their sense of social competence and self-esteem. Raymond Calvel added a third cause: the negative impact—the "harmfulness"—of the painful experience of World War II on consumer practices. Wartime bread, subject to rationing and of very poor quality, incited people to find substitutes and to develop other tastes. When peace was restored, many people never returned to their earlier level of bread consumption. Finally, the professionals invoked the orientation of consumption toward "small items": large loaves no longer suited the lifestyle or mentality of the French population. At best, bread was a kind of accompaniment to a meal: a 1977 survey noted that "bread appears less and less as a food that is indispensable to life."[1]

Although the state, in its capacity as regulator, stimulant, and under-writer, is not often invoked to explain the decline in consumption, it does play an important role, one that the trade surely takes into account. Politics is never absent from the history of bread. Between the nurturing prince and the providential state, the government of the Old Regime exercised a "bread policy"—more flexible in practice than is usually claimed—based on regulation of the grain and flour markets and controls on the price of bread. Symbolizing the involvement of power on the side of consumers, price controls had an economic as well as a psycho-political importance. In an article in early 1957, under the title (and profession of faith) "The Only Thing That Counts: Bread Consumption in France Is Declining," *Le petit meunier* suggested somewhat obliquely that the state's tireless interventionism was driving bakers, who were no longer inspired by their artisanal vocation, to lose interest in bread: "The further we go, the fewer bakers there are worthy of the name; they are just vendors of pastry and candy. For the good reason that making and selling bread does not provide them with a living wage. There is the scandal." Scandalized in turn by the way the millers viewed the bakery trade, members of the bakers' association called the milling business into question in their condemnation of "the politics of the symbolic low price of bread, which for too long has slowed down improvement in the quality of flour," thereby compromising bread quality.

Three decades later, without completely exonerating the bakers, an important miller, Philippe Viron, called the state into question directly. Between 1959 and 1990, consumption had fallen from 250 to 150 grams. Viron attributed this decline to the disappearance of a good-quality baguette, which resulted in turn from "price-fixing" by the state: price controls obliged bakers to "increase their productivity" by rushing into the race to mechanize, not always prudently. Developing his analysis somewhat hastily, Viron asserted that the new machines (especially dividers and shapers) imposed new procedures that virtually suppressed the first fermentation, the *pointage* that gives bread its flavor; baking in a rotating rack oven was the last straw. Why should consumers remain faithful to inferior bread?[2]

In the category of unfair arguments, according to our experts, the exemplary and intolerable case was the widespread belief that ordinary bread was harmful to one's health. Although we lack tools to measure the impact of the attack on bread with any precision, it seems certain that this belief weighed heavily in the steady decrease in consumption. It was of unprecedented force, and it claimed support from a large sector of the medical profession. The only bread that might have earned medical approval was the bread of "yesteryear," a place and a time inscribed in the imagination, impossible to subject to comparative examination. Covering a broad spectrum of issues, "scientific" warnings did not stop at blaming bread for undue weight gain (on this question, women's magazines were already advocating the cult of slenderness, relaying the viewpoint of the medical profession and conflating an aesthetic issue with a health problem); doctors accused it of causing cavities, tuberculosis, alcoholism, blood diseases, digestive disorders, and even cancer. We can identify a classic set of critiques inspired by a providentialist–naturalist vision: proponents did not seek to eliminate bread from the diet but rather to introduce a "complete" bread made from whole wheat grains — gems of nutritional value — and all or most of the husk. White bread was the enemy of this camp: from the late 1950s on, bread had never been so white. The decline in consumption constituted a "silent protest" against white bread, according to the author of the *Le scandale du pain*, who predicted that "well before the end of the current century no one would consume white bread any longer." Taken aback and furious, *Le Boulanger-Pâtissier* commented: "At a time when humanity is finally reaching the achievement of its old dream, white bread in profusion, medicine is proclaiming the virtues of black bread, the poor man's bread, made with bran."

Another more modern voice sought to appear as more rigorously scientific, focusing on what was added to bread rather than what was taken away. Despite its extravagances, this thesis, sketched out before World War II and amplified since, has an astonishingly contemporary flavor, anticipating what we now call food safety. Bread was said to cause illness because high-yield varieties of wheat were selected, submerged in chemical fertilizers, and treated with pesticides and other chemical products. These contaminated or unreliable flours — probably treated chemically once again at the mill, where "ameliorating" agents were already under investigation as pathogens — were used to make bread according to modern methods that were equally harmful: fermentation with manufactured yeast, a product denounced as "chemical," was replacing the natural, tried-and-true process based on sourdough, and a toxic fuel (oil) was replacing a noble and innocent one (wood) for baking.

The significance of these arguments becomes clear if we look back at the climate of the period. In late 1957, a school principal in Côtes-du-Nord refused to allow bread to be served in the school lunchroom, to protect the children's health. The following year, the National Bakery Confederation took the weekly magazine *La Presse* to court on a charge of slander; the magazine had treated bread as nothing less than "a fearful poison," not such a shocking accusation a few years after an incident in which mysterious deaths were associated with "cursed bread" in Pont-Saint-Esprit; in this small town near Avignon, several hundred people fell ill, scores experienced hallucinations, and "the entire population thought it had been poisoned by flour." According to a survey carried out in the early 1960s, four doctors out of five "recommended against or ruled out bread for their patients." In a country where "no ameliorating agent is tolerated in bread, there are doctors who seem to want to attribute all the ills of humanity to bread consumption," a professional publication complained bitterly in 1954, comparing the medical profession to the clergy taking on satanic evildoings in Loudun and elsewhere.[3]

According to a third hypothesis, consumers rejected bread not only because they considered it outmoded or devalorizing (nutritionally or socially), but because they found it of poor quality. This assertion was shocking because it contradicted a stereotype that fed a certain national pride: good French bread was the best bread in the world. Of course negative judgments on bread can be found going back to the eighteenth century, but these almost always involved bread for the poor, bread in the provinces, or bread produced under hardship conditions. It is striking to see the extent to which urban consumers of quite modest social rank under the Old Regime insisted on good bread, even when they did not have enough to eat. The classic bread riot resulted from an inadequate supply or high prices, but indignant consumers disappointed by the poor quality of the bread on offer also protested, and their reaction was not considered frivolous — precisely because poor quality was perceived as a provocation, even during food shortages.

When Did Bread Turn Bad?

But at what point did bread become bad, or, more precisely, at what point was it first denounced as bad? The chronology is of crucial importance in the construction of the vulgate of bad bread, for every generation of critics declares that the bread of its day is the only truly bad bread, and that it bears no resemblance to the bread of earlier times, which had not yet been corrupted or degraded. There is a good deal of mystification and very little rigor in this narrative, which operates by juxtaposing an Edenic moment with a fall from grace. Memory is short and discontinuous; science is mobilized as much to cut losses as to analyze and historicize the causes of the problem; marketing eagerly seizes on the situation to instrumentalize it. What people are praising or condemning is not bread itself but the way it is represented, and they are acting for ideological or practical reasons of which they may well be unaware.

For example, an article in the first issue of *Michel Montignac Magazine*, which focused chiefly on bread, includes the following assertions: "Until breadmaking was industrialized in early 1960s, French bread was viewed as a model, the envy of foreigners. Its quality has not stopped declining ever since, so that it is now among the worst in the world."[4] It may have been a model abroad, but not in France. In 1937, at the heart of what Philippe Viron regards as the golden age of the good baguette, the president of the Paris bakers' association, E. Guillée, wrote that "in fact bread has never been subject to so much debate, and especially its quality, which, according to some, is currently inferior to that of bread in earlier times." Of course, as other association spokespersons on the warpath against the treacherous past would have occasion to do, Guillée denounced as "pure legend [the idea] that today's bread does not [measure up] to that of the past." But even as he denounced the perfidy of nostalgia, he recognized that enough people were complaining about quality for it to constitute a real problem for the trade. At the same time, Émile Dufour, the author of a *Traité pratique de la panification* (Practical Treatise on Breadmaking), observed a relation between the decline of consumption and a deterioration in quality, although he imputed part of the responsibility to the attractiveness of meat, which was becoming increasingly affordable. Numerous associations militated in favor of increased bread consumption in the late 1920s, placing more and more stress on quality during the decade that followed. Many voices were raised against an approach that focused on "propaganda" as a solution to doubt, to the detriment of efforts to make truly qualitative improvements.[5]

World War II opened up a parenthesis that lasted well beyond the end of hostilities. But the question of bread quality arose fairly quickly. CNERNA was created in 1946, and one of its first missions was to look into the situation of bread.[6]

Confession

It would be unjust to say that the function of the bread commission set up by CNERNA was to "whitewash" bread. It brought together competent — and in some cases eminent — people of integrity, from various professional horizons, who were often rather combative; the transcripts of their meetings make it clear that the commission's members worked in a critical spirit. But they were also determined to clean up the territory so that the trade could regain its momentum. They sought to unmask and discredit the misinformation and outright lies that were handicapping the bread industry so badly: they wanted to establish (or reestablish) canons that would structure and define the practices of the trade, to give it not an immaculate conception but a new lease on life. Salvation lay in quality; to get there, artisanal bakers needed only renewed determination, for they already knew how to make good bread — it was in their very nature, even if they did not manage it every day. This exhortation-confession was heavy with pathos:

> We will put an end, believe me, to this decrease in consumption. If we proceed in such a way that those who still eat [bread] find it good, I believe there, and only there, is our salvation. If we decide to insist that tomorrow's daily bread be better than today's. If we want it better every day, lighter, better cooked, our clients will quickly take note, will appreciate it more and consume more. We will have saved our bread and our profession.[7]

While he criticized the exaggerations in such statements, Raymond Calvel reluctantly agreed that there was some truth in the claim that the quality of French bread had deteriorated. But the professor of breadmaking chose not to accuse bakers themselves, at least not directly. Writing on the eve of the wave of modernization in the industry (about which what he had to say was not always complimentary), he attributed the deficiency in quality in part to a diminution in the "already weak profit margin," implying that this resulted from state price-control policies, which "often prohibited indispensable investments that would make it possible to ensure a rational approach to fabrication." For him, the problem lay in part in the insufficiency of accessible information, so that even bakers with the best of intentions found themselves "having a hard time adapting to the technological evolution of production." A corporatist in the style of professors from Parmentier on, Calvel advocated not "training in baking rooms," which was too haphazard, but "training in schools," where basic principles were inculcated and the improvement of skills could be monitored.[8]

While the profession as a whole had little taste for critical introspection, certain voices in the bakery business cited working procedures among the reasons for the parallel decline in quality and in consumption. Everyone agreed that wartime conditions had led bakers to work badly and to do a poor job of transmitting their skills. After the war, they did all they could to work faster, produce more and whiter bread, and increase their productivity. The trade press recognized the dangers of an exaggerated "acceleration" of the production process. According to some commentators, this was a result of the state's insistence on "maintaining a low price for bread," an old political reflex. The press was echoing an accusation within the trade itself according to which the direct method of breadmaking, which had become virtually universal well before the war, was partly responsible for the decline in consumption.[9]

CNERNA Investigates and Reassures

Well before the formal appearance of the CNERNA commission's thousand-page report, *La qualité du pain*, the National Bakery Confederation's in-house journal published the gist of its conclusions, most of which were to the association's satisfaction.[10] Even the term "quality" is not entirely innocent. Without carefully defining quality, the commission made it clear that the notion could be approached from various and not necessarily compatible angles. Thus, for the farmer, quality was measured in terms of yield, resistance to disease, and suitability for mechanization—features that did not necessarily lead to a flour apt to produce good bread. The commission gave an accounting of the very significant changes undergone by the wheat industry in recent times: genetic selection by varieties, total replacement of natural fertilizers by chemical products, dependence on machines at every stage, and so on. While some of its members had criticized the already blind productivism of agriculture and others had expressed reservations about dependence on chemicals, the commission sought to be serene and reassuring. Yes, the entire industry needed to take into account the primordial importance of consumption, but it was important to remember that these new wheat varieties were not at all harmful and could in no way keep today's bread from rivaling the excellent bread of earlier times. Milling had changed as much as agriculture had in its methods of producing and storing flour, but neither the techniques for crushing and sifting nor the new blends should prevent millers from producing flour that would in turn produce superb breads.

Yet breadmaking, too, had changed considerably over the past half-century, especially in the way fermentation was managed. Here again, the commission tried to reassure its principal interlocutor, the French public, despite the highly technical nature of its deliberations. Mechanical kneading has no negative effects on bread quality; on the contrary, it has vastly improved the quality of working conditions for bakers, shop owners, and workers. The increasing importance of yeast and the declining use of sourdough, owing to use of the direct method, were more delicate matters. Intimately associated with traditional artisanal skill, sourdough culture had become a kind of guarantee of quality or, rather, an emblem of lost quality. At the same time, public "opinion," ill-informed and perhaps too easily aroused, confused yeast (sometimes called organic or baker's yeast, or still more frankly industrial yeast) with "chemical substances" such as Anglo-American baking powder. Hovering over agriculture and breadmaking alike, the word "chemical" had diabolical and terrifying connotations.

To exorcise fear and panic, the commission began by declaring that yeast, at least the yeast present in bread in France, was not a chemical substance: all chemical additives were prohibited in France (ascorbic acid—vitamin C—was obviously not viewed as a chemical substance, for its place in breadmaking was sacred, within certain precise limits, along with "natural" additives such as fava flour, soy, and malt). Even as it defended the present against the past, the commission sought to reassure consumers in another quite different realm to which they were particularly sensitive, that of health. Here, in the discussion of quality, taste took a back seat to safety. The commission contemplated establishing "limits of impurity," a notion that consumers found as disturbing then as they do now. No one was comfortable with the articulation of "acceptable standards" or "normal limits"—the expression borders on the oxymoronic—on pesticide or insecticide content or on other products whose toxicity is relativized with all the complacency of ultrapositivist science. Similarly, it was risky to evoke the copper content of bread, for it was hard to gain acceptance for the idea that copper occurred naturally in wheat.[11]

Without neglecting the trees, the commission's director Émile Terroine wanted above all to show the forest, to get consumers to understand, no matter what the badly or partially informed press might say, that the bread of the day was perfectly healthy. As far as that was concerned, the public seemed less interested in bread's ability to foster good health than in assurances that it was not harmful. Thus, for the bakers as well as the consumers, it was even more reassuring to declare that "the claim that bread leads to alcoholism and cancer has no scientific basis whatsoever" than to state that "doctors view bread as a food of the highest value in healthy individuals."[12]

Buoyed by the 1960–62 report, which was followed by the work of a second commission between 1965 and 1977, in the decade that followed the profession was preoccupied with modernization.[13] After some hesitation, it surfed on the huge wave of the new white bread, and it encouraged bakers to mechanize. One would have needed the gift of prophecy, during that period of optimism and faith in industrial progress, to determine the degree of illusion that was conveyed by this dream. A large part of the French population was afraid of missing the boat. To bakers as to many others, the siren of modernization seemed to speak a language that was as consistent as it was captivating. The choice was not between quality and ease of production, but between inertia leading to deadly stagnation and actions leading to creative renewal.

In the 1970s, the National Bakery Confederation set up an Institut national de la boulangerie-pâtisserie (National Bread and Pastry Institute) in Rouen. Its primary mission was to train bakers, providing basic instruction to neophytes and continuing education to people in the trade. After taking some time to get its bearings, it also became a center for research and reflection that has not always followed the association line. At the same time, severe critiques of excessive modernization were shaking up the profession. Raymond Calvel, for one, attributed the spectacular annual decrease in consumption (about 3 percent) to deviations that penalized taste and "disillusioned" consumers. Around 1980, "modern" bread in France, even for foreigners, was "no longer the bread we once knew and loved."[14]

A Confederation for Quality

After several years of vague, pious discourse that masked a certain disarray, the confederation began to ask itself whether the problem might not lie after all in public relations. Bakers are making "an effort in the area of quality day after day," confederation president F. Combe declared, but "in silence." Perhaps consumers ought to be "better informed in matters of quality" — in the final analysis a perfectly anodyne resolution. A priori, Combe welcomed mechanization with open arms: "Artisanal baking is fortunate enough to have access to suitable equipment that makes it possible to work dough and respect the traditional rules of our trade." The chief merit of the "artisanal equipment" alluded to here is that it rules out any wholesale rejection of machines. Still, its multiple nuances limit its impact considerably: "The maintenance and improvement of quality mean that equipment must not be substituted for the artisan's skill." In a similar vein, Combe noted that "the use of certain equipment betrays the artisanal vocation of the baker," and that "the quality of the bread made with certain types of machines was harmful to the image of our profession as a whole." It was rare for an association leader to speak so frankly to the rank and file about the path they had been following for some twenty years. He minced no words with producers, asking them to cooperate with bakers on a "serious study" of "the strengths and deficiencies of the equipment [they were being] offered."[15]

A few years later, the new president, Jean Paquet, said he wanted to make quality the confederation's "byword." This wish reflected not so much a Socratic analysis as an essentialist affirmation: we are better than our giant industrial rivals because we still practice artisanal baking. "Nothing equals the quality of bread made by a conscientious and highly skilled artisan," Paquet announced, as if this result were in some sense inevitable. "Only the artisan, through his training and experience, is able to master the tools to produce, from an always living dough, the traditional French bread that constitutes the nobility of our trade." However, he could not hide a real anguish, an uneasiness charged with twenty years of "progress" that was proving more and more ambiguous: "To be sure, this is not simple, in a period when the appeal of facility is great and when the sole criterion of productivity disconcerts those who refuse to produce bread that is all things to everyone." He warned his colleagues against a single-minded and seemingly profitable productivism that would overshadow quality, undermining the path to the future. And as early as 1983 he admitted that the confederation had "underestimate[d] the importance of the 'quality' factor."[16]

To highlight the confederation's renewed commitment, Paquet organized a "Congress for Quality." But, as we have seen, the term quality can hide a variety of concerns. As a common platform, it had to mobilize the troops behind serious demands rather than summoning them to undertake a demoralizing self-examination. Thus, in its first incarnation, quality was defined in economic terms: it was necessary "to do everything possible to gain recognition for the economic value of the high-quality artisanal product we are making." This allowed the president to do one of two things. He could criticize the state for imposing a sort of ceiling price through so-called moderation agreements, for "an insufficient price deprives us of the necessary means for high-quality fabrication" (this was a presumably reasonable and classically corporatist argument, four centuries old). Alternatively, by accepting the hypothesis that what would be in effect a single price "makes the notion of quality the sole argument at the level of competition," he could criticize the state for refusing to impose rules of fair competition that would prevent the big discount chains and industrial bakeries from spoiling everything by setting loss-leader prices (for example, the famous one-franc baguette).[17]

Bakers, to Arms! The Estates General of 1983

The meeting of the Estates General of artisanal bakers in 1983 was Jean Paquet's riskiest and most ambitious project. It was a matter of mobilizing public opinion, galvanizing the will of the major players in the wheat-flour-bread sector, and of inciting the state to support confederation policy. Shot through with contradictions and ambivalence, it was at once the sunshine operation on which the bakers' association prided itself and a high-level undertaking in marketing and manipulation. For the profession, it was the halting start of an appeal to bakers, who were invited to question their own procedures (in the end, this process took roughly two decades to achieve its aim) and who were reassured that they were already doing virtually all they could. These messages were combined with a more or less tacit critique of across-the-board mechanization and an injunction to complete the modernization of the baking rooms on one hand and an exhortation to remain artisanal on the other, the latter being the key to the bakers' difference in relation to the competition. Yet at the same time artisanal bakers were being asked to adopt the attitudes of businessmen rather than craftsmen. They were urged to stake everything on the quality of their product, but at the same time they were exhorted to stress the purely commercial dimension of their business, since they no longer had a captive clientele. Finally, bakers were enjoined to become aware of the crisis in the rest of the profession, but not to fall into a state of paralyzing gloom, while keeping in mind that this crisis — the perennial crisis — was a widespread phenomenon.

The message to the public was just as ambiguous. The image of bread had to be burnished, for the primordial objective of the confederation's massive campaign was to perk up consumption as quickly and as powerfully as possible. But to be credible, artisanal baking had to make its mea culpa in one way or another. Consumers had to be enlisted as wholly loyal clients of artisanal breadmaking; it was in their own interest and in France's interest, virtually a patriotic duty corresponding to cultural and economic needs alike. But those same consumers had to be made more demanding, and thus freer and more autonomous, by being better informed. The choice would be theirs, but they still had to be made to understand that they needed bread for health as well as for pleasure — not just any bread, but good bread, bread made the way artisans made it (or would make it, the way they used to; the message remains unclear on this crucial point, both for bakers and for their clients).

Consisting simultaneously of expert testimony, self-analysis, an advertising campaign, and a massive celebration of the trade, these Estates General announced not only the end of the old regime of bread but the determination to undertake a serious self-study, if not to make a break with the past. In this version of 1789 "light," Jean Paquet sought precisely to highlight the profession's determination to renew itself by comparing the bakers' association's effort to "assess the current state of artisanal baking" with the monarchy's attempt to assess France's condition by means of lists of grievances. Just as in 1789 the state sought to organize a social consensus in the general interest, "in the face of the general disarray of finances and states of mind," artisanal baking now sought to "improve the consensus" within the trade. In 1789, France placed its trust in the Estates General because it "felt that it was at a turning point in its history." According to Paquet, "breadmaking too [was] at a turning point in its history" and it hoped, thanks to the impetus given by its Estates General, "to arouse a new state of mind in artisanal baking."

Casting a critical glance at the practices of artisanal baking and its association, by "opening up a public debate on bread quality" the confederation president sought to bring the profession to as clear-cut a self-examination as the one that took place in 1789. This was the only way "to adapt ourselves to the evolution of our clients' taste," to learn how to sell in the new competitive commercial landscape, and to reaffirm the artisanal vocation of "true public service." In the spirit of 1789, everything had to be called into question, not merely the way bread was made and sold. At its most lyrical level, "the bakers' revolt," as it was christened by *Le Républicain Lorrain*, led to the societal choices that the French had to make: between "fair play" and "unfair competition," between neighborhood outlets and large-scale impersonal exchanges, between information-based consumption and mystification, between autonomy and artisanal creativity on one hand and industrial domination and asphyxiation on the other, between moorings in a long history that perpetuated enriching traditions and a blank slate subjected solely to the profit principle.[18]

The revolution Jean Paquet dreamed of was "a change in mentalities" involving artisans and consumers alike. In the end, the association called upon the French to maintain a sort of cultural exception, "the national character of artisanal French bread," as a vehicle for and guarantor of French values and French identity. The fall in consumption eventually accelerated the decline in the number of artisanal bakeries; more than ten thousand disappeared in thirty years. At the end of the day, one could imagine the Americanization, as it were, of the entire sector: it would be industrialized, depersonalized, standardized.[19]

A considerable degree of realism marked the confederation's thinking on the eve of the October 1983 meeting. Traditions and expectations notwithstanding, a preparatory document conceded that, clearly, "the French are not eternal bread-eaters. The level of consumption of bakery products will depend increasingly on their quality." Even if studies of motivation revealed the consumer's reticence toward the industrial version, which had "a bad image," it was necessary to recognize that "the difference between industrial bread and artisanal bread has shrunk." Calling the bakers "to arms" for the Estates General, the confederation's first thought was for the "weapon of quality": "Yes, quality, more quality, always quality," association president Jean Cabut insisted. Artisanal bakers had to reinforce this crucial difference with respect to industrial breadmaking, and at the same time they had to work on the quality of their service, the "distribution function," at the points where consumers seek human contact, social recognition, and safety. Torn between the impulse to impose a single, indisputable standard of quality (the republican approach?) and the impulse to relativize the notion of quality in relation to differences in age, sex, socioeconomic level, health, or eating habits among consumers (a sort of communitarianism?), bakers would increasingly have to engage in dialogue with their clients and work on educating them in bread and gastronomy. Henceforth, quality would be, by design, a multifaceted concept.[20]

For some participant-observers, the return to quality necessarily entailed an explicit rejection of certain forms of "progress." Guy Boulet, an innovative rural baker and humanist, saw the Estates General as the starting point for "an awareness of the negative effects of mechanization at the expense of quality." In his own way, Raymond Calvel distinguished sharply between positive and negative progress in the name of the quality of good French bread. For Calvel, there were "beneficial" stages (mechanical kneading, breadmaking "intelligently carried out" by the direct method, the "judicious" addition of ascorbic acid), others that "verged on being harmful" (baking on sheets or in wire molds, mechanical shaping, and controlled proofing, when these procedures "are ill-adapted or badly managed," and still others that were "frankly compromising" (the presence of fava flour, associated with "the widespread abuse of intensive kneading," and the excessive use of additives. Despite these significant and increasingly common critiques, the Estates General avoided taking a clear stance on breadmaking methods.[21]

Led by the sociologist Michel Crozier, who knew his way around in situations of social obstruction, a commission on bread and society explored a number of fascinating questions involving the quasi-institutional and symbolic role of bread in daily life. "How can a society be made of individuals?" Jean-Jacques Rousseau asked more than two hundred years ago. Speaking of city and country alike, Michel Crozier replied that his compatriots needed to weave into the social fabric bakeries close to home or bread trucks that deliver; like a sort of societal gluten, sources of bread constitute networks of sociability that structure daily life. Anyone at all inclined to follow Durkheim would have to take the sociocultural vocation of bread into account in regional planning. The commission counted on mobilizing appointed and elected officials at the local level to these ends.

Quality Running Rampant

Somewhere between a marketing ploy and a fundamental concern, the idea of quality was shaking up the profession. In late 1986, the Fédération régionale du Centre de la boulangerie announced a "quality charter" that would explain to the public that the signers were committing themselves to respect quality at several levels (hygienic, nutritional, organoleptic, and so on). The organizers also saw this as "an effective tool for struggling against a competition that strives to seize for its own advantage an image resulting from the efforts of artisanal bakers." The following year, Jean Paquet praised the publication of a decree instituting a "high council of artisanal quality." This reform recommended various ways to make the artisanal presentation or product — that is, the quality product, according to the underlying dogma — distinguish itself from the standardized products offered by the big chains.

At the same time and in the same spirit (commercial rather than critical), eleven departmental associations from Provence formed a group to promote quality artisanal bread, essentially in order to launch a "public relations campaign" — the bakers were modernizing their discourse — "to distinguish artisanal bakeries from the competition of bread vendors who used frozen dough, in order to restore the image of the profession and bring the faithless clientele back into the shops." Here the idea is not at all to ask questions about the way bread is made. The artisan "who takes the dough out of his kneading trough" — the poster for the campaign revealed that the secret of good bread lay in this magical gesture — is supposed to produce quality. A similar return to quality was announced at the other end of France a few years later, in the department of Nord-Pas-de-Calais. Mobilized here too by the competition of big discount chains, which had the effrontery to market a bread that was called "artisanal" but that was actually of "average quality," the bakers decided to go beyond words to action. "We have attended to quality by returning to a less industrialized bread," they confessed in all simplicity, partially repudiating the trajectory of thirty nonglorious years. "Our bread is yellower, more compact, and has more taste."[22]

Another approach to quality blended marketing and the attraction of the soil. There was a significant increase in specialty breads, which often incorporated grains other than wheat, used sourdough culture or a blend of fermenting agents, and followed recipes and procedures inspired, for example, by past practices, regional specialties, or consumer health concerns. As early as 1967, the Société auxiliaire de meunerie (Auxiliary Millers' Society) began to market a special premixed flour intended to speed up the production of rye bread. In the late 1960s, Raymond Calvel noted that so-called country and household loaves were finding more and more takers, although they were extremely uneven in quality. He warned against "floury transvestites," specialty breads made "with the same dough as regular bread, with a floury exterior." At the same time, the Grands Moulins de Paris were developing their Moul-Bie line, starring rye and country loaves; to support these new products, the company set up a customer service bureau offering "bailouts 24 hours a day throughout the territory." According to Gérard Delessard, president of the Paris bakers' association, the "passion for specialty breads" sprang up in the early 1980s. The (first) removal of government price controls gave bakers the prospect of selling more products with higher added value; they found imaginative ways to appeal to their clients with diversified offerings. All the mills began to propose blends made with various aromatics, fibers, dried fruit, seeds — some twenty different products in all. Specialty breads went from 4 percent of the total bread consumption in 1979 to more than 10 percent ten years later.

The main beneficiaries of this boom, according to Delessard, were the big chains (almost 50 percent of Carrefour's bakery sales came from its wide array of specialty breads) and the biggest artisanal bakeries, in particular the famous one belonging to Lionel Poilâne, the author of a highly informative book that lists more than eighty regional breads, some of which were reappearing in Paris storefronts as specialty items. Another baker, Claude Barinoil, boasted of producing twenty-eight different breads every day, including some that were not premixed but "kneaded the old-fashioned way," in order to satisfy a curious and demanding clientele. Pierre Demoncy, honored for the best baguette in Paris in 2001, offers forty kinds of specialty breads, of which sixteen are produced every day.

Not everyone is convinced that specialty breads serve the fundamental interests of artisanal baking and its quest for credible quality. Calvel approves of "diversity" but fears a "dispersion" that could confuse consumers and distract the baker from his primary task. The professor worries first and foremost about the baguette, the most authentic current expression of good French bread. "[The baguette] is not appreciated as much as it should be," he complained in 1990. "If bakers do not react," he warned, "we shall find ourselves facing the following paradox: a French baguette sold in Tokyo will be better than one sold in Paris." Jean-Luc Poujauran, a baker from an entirely different generation, nonetheless shares some of Calvel's values; he is troubled by "cosmetics and trickery," practices that "deceive the client and compromise the fairness of the competition." "Just by adding some little extra ingredient, one can sell for a higher price. This means we find breads made with anything and everything. The 'look' takes over: a nice plump loaf, swollen with yeast, dusted with a little flour, on display in an old-fashioned shop, may sell for 35 francs ($4.75) a kilo, as opposed to 18 francs ($2.44) a kilo for a country loaf in my shop."[23]

Organic breads may either be presented under the general heading of specialty breads or they may constitute a separate product line. The earliest "organic" production goes back to the beginning of the twentieth century. Most of the bakers who offered organic products sold bread at retail or were representatives of a large central shop. At the beginning of World War II, a well-known organic bread was thought to possess many healthful qualities and nutritional advantages; assigned a quasi-eugenic vocation, it was supposed to be able to "improve the race." The organic label had folkloric connotations and was not taken seriously for a long time; during the past decade or more, however, this reticence has been lessening as fear of manipulation, pollution, and toxicity in the food supply has increased. In response to the growing demand for bread that is naturally healthy and appetizing, many bakers make their own organic loaves. In Paris, excellent examples can be found in the shops of Basil Kamir, Éric Kayser, and Dominique Saibron, among others, and also in most Carrefour stores. The current king of organic bread in the capital is Michel Moisan: in his late sixties, son of a baker ("born in the trough"), Moisan sells only organic products in his "old-fashioned" shops, under his signature label "Le pain au naturel." Like the other outstanding specialists in this category, he uses only organically grown stone-ground flour; he disdains all additives and ameliorants, kneads slowly, and ferments with sourdough culture.[24]

The chief threat to the expansion of the new organic breadmaking is fraud; products falsely labeled organic undermine the credibility of the entire enterprise. Following in the wake of *Que choisir?* (a French equivalent of *Consumer Reports*) and several professional journals, the satirical newspaper *Le canard enchaîné* has unveiled some of the deceptions: "From 1996 to today, of some 500,000 tons of cereals bearing the 'AB' designation [*Agriculture biologique*, i.e., organic farming practices] that have been sold commercially in Europe, only 120,000 tons, according to an estimate made by the Bureau for the Repression of Fraud, were products of organic farming. The others were traditional cereals, no more organic than a menu designed for a bicycle racer."[25]

Doctor's Orders

One of the rare subjects on which virtually all bakers agreed was that the medical profession, by demonizing bread, had seriously exacerbated the decline in consumption. Earlier, in the 1930s, the Paris bakers' association had organized meetings with the federation of medical associations in the hope of finding common ground. The bakers wanted to promote the health advantages of bread; before giving their blessing, the doctors wanted bread to include more of the vitamins and trace elements contained in whole grains. Nothing came of these debates. After the war, the message that white bread was bad for one's health resurfaced and gained momentum. In 1957, Dr. Trémolières, a widely respected French nutritionist, published a text in *Le Petit Meunier* denouncing the "monstrous assertion" that "white bread caused cancer." CNERNA was determined to dispel the anxiety of healthy consumers by repeating that "nothing links bread to cancer"—inadvertent evidence of the weight attached to this popular fear. Commenting on the CNERNA report, a professor from the medical school in Lyon went so far as to discredit the bread of yesteryear: apart from its laxative effect and its power to evoke the war ordeal, there was nothing to be said in favor of dark bread as opposed to white; the latter was not lacking in fundamental nutritional properties. At least partially abandoning its classic defensive posture starting in 1958, the confederation chose health as the main theme of National Bread Week: "Eat bread and live well" was the slogan on posters. But the doctors failed to chime in, and the public hesitated. CNERNA's second contribution, published in 1979, demonstrated the high nutritional value of (white) bread and the absence of medical risk factors, but it had little impact. Although the report was praised by the confederation, it was ignored by the press at large.[26]

The profession kept on promoting the message, but it failed to pick up much steam. A 1983 advertising campaign, taking as its logo a loaf of bread drawn to look like a tree, promoted "the bread of life" that brings not only "health" but also "gastronomy" on a daily basis. Not much changed until the Estates General brought together "the greatest names in medicine"; according to Jean Paquet, these doctors were able to "state, with the accents of sincere conviction, before the press, radio, and television, that bread is the artisan of our health." Paquet declared that the "Bastille of health" had finally been taken, that "the ostracism [characteristic] of too many doctors . . . [was] a thing of the past."[27] Leaving their defensive attitude behind, trade leaders then went on the attack, without worrying about artisanal solidarity. In 1985, given the proven harmfulness of animal fats, a research foundation devoted to the nutritional role of cereal products denounced the housewife's preference for the butcher over the baker. The big international "Europain" bread show in 1986 celebrated bread's "rehabilitation" with a colloquium on "bread and nutrition" designed to bring the battle against "received ideas" to an end. Bread no longer had to settle for being an "accompaniment" to a meal; it could now impose itself as "necessary for a balanced diet." Association president Jean Cabut adopted a congratulatory tone in an editorial in late 1985: "Bread is no longer a poor relation; it has resumed its rightful place on the tables of our fellow citizens. To be sure, even more efforts in favor of Quality will be required, but the improvements already made in this area have been recognized by all."[28] The battle may have seemed to have been already won, but in fact there was another turning point in 1990, at the Entretiens de Bichat, a prestigious annual scientific meeting. Praised by outstanding specialists as "a complete food, healthy, extremely balanced and completely digest-ible," bread had fully regained its "honor." "It is not the Dreyfus Affair," *Le Pâtissier-Boulanger* observed with an admirable sense of proportion, "but there is beginning to be a resemblance." In a windfall for the trade, the experts recommended 350 grams a day for men and up to 250 grams for women. One hundred grams would supply vitamins and mineral salts, 8 grams of protein, 50 grams of complex carbohydrates ("slow sugars"), and less than 1 gram of fat! All this and only 250 calories: "no more worries about putting on weight."[29]

Unscrambled, the message now read: "Bread never made anyone gain weight." Any such accusation was "idiotic," according to the blunt assess-ment of Professor Guy-Grand, a nutritionist at the Hôtel-Dieu hospital. This shift in perspective allowed the profession to launch an advertising campaign that would have been inconceivable earlier: in magazines that came out during the spring and summer of 2001, we discover the slender, agile, seductive body of a young woman (un)dressed in underwear posing next to a delicious round loaf of bread (was it modesty that made the mar-keting departments decide that a baguette would be too phallic?). The caption spells it out: "These few lines will contradict what many people believe about bread." The text that follows, while it is a bit too overtly medical in tone, lauds the intelligent and balanced character of bread, which contributes not only to good health but also to the maintenance of a good figure. Here is the world on the other side of the looking glass! The baguette has in fact been reserved for the second target of the campaign: children are depicted as happy, healthy, and energetic thanks not to a tiger in their cornflakes but to the natural genius of French bread.[30]

While they were beginning to rehabilitate bread in the 1980s, medical experts avoided the risk of taking sides in the debate over dark bread versus light. Today, while bread is deemed healthy, it is being subjected to new research studies and to familiar nutritional inquiries. If bread in general is considered nutritionally preferable to many other foods, white bread is again being criticized as distinctly less good than dark bread from a health standpoint. Under pressure from public authorities, one recent study rec-ommends the widespread use of dark flours of the 80–110 type, rather than the T 55 type (ordinary; see "type of flour" in glossary) used in most baguettes in France. Dark bread wins out owing to its superior contribu-tion in fibers, minerals (magnesium and zinc in particular), vitamins (the whole gamut of B and E vitamins), and antioxidants (for example, poly-phenols). "The possibilities for improving bread are thus considerable," the authors conclude, "and the improvement of its nutritional image will make it possible to increase consumption."[31]

When Jean Cabut was forcefully playing the safety card, he could not have suspected the seismic impact that such a discourse would have ten years later, in the face of the rising anxiety among French consumers. Challenged by new threats on the health and technoscientific fronts, bread advocates found that it no longer sufficed to guarantee clean ovens (always "spotless") and shops (bakery clerks were advised by their association to wear gloves when handling bread). Charges that meat might be deadly owing to mad cow disease were not particularly subtle: *Les nouvelles de la boulangerie-pâtisserie* notes that "even cows are losing their minds," while "our compatriots, good Gauls that they are, are twisting their mustaches and asking themselves questions. They simply want to be sure of what they are eating." An editorial hammers the point home: "Bread has not gone mad." (Polemical advertising has a short memory: in earlier times, ergot-infected rye bread produced hallucinations and even dementia; more re-cently, the "cursed bread" of Pont-Saint-Esprit also seemed to drive people crazy, or even kill them.) Jean-Pierre Crouzet, confederation president in 2001, took the theme of nutritional anxiety to a new level: "The French confront the risks of bad food on a daily basis." It is time to show them how bread, the "symbol of our tradition where food is concerned, has what it takes to reconcile the consumer with his plate." In the same spirit, and of their own accord, millers and some bakers stressed the idea of traceability along the entire production chain, and they also forcefully rejected any agricultural use of genetically modified organisms.[32]

A Therapeutic Challenge

The call for self-examination was not unprecedented, but in the past it had always been accompanied by a whiff of elitism that left bakers mis-trustful. The most revealing instance remains the enterprise launched by Parmentier and Cadet de Vaux in the 1780s; they created a bakery school in the capital that sent out itinerant trainers, a sort of INBP before its time. But because it was created by outside experts, not by the guild itself or by professional bakers, the initiative was not well received by the base. In

1937, adopting a dramatic tone in his *Traité pratique de la panification*, Émile Dufour said: "I am issuing a cry of alarm: artisanal baking is headed for catastrophe if we do not come up with a remedy." Everywhere in France, "breadmaking leaves something to be desired." The fault lay in the "lack of professional knowledge on the part of too many head bakers." Close to the profession, Dufour vehemently rejected any solution proposed from the outside: "Let's leave baking to the bakers! To each his own trade; that way all jobs will be done well."[33]

The principal advocate of self-examination in the 1980s was Guy Boulet, early in his career as a militant bakers' association activist (begun in the rural world of his native Jura and continued at the national level).[34] Boulet shared Dufour's critical stance and his utopian propensities, but where Dufour looked to the past ("why would what was right in earlier times no longer be right today?"), Boulet kept his gaze firmly on the future, accepting the information age and other revolutionary developments without rejecting certain humanist values. Bakers had not kept up with the times. Ill-adapted to contemporary realities, they allowed the market to impose solutions that did not take into account either their values (which were tacitly disqualified as anachronistic) or their determination (which was thought to have atrophied). Like Dufour, Boulet believed that "our qualifications have broken down." Let us stop looking elsewhere, he said to his colleagues: "When a baker has problems, it is usually related to his competence, not to the environment."

The key to the "qualitative strategy" developed by Boulet was "a complete rethinking of the principles generally observed in artisanal baking" — a truly revolutionary perspective in professional breadmaking.[35] While the confederation found Boulet's path too iconoclastic, for a decade or more it had been openly espousing the idea of self-examination, if not on a global scale then sector by sector. As Gérard Delessard, president of the Paris federation in 1989, explained with humility, "we have to recognize what isn't working and call ourselves into question." Too many bakers saw this self-questioning as capitulation. On the contrary, he asserted, "being lucid is the opposite of giving up." A few years later, Delessard went further, warning his colleagues against the temptation to settle for tinkering, or even for a simple motivational slogan: "We must no longer hesitate to call ourselves into question, knowing that we can no longer keep on working according to ancient concepts, and that we shall be obliged to evolve if we want to succeed." The confederation's official journal detected "a cry from below" calling for the leaders to "rethink" the bakers' way of working, with the goal of achieving good quality. The bakers were beginning to understand that the bad ones among their ranks were going to bring down the good ones, that only the conquest of quality through merciless self-analysis could save the profession in the current bitterly competitive environment.[36]

Nothing better symbolized and embodied the confederation's commitment to the policy of self-examination than the "bread decree" of September 1993, the object of the long and intense lobbying effort that formally created the new bread type known as "bread in the French tradition." Both for the leaders and for the rank and file, this was a real test of their willingness to undertake critical introspection and make a break with past practice. Here was a new product, consecrated not by practice but by theory and — oddly — by law. To adopt this bread as a driving force for renewal necessarily implied a change in the way bread was made: a return to a long first fermentation or *pointage*, the suppression of additives that had made the process considerably easier, the risk of having to replace machine work by hand work at certain points, and so on. Yes, "such a procedure is perhaps *a little* more constraining," Delessard acknowledged, "but the result is unparalleled," especially "the incomparable flavor." The competition, in particular the industrial bakeries, could not offer such a product. This was the most powerful way of standing out, being out of the ordinary. But *Les Nouvelles de la Boulangerie-Pâtisserie* of June 1999 was excessively sanguine when it proclaimed that, "after the initial grumbling, 'bread in the French tradition' is recognized by all bakers for what it is: a label of quality and a booster of profitability." In fact, given its technical difficulties and increased costs, the new "bread in the French tradition" elicited more or less massive resistance from bakers, at least until the start of the new century.[37]

Another Challenge: From the Quality of Production to the Quality of Reproduction

While bakers were calling their working methods into question in an effort to produce better bread, they also had to reconsider their approach to producing new generations of bakers. For centuries, master bakers (or owners) were preoccupied with taming their "boys," in a permanent struggle for control of the labor market.[38] Bakers' assistants offered violent resistance to the system of mandatory placement by the guild (in the eighteenth century, several actually injured or killed the clerks responsible for assigning them to shops), and they chafed at the panoply of obstacles set up by the guild to make it difficult for them either to enter or to leave a given shop. At the same time, master bakers fiercely denounced the assistants' "cabals" intended to extort freedom of action in general as well as better salaries and working conditions in particular. Although the structure of work relations had begun to change by the end of the nineteenth century, up to World War I bakery workers "got together to struggle against the 'placers' and in favor of day labor."[39] While there was still friction between employees and employers after the war, the major issue from that point on was not so much the workers' fractiousness as their poverty. Following World War II, a double leitmotif ran through the discourse of the National Bakery Confederation: the insufficient number of workers and the inadequate quality of the young people who were joining the ranks.

In the twentieth century, as in the eighteenth, the usual path to the baking room, first as a worker, then perhaps later as the employer, started with a period of apprenticeship. During the Old Regime, an apprenticeship entailed a highly codified triangular relation between a young person's family, a master, and the guild; the terms were normally fixed by contract in the presence of a notary, and the apprenticeship was often closely supervised. The master was supposed to teach the secrets of his trade and not assign the young person (exclusively) to domestic tasks or mere unskilled manual labor; in return, the apprentice was supposed to "respect and honor" his master and "make his profit" during the standard three-year period of employment. Roughly half of all apprentices paid for the teaching and lodging they were to receive according to a ritually paternalist protocol. In the twentieth century, in contrast, apprenticeship was rarely governed by a written contract; in the breadmaking sphere, there were not even any legal protections.[40] An apprentice finishing his term in 1730 could brandish his *brevet*, a formal written attestation that he could now work as a journeyman. Mr. "D," an apprentice "bound" in 1930, confided to the oral historian Isabelle Bertaux-Wiaume: "I never had a paper proving that I had been a baker's apprentice, that I had completed my apprenticeship." At about the same time, Mr. "L" was complaining about his master in Pas-de-Calais: "He didn't teach you anything. I never learned a thing." The apprentice spent his time cleaning. "It was only in Paris [later, as a worker] that I could learn the trade." Apprentices learned things by watching and imitating. As Mr. "B" recounts: "One day the boss looks at me, he says to me: 'You're left-handed?' 'No, I'm not,' I tell him. 'So why do you hold your blade [used to mark the loaves] in your left hand?' 'Well, I'm copying you!' 'But I'm left-handed!' " Apprenticed at the age of thirteen, Mr. "V" worked up to fifteen hours a day, beginning at 3:00 A.M., and worked "from January 1 to December 31." At the end of his apprenticeship, he could knead and shape dough, "but he still didn't know how to put bread in the oven." (As soon as he mastered this task, the apprentice would ask to be paid at a higher rate.) Finally, few apprentices avoided beatings; these were a way of socializing young people to respect the schedule and the constraints of the baking room, and they also served to exact the supplement of "free labor" that was necessary for "the survival of the artisanal structure."[41]

According to Bertaux-Wiaume's study, the system of apprenticeship "through extortion of labor" lasted until the 1960s and 1970s. No doubt it seemed normal to many young people, typically from poor families, who somehow managed to get through it despite the beatings and extreme fatigue. Not a single one of the dozens of bakers I have interviewed remembered having been physically mistreated. Some complained of bosses who were less than competent and not very enterprising, but none of them had had an experience like that of Mr. "D," whose boss was a cruel, authoritarian "bandit." Of thirty-five "apprenticeship contracts signed in 1957 in the Jura"—after World War II, contracts seem to have come back into favor—six were canceled before the end and eighteen ended with the apprentice "passing the end-of-apprenticeship examination"; that too marked a return to a formal rite of passage. Although they are surely not representative, even today some apprentices complain of being treated badly. A Paris baker who prefers to remain anonymous denounces some of his colleagues as "scum" for the way they treat young workers: "You understand that after two years some apprentices have done nothing but cleaning; sometimes they've made croissants and even then. . . ." In 1995, echoing a reproach often articulated in the eighteenth century, P. Hurel, a bakery worker in Barcelonnette with a certificate of mastery (*brevet*) wrote: "Far too many Artisan-Bakers hire apprentices in order to have a cheap housekeeper and a maid!" He evoked his own experience: "As an apprentice, I never tended the oven, I never shaped loaves by hand . . . With my CAP [Certificat d'aptitude professionnelle] in my pocket, I didn't even know what sourdough was, or autolysis. They just handed me my certificate on a platter." At almost the same time, the scandalized wife of a baker in Marseille complained: "We tried an apprentice who didn't want to do the dishes or sweep up."

Other bakers point to more serious grievances, both with the apprentices and with the support system. They deplore the younger generation's lack of motivation, attention, and discipline. Apprentices often fail to come to work on time, or refuse to come before 6:00 A.M., invoking the rules, but then they leave on the dot at the end of the official workday, without any concern for how the work is going. Others learn too slowly and do their work carelessly. Employers protest against all the conditions imposed by the state (which is usurping the baker's supposedly paternalistic role) in order to ensure the comfort and well-being of the apprentices, who are treated as fragile or privileged beings (regulation showers in the baking room, inspections to guarantee respect for working hours, heavy school obligations that upset the rhythm and distribution of work, and so on).

The confederation, like all other artisanal agencies and like the state itself, has been concerned with the problem of apprenticeship for years. Impressed by the success of the German model, where apprenticeship is highly prized and is completely integrated into the system of training and recruitment, and where companies and schools work hand in hand, the state sees apprenticeship as critical for the future of the country, for growth, employment, and social cohesion. The artisanal sector, which boasts of being, collectively, the biggest business in France, is eager to restore prestige to manual labor and to the system of recruitment and training so as to guarantee its own survival. Among bakers, for whom the lack of a workforce is a chronic lament, a good deal of time has been spent on negative discourse; complaints focus on the tentacular state and its clumsy interventions, which allegedly prevent employers from making good use of their apprentices. Hence the clamorous campaign for an exception authorizing apprentice bakers to begin work at 4:00 A.M. rather than at 6:00, as required by law.[42]

At the confederation level, in the mid-1990s vice president Paul Gilles looked into the reorganization and revitalization of the apprenticeship system, with the help of Guy Boulet. Their one constant objective was to raise the level of recruitment, preferably getting apprentices when they had finished *troisième* (the equivalent of ninth grade). "Too many young people coming into the profession have flunked out of school," Gilles reported with regret; he was seeking the right way to convince parents of good students that breadmaking was a trade with a future. For Boulet, it was imperative to "stop taking the worst ones." It was time to end a recruitment system whose motto seemed to be: "You're not smart, you can be a baker." One of the best of the new generation of bakers, Thierry Rabineau, spoke very poignantly of the "psychological scar" borne for life by young people who come into the trade because they have been told: "You're no good, go work in a bakery." Failure in school is reproduced in "a kind of negativity" from which these bakers never escape. Noting the "calamitous" level of his students, Jean-Claude Mislanghe of the INBP reacts along the same lines: we are forming apprentices whose level is low to begin with, and even if the training is serious, the level remains low; two years later we'll produce low-level bakery workers, and ten years later low-level master bakers. This critique does not apply to everyone, the teacher insists, but it does fit "the majority." Mislanghe is strongly in favor of setting the entry threshold at the end of *troisième*: students could go on to prepare a CAP in breadmaking (or a BEP — brevet d'études professionnelles — in the food sector, with a concentration in bread), most typically in one of the hundred or more centers for apprenticeship training (Centres de Formation d'Apprentissage, or CFA) in metropolitan France.[43]

Spread over two years, this approach to apprenticeship requires signing a contract with an employer who commits himself to providing high-quality professional training for two years, both on site (1,500 hours in the baking room) and in class at the CFA (400 hours). (As in the eighteenth century, a third signatory underwrites and solemnizes the contract: no longer the community of master bakers, but the departmental director of work and employment.) The apprentice's schedule is theoretically flexible, allowing him or her to divide the 35 hours per week according to the needs of the employer and the demands of the school. And the new baccalaureate degree, the "Bac Pro," now offers another way to enter the profession without taking time off from school. With this degree, an ambitious young person may aspire to the *brevet de maîtrise*, a diploma awarded by the trade associations. Seeking reforms in all these diplomas, Guy Boulet recommends individualization of training programs, leaving room for young apprentices as well as for holders of the baccalaureate degree.[44]

Confederation president Jean-Pierre Crouzet agrees with Boulet, at least on this point. The whole training process has to be rethought. "The CAP as it stands no longer corresponds to the needs of our businesses," he argues. "Whereas at one time apprentices learned to produce a single item over three years, today they have to master a large number of products in two years." Many of the young people who earn the CAP are not prepared to go further, which leads to "discouragement" and "loss of motivation." The confederation proposes to reinforce the qualifications of young candidates by reducing the current content of the CAP "while requiring complete mastery of ordinary bread," and even, if Boulet's recommendations were to prevail, mastery of bread in the French tradition, the shining banner of the renewed artisanal bakery business. With a firmer grounding and intact self-esteem, the young worker would more readily commit to the trade and might consider taking further steps to enhance his skills. A more radical reform has also been discussed, one that would lead symbolically if not concretely to a significant departure: updating the image of both the bakery business (to make it more attractive to young people) and the apprenticeship process. "Apprenticeship still has an archaic image, and the very term discourages some from considering the profession," Crouzet remarks. "I would rather talk about training in alternation with schooling, training that would lead toward a real vocation." He has in mind a more flexible system that would allow a student to sign a one-year contract, renewable after a joint evaluation by teachers and the candidate. Once he had mastered the basics, the candidate who decided to go on would study fermentation in all its dimensions during the second year and special and regional products during the third; during the fourth year the candidate would learn to make *viennoiseries* and *sucré-salé* (sweet and savory products). "This would be a very complete four-year training program leading to full mastery of the entire profession," including the psychological elements and management, "at around age 25."[45]

Several schools are flourishing today. The most prestigious remains the old École des Grands Moulins de Paris, now somewhat more loosely tied to the giant of the milling industry; it is known for its dynamism in both recruiting and placement. The director, Jocelyne Gantois, is not a baker but an expert in agricultural food production; she brings a fresh approach that is nonetheless rigorous, owing in part to the high level of the faculty she recruits. The École Ferrandi, established by the Industrial Chamber of Commerce in Paris, prepares students for a number of food-related trades; its large breadmaking section is highly regarded. Christian Vabre, a Meilleur Ouvrier de France (MOF), is president of the Auvergne bakery federation and a vice president of the national confederation; passionate about training, he set up a bakery school in Aurillac over a decade ago. This school, the École française de boulangerie, accepts about ten students each year in a two-year program leading to the *brevet professionnel*; it organizes specialized internships and accommodates increasing numbers of foreigners who seek training in France.

The National Bread and Pastry Institute in Rouen, created by the confederation (perhaps prompted by the monopoly on excellence that had been claimed for a long time by a school run by millers), offers one of the best training programs in France, both for beginners and for practicing bakers who want to hone their skills. It is currently directed by Gérard Brochoire, one of the subtlest analysts of the profession in France. A discreet and cultivated man, Brochoire combines an acute sense of history and an intransigent realism with an active and critical faith in the future. A man with many projects, he has surrounded himself with the most charismatic instructors in France; together they have profoundly marked many of those with whom they have interacted, although they have not yet been able to do as much as would be necessary to renew the trade. Their collective goal is to "force people to get out of their rut," as Brochoire puts it. Taken in hand by teachers with strong personalities, but also stimulated by contacts with other aspiring or professional bakers and by the opportunity to exchange ideas, the institute's students learn proper methods and the ethic of ongoing self-assessment; the interns, who are already more or less experienced artisans, learn that "one can do things differently." Struggling against a complacent, corporatist logic, Brochoire and his team strive to show that passion for the trade is not outdated, but that it requires a critical mind.[46]

Banette, a brand name developed by millers, also boasts of its successful school, which focuses particularly on adults who want to change careers. To the great annoyance of the bakers' associations, Banette's diplomas are officially recognized by the state. The millers' group is obviously interested in handpicking candidates who will set up their shops under its banner. If we accept the legitimacy of the concept of retooling that is attracting more and more candidates (and prospective teachers), Banette's pride in its success is justified. In a sense, no one's "rethinking" is more serious than the conscious and conscientious commitment of a former sales manager, a former real estate agent, a former locksmith, or a former accountant. Other millers, such as Alexandre Viron, are contemplating ambitious educational projects at all levels, programs hinging on healthy, intelligent self-examination. Millers and baker association leaders alike are convinced that critical thinking and frank talk will attract better candidates and will end up projecting a more modern image of the profession.[47]

The Good Old Days?

If there are 38,000 bakers in France, as Bernard Ganachaud—one of the great bakers of his day—said to me over a decade ago, there are 38,000 ways to make bread. But those few artists or artisans who have resisted the general deterioration in quality have almost all followed Ganachaud and drawn their inspiration from what he calls the "return to the sources." Although modernity can help in various ways, it brings no more solutions at the beginning of the twenty-first century than the scientific recipes of "flour doctors" did at the end of the eighteenth. According to this logic, quality cannot be invented; it has to be *restored*. A radiant future presupposes a detour by way of the past. In 1987, the perspicacious and sardonic journalist Alain Schifres described the extraordinary fever of nostalgia that had artisanal baking in its grip:

> Bakers' ties with the past are not unambiguous. Most of them do not know much about what I would call the historical past, whose lessons require a critical approach and need to be corroborated by documentary evidence. Bakers tend to be interested in a more or less legendary past that has been formed by certain partial realities, consecrated by specific moral verities, and shaped by pressing needs of all sorts. This past is a fount of wisdom, available for absolution and guidance; it is also a treasure-trove of alibis. Like members of other guilds, bakers turn toward the past when they find the present troubling. They exhume (or create) traditions that may turn out to be useful. They draw on the past to orient (or reorient) themselves, but also to (re)educate the public.

They seek to recover something natural, something authentic, from the past, a capital of credibility that has been dilapidated. The past gives them the grounding for a new pact with their clientele.

"Do it the old way," Paul L'Hermine advises an aspiring baker (L'Hermine, one of the great Parisian bakers, returned to his native Brittany in 2000). For him, as for many of his colleagues, this doctrine is a fetish. In interviews with the author, he promoted his gamut of special breads "made the old-fashioned way, with sourdough, the way they used to do it." The major brand-name breads all make the same claims in their advertising. The Fleuriane baguette, now vanished, was made "in the old style." The big Soufflet-Pantin mills have developed a traditional bread of their own: "Baguépi Tradition—for your pleasure, tradition is reborn." Rétrodor dough is worked "the way it used to be." Banette, the pioneer among millers' brands, grew out of the conviction that "consumers increasingly want to rediscover the taste of bread made the old way."

The bakery across the street from where I live in Paris does not shrink from redundancy in calling its new baguette "old-style bread in the French tradition"; it would seem hard to take nostalgia further than this. But other efforts in the same direction have caught the attention of the press, echoing the theme of a return to the golden age. *Le Figaro*, for example, has described prodigies of *pointage*, four hours long, and bakers who turn up at the baking room at 10 P.M., a classic eighteenth-century practice that is definitely exceptional at the beginning of the twenty-first.

A powerful metaphor of polyvalent utility, "yesteryear" is at once rooted in time and atemporal, fixed in space and utopian, a concrete solution and a romantic fantasy. This yesteryear is a state of mind as much as a state of affairs associated with various positive images: solidity, reliability, honesty, virtue, performance. It reassures by locating what is good within a cumulative cultural experience and thus marking it as within reach: we were there once, so it shouldn't be too hard to get there again. The seductiveness of an uncorrupted, immaculate tradition betrays a deeper, more powerful desire that is by no means limited to bakers or to the French: a desire for sturdier values on which one might rely with confidence.

In 1987, Alain Schifres rightly demystified the "fairy-tale longing for yesteryear," asserting that "the original bread does not exist." Trade leaders and the experts in whom they had faith had already reached that position thirty years earlier, when nostalgia was undermining their attempts to regild the coat of arms of artisanal baking instead of reinforcing it. Paul Gringoire, the confederation president in the 1950s, spoke out against the counterproductive nostalgia that was leading to a systematic denigration of the trade. "Have you perhaps forgotten that you have aged?" he asked of those who dreamt of the bread of yesteryear. "These childhood memories are a bit fuzzy." A somewhat reductive neo-Freudian analysis published in Le Boulanger-Pâtissier around the same time goes further in counterattacking "the legend of 'the good bread we used to have.' " It began with a peremptory assertion: French bread "is unquestionably the best food of its type that has ever been produced" — healthier, more beautiful, more appetizing "than any made in the past." Why do people keep holding onto the "illusion" that once upon a time bread was wonderful? Because of an "eternally repeated and eternally unquenched desire" for "the good old days" to come back and fix everything. The human need to reconstitute the past "is the result of a premature, incomplete, or painful separation from the mother, a separation that leaves people, as they age, with nostalgia for the conditions of life [they knew] in their childhood." The nostalgic consumer (around fifty years old today) fixates on "the good bread of yesteryear" because "that's the bread his mother gave him. But his mother can't give it to him any longer."[48]

In 1958, in an effort to put an end once and for all to "lamentations over the myth of the good bread of yesteryear, the product of medieval farming without fertilizer, grinding with millstones, fermenting with sourdough, and baking with wood," the confederation relied on CNERNA's conclusions. The wheat of the 1950s, ground in cylinders and fermented with yeast, produced a white bread "as well made as in earlier times" if not frankly better. In the 1950s, nostalgia was a weapon in the war against white bread in particular, and this put the response of the "establishment" in rather sharp relief. Let us unmask this bread of yesteryear, a commentator wrote with heavy irony in 1957 in Le Pain Français:

> As a postscript, let us note the state's interest in materializing—that is, merchandising—nostalgia, more specifically the branch of the state that is more concerned with regulating business practices than with economic promotion and development. According to the Office of Competition, Consumption, and Repression of Fraud (DCCRF), an

agency that is extremely sensitive to the labels and declarations brandished by bakers (among others), "yesteryear" may not be appropriated
by just anyone at will. In particular, the inspectors focus on what they
see as excessive proliferation of the expression *à l'ancienne*, "old-style"
or "old-fashioned." In 2001, one of the best bakers in Paris, located in the
heart of the city near the old central market, received a letter from the
departmental director of the DCCRF spelling out his policy of controlled
nostalgia.

The 1990s: Getting a Grip, or Falling Apart?

In the early 1990s, artisanal breadmaking was in a ferment. Confronted by
"rapacious" millers as well as "unfair" big chain stores and "illegal" bake-
off terminals, it was in a state of continual activity, although "it"—essentially the associations—could not claim to represent all artisanal bakers.
Jean Paquet definitively relinquished the old corporatist prerogative of the
"neighborhood monopoly," the famous *métier de secteur*. Consumers had
become more selective, and they sought out the baker who "made the best
bread," wherever he might be. A 1998 SOFRES survey indicated that eight
of ten consumers were prepared to go farther from home and pay more to
buy good bread. An earlier study had already shown that a growing number "made distinctions among bakeries." While 85 percent of the French
population "cannot conceive of a meal without bread" and "bread remains
at the top of the list of products present on French tables," the French are
increasingly aware of their power as consumers, and they practice a more
critical and more demanding form of consumption known as "conscious."
They must be given better products, and new methods for communicating
information about quality have to be devised; word of mouth is no longer
sufficient in an increasingly diffuse and complex commercial landscape.
Now that the diversity of consumers has been fully recognized, how are
bakers to address them? Are consumers capable of telling good bread from
bad? This is an old argument among bakers and experts. Is good bread
necessarily what the buyers say it is, in the (speciously) democratic spirit
of the play of supply and demand, the universal suffrage of the marketplace? Or must consumers be educated? And if so, how can information
be distinguished from marketing ploys?[49]
    While the bread drama has not been exactly been played out behind

closed doors, it has often gone unreported by the nonspecialized press. In the late 1980s, the journalist Alain Schifres was one of the few who dared to state the problem bluntly and out loud: "[The baguette] is horribly disgusting. Ultrarapid fermentation, overkneading, fava flour, freezing. Bloated, hollow, dead white. Soggy or else stiff. Its crusts come off in sheets like diseased skin. It's the Court of Miracles under the breadseller's window."[50] And at roughly the same time, Jean-Pierre Coffe, a modern Brillat-Savarin with a fine palate, an ex-restaurant owner who had moved on to radio and television, drew attention by singing the praises of authenticity in food.

Coffe's *Au secours le goût* [Let's Rescue Taste!] published in 1992, conveys the strengths and weaknesses of its author. The book is passionate, exciting, perspicacious, hyperbolic, violent, and theatrical; it is sometimes superficial, often profound. Coffe denounces — among other things — not only the creeping mediocrity of bread, but those whom he blames for bread's decline, the villains whom he holds accountable for a personal affront and a crime against (French) humanity. What shame, what horror, what waste, when one is reduced to eating a baguette "without joy, without emotion, without appetite"! The bakers and the millers are at fault, of course, but also peasants, the state, consumers, and, more broadly, an organization and a way of life in which all these players are complicit. With his large media audience, Coffe was able to show that taste was anything but a frivolous matter. By making a lot of noise, he informed and alerted a lot of people, breaking what remained of the taboo on criticizing "national treasures" in public.[51]

Concerning the future of the profession, the sui generis practitioner Lionel Poilâne offered essentially the same analysis. He identified a potential double evolution: an opportunity (for the most dynamic members of the profession) and a very serious risk (for the most passive members) in the increasingly complex segmentation of the (new) market for bread. Schematically speaking, the orientation is becoming bipolar: on one hand, there are "top-of-the-line" products of high quality sold at a markedly higher price, and on the other hand there are less expensive products, a zone in which the big distributors already have a significant edge.[52]

In a recent editorial in *Médecine et Nutrition*, Dr. Monique Astier-Dumas suggests that bread in general has become top-of-the-line. The professionals may have written off her calculations and analysis as naive and reductive, but her argument is not without interest. At 5.20 francs (in 2001;

$0.71), the Banette came to about 24 francs ($3.26) per kilo at her ("pretty good") neighborhood bakery, where she could also get "very good" *ficelles* at around 30 francs ($4.07) per kilo. In the superdiscount grocery store next door, she found croissants at 22 francs ($2.98) per kilo and brioches at 19 francs ($2.58). At Auchan, she was astonished to find a kilo of *sablés* from Quercy for just 5.60 francs ($0.76). (Why didn't she look at the price of ordinary bread in this big chain store? She could have done the poor a favor and avoided turning the world upside down!) Wondering what this meant, she concluded that, just as the poor drink red wine in cafes where mineral water costs much more than wine, they are going to eat brioches rather than bread, which has become a luxury item: here we have "the triumph of Marie-Antoinette." And the doctor concludes: "Be a snob: eat bread, drink water. It is much better to be rich and healthy than poor and obese."[53]

chapter three

White Bread:
A Western Story

ENCODED BOTH AS A MATERIAL OBJECT AND A SYM-
bolic object, bread constituted a complex multiple register on which social, biological, and spiritual destinies
operated simultaneously. No food more powerfully illustrates the
play of "double incorporation" that characterizes the gesture of
eating. By ingesting bread, the eater incorporates it into his body
as nourishment. At the same time, the bread incorporates the eater into
its own universe, one that appears to be clearly defined and coherent but
that in fact produces contrary meanings. A sign of purity, an emblem of a
coveted social quality, and a stake of power for centuries, white bread was
never simply a source of energy and nutrition. For some, as a marker of
rank and a rampart against the "confusion of estates," it was a sort of Magi-
not line to be defended against the masses, the poorer classes, especially
those in cities, who readily acquired the dangerous and subversive taste
for luxury. For others, it was a form of permanent social anathema, the
key to a system of exclusion and control, a Bastille to be taken. Associated
with every virtue, competency, and prerogative, whiteness structured day-
to-day relations and exchanges. One of the great paradoxes of Paris life
was the extremely early access of much of the population to bread that
was at least partly white. Derided by provincial observers as selfish and
wasteful, in this respect Parisians were a privileged group under an Old
Regime in which privilege, obviously of very unequal intrinsic value and
very unequally distributed, nevertheless seems to have been the rule rather

than the exception. For Parisians, the vast majority of whom ate rather good middling (semiwhite) bread and sometimes even white bread every day, the French Revolution's ephemeral "bread of equality"—a dubious manna made from whole wheat, significantly complemented and adulterated, which must have resembled the "bread of deprivation" available during World War II—was as much a material regression as it was a moral and social triumph.

If "social" white bread gets everyone's vote, "nutritional" white bread has followed a more twisted path. Practical good sense and a whole cultural semiology argued for the superiority of white bread: how could refinement be construed as a sort of adulteration? Could purity be a form of degradation? To justify the hierarchical distinction, scholars under the Old Regime established a normative socioprofessional taxonomy of consumption. If white bread corresponded perfectly to the activities—which were rarely physically taxing—of the well-to-do classes, this was not the case for peasants or laborers putting in twelve, fourteen, even sixteen hours a day, often at very demanding work. The latter, according to the exegetes of socially differentiated nutrition, needed to rely on heavier breads, dark breads made of wheat often laced with rye (or occasionally with barley or buckwheat); these were thought to supply more energy, and, no less importantly, given the budgetary constraints of the families involved and the requirements of social discipline, they were thought to keep hunger pangs away much longer than white bread.

More or less with this rationale in mind, toward the end of the eighteenth century, the sociomoralist and proto-Taylorist scholars of subsistence would have liked to impose a form of whole-grain bread on Parisian workers, who had a penchant for breads that were lighter, hygienically and morally speaking. If dark bread was first of all a social instrument, a certain number of experts associated it with specific health-promoting attributes that were highly celebrated during the nineteenth century, in particular properties that favored digestion and intestinal transit. If well-being was at stake in the debate, material interests were involved as well. The state could save a considerable amount of money, for example, by adding bran to bread for the army, all in the name of health. The great bread scholar Parmentier did not manage—or did not dare—to settle the debate, even though he reminded his readers that the bran that "enriched" hybrid bread remained bran, a nonfood. The rehabilitation of bran and more generally of whole bread, either as a reflection of divine perfection, an old providentialist idea, or as an element of a naturalist or holistic philosophy that was not necessarily marked with the seal of religion, would come about in the nineteenth century, no doubt most dramatically in the United States, with the studies and preaching of Sylvester Graham, but also, by fits and starts, in France, where it eventually resulted in an authentic cultural and medical movement.

The World Turned Upside Down

Today we are witnessing a wholesale inversion of values, a sort of carnival of bread. Significant sectors of the so-called dominant classes prefer some kind of dark bread, which is considered more natural, healthier, and more in keeping with a certain lifestyle than an artificial superwhite bread which has been cosmetically treated and robbed of its ancient majesty. The phenomenon is droll, and historically unprecedented: these haute couture dark breads cost more than the ready-to-wear white versions. A resuscitated Parmentier would think he had landed in an insane asylum. The path toward the current bourgeois predilection for dark bread has been a somewhat contorted one. At the end of the war years, when ordinary bread, known disparagingly as "kaka," bore a strong resemblance to traditional dark bread, there was no question of rehabilitating it. To reverse this trend, a number of elements came into play: the prosperity of the Thirty Glorious Years; political ecology (moral and nutritional); hippies; the movement in favor of organic agriculture and food; the critique of consumer society in general and productivism in particular; the health concerns associated with overconsumption of fats, refined or "processed" foods, and chemical additives used to complete or replace natural substances; the growth of anxiety about food related to the use of hormones and antibiotics in animal husbandry, genetically modified organisms, and the outbreak of mad cow disease; the extraordinary rapidity of the spread of information, owing largely to the Internet; the reaffirmation of a bucolic nostalgia and an attachment to an idealized or imaginary cultural countryside with which food is associated; a growing disgust with fast food and all its symbols; old "slumming" reflexes disguised as a real philosophy of postmodern life; and the list could go on.

The polemics over what constituted truly good bread smoldered throughout the entire nineteenth century before a kind of moral and health-related lobby took over the debate. A "central commission on hygiene" made up of prominent specialists, two chemists, and twelve doctors concluded that dark bread was much healthier than white. In 1886, a Dr. Despaux warned that a breadmaking formula too oriented toward whiteness would foster both disease and social unrest. Small-scale millers who could not afford to go along with the large-scale shift to cylinders had an interest in attacking the white "pseudo-bread" robbed of the essential elements with which nature had endowed wheat. While the chemist Émile Fleurent claimed around 1911 that the move toward dark bread had lost its momentum in the face of scientific advances and the inexorable forward march of civilization ("one does not treat all of humanity as a pathological case"), two years later Dr. Albert Monteuuis of Nice published a brochure titled "Le pain blanc, péril national." During the 1930s, a group of commissions set up in Provence to study and promote good bread, speaking in the name of the trade and of science, sought to reconcile the professionals with the medical profession; they proposed to incorporate part of the wheat germ in bread. Whole wheat made the best flour in medical terms, but consumers did not like its taste; thus its spokesperson, Dr. Romant, sketched out "a happy medium" that led to "the victory of cream-colored over excessively white bread" (this formula would have a completely different meaning today). Dr. H. Thiébaut maintained in 1953 that moderation in the pursuit of health led to disaster, citing the work of "Professor Delbet, who has demonstrated scientifically that white bread causes cancer." The solution was a whole wheat bread incorporating the entire proteic sheath, an idea already advocated by Guillemet in the 1940s.[1]

More violent in tone and more extreme in its method, Georges Barbarin's Le scandale du pain, which appeared three years later, returns to Graham's holistic approach and anticipates José Bové's antiproductivism: "In fact, the resurrection of good bread presupposes a reform of the techniques of cultivation, harvesting, winnowing, storing, preserving, grinding, sifting, dressing, kneading, baking, and presentation." Far from being a fruit of civilization's forward march, white bread was a betrayal of progress: "If from one day to the next France is losing the intellectual primacy that used to go unchallenged, it is solely because France and the French have abandoned the widespread use of bread made the way their ancestors made it" and have succumbed to chemical and industrial white bread.

This false scientifico-technological progress would lead to an antibread and antilife stance, "nutritional chemification" based on the so-called direct method, with rapid kneading, ultrarapid fermentation, and "the use of dangerous yeasts." Instead of "this pitiful short-changed food," Barbarin proposed the providentialist solution: a dark bread including the entire wheat grain, which "constitutes a whole . . . the Creator's masterpiece."[2]

Dr. Terroine, head of the CNERNA commission, lambasted this sort of discourse—"the naturist mystique"—for its extreme naïveté. But while the exaggerated attractiveness of dark bread was irrational in its origins, and while "the state of psychosis against white bread" was harmful to society, several members nevertheless recognized that "the interest of a psychological order" aroused by this antipathy to white bread could not be totally ignored. The president of the National Bakery Confederation, Paul Gringoire, assured the public that his colleagues were ready to make dark bread if consumers really insisted on it: this would simply be a matter of good business sense. But "we don't believe it will happen," he added, and he seconded the conclusion of the Terroine commission: "Our white bread is an excellent food for healthy people." Better still, the good doctor had "liberated French bakers from the inferiority complex in which the libelous attacks on [white] bread had sought to keep them trapped."[3]

Bread in Wartime

Georges Barbarin denounced the "scandal of white bread" around the time a new phase in the conquest of white bread was getting under way. Schematically speaking, three stages in the social and spatial extension of white bread consumption in France can be identified. First, the popular urban (and particularly Parisian) offensive in the eighteenth century. Second, the occupation of the remainder of the French urban space and the beginning of the conquest of the countryside during the first half of the nineteenth century (the economic historian Alexander Gerschenkron depicts the parallel and intimately related advance of wheat consumption and the expansion of democracy elsewhere in Europe). Finally, the slow, uneven progression of white bread up to the 1930s and even beyond. In his *Chroniques alimentaires d'un monde qui s'en va*, Claude Thouvenot tells the story of a country priest in 1895 who offers a piece of good dark bread to a beggar who claims to be an unemployed worker. Instead of thanking the priest, the beggar says bitterly: "You can keep your bread. Workers without jobs are already unhappy enough, we don't have to let you insult us and treat us like animals — because that's dog's bread you have there."[4] By the time France collapsed, it was very largely if not entirely a white bread country. The Occupation would change all that, bringing the country back to a level that it had not known for a long time. For various reasons, white bread did not get its revenge until the 1950s.

The war of 1914–1918 — but all wars throw the food supply system into chaos — had deprived the French of the "pure wheat" bread to which they had been accustomed. According to E. Guillée, president of the bakers' association in Paris during the 1930s, in a somewhat confused speech, "the legend of bad bread" (that quasi-truth that dared not speak its name and was already troubling his colleagues) "was born of the sad war years" (thus the bakers were largely exempted from responsibility). But the legend grew during the postwar period, at a time when the bakers had "made the error — this time it was their own fault — of failing to make a clean sweep of the substitute products that were still being used to excess." Various committees had worked during the 1930s to stimulate renewed consumption: a propaganda committee, a central committee on flours and bread, followed in 1939 by the first national congress on good bread. Suffering from a short memory, the business as a whole, and especially the breadmaking sector, had lost sight of these efforts forty years later when it found itself in unexpected difficulty. On the eve of World War II, a professional journal connected "the crisis in bread sales" to inadequate education, stressing the need for more and better schools. Even before the arrival of the Germans, then, this was not the best of all possible worlds. If the legend of bad bread was revived in 1939–1944, the bleak life encountered day in, day out, was what left the deepest mark. And artisanal baking seemed to confirm association president Guillée's fetish-slogan: "When we stop making progress, we go backward."[5]

Bread was a sticky, inedible dough, according to author Roger Martin du Gard. And he probably had access to a bread of better quality than the average Frenchman, whose dark bread was gluey and had an unpleasant smell. "The whole wheat bread of the Occupation will remain among our worst memories of the war years," Raymond Geoffroy commented in 1948; he was one of the foremost scholars of the trade, though his work got little attention. He added a little sarcastically: "And yet, if we believed the enthusiastic statements of the partisans of whole grain bread, we should have been expecting a great improvement in public health." The Liberation was unable to liberate France from bad bread for structural reasons, especially the dearth of French cereal stocks. People thus continued to eat a dark bread made from wheat flour extracted at 85 percent and supplemented with soy, barley, and rye flours. During the summer of 1947, part of the country went on a diet of yellow bread, "worse than the bread under the Occupation." This was an accident resulting not just from the general poverty but from a specific linguistic blunder: French bureaucrats had ordered "corn" from the Americans, using a generic word understood to mean "wheat" in British English; to the Americans, it meant only maize.[6]

These problems were compounded by the bakers' own bad habits in times of food shortages. After having to make bad bread in an unfavorable climate, "the practitioners lost their taste for careful work," Raymond Calvel wrote; "most got in the habit of rushing sloppily through the process." Several generations of apprentices "were subjected to an exceptional education, full of gaps, seriously incomplete." Finally, the custom of paying workers by the piece encouraged them to work too quickly to ensure good quality. Did Calvel, despite his natural optimism, paint too dark a picture? We know, for example, that the shortage of yeast during the war obliged many bakers to go back to the demanding work with sourdough, a process that many had more or less forgotten (to help them, the Paris association very intelligently drafted and distributed a guide for the purpose).

When the war ended, for the principal players, the bakers, things were probably not quite so clear. More or less battered, still bound by various restrictive regulations in the wake of the hostilities, finding it difficult to recruit workers in a revitalized labor market, bakers found consolation in telling themselves not that they should question what they were doing, but rather that they should wait for the end of the cycle of bad luck. The trade press focused on political and macroeconomic questions, paying very little attention to the practice of the craft itself, which it did not view as in crisis. With better raw materials, bakers did not doubt for a moment that they would be able to make better bread—bread that would have to be, first and foremost, entirely unlike the wartime product. The shift had to come as quickly as possible. For the public, this would be the irrefutable sign that good times had returned.[7]

The White Bread Western

The break finally came around the mid-1950s, thanks to the application of a breadmaking method—intensified kneading—that was to transform artisanal baking profoundly by creating a whiter-than-white white bread. Its history is a real mock Western, for it got its start in western France. Every version of what one might call the origins legend of white bread begins with an accident, as if routine artisanal breadmaking could only advance through chance discoveries. The first narrative: a bakery worker in Mauges (Charentais) who had been dozing on the job managed to produce a markedly more developed and whiter bread with a dough that had been kneaded much longer than it was supposed to be. There is a more heroic variant of the tale that does not reward a moral lapse; in this version, the cause was the excessive speed applied to a kneading machine when an electrician used a more powerful motor to make emergency repairs for a baker whose kneader had stopped working. The third scenario has become the canonical one; it relates the epic of Joseph Albert, also a child of the west, who learned to knead by hand as an apprentice in 1919. Ten years later, his boss replaced the old gas motor on his kneading machine with an electric one. Starting up the machine that night, Joseph observed that it worked extraordinarily fast. Although the dough seemed to have suffered, he went ahead and made bread from it, and it gave "bread like nobody had ever seen before," exceptionally voluminous and with magnificent slashes. The details of the story become fuzzy, though, because the secret of that night seems not to have been exploited for a quarter of a century. Joseph Albert became a home distiller and took on replacement jobs in baking rooms. Not until 1954 did he offer—exclusively to bakers of the region—"a new fabrication technique" that combined rapid kneading with a large dose of prefermented dough plus baker's yeast to compensate for the virtual suppression of the first fermentation, or *pointage*.[8]

Although this whiter and more voluminous bread seems to have had a seismic effect on the rural clientele, the news spread slowly, as a growing rumor that was more disturbing than enlightening. "It was at the beginning of the 1955–1956 campaign that the first echoes of a bread being made in the west, a bread characterized by its lightness and the whiteness of its crumb, began to reach me at the École [de la meunerie]," Raymond Calvel noted. A baker from Maine-et-Loire, Leber, suspicious that chemical products were being used to get such results, was the first to talk about it: "Studies were done at the School and elsewhere; they eventually disproved this hypothesis."

Between July 8 and July 13, 1957, Professor Calvel visited baking rooms in the Vendée and Anjou regions to evaluate these innovations. In Albert's establishment and the others, he found roughly the same techniques: breadmaking with prefermented dough supplemented by a hefty dose of yeast; the use of very cold running water to compensate for the high temperatures of the dough (a phenomenon that would lead to the invention of the first water cooling machine designed for white bread by an equipment specialist in the west); accelerated and extended kneading; dough of a slightly soft or "bastardized" consistency; virtually no *pointage*; the *apprêt* (second fermentation) considerably lengthened. Calvel noted results that were also very similar: a well-risen bread, astonishingly voluminous, with pronounced slashes; a crumb texture that was sometimes a bit too regular, but very white; an occasional lack of flavor, although this deficiency was not "general" (later, Calvel would prove less optimistic and less generous in his assessment); and good keeping qualities. The dough's plastic aspects impressed Calvel: the dough was cohesive and very smooth, not at all "burned," spectacularly white, incorporating more air than usual, holding its shape well in the oven ("of exceptional tolerance").

In 1957, Calvel's conclusion was quite positive, though with an undertone of circumspect hesitation. The first point: was this an improvement in the way bread was made? Undeniably, in relation to the ordinary bread of the day, western bread was consistently more attractive and certainly whiter (for the time being, our expert attributed its whiteness to oxygenation of the dough during kneading; he later drastically modified his analysis and the assessment it entailed). Still, he was not absolutely convinced that beauty and goodness were compatible with this "lifeless white," for a creamy white tint was "one of the fundamental characteristics of our French bread." The second point: the sociopsychological implications for the profession and allied trades. Thanks to this "new way of working —for it is not simply a matter of accelerated kneading—certain bakers are rediscovering their vocation," and even skeptics are overcome "by a healthy curiosity." But Calvel feared, as did the bakers' association at certain points, that the equipment suppliers, wanting to make the bakers' task easier, were sometimes carried away by a "zeal that was not simply technological."[9]

When the Western tale is recounted by an indigenous actor, it becomes more impressive still. Before he adopted what was known locally as the "white-bread" method, R. Bousquet, a baker at La Grève-sur-Mignon in Charente-Maritime, was not satisfied with the results of his own daily work. When he heard a rumor that a new approach was modifying the basic premises of breadmaking, he called upon an itinerant demonstrator. When Bousquet's attempt to use the new method failed, the demonstrator blamed an ill-fitting arm on the kneading machine, and an overly "flat" flour that would never allow him to achieve good results; he advised Bousquet that a certain miller from Deux-Sèvres was the only one who made a suitable product. "But I later learned that the miller in question had involved the demonstrator in the sale of his flour," Bousquet confided; he added — let us not confuse the good guys with the bad guys in this Western — that he was not talking about Joseph Albert, whose on-site trials had always been successful. Bousquet had more confidence in some of his colleagues, in particular Cordon, a baker in Clavette, who had successfully produced white bread and with whom Bousquet exchanged ideas, test results, and encouragements. In a corporation that had been torn since the sixteenth century between the collective interest of the masters, understood in the spirit of a confraternity, and the particular interests of those who yielded to the siren of the marketplace, Bousquet remarked that colleagues who had already abandoned the new method in frustration — for the operation proved to be more difficult than the experts claimed — "often failed owing to an overly pronounced individualism." The essential dimension of a Western is respected: it has a moral.[10]

Bousquet's eventual success in making white bread can be attributed to that spirit of exchange, to his scrupulous attention to procedures (using a thermometer), and to the recipe (observing the subtle effect of yeast on sourdough); to the great displeasure of the equipment salesmen, it could not be attributed to the purchase of a new kneading machine. The old machines — Bousquet's dated from 1933, Cordon's from the 1920s — simply had to be adapted. In contrast, the recipe, which essentially eliminated fermentation in vats, made it easy to move to a new stage in mechanization, division, and weighing. Bousquet and Cordon experimented with a new ameliorant based on ascorbic acid (probably Nerfarine, advertised extravagantly by Vitex) that was supposed to be good for making white bread, and they did not observe "any notable improvement," an interesting attestation if we think of the degree to which a large sector of the profession was about to become dependent on that same acid.[11] As for the quality of the white bread that he eventually managed to produce, Bousquet was thrilled. Better developed by 15 to 20 percent than bread made according to the old method, lighter, with well-demarcated slashes, this bread "is agreeable to look at and, in a word, appetizing." Needless to say, its crumb, was whiter, "nicely aerated, supple and silky." The taste was less acid, "more discreet," and the bread had good keeping qualities.

The protagonist of this made-for-Hollywood tale is beyond all doubt an exceptional man and artisan. What could not be foreseen at the end of the 1950s, however, is that, transposed to the national level, this success story would turn into a disaster that would affect the entire profession for the next quarter century. At the end of the summer of 1957, a rumor about this new white bread escaped from the laboratories of the trade schools to make front-page news in two of the major trade papers, *Le Petit Meunier* and *La Boulangerie Française*. These both published the same text, a highly pedagogical paper by Raymond Geoffroy aimed at demystifying "that revolution" of a "whiter" bread hatched in the baking rooms of Vendée (a region accustomed to fighting against revolutions, but under a white flag!). Among the "uninitiated" bakers and millers, "some shouted 'fraud'; others were incredulous and shrugged their shoulders, according to the agricultural food specialist, but it seems that that practice is beginning to spread and threatens to make its own tour of France." Like Calvel and Guinet, Geoffroy announced the bread's color at the outset: this was real bread, "pleasant, well raised, light, and white," made without sorcery or fraud by an accelerated kneading that oxygenated the dough and whitened it "naturally." While Geoffroy set himself apart from the others by declaring that the product was "pleasing to eat" and that it constituted "an improvement in bread quality," he explained the process in terms that would be taken up again later by all the specialists when they denounced the harmful effects of this anecdotal revolution that was to disrupt virtually all artisanal baking throughout France. Geoffroy seems to have been the first to explain the oxygenation and whitening as a function of the enzymatic action of lipoxygenase, a diastase that is found naturally in wheat flour, but which is even more effective in combination with fava and soy flours.

The fruit of a discovery made by chance (Geoffroy repeats the founding narrative), this method is in fact less original than it appears, for it marks a return to a technique patented by two English bakers in 1948 (many years later, Geoffroy attributed the innovation to Americans, who had experimented earlier with the action of lipoxygenase; he had not succeeded in his own experiments with that technique, as he acknowledged later, because he had not made the kneading go fast enough). Although he was convinced that the new method was effective, Geoffroy wondered whether it was truly useful. On one hand, the reconstruction and redevelopment of France augured a lowered rate of abstraction of flours, which would "bring about a favorable change in color." On the other hand (and this is Geoffroy's least inspired argument, for he completely ignores consumer expectations and seems to reduce everything to a cost-benefit analysis), if artisanal baking in its entirety were to adopt the new method, "no personal advantage would result for its members," who would risk losing money on the modernization of their baking rooms.[12]

The Long Road to High-Speed Kneading

The baker is still left *dans le pétrin*, in trouble in the kneading trough: this is his lot, his ontological condition. Until very recently (and even then, not unproblematically), he has never had an easy relation with his kneader, an emblematic and indispensable tool of the trade, but a treacherous one, because it enslaves and exhausts its owner. When people used to say that to be a baker you had to be big, strong, and stupid, they were probably thinking about the kneading process, a daily task of Herculean proportions done by hand (less often with the help of a sort of paddle or with the feet (thanks to a suspended trapeze device) in a long four-legged wooden trough. Until World War I, apprentices were still trained to knead by hand. This required considerable strength, because it involved manipulating up to 100 kilos or more; it also required a certain delicacy, for the worker had to knead, churn, and mix without doing any damage, in order to reach the point when the dough was smooth and ready to ferment—a fleeting moment, difficult to gauge. When a baker, in one of the versified expressions of misery reiterated from generation to generation, complained that his trade was harder on the health than most, he was thinking about the kneading process, the obligation to lift huge weights and to work quickly for many hours. Difficult to master, kneading was not the most prestigious task carried out in the baking room; that honor fell to those who moved bread in and out of the oven. Despotic masters delayed teaching these gestures to their apprentices as long as they could, precisely in order to keep them working at the apprentice level as long as possible. In the eighteenth century, in the small shops, the master often asked his brigadier, the chief assistant, to take care of the thankless task that usually fell to the *geindre* or "groaner," the number two man in the baking room.

As early as the eighteenth century, bakers began to imagine and even to build kneading machines to reduce the imperfections of hand work (there were enormous variations in technique, strength, and care, and thus in the results) and to lighten the burden. Jean-Baptiste Lembert, a baker in Paris, built one of the first functional models in 1796; he won several competitions with his invention, and he was immortalized much later by Lionel Poilâne, who put a reproduction of the lembertine on the bags he used for his wonderful bread. Lembert's machine was simple to use — an untrained aid could turn the handle while the baker's boy took care of other tasks — and it economized on flour (less waste), labor (less time), workers' health (less painful effort, less flour inhaled, greater professional and overall longevity), and public health, a question that weighed more and more heavily in the debate (less perspiration dampening and potentially infecting the dough; later calculations determined that, for 172 kilos of dough, the *geindre* lost 200 grams of sweat in the first kneading, 300 in the second). And, no less importantly, the lembertine produced "a bread of superior quality, always uniform." Dozens of machines followed, offering other propulsion systems ("mechanical drives" that turned as many as eighty times per minute), other mechanisms for kneading (incorporating more air and stimulating fermentation), other materials (iron teeth instead of wooden arms), better distinction among processes in imitation of the steps involved in hand kneading (dilution was restored, for example). All these inventions were based on better scientific information about the plastic and chemical properties of dough, but virtually all of them led to the same advantages attributed to Lembert's machine: economy, simplicity, consistency, humanity, health, yield, and quality.[13]

Despite these advances, "mechanical kneaders did not achieve the success they deserved," as one observer noted at the end of the nineteenth century; indeed, they aroused considerable resistance. One might have thought that the masters, especially those in cities, would have been overwhelmingly well disposed. Apart from the economic, technological, and health arguments, mechanization ought to have protected bakers against "the frequent and dangerous coalitions of bakers' boys" — in other words, against strikes for higher wages or better working conditions. But many bakers were not interested: they were deterred by the cost of purchasing, amortizing, and maintaining the machine, along with the cost of energy, the price of insurance, and the increase in their business tax bracket; and after all that, a mechanical kneader still required a worker "who knew his dough."

Beginning in the late 1830s, a "coalition" of bakers' boys violently rejected the idea of mechanization, in a Luddite reflex growing out of an entirely reasonable fear that the process could put them out of work. Moreover, turning a handle proved to be as tiring as kneading by hand; the argument of physical relief became convincing only when motors were added toward the end of the century. Not until the eve of World War I did workers accept the idea that kneading machines did not threaten their jobs. But some still felt alienated, cut off from their own mastery of the process; their wounded self-esteem and their feeling of marginalization made them recalcitrant. Building owners noisily opposed the noise caused by the motors, especially the one known infelicitously as "the exploder." Consumers, for their part, were suspicious of "machine-made bread"; they viewed it as adulterated, unnatural, even harmful to health, and in any case less good, because it was heavier and less flavorful. One Paris baker described bringing in his kneading machine in the middle of the night, for fear that his clientele would find out and "abandon" him.[14]

In 1904, only two bakeries in Paris used mechanical kneaders. In 1908–1909, the Paris bakers' association organized a long series of studies comparing hand and machine kneading in order to enlighten the profession as to the relative advantages of the two methods. The special commission, after trying fourteen different models of kneading machines, concluded that bread made "mechanically" was identical in yield and quality to the handmade product. Still, on the eve of World War I only 6,000 of the 45,000 bakery shops in France seem to have been equipped with kneading machines. A baker named Proust from the department of Vienne who had settled in the Paris region reports that up to 1914 he kneaded by hand with the help of his wife. The mechanization of kneading really took off after the war, much more rapidly and extensively in cities than in the country-side. Linked to the extension of electricity, the adoption of machines also depended on a certain degree of awareness. Guy Boulet, one of the most important figures in rural breadmaking and in bakers' associations in the past half-century, stresses that a stubborn refusal to mechanize kneading condemned a baker to go out of business.[15]

France Whitened—and Whitewashed

It had taken much more than a century to shift to mechanized kneading; hardly more than a decade was needed to shift to the new white bread. The new method spread so rapidly in large part because equipment sup-pliers and millers seized upon it as a potential gold mine. The small and medium-size mills sent out demonstrators whose message linked the pros-pect of success in the baking room to the correct choice of flours. These flours probably contained fava beans, guaranteeing even stronger oxida-tion under the effect of "overkneading," as Geoffroy called the doubling of speed and duration. The Grands Moulins de Paris offered a "special flour for rapid kneading" at no increase in price "if the client asked for it specifi-cally when he placed his order." Several companies quickly put two-speed kneading machines on the market, with brakes and other devices facili-tating the intensive approach, along with the water cooling systems we have already seen. Yeast merchants were not left behind; they promoted recipes calling for still more yeast than had been initially recommended by the vanguard of the white bread method.[16]

Guy Boulet, anchored in the Franche-Comté countryside, offers a mar-velous account of his conversion to white bread, although his strong retro-spective regret distorts the story somewhat, just as the new method "de-natured" his bread. Still, this ex post facto judgment of the phenomenon was not at all obvious to bakers and consumers at the time.

In 1960, a new market orientation got me interested in the Rex knead-ing machine (with a rounded basin, an oblique arm, and two speeds) and in the "white bread" method that made it possible to start with T55 (ordinary) flour and get better development, a much whiter crumb, and a finer crust: all these criteria attracted the consumers of the day *despite the drawback of a total lack of taste.*[17]

Noting the success that the method had brought one of the bakers for whom he worked, Boulet urged his father to install this type of kneading machine in his own baking room. When he came back from military service, Boulet had "a great deal of success" making white bread: "Clients from outside my regular area more than made up for the decline in consumption related to the increase in volume [a phenomenon that Bousquet had not encountered in the west], all the more so in that my closest colleagues, who were older than I, remained faithful to their traditional production methods for a long time."

And White Became Black

Experts in the two major professional schools in Paris, Roland Guinet and Raymond Calvel, did not condemn these grassroots practices out of hand. On the contrary, both of them welcomed initiatives emerging from the local level in the rather dreary postwar atmosphere. And yet the picture quickly grew bleak. Once the specialists focused their attention on the new method, their research and reflections during the three or four years following the little Western revolution led to increasingly severe criticisms. In 1961, Guinet expressed doubts both about the intrinsic value of the results of intensive kneading and about its impact on consumers. While white bread may be more voluminous and grows stale less quickly, "not everyone finds this white color agreeable" and the bread has lost "part of its taste."[18]

It took Calvel another decade or so to articulate fully the theme with which he is most closely associated: the "denaturing" of the ideal type of French bread to which he has devoted his career and which inhabits his imagination. Writing in 1975, he noted his own astonishment at the passage "without transition" from underkneading to overkneading, in a profession so often reproached for its resistance to change. He acknowledged some positive points, but for Calvel "the generalization of intensive kneading" produced a negative balance sheet, on the whole: "Whereas the crumb of a loaf produced from a lightly or very lightly oxidized dough remains creamy or slightly creamy and retains its natural flavor, the crumb of a loaf that results from overkneaded and highly oxidized dough is lacking in color, bleached, *denatured*; this would be of little moment except that the flavor is significantly decreased and *denatured* in its own right; it is often actually unpleasant."

The oxidation would be less accentuated, Calvel maintained, if fava flour were not added, for, as people said in the trade, that biological adjuvant "increased the oxidation, decoloration, and corruption of the resultant flavor tenfold." Calvel denounced it later for having made it easier to introduce a radical reduction in the first fermentation, the one that generates the organic acids that enrich the aromas and in part determine taste. As it happens, bakers have been on familiar terms with fava beans for a long time; their traces have been found as early as the eighteenth century if not before, first of all as an agent of fraud, used to "cut" or fill out good flour or to "repair" degraded flour, and then as an ameliorant used to facilitate work with flour lacking in elasticity. A dose of 2 percent fava flour in wheat flour was a common practice among the millers serving the Paris region toward the end of the nineteenth century, as it is a very frequent practice today, even in the so-called flour in the French tradition.[19]

In 1960, Raymond Geoffroy, who was for a time the director of the laboratory of the Grands Moulins de Paris, defended fava beans, whose action he depicted as "beneficial to bread," as they favored alcoholic fermentation and produced a finer, more golden crust (he said nothing about the whitening of the crumb). The following year, Calvel echoed his position, recommending from 1 to 1.5 percent fava bean flour as "a precious ameliorant" in the process of accentuated kneading. During the following decade, Calvel changed his religion, no doubt because of research demonstrating the harmful effect of fava flour through the action of lipoxygenase, an enzyme that catalyzed the oxidation of unsaturated fatty acids; this process alters the taste at the same time as it whitens the bread and increases its volume, in synergy with the intensification of kneading. In 1992 he declared: "I was the only one, for more than fifteen years, to speak out against the use of fava flour and the abuse of overkneading"; these practices, combined, were followed by "99% of the millers and bakers" and had a "catastrophic" impact on "the taste of French bread."

Fava beans were the principal enemy, because when intensified kneading was performed without them, the bread would remain somewhat creamy and its taste would be "relatively unchanged." Fava flour was also a diabolical enemy because, although obviously deleterious, "as [it] is useful at first, we can no longer do without it." The addition of fava flour has numerous effects: among other things, it facilitates the "machinability" of the dough, by giving it a better resistance to the gaseous pressure that announces fermentation (bakers call this "tolerance"). In association with other types of dependency, moreover, the white bread method seems to provide "the opportunity to spread the use of other ameliorants"; in Calvel's view, these latter are not at all harmful, especially ascorbic acid, a veritable crutch for bakers. It accelerates the maturation of the dough, "thus making it possible to reduce the length of time needed for bread-making," and it increases the tolerance of the *pâtons* — which rise when they are baked — at little cost, Calvel insists, because "it very slightly favors the whitening of the crumb, but it has practically no effect on the taste of the loaf."[20]

Just who was going against the tide of progress, the promoters of the white bread method or the method's critics? The question was raised by Geoffroy, the only specialist in the business, it seemed, who energetically defended intensive kneading. "Despite the jeremiads of some who are stuck in the past," he wrote in 1972, "accelerated kneading has won out all over France and abroad, owing to the quality of the breads obtained, despite a slight loss in aroma that has not been noticed by consumers." Playing a dyed-in-the-wool populist (but here he put his finger on a problem that has never been resolved, even in the survey-obsessed era that followed some twenty-five years later), Geoffroy claimed that public opinion had as much impact on bakers as easing the work load: "It was the public's preference for this bread that obliged the artisanal baking business to adopt accelerated kneading: *vox populi, vox dei.*" Alongside the advantages, the "slight lack in flavor" did not carry much weight. Of course the baker had to follow rules, had to avoid exaggerating the dose of yeast that worsened the decline in taste, and had to remember to add salt at the end, since this helped to mask the taste problem. Three years later, Geoffroy was still celebrating the "spectacular" results of this method, in terms of workplace organization and also the beauty of the product. For it was unequivocally a matter of "progress achieved in the quality of bread." Geoffroy was no longer prepared even to concede much on the issue of taste: "The flavor is slightly diminished in warm bread, but the difference disappears when the bread sweats down." This method embodied the principles of speed and goodness that defined the destiny of breadmaking: "rapidity and simplicity of breadmaking operations subjected to the imperative of improving *the quality of the bread*." Geoffroy deplored the quarrel between Ancients and Moderns: those who dreamed about "going back in time," those "hypocritical detractors," and those for whom "progress lies ahead and not in a return to the past."[21]

By the early 1970s, the white bread method seems to have locked in the profession, even if Geoffroy's claim that it was practiced by 95 percent of the trade seems hyperbolic. The popularization of intensive kneading imposed rules, work procedures, and the acquisition of appropriate equipment. As Raymond Calvel—who did not see himself at all as a reactionary—noted, "to say that bakers can no longer avoid [this method] and are henceforth condemned to use it is probably excessive, but there is a good deal of truth in it." Bakers were modifying their way of working to adapt to the results of excessive oxidation; the dough developed more rapidly and showed increased strength and tolerance. The new recipe implied drastically decreasing or even eliminating the *pointage*; in exchange, it called for a considerable increase in the *apprêt*. While the elimination of pointage shortened production time, Calvel noted with regret that it mutilated the taste of the bread, and the baker's temptation to reduce the apprêt—which takes a lot of time and space—by increasing the dose of yeast did not help.

Aware of a serious problem of quality in the new method, some professionals modified their procedures, diminishing kneading time and extending the *pointage* to sixty or even ninety minutes. Even though he acknowledged the emergence of this compromise method, called "improved kneading," as a positive sign, Calvel judged that its effects could only be "very limited." This is chiefly because, "in spite of everything, the baker is always looking for a bread with substantial volume" (Calvel denounces such breads elsewhere as "obese and diseased"), and because "a dough that has not been allowed to ferment very long at the point when the *pâtons* are divided and shaped makes it vastly easier to use contemporary mechanical means." Adding fava flour to encourage oxidation, incorporating salt—which slows it down—at the very end (in increased quantities, to combat tastelessness), taking advantage of an easier work procedure, the baker will be unable to remain below the threshold of kneading intensity that could preserve the quality of the finished product.[22]

Westernization, Modernization, Mechanization

If the spread of the mechanical kneader marked the definitive entry of artisanal baking into modernity, the adoption of the western method unleashed a wave of modernization that came about via the mechanization of other steps in the breadmaking process. To understand this torrent of changes, we must above all avoid looking at it through the prism of retrospective wisdom that interprets it as the second fall of *homo faber*, the betrayal of the artisanal vocation, or the Trojan horse of decadence. Restored to its historical context, this movement looks more like a logical, if not inexorable, cycle of development. It did not proceed by way of a malicious plot carried out by greedy equipment manufacturers and various predatory suppliers at the expense of bakers unable to defend themselves or to get their bearings. It resulted from a genuine complicity and from the "normal" interplay of supply and demand, an interplay that was as much cultural and psychological as economic and material. On the whole, this spasm of modernization was experienced as a positive development by bakers, most of whom had a fairly clear sense of their own interests, in the perspective of a resuscitated France mobilized in pursuit of progress — progress that would be straightforward, efficient in the American style, bringing rapid gratifications and propelling the country into a future full of advances. Retrospectively, these interests strike us today as decoys translating a hollow vision of the world and constituting a trap for the profession and its allies. But few people held such a view at the beginning of the Thirty Glorious Years. The disastrous spiral and the lack of awareness that can be denounced today seemed at that time to be matters of emancipation, rational organization, and far-reaching strategy.

The confederation, seconded by the banks, encouraged bakers to invest in modernization; mechanization would guarantee the survival of the artisans, who would thus be better able to resist industrial competition. Two-speed kneaders proliferated, making it virtually a requirement to install automatic cooled-water injection. Strengthened in its physical and chemical properties by the white-bread method, whose tonic effects were amplified by the addition of ascorbic acid, the reinvigorated dough could now withstand the ravages of mechanized dividing and shaping. The *pâtons* could also cope with the stress of automatic placement via conveyor belts in multilevel gas or electric ovens featuring built-in vaporizers or via wheeled carts into rotary rack ovens baking perfectly uniform baguettes in metallic molds.

The real key to success lay in the improvement of the holding quality of the dough, allowing deferred baking: the use of refrigeration preserved the fermented dough and thus could delay the moment when the *pâtons* went into the oven. This revolutionary technique announced the practical mastery of fermentation. Toward the end of the 1960s, still another man from the west, Norbert Cosmao, a refrigerator manufacturer in Nantes, proposed a fermentation chamber ("Panem") equipped with an electronic programmer; this device allowed bakers to block fermentation for up to forty-eight hours and then restart the process. In a paradoxical way, "social progress" also encouraged the process of modernizing baking rooms. In order to finance salary increases for the workers, supplementary pay for holidays and weekends, and vacation pay, the state modified the fixed tax on ordinary bread, and this allowed bakers to increase their margins. Many bakers, handicapped by a shortage of workers and troubled by the cost of the workforce, invested their profits in mechanization.[23]

A better yield produced good profits, destined to feed a new wave of mechanization and to amplify a certain professional concentration, under the impetus of a decline in consumption. The figure went from 55,000 shops in 1960 to 48,500 in 1966; many small and not very profitable rural shops, unable to afford the modern equipment, went under for good. However, the immediate and provisional balance sheets did not take into account some more subtle but ultimately more decisive costs of the white mechanization that had quickly gone beyond the requirements of the new method. Bakers were becoming entangled in an all the more insidious predicament in that it took on the appearances of a progressive and thus reassuring rationalization. Behind this evolution, considerable danger lurked.

Experts like Calvel and Guinet began fairly quickly to denounce the perverse effects of progress, especially in its impact on bread quality. Historically, the cultural and institutional relays between the Parmentiers on one hand and the professionals at the base on the other have always been weak. High-level science, even when it operates within entities specifically intended for the enlightenment of practitioners, does not communicate easily or quickly with the latter. Here is a language problem in a double sense: it is a matter not only of making specific information accessible and intelligible, but of surmounting the suspicion if not outright rejection nourished by ordinary knowledge with respect to esoteric knowledge. Information and (implicit) directives coming from on high do not necessarily seem relevant to those who put their hands (or their machines) to work every day, several times a day, in their own baking rooms, for a business that has to be profitable and competitive. The gap between ideal knowledge and the practical sense of survival can be enormous. Even when the challenge comes from one of the great teachers of the profession, someone closer than the researchers are to the bakers' everyday concerns, skepticism is frequently the first response. Popular culture, reinforced by experience and proud of its independence, resists being subjected to the learned or dominant culture. In the case in point, during the 1960s and 1970s, critical discourse remained quite marginal, and, in a France on its way to being a society of consumption and mechanization, it seemed out of place, dated, even a killjoy.[24]

chapter four

The Enemy

IN THE CORPORATIST MODEL OF THE OLD REGIME, which continued to condition the structure of artisanal baking and the behavior of bakers, especially in Paris, competition in the strict sense was forbidden. In exchange for licensing by the state, the community of master bakers agreed to provide an uninterrupted bread supply, promising good quality and honest weight, sufficient quantity, and reasonable prices. The privileges bakers enjoyed were justified by the public service they ensured. However, in the name of the same public service, through the intermediary of the royal police, the state tolerated or even encouraged certain forms of competition that violated its own rules. On the face of things, how in good conscience could anyone fail to welcome additions to the supply of this fundamentally necessary foodstuff on which the life of the vast majority of the inhabitants and the political stability of the state depended? In the capital, for instance, the police authorized an enormous contingent of bakers who were not masters to set up shop in the Faubourg Saint-Antoine, a so-called privileged space where one could practice almost any trade without belonging to a guild; although the guilds were not closed, access to them was rationed by a variety of means (money, kinship, connections, and so on). The state also looked favorably on the twice-weekly bread sales by so-called itinerant bakers who came to city markets from dozens of small towns and villages around the capital (Versailles, Gonesse, Le Bourget, Saint-Germain-en-Laye, and so on). The guild of master bakers did everything it could to limit if not to eliminate this competition, struggling to impose its administrative oversight on the outliers on one hand and to exercise tight control over the types of bread sold by the itinerants and the conditions of sale on the other.

Seizures of property, commando operations, lawsuits, lobbying, influence peddling: all means were good, but they hit the mark only rarely, and around the edges. Theoretically, artisans who did not belong to the community of masters had no legitimacy, no unchallengeable right to practice their trade, and no recognized competence—that is, they were "without quality." The guild's only real successes against this competition involved small fry: journeymen bakers who made bread illegally using the ovens of absent, greedy, or merely cooperative masters, or petty retailers who bought bread in the city or elsewhere and resold it on the street. Competition from outside the city walls and from itinerant bakers was protected by the state, because it was not viewed as a commercial threat to the master bakers; in hard times (during grain or flour shortages, economic crises, so-called innocent bankruptcies, and so forth) the state was always prepared to offer them material aid. But in order to reassure the master bakers, who viewed this competition as illegal and unjust, the police were expected to enforce principles of fair play. Outsiders and itinerants had to obey the same rules and satisfy the same production standards as guild members. These "bakers-without-quality" already escaped certain taxes and charges that master bakers had to pay; the latter also suffered from much higher operating costs (among other expenses, they often paid high rents for their shops and baking rooms in the city). Even the state, opportunistic in the name of the public interest, could not tolerate the cruel paradox of granting more practical advantages to the quality-less rivals than to the bakers who were privileged by their status and by law.

The alarmist talk and the endless squabbles notwithstanding, under the Old Regime master bakers generally did not suffer too much from the more or less regulated competition. The bakers' guild, officially abolished during the Revolution, reappeared in the early nineteenth century according to a seemingly new logic that in fact essentially replicated the traditional paradigm. In Paris, Lyon, and other cities, specific authorizations were required to exercise the bakery trade, and the baker had specific duties to carry out, always in the name of public service. The itinerants continued to play their crucial complementary role. On several occasions, in Paris and in Lyon, the authorities envisioned breadmaking concessions that were almost industrial in scope, for example, under the auspices of public assistance, on whose grounds gigantic baking rooms had already been built in the eighteenth century. In records of the debates over these matters, we can already see at least the outlines of the tension between an industrial approach, which was thought to be better able to ensure a regular supply of bread at sensible prices, and the comfort of neighborhood shops run by a baker who lives near his customers and shares their interests, gives credit, and sometimes sets prices on a socially differentiated scale.

The New American-Style Competition

In the twentieth century, artisanal baking was not seriously threatened until the postwar period known as the Thirty Glorious Years. Up to then, it had encountered only false alarms or relatively minor inconveniences. A 1939 text called *Pour le boulanger* (For the Baker) warned against a kind of social Darwinism that threatened all the values of French society. "We are becoming Americanized," the author announced with regret, "and if we do not Americanize ourselves, others will do it for us." In other words, "industrial organization" was about to undermine the artisanal model of fabrication and distribution. The bakers' only hope, according to this author, lay in the French fondness for fresh bread at least once a day, "bread straight out of the oven." Around 1950, the associations mounted a campaign against a more concrete and less apocalyptic threat: the proliferating "cold shops" for bread (retail outlets with no on-premise baking), set up by greedy bakers or intruders, constituted a form of competition lacking in quality and therefore intolerable. This was the artisanal version of the industrial depot that was to proliferate some forty years later under the name of "bake-off terminal." But the emergence of a company such as Jacquet, whose presliced and prepackaged bread was mainly intended for American soldiers based in France, did not seem to worry the leaders of the profession very much.[1]

Industrialized breadmaking gained ground slowly, finding new customers first by way of supermarkets, collectivities, and the restaurant business (companies and chains). Above a threshold of about 700,000 kilos of flour per year, a bakery was deemed industrial: this meant a production that was ten, twenty, or even thirty times greater than that of the artisanal baker. In the mid-1980s, out of 225 industrial-level companies, half exceeded the million-kilo mark, representing 8.5 percent of the national bread market. Some fifteen companies did more than 50 million francs ($5,611,500) in sales per year. Altogether, the industry employed about 15,000 people. In the early years, these factories made bread according to more or less artisanal methods, even though the scale and degree of mechanization betrayed the traditional norms.

The great industrial innovation was frozen dough; this opened up new markets that threatened artisanal bakers more directly on their home turf. The last-born of the vectors of distribution, bake-off terminals depended exclusively on frozen raw or partially cooked dough. They did not require large spaces or big investments, and the skills needed to operate them were quite limited and quickly mastered. These "hot spots" selling bread-without-quality often sprang up in the immediate vicinity of artisanal bakers. False bakers' boys "made" bread all day long in a theatrical ambiance; the bread was always hot and fresh, and the air was infused with the pleasant aroma of baking. This artisanal mimicry succeeded in attracting customers, especially because bread prices were much lower than those of the artisan hidden away in his underground baking room. At the end of the 1980s, eight hundred terminals were at work transforming 60,000 tons of dough, almost 2 percent of the national bread production, and with 30,000 tons, around 10 percent of pastry. Around 1995, the number of terminals was estimated at about 5,200; most of them served as production units in supermarkets and big chain stores.

Large and medium-size chain stores constituted the other major pole of competition. They relied on three different distribution systems. The most classic one was the "cold shop" (sometimes an in-store department or counter) where artisanal or industrial bread was resold. This mode involved about a quarter of the big chain stores and almost 90 percent of the supermarkets. The second system was that of the bake-off terminal. The third, costly to start up but profitable, was the integrated laboratory, that is, the installation of a real on-site baking room where professionals did their work. Around 1992, 60 percent of the 1,050 big chain stores had their own bakeries; the others opted for terminals. Today, placing their bets on quality with the same arguments and the same claims as the artisans, more and more of the chains rely on the laboratory, a carefully staged baking room with a big refracting soleplate oven in the middle of the manufacturing space, kneading machines and work tables on each side, and giant

Table 2. Market Share of Breadmaking in France, 1991–2000 (percent of total)

Category	Year									
	1991	1992	1993	1994	1995	1996	1997	1998	1999	200
Artisanal baking	78.6	77.7	76.7	75.3	74.4	73.3	72.3	71.3	70.3	71.
Industrial baking, frozen products	15.1	15.7	16.1	17.3	17.9	19.0	19.5	20.3	21.4	20.
In-store baking (chains)	5.9	6.2	6.8	7.1	7.4	7.6	7.9	8.1	8.1	7.

ugly rotating rack ovens more or less hidden in the background. Government regulations require ventilation systems that prevent the cooking odors from penetrating the store, but the client still has the impression that he is seeing bread made before his eyes. These baking rooms were among the first in France to propose a wide range of special breads, offered fresh for every taste, every day.[2]

Artisanal baking has long been preoccupied, even obsessed, with the decline in consumption. In 1950, there were 49,000 bakery shops; ten years later, there seem to have been 55,000. In 1984, only 39,000 remained, and half of these still made home deliveries. Between 60 percent and 80 percent of the owners were once journeymen in the great corporatist tradition. Statistics from Gironde are revealing in this regard: there were 1,080 artisanal bakers in 1955, 655 in 1985. The number of bakeries fell from 37,800 in 1987 to 35,000 in 1996 and to 33,000 in 2000. This forced compression, attributable in its early phases to the decline in consumption, was compounded by a perhaps even harsher blow beginning in 1965–1970, the loss of market shares to new competitors in an already somewhat unfavorable climate. In 1988, artisanal baking accounted for 86 percent of the bread made in France, industrial baking 8.5 percent, chain stores 3.1 percent, and terminals 1.9 percent. Up to the very end of the twentieth century, the figures for the 1990s betray a constant, disconcerting decline for the thousands of artisans struggling to survive.[3]

Bakers are not accustomed to competition from the outside. Even within their guild, the founding idea of limiting competition so that all members can make a decent living has never been abandoned. In February 1939, workers joined with owners to demand that no new bakeries be allowed in Paris. After the Liberation, the national confederation repeatedly requested "a professional statute [that] would limit the creation of new sites of manufacturing and selling." The sectorial principle continued to mitigate the risk of direct confrontation with a colleague. Faced with their new rivals, however, artisanal bakers found themselves taken aback or furious. They consoled themselves with the idea that history, their skills, and public opinion were necessarily on their side, although they were not always persuaded by their own rhetoric. They made fun of people who thought they could "turn themselves into bakers" thanks to the "revolution" of frozen dough. "Baker friends, remain true to yourselves, don't let yourselves be deceived, and trust to time: frozen bread, hot spots, and other inventions of modern marketing will just pass on and disappear," the confederation house organ promised.[4]

The blight of the huge chain stores and the maneuvers of bread retailers upset everyone in the trade. Claude Mourigal, president of the Corrèze bakers' federation, remembered a happier time when he made the rounds with his father in an old Renault truck loaded with big *tourtes*. "Faithful clients were waiting for the baker, and the baker kept his daily appointment just as faithfully." But changes came rushing in: chain stores, spoiler prices, steamroller marketing. "Soon people will stop eating our bread, and we're the ones who'll be devoured," Mourigal lamented. "We need to be protected," he said aloud, addressing the political authorities, "yes, protected from those chain store monsters, from all those financial groups that are penetrating our sales circuits, our own territory, belonging to us, the small bakers." Otherwise, Mourigal warned his compatriots: "They too will have lost the real sense of life 'in the French style,' a life that came out of a rural world that has changed too fast and that is even forgetting the taste of good bread." To express her anger against the "contemporary scourges," Isabelle Azaïs, a baker in Saône-et-Loire, wrote and published a small book titled *On a perdu le boulanger* [We've Lost the Baker]. Around 2050, in a small town, little Mathilde asks her grandmother: "Tell me, Grandma, what's a baker?" "Ah," the grandmother replies, "it's a whole world gone by."[5] Rural artisanal bakers seem to have suffered more from chain store competition than have their urban counterparts.[6]

The Rules of Competition, or "Fair Play"

With regard to competition, the profession showed profound ambivalence. Competition was acceptable, bakers allowed, provided that it was fair and honest—but from the hard-nosed, hypermodern vantage point of certain captains of industry, hussars of large-scale distribution, and foot soldiers of finance, the normative notions of fairness and honesty were seriously outdated. The associations complained bitterly that the competition was unfair, that it heavily penalized good citizens and privileged the interlopers. The adversary, born in a simultaneously permissive and Darwinian age, had no scruples, no sense of fair play, and, worse, no respect for explicit rules. "Artisanal baking is threatened by this profoundly unfair competition," Jean Paquet confided to François Mitterrand in 1983. The discounting practiced systematically by the big chains—the famous one-franc baguette—was nothing less than an "attempt to destabilize artisanal baking."

Loss-leader pricing was only the most spectacular example of "the increasingly abusive and unfair competition." Another manifestation that bakers in the field found enormously troubling was the refusal to respect the practice of closing one day a week. Mandated by law, the weekly closing, devised to give the overworked staff and owner some rest, would be unprejudicial so long as it was uniformly respected. Yet in spite of ministerial pronouncements, prefectoral decrees, and court decisions, the terminals, chains, and discount houses ignored the requirement. The bakers' associations brought legal action against the scofflaws throughout France. In Paris, bakers went into the streets to protest the Holder Group's 7/7 policy, applied both in its Paul string of bakeries (baking rooms and cold shops) and in its Saint-Preux brand of bake-off terminals.[7]

"We are not asking for a monopoly," Jean Paquet insisted. But in spite of the politically correct and somewhat consoling assertion that fair competition was "stimulating," at bottom the associations and the bakers at the base were more or less allergic to it. In the first place, unless competition were highly regulated, could it ever be entirely fair? Even if it were technically honest, if it were "unbridled" in its spirit, did it not threaten not only the artisanal trade but also a certain idea of socioeconomic life shared by the (silent) majority of the French population? Unlimited competition led to disorder; manipulation if not outright deceit in advertising drowned out everything and glossed over the deterioration and even the adulteration of the products. In the late 1970s, confederation president Combe spoke out "against the repeated aggressions of the industrial enterprises" which were offering false products, that is, products bearing a superficial resemblance to artisanal products known by the same names: "They are quite simply usurping the reputation earned . . . by artisanal production."[8]

To the extent that it threatened the very existence of artisanal baking— 175,000 people in all—and that by degrees it was destroying a form of society and the way of life it supported, any competition was fundamentally illegitimate and tragic, in the eyes of several generations of association leaders. Like the eighteenth-century abbot Galiani, a great critic of physiocratic liberalism although with different goals, these leaders did not believe that bread could be considered comparable to any other article of commerce. Embedded in a value system consubstantial with the very identity of France, bread belonged to another category of analysis altogether. After struggling for centuries against the state control that prevented them from functioning as economic agents like other merchants, who were free to set up shop as they pleased, produce what they chose, and post the prices they wanted to receive, bakers themselves recognized that their historically exceptional status was absolutely necessary, even if they had often chafed under it. "Yes, we need freedom," one proclaimed, in the spirit of Galiani or Jacques Necker, the Swiss Protestant banker who as Louis XVI's prime minister was seeking a middle ground, a synthesis between Colbert and Turgot; "yes to competition as well, these are the driving forces of society and they are stimulating elements, but a hundred times *no* to anarchy, I mean untrammeled liberalism"—a pleonasm for many bakers.[9]

Depression

The reaction of the artisanal baking business to competition starting in the 1970s can be likened to a certain French response to globalization: "We noticed, a bit late, that our old Europe was not America." It did seem as though, almost without noticing it and in any event without being able to resist, the French were about to lose a world to which they were profoundly attached. The feeling of helplessness that began to invade the profession worried the associations: "A gnawing anxiety" set in among bakers, "a nameless despair" that cast "a sort of doubt on the future of the trade." To fight off this depression, the confederation had no remedy but the bakers' will to survive. Giving in to melancholy would amount to helping the enemy. Harping upon the idea that they could still carry the day, confederation leaders Jean Paquet and Jean Cabut urged bakers to resist "sterile morosity," "sterile pessimism."[10]

While many bakers felt as though they had "been through the wringer" and "marginalized," humor (though rather black at times) did not abandon the profession entirely. Here is one allegorical evocation of the anxiety stirred up by competition:

> One day the head of Coca-Cola's advertising department calls on the Pope. "Your Holiness, we can offer you 5 million a month if you'll change the line in the Lord's Prayer that goes 'give us this day our daily bread' to 'give us this day our daily Coke . . .' "
>
> After a moment's pause, the Holy Father replies: "We cannot do that, my son . . ."
>
> A few months later, Coca-Cola comes back with a new offer, upping the ante: "Your Holiness, we can offer you 50 million a month if you'll change 'give us this day our daily bread' to 'give us this day our daily Coke . . .' " After a pause, the Holy Father turns to his secretary and asks: "Just when does our contract with the bakers expire?"[11]

Since the chain stores and the industrial bakeries showed no moderation, betrayed no willingness to discuss or negotiate, artisanal bakers had no choice: they had to "fight." In "the merciless war being waged by [the chains]," Cabut reminded his colleagues, the enemy had just one ambition: "to take us down to the level of mere distributors," to reduce proud, independent artisans to a modern form of servitude. The profession represented itself, in 1990, as "under attack from all sides." Paquet and Cabut, like Combe, called for an "aggressive" response. But in what form? By what means?[12]

Sounding the Alarm

After sounding the alarm, the associations tried to organize more concrete responses. To mount a lasting, effective campaign against their adversaries, they had to ensure support from three different camps: the bakers themselves, representatives of adjacent trades (millers in particular), and the state. First of all, their own members. Affected very unevenly, bakers were not all aware of the danger, the confederation house organ noted; the editors oscillated for their part between alarmist messages and appeals for collective lucidity, in the name of a necessary solidarity, for, in the long run, "no artisanal baker is safe." The confederation sought "a triggering event" that would come to the rescue and wake everybody up. But when association leaders spoke of getting a "second wind," many bakers had the feeling they had already been through that in the 1960s, with the frenetic and costly move to modernize. They were told to "look at their baking rooms and shops with new eyes and take care of simple things right away, by perfecting new methods, new recipes, different presentations, a judicious use [of new ingredients]—in short, by infusing the enterprise with new life, for the artisanal baker still has cards to play." They must have wondered how often they were supposed to reinvent themselves. But the only possible winning strategy was to play the quality card, emphasizing what they had to offer as artisans.[13]

The "quality effort" that Combe asked for, the "winning quality" that Paquet urged upon bakers, was the way to save artisanal baking at once from itself (as we saw in chapter 2) and from its adversaries.[14] In a first phase, consumers had to be shown that the artisanal bakers could do better than they had been doing. This was up to them. The exact chronology was unimportant, as was the historical exactitude of the narrative. The bakers had to confess and clarify, then expiate and take responsibility, and finally improve and inform. In a second phase, the artisanal bakers needed to prove that they could do better than the others. The associations placed their bets first of all on information. If consumers understood what was involved, they would make the right choice. Hence a campaign urging them to "trust [their] artisanal baker" and not to "buy [their] bread just anywhere." Posters were distributed warning the public that "a bake-off terminal is not a traditional bakery." The bread sold in a terminal "results from cooking a loaf of frozen dough that has been produced industrially by another manufacturer." Some artisans thought that this pedagogical information, while necessary, was not sufficient to arouse public awareness. Nearly eighty artisanal bakers from around Angers "laid siege" to a bake-off terminal, blocking access and denouncing it for "provocations" and "cheating." This involved one of the two hundred terminals supplied with frozen *pâtons* by the Épi gaulois factory in Aveyron, a label that dared to boast of "the secret of good bread" and refused to follow the regulation requiring a weekly closing.[15]

The Cult of the Artisan

It may have been fair enough in time of war to demonize the enemy, but it was probably more productive in the long run to glorify the merits and the specificities of the artisanal baker. The public must not be allowed to underestimate the role of human capital in the production of quality. By stressing their difference, the bakers forged a cult of the artisan. The artisan was the bridge between past and present; he stood for the perpetuation of ancestral values, the beautiful and the true, the engendering of life itself in a natural and personalized breadmaking process. Only the artisan "knows" the dough, almost in the biblical sense. Only the artisan has the "know-how" required to achieve "authenticity" in breadmaking. Inspired by "his love of the trade," by his "enthusiasm," only the artisan refuses to settle for "facility" and "mediocrity."[16]

The artisans found their rivals' hypocrisy and pretentiousness unbearable. "When we hear Michel-Édouard Leclerc [president of one of France's largest chain stores] declare that 'we are artisans,'" one baker remarked, "it's enough to send chills down your spine." "There is as much difference between artisanal and industrial baking," another commented, "as between a three-star and a fast-food restaurant."[17]

While the apotheosis of the artisan rendered a therapeutic service to the guild and helped with marketing, the way bakers were represented posed a problem to the extent that it no longer strictly corresponded to reality. In 1985, *Le Boulanger-Pâtissier* declared: "Technical progress, increased productivity, and reduction in work time do not impair the work of an artisan." This optimistic modernist line was criticized in 1993 by one of the best teachers in the trade, Jean-Claude Mislanghe, who was concerned about certain practices that were leading many bakers far away from classic artisanal quality: "By always working mechanically, one forgets the gestures and the feel of the dough," he warned. "The baker who shapes his dough by hand sets himself apart from industrial baking and mass distribution in the eyes of his clients." At a time when some of the big chains were appropriating the old methods, some artisanal bakers were industrializing. "How can we set ourselves apart from the competition," Mislanghe asked, "when we are using the same raw materials, the same kneading and fermentation methods, and the same ovens?"

This tension took a strident turn in 1985 when a journalist from *Le Monde* used breadmaking as the illustration par excellence of "the trades that were dying out." She explained how "the baker [is] dispossessed of his know-how" while holding onto a mythical image of his artisanal essence: "The baker is by definition the one who possesses mastery both of the art of handling dough and the technique of baking. These last twenty years, with mechanical kneaders and cyclothermic ovens, and now precooked frozen dough, the reality has definitely changed."[18]

Nevertheless, the bipolar view that consigns industrial baking to the antipodes of artisanal baking—hell and heaven probably express the opposition better—is not immune from all criticism. Not everyone subscribes to the passionate radicalism of Philippe Viron, for whom "the industrial baguette is an embarrassment for the profession and for France." *La Filière Gourmande*, whose artisanal sympathies were underscored by the regular collaboration of one of the great artisanal bakers, Jean-Luc Poujauran, adopted a conciliatory line, stressing what links the industrialists and the artisans—including a common concern for quality—rather than what separates them. This publication reported that the chief executive officer of Sofrapain, a large industrial bakery employing 600 people, heads the Île-de-France branch of the French Movement for Quality, a lobby for product excellence. It is better for bakers of all sorts to unite against a common enemy, the manufacturers of corn flakes and other cereal products that attract many consumers. "The Manichean split between artisan and industrialist will shrink," *La Filière Gourmande* predicted in the summer of 2000. Its new realism is seconded by one of the best bakers of the new generation in Paris, Hervé Malineau, whose career, it must be said, is quite atypical. Before opening his three shops in the capital, he worked for Jacquet for eighteen years, much of the time in research and development. "Jacquet had me up to my neck in bread, and gave me my passion for a good product," he reports. "The image of the good artisan and the bad industrialist is now completely outdated."[19]

Jean-Pierre Crouzet and the Business of Breadmaking

An agent of renewal but not a rebel, Jean-Pierre Crouzet, the current confederation president, has not abjured the Manichean faith but seeks to
avoid its immobilizing and backward-looking effects. To stand up to the
competition, artisans have to become "managers of their own businesses."
The goal henceforth is "to make it understood that a bakery is a real business" and to defend not the nostalgia of a trade but the dynamism of a
bakery business." If this is not a break with the past, it is a fairly harsh
updating, implicitly a way to bring the artisan entrepreneur closer to his
entrepreneur adversary.

To cling to the "overly restrictive" perspective of the artisan was to con-
sign the trade to the "ecomuseum," according to Crouzet. Henceforth,
artisanal baking needs to be viewed, in the Rhineland fashion, "as a small
or medium-size business." This does not mean selling its soul. The mistake many bakers and some sectors of the public make is to associate the
idea of artisanal baking with a nonchalant attitude toward management.[20]

Crouzet, on the strength of his reelection in 2001, is betting on the re-
juvenation and renewal of the association and the profession (a realist, he
does not confuse the two). And this is not simply a pious hope: at a recent
meeting in western France, 85 of the 140 participants were in their thirties.
These young bakers are neither protectionists nor chauvinists. They believe in their future; they are not bakers simply because they could not do
anything else. Someone who succeeds is not a bad baker, in their eyes. For
them, competition is "normal"; one has to adapt to it.

Family, Firm, Fidelity

One of the results—perhaps also one of the causes—of the competition
that shook artisanal baking was the "infidelity" of the clientele. Bakers
experienced this as a kind of personal betrayal. According to association
doctrine, bakers' wives are supposed to be "sales technicians"; they "play
a role that truly makes them as important as their baker husbands. They
are business executives . . . [with] responsibility for sales, relations with
suppliers, and product presentation." In the face of acute competition,
however, both commercialization and marketing have become points of
vulnerability.[21]

Historically, the baker's wife took care of everything that happened in the shop; she handled the accounts and the competition. In the eighteenth century, the baker's wife slept at night, but she turned up in the shop at 6:00 A.M. to organize home deliveries, to put out the bread for sale, and to prepare the bread crumbs, croutons, and embers to be sold retail. Installed behind the counter, she chatted with clients, making sure to keep them happy and faithful to the house. She decided, often on her own, whether to grant credit to a given client, and if so, how much. She was also charged with the delicate mission of collecting payment without upsetting the customers. In Paris, in May 1726, Dame Chaudron, who wanted to collect payment for nearly 200 pounds of bread she had supplied, was beaten up by M. Gentil, who wasn't so gentle after all, and who then sullied her honor by calling her a "whore" and a "sodomite." The baker's wife also often dealt with suppliers; court records show bakers attesting that they could not manage their affairs without the constant participation of their wives.[22]

In the eighteenth century, each baker considered his clientele as his own private property. Very complex ties were woven so as "not to lose regulars." The "professional jealousy" that drove a baker (or his wife) to usurp someone else's client was very badly received. Dame Thuillier could not tolerate the perfidy of the baker's wife across the way, who tried to seduce one of her best clients by offering her the "present of a cake." A three-year-long vendetta between two bakers' wives troubled the precarious calm of one wide street, Faubourg-Saint-Antoine. Madame Royer stopped trying to hide her "hatred" for Madame Leprin or her professional jealousy; she struck her in the chest and told everyone who would listen that people should have nothing to do with that "crook, robber, flour thief."[23]

If artisanal baking has been a business ever since, the family still constitutes the firm. Even the young turks who are transforming the bakery landscape in Paris today rely on their wives. We are familiar with the lament of Pagnol's baker: "How do you expect me to make bread? My sourdough has left me." Giono's baker explains to the schoolteacher, who has misunderstood, that "it's the baker's wife who makes bread." Jean Paquet's lyrical version, composed in 1985, is no doubt hyperbolic, but it tells us a great deal about the representations that continue to condition the behaviors and mindset of the people in the trade:

Artisanal baking is the work of a couple. Both spouses bring their ability, their devotion, their clairvoyance. It is also a family atmosphere consisting of constant solidarity. . . . It is a circle of life that has resisted the passage of time so well that even today, in a world that keeps endlessly running after vanished moral values, it remains a model of successful family structure.

During the same period, the president of the Gironde association, André Baril, maintained that "the success of a couple determines the success of a bakery. And yet it is a trade with constraints. The husband and wife do not have the same hours. Most often, they cross paths in the stairwell. One wonders when and how they can produce children." Without citing specific references, the confederation house organ claims that studies show that the man represents only 30 percent of the success of a bakery. "The rest has to be credited to his spouse, the indispensable link to the clientele." [24]

Owing to the competition from the big chains and the terminals, what is generically called "welcoming" became a priority for the profession. As early as 1954, association leaders were stressing the importance of conviviality: bakers had to "sell bread, yes, but more than bread." The end-of-century incantations were not far off: "The clients need warmth, smiles, availability, and an attentive ear." The organization of bakers' wives within the confederation tried to make women aware of the need to pay more attention to reception. This group and its regional equivalents organize internships and award trophies and prizes. [25]

Yet how many times, when you ask the baker's wife if the bread is made with sourdough, she says no, it's pure wheat. How many women can explain what bread in the French tradition is? There are exceptions, of course, such as Florence Lebehot, on the western edge of the thirteenth arrondissement, whom I frequent regularly because she knows what goes on in the baking room. On the other side of Paris, another energetic Banette seller, Maryse Portier, running a shop five times as large, trains the sales staff herself. The ability to communicate is all the more strategically important since a branch of the Pétrin Ribéïrou chain has been operating nearby for several years; this group is distinguished by the way it eliminates barriers and puts consumers in direct contact with the production site. Thierry Bouvier in Rennes, adopting the competition's tricks (in this case the catalogues of the enemy chain), offers the clients a fifteen-page newspaper describing his breads. Whether because they themselves lack expertise or because they are afraid to be too authoritative, most of the women running bakery shops (and their saleswomen) miss the precious opportunity to use their knowledge as well as their charm to educate their clients and ensure their informed fidelity.[26]

Fidelity, Loyalty, and Betrayals

Few values have as much resonance among bakers as fidelity, in relation of course to their clients and their suppliers but also to one another. In the context of their struggle against new enemies, bakers were disturbed when their own colleagues betrayed the prevailing ethic of the profession. "They say that people are deserting their bakers, that they're turning to the big chains, and it's true!" This charge was made by a baker from Le Mans writing for *Toque Magazine*, a newspaper whose complaints some-times served political purposes but were often sincere and revealing. He continued: "But I think certain artisans have done everything they could to make this happen: passing off frozen bread without admitting it, or yester-day's bread . . . these are things that a baker or pastry chef worthy of the name should not do." The practice of freezing bread had been denounced at the time of the Estates General as an attack on quality that could only encourage the competition, but it was defended by bakers whose clientele was seasonal or who were understaffed; it remained highly controversial. The code of professional practice did not prohibit freezing, which was de-scribed dryly as "a recent, little-used process that allows the profession to organize its work better." While the confederation avoided the issue, for fear of raising doubts about its commitment to quality, Raymond Calvel saw considerable advantages in the technique as a tool for rationalizing work procedures, and he insisted that "[frozen] bread suffered hardly at all from the physical operation to which it was subjected." In the legislative debate about the proposed law defining the profession of baker in 1998, several deputies argued that the bakers in their regions needed this tech-nique. "In the Vaucluse, 95 percent of them . . . wanted to freeze, among other things, the surplus dough produced for their special breads," accord-ing to Thierry Mariani. His Alsatian colleague Jean-Jacques Weber wanted to protect bakers' freedom to freeze their unsold loaves on a daily basis.

The government minister involved, Marylise Lebranchu, pointed out that "the bakery confederation [did] not want this," and the deputy sponsoring the legislation warned Mariani: "If your amendment were adopted, it would cast suspicion on the quality of all their bread." "Carrefour and Auchan can thank you!" retorted the deputy from Vaucluse.[27]

In 1980, confederation president Combe had already proposed a definition of the artisanal baker in the context of the war against the interlopers: "I stressed that the brand image of our trade made it our duty to make the products we sell ourselves. I insisted that we must under no circumstances turn ourselves into re-sellers." But in 1997, La Filière Gourmande reported that 9 percent of artisanal bakers sold pastries made from frozen dough. Representatives of two large mills mentioned significantly higher figures; according to them, half of the products sold were frozen goods. There is reason to believe that the figure is even higher today.[28]

Among the most odious betrayals, in the twentieth century as in the eighteenth, were direct attacks on colleagues. Some forty years ago, a fifty-year-old baker found himself on the brink of professional catastrophe in a village on the border between the departments of Creuse and Indre. For some reason, his dough would not rise. Half of his batches failed, and his clients were turning in increasing numbers to the other bakery in the village, run by an old woman. After the baker in difficulty had changed his source of flour, made new sourdough starters, and had his water tested, to no avail, his jealousy led him to conclude that his rival had laid a curse on him to take away his clientele and ruin his business. On the advice of some local experts in curse breaking, he decided to turn the tables. He knew that his suspicions were well founded when his competitor suddenly fell ill and had to give up her shop almost immediately after he had sacrificed a black rooster according to a ritual intended to turn the fowl's diabolical power against her.[29]

Other victims of dishonest competition turned to the associations or the press rather than to witchcraft. In Mollans-sur-Ouvèze (Drôme), a recently established baker began to "sow doubt" among his rival's clients, implying, according to the rival, "that [he] did not make [his] own bread and had it delivered ready to bake." Elsewhere a male baker accused a female baker of maintaining a cold shop instead of making her own bread and punished her with a gesture of symbolic violence: he destroyed her "bakery" sign. There was a more complicated confrontation between R. Grillon and

L. Messerlin, two bakers in Draguignan. Grillon accused his rival, who was moreover the president of the Var association, of inventing subterfuges to get around the obligatory weekly closing and of having set up shop in the same neighborhood in order to destroy him and put him out of business. Messerlin denied the accusations, presenting himself as an ardent defender of true-blue artisanal baking and disqualifying his competitor on moral grounds because he made bread under the Banette label and was thus an agent of "a national chain." The accused, outraged by this bad faith, responded: "I do not hide behind the Banette identity, I make good bread in broad daylight at the Grillon bakery, whether M. Messerlin likes it or not."[30]

The State: Arbiter or Protector?

In its great battle, artisanal baking counted more on the state than on its trade partners, despite a history studded with conflict. The two parties went way back; their relations had been more intimate in the eighteenth century than they were in the twentieth. The state no longer played the role of a prince feeding his people, but bread continued to exercise a symbolic role to which the authorities were not indifferent. During the Thirty Glorious Years, the state evinced a genuine willingness to pull back from its regulatory and protectionist controls alike, in particular by freeing the price of bread, the last formal vestige of the old social contract. Artisanal bakers had been pressing for this freedom for ages, but at the same time they did not really want to be abandoned to market forces. Once liberated, they did not want to lose their status as moral guardians of a certain tradition, a certain way of life. The state had unfailingly celebrated this privileged status — after all, there were tens of thousands of bakers whose political and cultural influence, like that of the peasants, had always far outstripped their sheer numbers — until the late 1960s when it began to allocate large subsidies to developers of factory-scale industrial bakeries. The confederation complained bitterly that the state now seemed to favor the planned extinction of the artisanal sector.[31]

For reasons that go well beyond the particular case of bakers, the state gradually modified its position, putting postmodern brakes on its idea of "American-style" progress. Wholesale industrialization, on the levels of production and distribution alike, threatened to disfigure France. Officials began to realize that modernization was neither socially neutral nor culturally innocent. It became clear that the bakers' pleas went beyond mere corporatism and wistful archaism. Artisanal baking seemed at last to have the wind in its sails by the early 1990s. At the very moment when Edouard Balladur's bread decree reconsecrated artisanal bread as an object of public utility and classified it as a historical monument, as it were, the government froze new constructions of big box stores. That enemy was not eliminated, but artisanal baking had the virtual certainty that the competition could not open aggressive new fronts. Three years later, the government struck at the existing (and prospering) chain stores, reducing their ability to draw clients away from the artisans. The latter had been complaining loud and long against the chains' "unfair" strategy of selling bread at a loss for the sole purpose of attracting clients ("an island of loss in an ocean of profit," as one observer put it). In 1996, Yves Galland, the secretary of state responsible for this area, presented a draft law on competition, declaring that sixty centimes for a baguette "is a dangerous price": "If we allow this to spread, we will run the risk of ruining a profession." The Galland law was passed in July 1996; its goal was to redefine the rules of fairness and to combat the new low prices that were "destructuring the economic fabric." While they were not completely safe, the artisanal bakers were nevertheless much better protected against what they called "killer pricing."

In 1998, a handful of rightist deputies proposed an amendment to a law redefining the profession of baker that would have severely limited the exercise of this trade in the chain stores. The uncomfortable response of the Socialist sponsor of the legislation suggests that the besieged artisans had made some headway in terms of public opinion:

> I am trying, like you, to protect the artisanal bakers, but I do not agree with your amendment. I do not see any drawback, for my part, in the installation of a bakery on the premises of a supermarket or a chain store, so long as the terms of the law are respected, and the bread is well made, baked and sold on the spot, without freezing or excessive cooling. Our intention is not to control relations between artisans and the big box stores: this is a matter for legislation on commercial urbanism! [*Protests from the benches of the RPR and UDF groups.*] [Rassemblement pour la République and Union pour la Démocratie Française, both right-wing

political parties.] Or else, if you want to forbid the sale of bread in the big chain stores, these stores will have to be closed! No one wants to settle this matter more than I do, but we will not do it by going against the Constitution.[32]

As we shall see in the following chapter, the profession received favorable treatment from the Balladur and Juppé governments (1993–95 and 1995–97, respectively), especially thanks to the energetic involvement of Jean-Pierre Raffarin during his stint in the ministry responsible for the artisanate. The associations referred to him as "[their] minister," and Raffarin gave numerous signs of his attachment not only to the artisanate in general as an economic force and a social structure, but to bread in particular, on one hand as a historical and spiritual symbol and on the other as a source of pleasure. The bakers were pleased to see Jacques Chirac become president, because he had staunchly defended them during all the years he had served as mayor of Paris: "It is out of the question to compare the artisanal bread that comes from a bakery with the stuff that comes from a bake-off terminal; that has nothing in common with bread, or with any self-respecting food," President Chirac proclaimed to a delegation of bakers, offering a healing "balm for their hearts."[33]

The Industry

For the most orthodox artisanal bakers, industrial production represents the antithesis of the profession in its legitimate, canonical, mythified form; it is the ultimate betrayal for one of their own to move in that direction. As it happens, in the beginning—and the beginning was not so long ago— virtually all industrial bakers came from the artisanal ranks and knew exactly what was involved in making bread, from A to Z. In the early years, industrial bakers produced only fresh bread; the arrival of frozen products changed everything. From a market share of 10 percent in 1985, the industry boasted 23 percent in 2000. Bread amounted to 70 percent of the industrial production, Viennese pastries 25 percent, and other pastries barely 5 percent. "The industry" consists of some 200 to 220 businesses. In 2002, about 60 percent of the industry's clients were chain stores; restaurants accounted for 23 percent; and sales to individuals, chiefly through bake-off terminals, made up 12 percent. Of the industry's products, 39 percent were frozen, 36 percent fresh, 10 percent prebaked, and 15 percent prepackaged.[34]

At the outset, the industrialists' union was a small association of people who knew each other well and got together for dinner about three times a year. The association began to become more professional around 1981 under the influence of Nicole Watelet, the general secretary; a master's degree in history had given her a sense of perspective, years of teaching experience had given her a pedagogical style, and some business training had familiarized her with principles of organization and management.[35]

Watelet has a lucid view that is not without a certain ordinary Machiavellianism. Two lapidary formulas sum up her analysis: "We aren't trying to kill off the fishermen," and "If we wanted to squash them, we would lose." Given the place of the artisanate in the national imagination and the affective (atavistic) relation of the French populace to traditional bread, Watelet concludes unambiguously that the industry needs the artisans.

While it is unrealistic to expect a formalization of the division of labor, Watelet is betting on an eventual complicity on the part of the younger artisans, whom she sees as well disposed to this sort of coexistence owing to their own realism (since they did not live through the most traumatizing confrontations with the enemy, they can afford to be more coolly analytical) and also to their reluctance to spend twenty hours a day in the baking room. The division would be partly sociogeographic: rural areas are of virtually no interest to the industrialists, who are ready to turn them over to the guardians of tradition (although the experience of Guy Boulet in Franche-Comté, where the industry has penetrated to the heart of the countryside, casts some doubt on the sincerity of this theoretical renunciation). The division would also take place in production, dealing a hard blow to the artisanal ethic (which skeptics would call a fiction). "We're taking over the products that are hardest for you to handle": this is the industry's proposal to the artisans, who have difficulty juggling all the specialty breads and various types of pastries while they also make ordinary bread—a process that has become more demanding for those who have gone back to "traditional" methods. The "vast hypocrisy" of artisanal baking irritates the industrialists, for "enormous numbers" of artisans are already, shamefully, using frozen loaves to produce specialty breads, simply because it is too complicated and too expensive to produce everything their clients ask for on a daily basis (the industrial association claims that 80 percent of the specialty breads sold by artisans are actually made by its own members), not to mention the frozen Viennese pastries that are offered by many baking rooms.

For psychological as well as commercial reasons, industrial producers insist on being recognized as full-fledged bakers, brothers in their baking rooms, whatever the scale. They resented the attempt on the part of artisanal baking to confiscate for its own exclusive use the labels "baker" and "bakery," an attempt that achieved its aims in 1998 after several years of legal wrangling that we shall look at more closely in chapter 5. For the artisans, it was a symbolic way of killing off their enemy, driving him out of the sacred activity of producing *authentic* bread. It was also a way of showing their political influence, for while the measure—first promulgated in late 1995—that restricted these designations to artisans aroused the disapproval of the Conseil d'État after a complaint by the association of industrial bakers, it was reformulated and reissued by a left-wing government in 1998. This second version limited the practical consequences to the industrialists, for it no longer prohibited them from calling themselves bakers for purposes of export—a key point, since the whole credibility of the export business depends on the golden legend of French breadmaking. If the challenge to their "professionalism" wounded the industrialists in an initial phase, they had no difficulty adjusting their sights in the bake-off terminals and the chains by using substitute brand names (such as Épi gaulois and Pomme de pain), as the Direction générale de la concurrence, de la consommation et de la répression des fraudes (DGCCRF) has noted.[36] Nicole Watelet takes sly pleasure in remarking that the most dynamic artisans, including the current confederation president, are more bothered by these regulations than the industrialists are, since they can no longer use the designation "bakery" for their branches or outlets (cold shops supplied by the baking rooms located in their principal outlet). The only ones who profit from this artisanal triumph, she adds, are the big box stores with their own bakeries, since they can emphasize their "bakery" status as a marketing tool.

Another point of conflict between the artisans and the industrialists was the obligatory weekly closing. The artisans' association extracted this concession from the state, after years of resistance to the regulation when

bakery workers were demanding it from their bosses. The sacred (and politically consecrated) day of rest was sheer hypocrisy from the industry
standpoint; the industrialists claimed that artisans continued to bake or
deliver their bread despite the fact that their shops were closed.[37]

The most significant ground on which artisans and industrialists meet,
according to Watelet, is that of quality—precisely the point where artisanal bakers saw an abyss of separation. In their own way, the industrialists have been able to develop parbaking techniques making it possible
to produce good bread. Watelet is quite prepared to acknowledge that
industrial bread has been "insipid" for a long time—like much artisanal
bread, moreover: "Everyone was making bad bread; it is not right to single
us out." Like the artisans, the industrialists rediscovered taste, which became the key to their strategy of "quality," an objective that was as much
industrial as artisanal. The bard of the discourse of industrial excellence,
Claude Gamel, general director of the Moly enterprises (200 stores bearing the Épi gaulois or Délice du mitron banner, mainly in Aquitaine and
Midi-Pyrénées), defends his country loaf tooth and nail: "We use the same
kneading machines and the same raw materials as the artisans. Flour without ascorbic acid, without fava or soy flour. The only difference is that we
freeze the dough in order to be able to offer bread at any hour of the day.
The notion of services [is] inseparable from that of quality."[38]

Clearly, this "single difference" of freezing is at the heart of the debate
between artisans and industrialists. Frozen breads are very far removed
from the degree of fermentation normally considered optimal for making
bread according to the direct method. What is involved, then, is partial
prefermentation: most of the development of the *pâton* takes place during
baking. Yet artisanal wisdom stresses the primacy of fermentation in the
production of taste. The official line of industrial baking claims that, after
the brief interruption in the process, "the dough resumes its work at the
same point without being affected." However, scientists note a decrease
in rising after thawing, owing to an alteration in the gluten or to the loss
of the yeast's fermenting power attributable to cold stress. Compensating
by increasing the proportion of yeast risks harming the taste. The industrialists count on solving this problem via a technological solution. The
question of restarting the process in bake-off terminals remains: first, the
duration of the phases of freezing and fermentation (three hours mini-

mum?), and then second, the technical know-how required of the staff on duty, in particular their ability to evaluate the degree of fermentation and to scarify the *pâtons* before baking. By the mid-1990s, certain industrialists heralded the blast freezing and precooked technology of parbaking as the most promising avenue.[39]

Raw or partially precooked, deep-frozen bread is no doubt the "enemy" product that shook the artisans most, the one on which they focused their anger, scorn, and fear. This bread was sold in bake-off terminals, the Sodom and Gomorrah of artisanal baking at the end of the twentieth century, a vector of the corruption of values and the contagion of the depression inspired by the introduction of terminals. These terminals proliferated during the 1980s and were deeply disturbing to the artisans, whose anguish over their business prospects and their very identity was clearly articulated by Jean Cabut in his report to the Conseil économique et social, a prestigious state advisory commission, in 1988. At that point, there were already 800 terminals in place; 3,500 were projected before the end of the 1990s. In 2002, there were over 5,000 (without counting the ones integrated into supermarkets and other points of mass distribution), a triumphal sign of the advance of industrial baking.[40]

Despite their distance from the consumer, the industrialists could not remain indifferent to the concerns of the public, not only about taste but about the safety of the raw materials and the stages of production. In the logic of modernity and postmodernity, consumers might easily suspect that industrialists took less interest in that aspect of quality than artisans. In fact, like the latter, industrialists are increasingly attentive to consumer anxiety about food safety. They give detailed instructions to their millers, they devise traceability projects, and they try to use fewer additives.

On the qualitative register, Hervé Malineau, one of the most gifted bakers of the new generation, offers lucid testimony. Trained in biochemistry and nutrition, he spent eighteen years with Jacquet, one of the major industrial bread-producing firms, before recycling himself in artisanal baking. Malineau vigorously rejects the facile stereotypes that contrast artisanal bakers embodying quality ("necessarily good") with industrialists infatuated with mass-market mediocrity ("automatically bad"). "Arrogant and complacent," the artisans were addicted to scapegoating their rivals rather than questioning their own technical and commercial stagnation. As for the industrialists, Malineau noted positive as well as negative factors: much imagination and rigor alongside simplistic procrustean solutions.[41]

For the future, Nicole Watelet is optimistic. Industrial baking will continue to progress, in France—at the expense of artisanal baking, naturally—and in the export market. Industrialists are well aware that they cannot compete with artisans in terms of their public image. Moreover, at the worst moment of their clash with the artisans, and even when they were being reviled in the press and savaged by their adversaries, industrial baking did not suffer in the marketplace; in four years it increased its market share from 17 percent to 21 percent. Until now, the industrialists have refused to put their money into advertising or public relations. Their investments are colossal, for the logic here—as in many other industries, especially in the current climate—is that one has to be big to survive and grow.

Like the artisans, the industrialists have trouble recruiting. It is a demanding business: the factory runs day and night, all year long, holidays included. The shift to a thirty-five-hour work week in 2001–2002 exacerbated the industry's problems (many employees normally worked forty-two hours), and their poor brand image did not facilitate the articulation of a real politics of training. On the strength of its specificity, the industrial branch developed its own Certificat d'aptitude professionnelle (CAP), with a somewhat Orwellian title, Opavi (Opérateur de produits panifiés et viennoiseries industrielles [Operator of Bread Products and Industrial Viennese Pastries]). The Forbopain school, which delivered the diploma, offered two tracks for preparation with an apprenticeship contract in one year or two, depending on the level of prior schooling. So far, the results are mixed.[42]

The most delicate moment will no doubt come with the transition to the next generation, when the founders and promoters of the first wave, almost all broken in as artisanal bakers and often passionate about bread, will make room for people who are much closer to management than to production, trained perhaps in a business school rather than a baking room. Will their mastery of finance and marketing compensate for a deficit in the culture of the profession and in historical sensitivity to the product they are selling? Here is where the banalization of bread may well catch them in their own trap.

The End of the Anathema? The Big Box Stores

Borne by the great wave of postwar modernization, mass distribution responded to a social logic that artisans, bakers among others, were completely powerless to resist. There was a new social structure, a new way of life. People were more mobile, in a bigger hurry, less anchored in the classic family routines; they began to organize their daily lives differently. The massive arrival of women in the workforce probably constituted the decisive moment in the flourishing of mass distribution. Instead of doing their shopping every day in six different stores, women were more and more tempted to do everything in a supermarket on their way home from work once or twice a week.

Very visible and omnipresent, the big box stores embodied evil, in the eyes of the artisans, just as the bake-off terminals did. Under the title "Bread Discredited," Raymond Calvel describes a visit in the mid-1980s to a big discount store southwest of Paris, a "spectacle of desolation . . . so painful it was sickening."

> The baked products, baguettes, long loaves, so-called country loaves, rye bread and more, were there to greet me, like the miserable, pitiful cohort one can imagine, spilling over from the crossroads of a court of miracles [where beggars gathered].
>
> Ah! The baguettes . . . skinny, smooth sticks, with visible scabs from aborted scarification, with a greyish crust, skimpily packaged, in the sort of perforated plastic paper that serves as a wrapper and that, all by itself, in this state, gives a leprous look.

The crumb, according to this commentator, is dense, very white, lacking in odor and taste, pathetic when chewed; it leaves the consumer "hungry and disoriented." Country loaves and other specialty breads are "flat as boards," often deformed, with dull crusts, "almost apologizing for being there, in such a pitiful state." If the big chains hoped to achieve an acceptable level of quality, their breadmaking would have to be "taken care of by qualified bakers" and not by the discount grocery business. Without "love and the refined skills of the trade," there could be no good bread. Ten years later, Calvel acknowledged that "certain big chains [had] understood this": "I have been told that in La Rochelle, the best bread is sold at the Centre Leclerc."[43]

The Carrefour Case

Everywhere in France, artisans, industrialists, millers, association leaders, and others have received me readily and spoken openly and spontaneously, allowing me complete freedom to report and assess their statements. Only Carrefour attempted to impose conditions of control that were unacceptable in the framework of a study such as this one. As I was not able to discuss the issues with the directors responsible for the choices and the policies of this huge distribution network, I had to pursue my investigation at the base, in several of the store's baking rooms, and in the professional press. In a word, there is no necessary link between the "moral" quality of a company's leadership and the quality of its bread.

Carrefour owes its success in the bread realm to a sound strategic choice: they entrusted the renovation of the whole sector to a very great baker. Following the advice of Jean-Pierre Coffe, Gabriel Binetti, the national director in charge of fresh products, proposed to hire Dominique Saibron right after the latter had sold his shop on Place Brancusi in Paris — a very popular bakery, patronized by Coffe and Binetti among others. Hostile to mass distribution, like most artisans, Saibron did not sign on right away. Carrefour executives had to convince him that they were seriously committed to quality. Accepting a one-year contract, faced with the enormity of the task and the interest of the challenge, Saibron ended up staying six years. Even after he opened a new shop on Rue Monge, he continued to advise Carrefour on everything related to its bakery line, in France and abroad.

Before Saibron's arrival, Carrefour made its own bread; most of its stores had been equipped with baking rooms (114 of 117, in early 1996). While Marcel Montaigne (the legendary demonstrator of the Decollogne-Lococq mill, which supplied the Poilâne brothers and Jean-Luc Poujauran, among others) had discreetly introduced the organic round loaf baked in a soleplate oven in a handful of big box stores in the early 1990s, Carrefour's ordinary bread was strictly mediocre. In particular, Carrefour produced an ultrawhite baguette, "washed out," in Clavel's terms, without taste or aroma, made from undistinguished flour, boosted with additives, baked on a quasi-industrial scale and at an industrial cadence in a rotating rack oven.

Confronted with the rising preoccupation with quality on the part of the artisans, who were frequently pushed by their millers, and aware of his own clients' preference for a so-called artisanal bread, Gabriel Binetti sought a return to tradition ("we are artisans, not factories") that would not prevent Carrefour from "remaining productive." This was like trying to square the circle in the bakery business, but it was the sine qua non of competitive capitalism: to achieve quality and quantity at once, to be both (ostensibly) "ancestral" and (surreptitiously) productivist. This means having equipment capable of reconciling the two objectives, including a shaper with rollers that produced a back-and-forth movement "very close to the traditional movements of the baker" and a stone hearth oven that looked quite ancestral and produced results to match (fabricating homemade products). The oven was set up center stage in the baking room–theater of every store, symbolically if not actually concealing the gigantic rotating rack ovens in the background.[44]

While he was well aware of the weaknesses in Carrefour's breadmaking processes, Dominique Saibron quickly came to understand that the chain had the economic (and ideological) capacity to "be better than the artisans." But the company would have to introduce profound changes in the way its personnel thought about and produced bread. First of all, they would have to get good flour; as a pastry chef by training, responsible for Carrefour's pastry as well as its breadmaking operations, Saibron militated in favor of getting high-quality raw materials in all areas: unadulterated cacao, fresh fruit. And then any product not sold within twenty-four hours would have to be discarded. Given the enormous volume of its orders, Carrefour was in a position to get from the most demanding millers a much better price than the most faithful artisan could negotiate. The company did not go as far as its technical counselor would have liked, when he asked for flour with no additives whatsoever. But he inaugurated a new product line built around an "old-style" baguette (the designation à l'ancienne was quickly challenged by government authorities) and also a pavé; Carrefour's "bread in the French tradition" was produced according to a formula that had been perfected over time after hundreds of trials. Using a small amount of yeast, it gave the bread a long first fermentation that took place during a modified slow rise; the loaves had to go into the oven half an hour after they came out of the fermentation chamber.

This "traditional" bread, sold for 4 francs ($0.54) a loaf in 2001, may be the Carrefour bread of the future, and while a certain number of stores began to offer it as their ordinary bread, Saibron did not abandon the ordinary baguette — but he transformed it. Made with yeast by the direct method and baked in a rotating rack oven, it bears the stigmata of the bad old days. However, it is made with "traditional" flour, without additives or adjuvants. Without being boosted by vitamin c, this baguette has aromas and taste. The absence of ascorbic acid is also translated by a reduction in volume, which worried consumers at first, as much on the aesthetic level (the bread has a frugal appearance) as on the economic level (it may be perceived as underweight). But I found it better in the mouth than most ordinary baguettes, and at about 2.50 francs ($0.34) apiece in 2001, it was an outstanding bargain.

In the early stages, organic principles were doubtless responsible for the reputation of Carrefour's bread. Saibron rationalized the manufacturing process, establishing distinct stages, each one subject to special surveillance and control. Already familiar with the Decollogne-Lecocq mill, Carrefour's supplier, he organized small-group internships there for department heads from all the stores, to train them in working with the delicate and demanding sourdough. One or two months later, Saibron paid a visit to each intern's baking room to verify that the method and the recipe were being followed, and to encourage the bakers. Each team had to refresh the leaven matrix every day and check its temperature — as they had to do, in fact, for all the doughs. Noted in work records, this information allowed the department heads and the fifteen monitors who traveled throughout France for Carrefour to diagnose and correct any deficiencies.

One of the big problems in a gigantic chain in which each store has its own baking room and many teams whose members have quite disparate backgrounds was the regularity of the production process. All Saibron's recipes were written down, articulated in simple and precise terms. He was after rigor, which implied above all properly trained bakers who were ready to follow to the letter the process indicated for each type of bread. While Carrefour, like all bakeries, has recruitment problems, the teams in many of its baking rooms are fairly stable; most of their employees already work on a thirty-five-hour-per-week schedule, and certain bakers earn over $1,883 a month, which is viewed as a good salary in the trade.

After devising and setting up this new system, Dominique Saibron devoted himself to perfecting it. He constantly reviewed his own methods, cor-

Éric Kayser. © Perrin.

Dominique Saibron. © Perrin.

Pouring in liquid sourdough: a fermentation technique that identifies Éric Kayser's breadmaking method. © Perrin.

The essence of the dough to come for Dominiqu Saibron's baguette, prepared twenty-four to forty eight hours in advance. © Perrin.

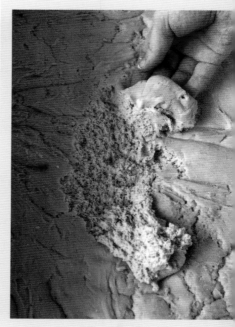

Mixing liquid sourdough with dough that has spent thirty minutes in autolysis (after five minutes of kneading, the mixture of flour and water is allowed to rest in order to relax the dough). © Perrin.

Organic sourdough, reactivated daily; the basis fo all organic breads. © Perrin.

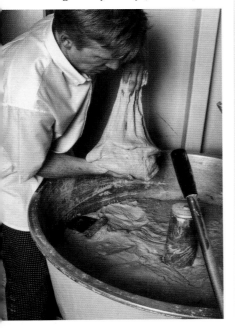

...ading: the dough is smooth and soft. © Perrin.

Incorporating the ingredients in the kneading vat: here, pouring in type 80 flour (85 percent extraction). © Perrin.

...ighing the very supple dough. © Perrin.

Starting to knead organic bread, slowly and briefly. © Perrin.

Shaping *tourtes* in wicker baskets (*bannetons*). © Perrin.

First fermentation in bulk (*pointage*); after kneadi the long fermentation that produces aromas and flavors. © Perrin.

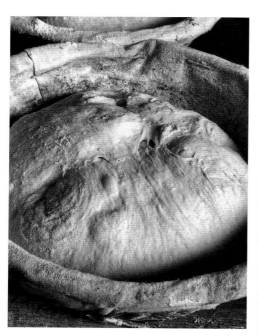

Second fermentation (*apprêt*) of a tourte. © Perrin.

Cutting the dough by hand. © Perrin.

Breadmaking the Kayser way (continued)

Breadmaking the Saibron way (continued)

ng a mechanical divider to produce unbaked
ves of equal weight. © Perrin.

Hand shaping of round loaves. © Perrin.

ping the baguette with two hands. © Perrin.

Laying out loaves for the second fermentation
(*apprêt*). © Perrin.

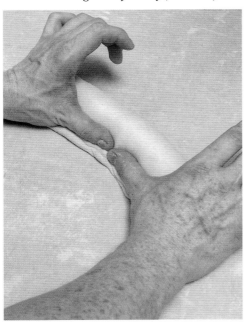

Lengthening and stretching the dough for a baguette. © Perrin.

Slashing: the knife-strokes represent the baker's signature, added just before the loaves go into the oven. © Perrin.

Bread on display in Éric Kayser's shop. © Perrin.

Cross-section of one of Dominique Saibron's loaves: a creamy crumb, with irregular cavities (*alvéolage*). © Perrin.

Well-caramelized baguettes coming out of an oven with a heat-reflecting hearth: the traditional method of baking. © Perrin.

Dominique Saibron breathes in the aromas of bread fresh out of the oven. © Perrin.

Dominique Saibron. © Perrin.

Éric Kayser. © Perrin.

rected the bakers' gestures in their own baking rooms, and experimented with new equipment. During the Saibron era, Carrefour attained a remarkable level of excellence. Its round organic loaf seduced by its richness, its rustic aroma, its agreeable texture in the mouth. Its breads in the French tradition boasted a good balance between crust and crumb, an intoxicating wheat flavor, a crispy sensation that endured, a whiff of very tonic freshness. Since Saibron's departure a few years ago, it is clear that Carrefour has not managed fully to institutionalize his methods and his rigor. The quality today is much more uneven; the baguette in the French tradition is often quite disappointing, and the everyday baguette has rejoined the ranks of the ordinary.

The Auchan Alternative

At Auchan, one of Carrefour's major rivals, rooted in the north of France, the impetus for renewal came somewhat later and in a structural context that was less favorable to a vital in-depth transformation. As *La filière gourmande* noted, Auchan undoubtedly "wanted to shed the image of a company engaged in mass production with no concern for quality." But although as much as 20 percent of this giant firm was owned by a single family, it was as decentralized in its organization as its rival was hypercentralized. Every store was viewed as an individual profit center. The manager of any Auchan store could resist the company's overall strategy. With more discussion on the inside and on the periphery, and few firm directives from the center, change came more slowly. Even if Auchan had found its Saibron (a political and technical choice that the chain did not make), it is not obvious that such a person could have transformed the hundred or so stores (out of 120) that had baking rooms.[45]

Although Auchan did not have a great alchemist-baker like Saibron, it can be congratulated for putting its bread and pastry line in the hands of a perceptive, well-informed, and strong-minded "manager," Marie-Georges Colombe. A specialist in agro-alimentary marketing, charcuterie in particular, she prepared herself for her new mission in one of the best schools for continuing education, Banette, where she spent three years. She has a firm grasp of the institutional evolution of the market and the anthropology of consumption. She identifies three distinct periods. From 1960 to 1980, a period of exaggerated consumerism when all sorts of things were sold and were easy to sell, the dominant logic was "a logic of productivity, not of quality." During the following decade, selling became more difficult when consumer spending became more differentiated and consumers became more prudent. In the 1990s, food products made slow gains. To sell more, businesses had to become "more relevant," had to understand that there was no longer just one client but a range of consumers with varying propensities. Given a segmented market, companies had to fine-tune their approach in order to optimize sales to "multiple consumers."

The breadmaking business followed the same trajectory, but it is an "atypical department": before it was segmented, the market was already structurally — one might almost say culturally — atomized. Its clients had an a priori preference for "their" baker, an artisan, and above all for a site embodying proximity and freshness. If mass distribution looked to many interested parties like the principal antagonist of artisanal baking, the chief enemy of the mass-market bakery was the very nature of the product and its low unit value. The average consumer made 250 purchases per year, spending well over $375. This meant an enormous market. Logically, Auchan ought to have positioned itself as a complement to artisanal baking. But consumer habits were changing, along with the social demographics.

Marie-Georges Colombe offers two contrasting examples in this connection. In the Lille region, consumers prefer a very white, voluminous baguette. The artisan here, who does not cook all day long, does not seem to be defined either by the freshness of his products or by service, for his range of products is fairly narrow. Confronting such artisans who are not adapting very well to modern life, Auchan can try its luck by playing the card of a return to authenticity. The company has no problem of practical or symbolic legitimacy to contend with, under these circumstances. By producing good bread and inviting its clients to buy six or seven loaves at once and freeze them on a weekly basis, Auchan can "squeeze out the artisan." The situation in Lyon is totally different. Bread culture is focused less on white bread; there is more diversity, an interest in darker bread or bread made with sourdough. In this community, which is richly endowed with an artisanal fabric, the atmosphere is propitious for the neighborhood baker who can boast of the quality and freshness of his products. Here, where artisans have a corner on legitimacy, Auchan has a hard time overcoming the obstacles.

To make gains in the 1990s, a period of individuality and multiplicity, Auchan had to put forward its dual identity, artisanal and industrial, taking its inspiration in part from *the* paradigm of bakery success: Francis Holder, founder of the Paul chain, an entrepreneur moored like Auchan in the north, who managed to articulate a double identity as a master of artisanal and industrial production. For Auchan, this meant, for example, keeping their giant rotating rack ovens, but adding traditional artisanal ovens. This led to the "bread of yesteryear" campaign launched around 1996, respecting "a breadmaking process called 'old-style' " that included slow kneading and manual shaping.[46]

The logic behind the decision to promote this old-style bread rather than to go ahead and make a "bread in the French tradition" following the new government regulations does not seem to me entirely convincing. The flour used was very similar to what was used for "traditional" bread (without fava flour) and the breadmaking process eschewed ascorbic acid and incorporated slow proofing. The evocative but nebulous labels "old-style" and "of yesteryear" came to pose problems for Auchan. The national commission responsible for certifying labels and the DGCCRF challenged their use and required the chain to abandon them.

The Saga of Francis Holder

For the artisans, Francis Holder is the enemy not only because he is an industrialist, supplying the large and medium-size chains and bake-off terminals, but because he is a very gifted artisan who operates like no other on an industrial and ultramodern scale, thus blurring the border between the two categories. Like any anomaly that results from a taxonomic transgression, Holder is particularly feared and despised. His boldness as a businessman is astonishing, but so is the excellence of his products, which are omnipresent in many parts of metropolitan France.

It is a shame to resort to journalistic shortcuts and reduce this wholly exceptional trajectory—perhaps the finest success story in French breadmaking, along with that of Lionel Poilâne—to a bottom line, even if the sum of approximately 1.5 billion francs (nearly $204 million) in annual sales at the very beginning of the new century is very impressive. Holder is a true self-made man (an itinerary that carries less social value in France than in the United States); he is the grandson of a Polish-Ukrainian immigrant on his father's side, and his rise could have begun just as well on New York's Lower East Side at the beginning of the twentieth century, though presumably not in a baking room. The son of a breadmaker and pastry chef, the grandson and great-grandson of bakers on his mother's side, Holder is a man of the north, the great seedbed of entrepreneurial success stories in France. He presides over the Holder Group, which employed more than 4,000 people at the end of the century. This group includes the Paul label (accounting for 67 percent of its proceeds), the jewel of the lot, with 255 shops in forty-three departments in France in 2000, and more than twenty abroad. It also includes the Moulin Bleu, its industrial division (24 percent); Saint-Preux, a new franchise chain (2 percent); Ladurée (7 percent), a chain of elegant pastry shops/tea shops/restaurants (here the company took over — as it did with Paul, moreover — and is making good use of an already-prestigious brand name, a "house of quality founded in 1889"); and Panétude, an "engineering bureau" responsible for creating and maintaining the group's stores.[47] A new concept called "La Manufacture du Pain," deploying a recently developed raw-frozen technology, is scheduled for implementation in 2005–2006.

Probably because he remains very conscious of his origins, Francis Holder is attached to his country and his culture, even though he frequently fulminates against the constraints that tie businessmen's hands in France, and even though the United States, the site of one of his rare failures, tempts him to participate metaphorically in the dream of the continuing conquest of new spaces. It was neither a marketing ploy nor a decorative impulse that led "*Franc*-is" Holder to adopt as his group's logo — summing up his own trajectory, as it were — two bouquets of wheat sheaves in the form of an H wrapped in a tricolor band, the marriage of the symbol of life and the emblem of national belonging, of "the glory and freedom of the fatherland," as Lamartine put it. If a powerful identification with French civilization is striking in Holder's case, one also finds a strong desire for social revenge, not the expression of the egalitarian ambition of 1793, but of the demand for personal freedom of 1789. When a journalist from *Le Point* asked him recently where he came by his inclination to aim so high, Holder portrayed himself as an outsider in relation to the "inheritors" who dominate France's sociocultural and economic landscape. He sees himself as he was as a little boy, going to Saint-Pierre, the school where the wealthiest northern industrialists sent their sons: "They all had lots of factory chimneys; all I had was my father's baking room. That was my dream: to have a factory chimney."[48] "I'll show them" quickly became a kind of raison d'être, a source of energy and inspiration. Today Francis Holder can receive his privileged schoolmates in one of the magnificent salons of his luxurious restaurant and pastry shop on the Champs-Elysées; Ladurée is located in a Napoleonic palace.

The tricolor band of his logo evokes other collective and institutional origins, those of modern France, and while there is nothing revolutionary about Francis Holder except his way of creating and managing his businesses, it is striking that two of the most important dates in his professional genealogy, mentioned in his press releases, mark the centenary moment of the French Revolution: in 1889, Charlemagne Mayot and his wife, Holder's maternal grandparents, started a small bakery on Rue de la Mackellerie in Croix, near Lille, thus founding a family dynasty of bakers, and 1889 is the year when the Paul bakery was created, on Place de Strasbourg in Lille. Julien Holder — who had married Suzanne Mayot in 1935 and who had abandoned the bakery at one point because the work was "too hard" — bought the Paul business and started it up again after World War II.

Julien Holder had no sooner managed to get the business back on its feet than he died, in 1956; he had just had time to pass his knowledge along to his son Francis, who had begun to work in the baking room three years earlier. Paul was prospering, but the young man had to interrupt his activity to do two and a half years of military service. While Algeria posed a stiffer challenge than the baking room, Francis Holder acknowledged later that for him it was an eye-opening and adventurous period that offered a striking contrast to the closed world of the bakery. Distancing allowed him to get a clearer perspective, to forge a less local ambition, to broaden the scope of his culture and his imagination.[49] When he returned, he sketched out a dual undertaking that prefigured the outline of his future empire. On one hand, borrowing money from his mother, in 1963 he opened the first Paul subsidiary, a store supplied by the mother house. On the other hand, he opened a series of workshops, each bigger than the last, to supply new clients, especially the big mass-market companies: Les Nouvelles Galeries, Monoprix, Auchan, the first Novotel. From an exiguous baking room of 20 square meters to a sprawling factory space of 4,000 square meters was quite a vertiginous leap!

The biggest challenge probably lay on the artisanal side. With capital and clients, good manufacturing tools (readily available in Europe if not in France), and a sensitivity to the evolution of demand (Holder put so-called specialty breads in large and medium-size chains as early as 1968), industrial expansion proceeded virtually on its own steam. The bread sold in chain stores at the time, noticeably less expensive than artisanal bread, did not warrant any compliments for its excellence, even when it was sup-plied by Holder enterprises. Ahead of his time, Holder sensed that, in the return to ancestral sources, at the symbolic and practical level (marketing and production, appearance and reality), there was a niche to be filled. But even before he changed his breadmaking techniques, he had begun to expand the Paul network, without a precise marketing plan, following developers of shopping centers.

The opening of the emblematic Paul, the precursor of the new model, took place in Lille, on Rue de Paris, in 1972.[50] It was a theater bakery, with the baking room in plain sight; there was no curtain between the spec-tators and the actors; it was also a transparent bakery where one could observe and even monitor the artisanal hand and the quest for old-style quality. Thanks to his reputation, Holder was aware that he could take additional market shares in "cold shops" without a baking room, to be supplied by the nearest Paul shop; this small step backward was scarcely visible on the public's radar (he says that today more than half the Paul shops have baking rooms). In the late 1980s, he decided to give a com-plementary personality to certain stores, by opening a tearoom and a res-taurant area, a sort of French-style fast food in an infinitely more elegant environment than McDonald's.

The site, the décor and atmosphere, and the concept are the elements that have structured the prodigious expansion of the Paul chain over thirty-five years. Although Paul was an essential component of the larger Holder enterprise, it was ultimately the easiest one of all. Holder's genius lay in knowing how to resist an overemphasis on marketing. Lasting and con-tagious success could only be based on the excellence of the products. Constantly keeping in mind his parents' attachment to quality, he wanted to make this Paul's signature. The banalization of bread pained him. The entire wheat-flour-bread production network seemed to forget the ulti-mate consumer. Holder, who had been making white bread like everyone else, practicing intensive kneading and paying little attention to the flours and mixes supplied by the mills, decided to proceed differently.

First, on the supply side, he changed the relation between bakers and farmers. The latter, paid for 100-kilo units, good or bad, had no intention of planting high-value wheat for breadmaking when its yield might be much less than that of the standard types. The Holder recipe entailed not only an audacious idea, going against the tide, but especially the stubborn determination to carry it out. Holder resolved to bring back an ancient variety of wheat called Camp Rémy, a tender wheat of which his father had been fond. No one believed in it, in the beginning, and even today a wholesale Camp Rémy strategy seems imprudent, even unreasonable, to many millers and bakers. Having gotten hold of seeds and set up a system to reconstitute a reserve supply, Holder negotiated with dozens of farmers ready to play the game. Anticipating the practices known today as rational farming, sensitive to the need to protect the environment (another connotation of the word "nature" appreciated by the Holder Group) and to the imperatives of traceability, he imposed rules and controls concerning the fertilizers, the products authorized to treat the grains, the timing of harvests, and so on. In 2000, more than 200 farmers, bound by contract, supplied the group with 14.1 million kilos per year. The group found six millers who also accepted constraints, including the obligation to store Camp Rémy separately and to give at least three weeks of "floor time" (rest) to the flour so that it would produce "its effect," as millers said in the eighteenth century, that is, ripen and improve.

Always motivated by memory and intuition rather than by academic science (which came later; he is anything but a primitivist), Holder sought to convince his millers to stop "cooking" the wheat, that is, to stop heating it. Finally, he asked the millers to incorporate a bit of wheat germ into the flour. Given the preoccupations of late-twentieth-century consumers, who were becoming more and more anxious omnivores, offering a delicious bread was not enough. "Paul, concerned for your health, gives priority to the safety of your food"; the group sought to meet this commitment by controlling the entire network.

Very early in relation to the (other) artisans, Francis Holder ruled out additives in his flour; this was another bold decision, since the absence of adjuvants or ameliorants made the work more difficult, in a milieu where

it was already difficult to recruit motivated and reliable bakers. (It is hard
to imagine a job posting that would read "Come work at Paul; the dough
will be harder to handle than anywhere else!") Holder laid claim to quality
with the self-interest of a businessman, the confidence of a connoisseur,
and also the pride of a moralist, as if he had the duty to guard the authentic tradition; just as his pastry cream was not reconstituted powder and
his fruit was real fruit, his flour met the criteria for flour "in the French
tradition," four years before the promulgation of the edict formalizing the
taxonomy and opening the artisanal path to a new qualitative undertaking.

How, finally, should dough be worked? "By feel," Holder acknowledged, before having the method confirmed by other bakers and before
codifying it in a recipe or work procedure, for the boss cannot expect that
everyone will have the same set of skills and the same feel. He cannot seriously instruct his bakers to go outside and measure the temperature and
the wind before starting each kneading, as his father did. When Holder
talks about breadmaking, he gestures with his hands and his body, his
eyes sparkle and dance, and his face lights up. Affect seems to win out
over technique. But he knows what he is doing, and when he says that
the dough needs to ferment for a long time and to be punched down several times, until it resembles "a woman's buttocks," his collaborators know
what he means.

The fiction is that in each Paul outlet where there is a baking room,
"Paul" himself is there making the bread. The baker has at least a CAP and
some experience, but he has been retrained in house, and he can count on
the considerable resources of the group to support his development. The
Paul in my neighborhood, for example, relies on Hervé, who has been
a baker and pastrymaker for more than eleven years and a monitor with
Paul for five years. Responsible for quality control in about fifteen stores
in the chain, every two months he spends three days verifying the respect
for the work plan manifested for all products in every shop. He makes cor-
rections, teaches tricks of the trade, reorganizes the work in part, and is
vigilant about hygiene. While Hervé trains workers in production methods, he is also concerned with packaging and sales pitches. Much more
than in most artisans' shops, the clerks in Paul shops whom I have questioned have a fairly clear idea about the products they are selling.[51]

The breadmaking process—"in pure respect for the artisanal methods" — starts with a slow but not very long kneading. Only a small amount of yeast is used, and a considerable amount of water (70–80 percent). The first fermentation is lengthy — up to two and a half hours — and the second one brief; for the organoleptic value of bread, everything plays out in the fermentation process. To keep the dough from tearing and to retain the carbonic acid, the agent that makes the dough rise, hand shaping is advocated, an artisanal stamp par excellence. Baking is done in an electric oven on a fixed hearth; the original brick, wood-burning model caused too many environmental problems. Paul's bread has a creamy crumb, wildly irregular alveolage, a crackling crust, a very agreeable taste of wheat with hazelnut highlights, sometimes completed by a toasty aroma; it comes in several different shapes (for example, paulette, pistol, thread, flute, polka) and in a variety of flavors or inflections (it may be made with sesame seeds, bacon bits, onions, olives, and so on). The entire Paul matrix gave rise to forty-two different loaves in 2001, but the list continues to expand.

Never far from his experimental baking room at La Madeleine, the seat of the society located near Lille, Francis Holder continues to be closely involved in the business. While he no longer develops new products himself, he pays close attention to those developed by his staff. Some breads are undoubtedly destined to be modified or retired in favor of others. His computer system allows him to follow the performance of every product at any time, as it varies according to the habits and social demography of a given region. More than twenty regional directors have France covered, establishing the objectives to be achieved. They have to instill in every store the determination to do better, an eternal quest for productivity and profitability. "Here, everything is very organized," according to Jean-Paul Gagnère, head of a Paul shop in Tours. "First, there is no waste in the use of ingredients. Next, every employee has his own protocols to follow: he knows what he is supposed to do and what he brings in in terms of proceeds. So, for example, the sales clerk can get after the pastry chef if she has nothing to sell. We are all in the same boat."[52] This is not the gentle solidarity of a phalanstery. But the staff often appears highly motivated, and, given premises of equal size, Paul's sales are three times greater than those of a traditional bakery: 5–6 million francs ($678,277–$813,932) per year, rising to 18 million ($2,441,797) for the shop on Rue de Buci in Paris, a chic Left Bank address. Today, Holder is one of the leaders in the field of precooked deep-frozen products. Made entirely by machines designed to give the dough a serious proofing and a relatively gentle shaping, the loaves are three-quarters baked and then finished on site, in terminal ovens, to give them crust and to optimize their freshness in the client's eyes.

This technology has recently given rise to a completely new project, launched in 1998: a group of stores, mainly held by franchisees, under the Saint-Preux name.[53] Whether or not the name alludes to the character in Rousseau's *La Nouvelle Héloïse*, Holder definitely intends it (although in a very nebulous way) as a sign "of a powerful identity as an eighteenth-century bakery." Despite the ever-so-slightly aristocratic name (the sign is a shield with a coat of arms), the project is democratic in its aims, aspiring to win over "lively, densely populated neighborhoods." With wooden counters and tables, red-painted exposed beams and ochre walls, Saint-Preux offers "a particularly warm and convivial atmosphere" in which clients can buy bread, Viennese pastry, other pastry, and sandwiches. We are far removed from the early days of deep-freezing. The bread is appetizing, lacking in aromatic backbone but tasty and attractive, and it does not turn stale within the hour. The Saint-Preux high-end terminals are franchise operations; it remains to be seen whether the investors will manifest the will and capacity to execute rigorously the procedures that the Holder Group wishfully claims will link this formula to "the good recipes of yesteryear."

Playing simultaneously on the registers of master artisan of yore and cutting-edge captain of industry, Francis Holder projects a future in which the gap between the two will be blurred if not bridged. In 2005, he began renovation and construction on massive new headquarters near the old Madeleine, a vast breadmaking campus in a verdant park traversed by a picturesque creek that will centralize his operations: artisanal, industrial, design, engineering, managerial, and so forth. Beyond important factory innovations on the parbaking side and the installation of a superb retro-hypermodern experimental baking room, the campus will feature a large school for the training of Paul bakers and other personnel. Drawing on outside capital, Paul continues to expand in railroad stations and airports and in foreign sites, from Marrakech to Miami. China is inexorably on the horizon, but emotionally the reconquest of the United States is dearest to

Holder's heart. The American Pauls will use Saint-Preux technology; it will be interesting to see how "French" parbaking fares in a market where an indigenous industry (e.g., Au Bon Pain, LaBrea) is already well established. Here Holder will face no identity problems, for in the United States parbaked bread passes as an *artisanal* creation. Only in America . . .[54]

chapter five

Bakeries and the State

T HE STATE TAKES AN INTEREST IN BREADMAKING today for many different reasons and on many different fronts. Politically, on the local and national levels alike, breadmakers constitute an influential clientele whose weight is quite disproportionate to the actual number of its agents. Symbolically, bakeries convey memories and values that no politician can ignore. Socially, bakeries play a major role in the construction of the everyday order, the conviviality of a neighborhood or a village, and thus of the social bond. No urban or regional planning project can be conceived without taking bakeries into account. Even economically, with its network of associated industries, the bakery business is not insignificant. As for the attitude of bakers toward the state, it remains ambivalent and fluctuating. The average baker—whether Maréchalist or Gaullist, Poujadist or Socialist—tends to see the state as a tentacular, intrusive, asphyxiating, excessive force that imposes taxes and regulations.[1] But even as they energetically demand their freedom, bakers also strongly desire protection. Like it or not, the state and the baking business are locked in an intimate, sometimes symbiotic, often conflictual relationship. But what is at stake today in this sometimes turbulent liaison is nothing like what was at stake in the past.

The Tyranny of Grain

Under the Old Regime, social life in France depended on cereals in every respect. Grain dominated the economy. Beyond its determining role in the agricultural sector, it influenced the development of commerce and industry, directly or indirectly; it regulated employment and constituted an essential source of revenue for the state, the church, the nobility, and a large sector of the third estate. Subsistence needs gave the tyranny of cereals its most pitiless expression. The populace lived essentially on wheat, and this dependence was an obsession as well as a servitude, for the cereal economy is one of scarcity and uncertainty; it engenders a psychology of chronic insecurity and holds society hostage. The result is an anguishing subjection to the whims of an environment that one can neither master nor tame. The structuring role of fear was obvious in its triangular Parisian incarnation: at one extreme of the base there were the people terrified to be at the mercy of bakers who seemed prepared to let them "die of hunger" in order to satisfy their greed; at the other extreme there were these same bakers, very conscious of their vulnerability and taken aback by "this so deeply rooted hatred" in the heart of the consuming populace; and at the top there was the state with its police force, the "great tremblors" of the Old Regime, which kept watch, negotiated, and attempted to work things out.[2]

Whereas the tyranny of cereals reinforced the deep rifts between the haves and the have-nots, consumers and producers, city and country, the obsession with subsistence also forged strange bonds of solidarity between the governors and the governed. At all levels, the state was as concerned about the food supply as were consumers. Subsistence constituted the main common interest that bound them together. Their shared desire to meet subsistence needs served in a way as a mutual guarantee of fidelity and responsibility. A particularly disastrous harvest or a series of inadequate ones, in addition to determining the ration and the price of survival, produced a terribly disorganizing effect that had repercussions in every area: social, economic, and psychological. The state strove to do everything in its power to avoid this sort of disorder, or at least to limit the damage. It anxiously followed the phases of the harvest cycle, as if vigilance itself were a mode of prophylaxis, as in some propitiatory rite. Ensuring an adequate food supply was a political problem; no issue had as much power to mobilize or destabilize as penury, or the fear of going without.

The Social Contract

"The subsistence of the people is the most essential matter with which the Administration must concern itself," affirmed Jacques Necker, a philosopher, minister, banker, and grain speculator. And except for two brief free-market interludes, this commitment to France's consumer population was the unchallenged foundation of government policy under the Old Regime. This policy was in fact dictated by the conviction that social stability would be ensured only if the food supply were also guaranteed. History seems to have demonstrated convincingly that hunger and scarcity had "preceded, prepared, and caused" serious and sometimes fatal disorders, in Rome, Constantinople, and China. Without order, the authorities could not hold onto their power, and society could not maintain its cohesiveness. The necessary condition for order, in the words of a regional agent of the state, "was to provide for the people's subsistence, without which there is no law or power that can contain them."[3]

To ensure a sufficient food supply was not only in the interest of the state but also one of its obligations, in conformity with the doctrine that gradually came to preside over the relations between the governors and the governed, a doctrine I have called the social contract. In this solemn exchange, which defined and structured the relations between the state and society under the Old Regime, the consumer populace subjected itself to taxation, conscription, and other levies; its members subscribed to a more general commitment to submission in exchange for the assurance that they would not be allowed to starve to death. A nurturing prince, embodiment of the state, the king became not the provider of food on a daily basis (although he had supervisory power over the arrangements set up for that purpose), but the baker of last resort. The women who marched to Versailles in October 1789 to demand that the contract be respected, by bringing the baker, the baker's wife, and their little baker's boy back to the capital, understood the king's role and its meaning perfectly well. The same thing held true for the Parisians and the peasants from the hinterlands who, during the wheat riots in May 1775, known as "the Flour War," shouted "Long live the King, and may bread [prices] go down!" —

in a nutshell, a whole political doctrine based on a mix of deference and reciprocity. This hope had a chilling underside: when the riots were running their course and the new monarch was preparing to be crowned in Reims, the threat was clear, announced on placards: "If bread prices don't go down, we shall exterminate the king and wipe out the Bourbon line."

It is not surprising that throughout the regions shaken by the uprisings, between the heart of Burgundy and the Normandy borders, rumor had it that Louis XV had fixed the price of grain at 12 pounds 10 sous and bread at 2 sous a pound. A water carrier from Rue Mazarine in Paris, accused of entering a bakery and refusing to pay more than 8 sous 4 deniers for a four-pound loaf, protested that he was conforming to the will and the order of the king, the supreme price-fixing authority. And indeed, yielding to intense pressure from angry demonstrators, the young governor of Versailles had fixed the price "in the name of the king" at 2 sous a pound—the mythical and historical fair price inscribed in memory. Under these conditions, who could blame the poor 23-year-old Parisian who offered to pay 12 sous for a 6-pound loaf although the baker was asking 16 sous? He had learned prosaically from his butcher that the night before, under solemn circumstances, "bread was officially priced at 2 sous a pound and . . . that was what convinced him to want to pay only this much." Marie-Catherine David had a similar excuse; arguing with an itinerant baker in his stall in Neuilly, she declared that the king's word could not be contradicted.[4]

When the police, as the implementation agent of the state's rules and regulations, failed in its duties and did not manage to calm the fluctuations in bread price or to avoid short-term scarcity, the king had no choice but to intervene. Such was the very definition of royalty, to borrow the words of the police assembly convened by the Paris Parlement during the upheavals in 1768—a crisis that had been seriously exacerbated if not actually triggered by the government's revolutionary decision to remove grain and flour from police control (or, to put things in more familiar terms, by the monarch's decision to "emancipate" his children from their age-old dependency). "Be a king," clamored the magistrates, by which they meant: "Assume your paternal obligations."[5]

To be king was to assume the traditional responsibilities of royalty and above all the obligation to honor the social contract concerning subsistence. When the consumer population was confronted with catastrophe, it was incumbent upon the monarch, embodying the state, to intervene, first as regulator and avenger, and then, if necessary, as supplier. In the early days of the Revolution, the count of Saint-Priest strove to convince a band of Parisian women that famine was the result of accidents beyond the control of Louis XVI ("it was no more up to the King to make wheat grow than to make rain fall"); he was not very credible, given the widely shared image of a powerful royalty and a sanctified social contract. In the aftermath of the Flour War, Voltaire pinpointed the difficulty when he put words in the monarch's mouth: "The Good Lord made me King of France, he didn't make me the Great Breadmaker." And the modern royal reasoner was made to add, in harmony with Turgot's liberalism: "I want to be the protector of my nation, not its regulatory oppressor."[6]

The pathos goes up a notch in an anonymous memoir written during the fall of 1789 in the middle of a major food supply crisis, while polemics were raging between Jean-Jacques Rutledge, a noble military officer who had exchanged his sword for a pen dipped in vitriol and expressed himself in the name of the bakers of Paris, and the Leleu brothers, who had been charged by Turgot with setting up an emergency supply of grain and flour for the capital after the Flour War. Furious to see these entrepreneurs invoking the sacred name of the king, the symbol of his intangible commitments to his people, in order to mask their odious speculative machinations and to transform innocent bakers into scapegoats, the anonymous author wrote: "Is it because these men (I am mistaken, for they are hydras), these men, I say, use the sacred name of the King, a name they bandy about and use only too often to shout everywhere, at all times and in all places: this wheat is for the King's storehouses. But are people unaware, do they not know, that the King is the father of the people, and how can a father allow himself to make his children starve to death? This cannot be believed, it is a clear falsehood."[7]

The Bakery Police of Yesteryear

"Temper their greed for profits as much as possible": this was the byword of Commissioner Nicolas Delamare, the great codifier of police regulations at the end of the seventeenth century, in his dealings with bakers. La Reynie, the lieutenant general of police at the time, never tired of reminding bakers that they would be "severely chastised" if they did not fulfill their responsibility to provide an adequate supply of bread. For La Reynie's successor, d'Argenson, the bakers often behaved like "the cruelest enemies of the people." He often warned that "it would be dangerous to be unable to suppress the bakers' insolence." Hérault, the police lieutenant as of late 1725, considered it urgent to administer "exemplary punishment" for the "hypocrisy" and "greed" that victimized the public.

The approach to bakers was applied to grain and flour merchants as well; for reasons of state and out of humanitarian concerns, the people's food supply had to be protected. In its strategy of containment, the police treated both groups as public servants rather than as mere commercial actors. If they failed in their duties, the public would explode in a more or less legitimate "fury." A popular insurrection in the context of a shortage would doubly compromise the public order.

From the point of view of the police, it was part of the bakers' duty to keep their shops and stalls supplied, whatever difficulties and ordeals they might be facing. Nothing could dispense them from this obligation, and certainly not the ordinary paroxysm of scarcity. If they were compelled to reduce their production, their wealthiest clients were to be the first to suffer; despite the big demand for specialty loaves, bakers were to stop making them and, in the same spirit, were to use their grain to make less white bread and more dark. Police authorities exhorted them to use their ingenuity to find merchandise, and they were ready to supply grain and flour themselves if bakers could not do so for want of means or credit. In times of abundance, the police allowed them to make nice profits, even compensatory bonuses. In times of crisis, on the contrary, they were supposed to "be content with modest gains," or, if necessary, accept a loss that would be compensated one way or another. Until the mid-nineteenth century, they were forbidden to leave the profession, especially in hard times, without authorization. The authorities ordinarily required three to six months' notice, even if in reality two weeks were often enough.

Delamare brought "the bakery police" back to a triple objective: to produce "good bread, have enough of it, and [sell it] at a fair price." Bakers were supposed to have scales in plain sight in their shops or stalls, in order to allow the most demanding clients to verify the weight of the merchandise. In markets, each baker was supposed to display the number of his stall clearly to make it easier for clients to lodge complaints. The bread was supposed to manifest an "appropriate degree of baking" and to be of good quality; the bakers were to make sure that their bread was not made of "spoiled flour that would be harmful to those who ate it"—their clients were well positioned to make their own judgments. Finally, bakers could not exercise certain professions deemed "incompatible" with their functions, in particular speculative trading in grain and flour. But all these injunctions were at the service of a larger, all-encompassing goal: price control.

Recalcitrant or rebellious bakers were exposed to a whole gamut of collective or individual sanctions. Throughout the eighteenth century, police lieutenants threatened to set up public ovens that would compete for the bakers' clientele if the latter did not guarantee or increase their supply. By widely publicizing violations and ignominious actions (for example, by posting 200 notices describing one master baker's adulteration of flour or another's practice of fudging weights), the authorities shamed the "evildoers" in public. Less often, the police humiliated them by placing them in the stocks or making them run through the marketplace wearing a placard declaring their perfidy: "Baker defying justice, selling bread above the price set by the police and at false weights." Another way of tormenting refractory bakers was to hint that the police would not protect them against the likely "furor of the populace" the next time prices went up, even if the increase in question was authorized. In the 1850s, some Paris bakers were still in favor of an official price schedule that protected them from public ire.

Crackdown on Fraud

With perhaps more means at their disposal than the services for countering fraud (DGCCRF/DDCCRF—Les directions départementales de la concurrence, de la consommation et de la répression des fraudes) have today, under the Old Regime the state oversaw bread quality. The keystone of all the regulations remained the sixteenth-century directive requiring that the bread be "without adulterants, well developed, fermented and baked, as it should be." Delamare used three criteria that were only refinements on the inherited base: the flour to be kneaded had to come from "good wheat," neither "sour" nor "overheated and rotten or spoiled"; next, the dough had to be "well raised"; finally, the bread had to be "baked just long enough." Abbot Terray, a minister in the early 1770s, readily conceded that "the poor quality of bread" was one of the chief causes of the widespread subsistence riots. In September 1789, a rumor went around that some bakers were selling bread "mixed with lime." It is not surprising to learn that the "poor quality of bread" was one of the vehement leitmotifs of the women who marched on Versailles the following month: "We'll make the Austrian [queen] eat it, and we'll cut off her head." "Alum, soap, and flour together / There's the bread you eat every day" remained a classic satirical couplet until the twentieth century.

Put a baker on the scale after he dies, the adage went; he won't make his weight. Selling underweight bread was among the bakers' most common infractions. It was an "almost general fraud," the author of one manual observed toward the end of the eighteenth century. "To the shame of the Bakers, one rarely finds a Bread that weighs its weight," a Parisian observed in 1791. However, the problem did not end with the Old Regime. "Is it possible," a member of the Paris municipal council asked in 1859, "that in a state of civilization such as our own, when someone wants to buy a one-kilogram loaf of bread, . . . he has great difficulty getting the weight?" Twenty years later, an editorialist of Le Petit Parisien invoked a classic children's riddle: what is heavier, a pound of feathers or a pound of lead? There was always the risk of falling into the trap and answering "a pound of lead." "But if someone were to ask us the difference between a pound of ordinary bread and a pound of white bread, would we not be justified in responding that they have something in common: neither usually weighs a full pound."[8]

In Paris, bread was not weighed at the time of sale. A mark indicated its weight, and it was sold at the price corresponding to the weight announced. The police viewed cheating on weight as a very serious infraction. Intolerable in itself, dishonesty was judged as dangerous as it was reprehensible in areas which, like that of food supply, involved "the public good." It undermined consumer confidence in the authorities no less than in the bakers. It is thus not surprising that the police did not hesitate to see false weights as "a theft from the public" motivated by greed and bad faith. Diderot told the Empress Catherine the story of a Turkish judge who was interrupted during a meal because a baker who cheated on weight had been arrested. "They had informed me that a baker sold his bread short," the judge said. "I went to his house. His bread was weighed and found wanting. His oven was blazing; I had him seized and thrown in, and the matter was settled." And the judge explained to his shocked listeners the reason for this manifestly cruel gesture: "His was a public theft that fell on the most wretched people in the land, those who buy their bread by the pound. You subject the man who breaks into the financier's safe to the wheel, and you don't want me to burn the man who steals bread from the poor."

French justice was much less brutal. According to the statutes, the heaviest punishment for cheating on weight was the loss of the title "master." More often, the baker's shop was closed and "walled in." The ordinary sanction applied to all categories of bakers was a fine, highly variable in amount: from 3 to 3,000 pounds, during the eighteenth century. In addition, virtually all bakers caught in the act of selling short had their bread confiscated immediately; it was often cut up in a humiliating ritual and distributed to the poor. The bakers considered accusations of false weight as profoundly unjust. The weakest argument was articulated by Félix, a baker from Rue Saint-Jacques in Paris, to Commissioner Roland: "It was the journeymen's fault." The arguments of the bakers who acknowledged that they were technically unable to guarantee the proper weight were much more convincing. Master Estienne Mongeret protested that he was not responsible; he had not intended to cheat. The false weight of which he was accused resulted "from overcooking the bread and the heat that dries it out." His colleague Edière proclaimed his innocence in similar terms: "It resulted from the fact that the bread was cooked too long and was stale." A century later, Jacob, a baking expert, invoked the same argument before an investigatory commission to explain why he could not anticipate and control weight.

Price Controls

Late-twentieth-century bakers and their eighteenth-century counterparts were similarly subject to public pricing policies. To settle the question of bread, the authorities of the Old Regime had gotten into the habit of fixing sales prices in large sections of the kingdom. Announced by the Bible, put to work in classical Antiquity, this time-honored strategy had been perfected at the dawn of modern times, in particular by the English and the Italians. Price-fixing, or *taxation*, as it was called in France, lent itself either to systematic application, in the form of a very elaborate price schedule covering all possible levels, or to a simpler and more summary practice, the establishment of a fixed or mobile price ceiling.

If "taxation" was never the object of a sociopolitical consensus in the eighteenth century, the police customarily justified it as a necessary evil. In this the police shared the conviction of numerous moralists: merchants selling products of "prime necessity" must not be allowed to hold society hostage to their unquenchable greed. But not everyone agreed that "the path of authority" was the best way to achieve "a just price," which is, according to the definition of Commissioner Lemaire, "a reasonable price . . . and within the reach of the people." Answering Narbonne, the commissioner in Versailles who loudly demanded a permanent maximum price for Paris ("it would be good for the whole country"), various specialists on the food supply, including Commissioner Delamare and Inspector Poussot from Les Halles, warned that the cure would be worse than the disease, for the supply, far from being increased, would go elsewhere. "Never fix the price of wheat or bread in the middle of the cruelest famine," Abbot Galiani, an implacable adversary of the physiocrats' free-market scholasticism, advised police lieutenant Sartine around 1770.

Throughout the Age of Enlightenment and during a good part of the nineteenth century, the authorities remained divided on the critical question of setting the price of bread. They did not view the question in strictly objective terms having to do with the organization of the food supply. They saw perfectly well that the question of bread was as much a matter of public opinion as of price (and supply), and that price shaped public opinion just as public opinion conditioned price. It was difficult to explain to consumers that visible inaction on the part of the authorities served their interests better than aggressive intervention—in the case in point, price-setting. Emphasizing the political stakes in the control of bread prices, the scientist Mathieu Tillet, speaking to the Academy of Sciences in 1781, maintained not only that price-setting protected the public from uncertainty and worry and sheltered bakers from popular fury and revenge, but that it also protected the state, including public authorities at all levels, against "the anger of opinion." Reversing Tillet's argument, according to which the absence of a fixed price incited people to hold the state responsible for penury, the mathematician and philosopher Condorcet considered that the pernicious use of price-setting got the people used to "holding its magistrates responsible for the high price of subsistence items." Far from preserving them from the ravages of public opinion, price-setting held them hostage to its whims. Far from sparing the people misery, fixed prices were apt to produce "real scarcity"—rather than "perceived scarcity"—by encouraging frightened suppliers to conceal their goods. And, more seriously, it offered "dissidents the only way to stir up the population" and thus to undermine the stability of the state.

Throughout the kingdom, bakers denounced these constraints and resisted them in a variety of ways. First of all, price-setting was "an injustice," if not simply "theft." In more concrete and specific terms, the bakers of Chateau-Thierry complained that the fixed price was based on an artificially low price for grain, lower than the price at which they could get flour to make an acceptable bread. Paris bakers warned that the policy of price-setting forced them to "skimp on the quality" of flour, and that "there [was] reason to fear that the complaints of the Public were thus very considerable and very well founded." Frustrated, angry, and even emboldened by the crisis that seemed to reinforce their means of pressure in the short run, the bakers sometimes burnished their ultimate weapon, the threat that they would stop baking. In 1725, the bakers of Rennes organized a kind of strike, refusing to bake as long as the police did not put a stop to price controls. In 1770, the bakers of Arpajon threatened to close up shop if prices remained fixed.

A century later, in the name of the entire profession, Victor Borie compared the fate of bakers to that of the Jews, who were "allowed to enjoy common rights," and the blacks, who had been "emancipated." Fixed prices denied bakers "the equality of rights" from which all other citizens benefited, reducing them to the status of "slaves" and "pariahs of modern society." A hundred years after that, when bread no longer mattered much on the strictly nutritional level, Paris nevertheless came to the boiling point when bakers staged a strike lasting several days to protest against price ceilings and other administrative constraints. Two thousand bakers gathered at Mutualité, some brandishing sticks to which they had tied sacks of flour, and clamored, in a classic Thomist idiom: "Bread has its fair price; bakeries want to survive."[9]

From a Community of Master Bakers
to a State Corporation

In the eighteenth century, in Paris and in many other cities, the master bakers' guild, which had recently come to be called a corporation, concerned itself first and foremost with the interests of its members. It also carried out policing functions on behalf of the state. This was a matter of give and take: in exchange for the granting of a monopoly, a very attenuated one in the capital, and in the name of the general interest. The leaders of the community made sure the duties of public service were carried out. Thanks to this collaboration, the guild enjoyed real autonomy in managing its internal affairs, recruitment in particular, and it was able to negotiate with the authorities to obtain a less onerous fixed price or to favor its competitive position with respect to its nonincorporated rivals. Abolished for a brief moment, as were virtually all corporations, by the ultraliberal minister Turgot in February 1776, the guild of master bakers was reestablished several months later along new lines, in a model applicable to the entire corporatist universe. Standardized in their organization, subject to close financial and political oversight, purged of the cultural and symbolic specificities that guaranteed their cohesiveness, deprived of direct control over recruitment, which had been the token of their self-esteem and their collective honor, the new corporations were all more or less colonized by the state, bakers more than the others, given the quite particular character of their vocation as providers of the foodstuff of prime necessity.

The bureaucratization of the baking business was interrupted by the Revolution, for ideological reasons (the belated official triumph of individualist liberalism was concretized by the "definitive" suppression of the corporations) and also for practical reasons (the recurrence of crises in the food supply in a climate of civil and international war, real or imaginary plots, popular outcries, and general disorganization).

In the arsenal of the Revolutionary authorities responsible for managing food supplies, apart from new ideological tools of real significance and an astonishing mobilization of paramilitary forces in rooting out hoarders, the weapons of the Old Regime remained entirely relevant. The "maximum," emblem of the Jacobin social commitment extorted by the sans culottes, was nothing but the fixed price or ceiling routinely practiced before 1789 and henceforth generalized. The moral economy of the Old Regime strangely resembled the egalitarian ethic of the new, but the latter took root in very different soil. The social contract of subsistence continued to constrain the sovereign, in an intimate bond with the people, but from now on the people themselves were sovereign. In this regard the role of the state did not change a bit: sacrificing liberal dogma to public safety, it toiled as before to limit the ravages of subsistence crises and keep a handle on prices. Authorities quickly returned to the bureaucratized corporatist model as the primary mechanism for policing bakers, particularly in the capital. They facilitated the creation of a baker's association (*syndicat*), which addressed the needs of the state rather than the professional priorities of the artisans. Its main function was to ensure the application of the new regulations, especially the obligatory supply that every baker had to furnish: a large quantity of flour deposited in a public storehouse and another amount stored on his own premises. Considerably reinforcing the material and psychological security of the city, this system, linked to a price-fixing mechanism, led to a significant reduction in the number of bakeries and ensured a much higher annual sales figure. In comparison to the Old Regime, the logic was anything but corporatist.

The association leaders, more and more involved in the everyday management of bakery affairs, had the problem of reconciling their administrative duties with their specifically corporatist concerns. On one hand, they carried out inspections along with the police to reinforce the subordination of the bakers' boys (work passport [*livret*], mandatory job placement, and so on) and to suppress the illegal competition of resellers (*regrattiers*); they also pressured shop owners to respect the preexisting obligation to get approval from the police prefect in order to enter or leave the trade. On the other hand, they organized a system of collective compensation for bakers who had been compelled by the authorities to give up their professional activity, deemed too tenuous; they fought to preserve the privileges that were supposed to make up for the constraints to which bakers were subjected (exemption from the business tax, an advantage lost in 1814); they tried to stabilize the obligatory stockpiling (brutally increased in 1818); they set up a common baking room that allowed colleagues going through hard times to bake their bread. An excellent recent study unmasks the association's idealized retrospective depiction of its own role as vigorous defender of the interests of the profession from the start. An agent of power, the association tried to get bakers to play the game, ensuring the diffusion of official directives without ever criticizing them.[10]

Price-setting was sometimes spasmodic and unpredictable, in the style of the Old Regime, and sometimes more systematic; on the practical level, it constituted one of the bakers' greatest concerns throughout the nineteenth century. Yet even though bakers vigorously challenged the specific assessments that led to the new system of periodic price-setting starting in 1823 (in particular the estimations of the amount of bread yielded by a given amount of flour and the establishment of the "baking bonus" covering expenses and benefits and replacing the mechanism of negotiated compensations that had been more advantageous for the bakers), they were more critical of the particular modalities of price-setting than of price-setting itself. Even though price-setting obliged the average baker — "seen as a serf of the Administration," according to Ambroise Morel, association leader and historian of the baking business in the early twentieth century — to fall back on baking agreements (marchés de cuisson) and thus made him dependent on the millers, who paid a fixed rate for the transformation of each sack of flour delivered, the system often worked in his own interest. While the prospect of liberalization was growing more concrete, the syndicate leaders were more apt to invoke the threat to the public order than the imperative to emancipate the baking business. "The bakers did not want their utopia to be realized," the young historian Nicolas Martin notes; "it was better for it to remain a 'dream.'" A lawyer representing bakers in the mid-nineteenth century adopted a position that would resurface among a certain number of bakers 120 years later, in the wake of the "definitive" liberation of prices, the realization of a utopia that was not quite the Garden of Eden: "The uniformity of prices, the convenience of service strike me as conditions for tranquillity."[11]

The new factor, which modified the relations between the state and the bakery business in the long run, was the gradual improvement in the standard of living and the dietary diversification that deprived bread of a significant portion of its coercive power.

"Modern" Price-Setting

"Officially" abrogated in 1863, price-setting nevertheless persisted in the twentieth century, in part a glorious anachronism paying homage to the long history of the state (from paternalist institution to welfare state), but in part a lucid policy that took into account the expectations of a highly differentiated and stratified population undergoing modernization at varying rates, the durably disorganizing impact of two wars and a world-wide economic depression, and the imperatives of the recurring struggle against inflation. Mayors had traditionally set prices, but starting in 1924 the task fell to prefects. After the price code was drawn up in 1945, prefects theoretically still had price-setting authority, but in practice the central government made the decisions and transmitted its instructions to the departments. After opting for discretion in the immediate postwar period, in the 1950s the National Bakery Confederation relaunched a searing critique that became the refrain of the bakers' dialogue with the state. Mesmerized by the symbolism that tied its hands and permeated its thinking, the state lost sight of the realities that the artisans were having to confront. It was guilty of a double error of judgment; it refused to understand that public "opinion" had for a long time been more interested in the quality of bread than in its price (an observation that has a cruelly ironic ring some half a century later), and it was unwilling to recognize the concessions that the bakers had already made. President Gringoire attributed the profession's immobility directly to price-setting. Paralyzed by this practice, the consensual scapegoat of the profession, bakers could not modernize, invest, or improve the quality of their production.[12]

In 1859, many bakers agreed with Ferrand, the inspector general of exchanges and markets, when he said: "As for price-setting, this is the way to maintain bread quality, because competition is established around quality and not price." One hundred years later, Paul Gringoire, testifying before CNERNA, whose objective was precisely to evaluate the quality of bread in France, asserted that "the low price of bread has slowed improvement in the quality of flour, and consequently in the quality of bread, for too long. It has sometimes led us to an excessive acceleration of the bread-making process, which was thus less costly," an acceleration that was to expand under the impetus of the wind from the west. Somewhat later, Guy Boulet, a rural baker from the east, took the opposite stance in the price-setting stagnation argument. He deplored "the choice of productivity imposed by price-setting." Instead of straightforwardly preventing investment, price-setting pushed bakers to modernize blindly, one might say mechanically, "according to the simplistic notion that what is modern necessarily replaces what is ancient." According to this logic, bread quality was suffering not for want of means of modernization, but because of the industrialization of baking rooms that had been imposed in part by price-setting. Did Boulet underestimate, retrospectively, the shackles that a completely antiquated baking room imposed and the feeling of impotence aroused by price-setting among many bakers at the very beginning of the Thirty Glorious Years? In 1980, right after the (provisional) suppression of price controls, when confederation president Francis Combe foresaw the return of high-quality bread thanks to the suppression of the "straightjacket" of price controls which "required [the baker] to purchase flour at the best price" instead of being able to "demand the best quality from his miller," was he putting his finger on the problem or was he exonerating the artisan from all responsiblity for the decline in quality by attributing this regressive move to the state?[13]

For Guy Boulet, price-setting was not simply the story of a tentacular Jacobin state dictating prices year after year from on high. He notes "the determining role of our regional association and of the National Confederation on the price of bread. Everything depended on those two agencies alone, and the daily volume at the cash register depended on their actions." The result of price-setting that was as much negotiated as prescribed (if not more) was usually unfavorable to rural bakers, according to Boulet (which prompted him, among other reasons to become an association militant). He cites the following example: newly elected to the presidency of the confederation in 1972, Combe requested a meeting with the minister and obtained an increase of 5 centimes on all categories of bread, clearly favoring the 300-gram urban baguette as opposed to the 2-kilo rural loaf.

From the eighteenth century on, except in times of great crisis or administrative outrage, price-setting was ordinarily the result of a discussion and subject to revision during the course of the year (more often before 1900 than afterward) as conditions evolved. Every year, in late spring, the confederation began to prepare a dossier that brought together data on production costs (salaries, utilities, rents, and so on), and on projections for the harvest and the price of wheat and flour. In August 1976, after a three-hour "debate" with the director general of prices, to whom he had presented his dossier, Combe announced that he had obtained a more favorable result than the solution initially proposed by the government. (Did the state prove to be as understanding with regard to the delicate political situation of the association leaders in the mid-twentieth century as the lieutenant general of the police, representing the state, with regard to the guild leaders in the eighteenth century?) Noting with great satisfaction the small impact the 10-centime increase had on public opinion (during a period of inflation, it should be added), the association hastened to draw the classic lesson: "Might the price of bread have lost the importance it once had in consumers' minds? This is what the Bakery profession desires and hopes. It has suffered too much in the past from the taboo on the price of bread not to take justifiable pleasure in this shift of opinion."[14]

Historically, bakers subjected to price controls were always granted compensations of one sort or another. After lifting price controls, the state pressured bakers into adopting "an agreement on moderation" in 1983. "Bitterly negotiated," this "disguised price-setting" would have gone over better if the confederation had been able to win other concessions relating to its major concerns, "abusive and unfair competition." But it never ceased to insist that in any case it preferred to accept a bad agreement, the product of an exchange of views, rather than leave the door wide open to authoritarian regulations.[15]

"A Revolution"

"The price of bread is free," proclaimed the headline of the confederation newspaper on August 12, 1978. A drawing shows a statue of liberty holding a round loaf in her left hand and a quite phallic baguette in her right hand. "Price controls are dead," another newspaper rejoiced. There was talk everywhere not only of "revolution" but of "impossible dream," "utopia," and "myth." However, confederation president Combe, praised for his exceptional combativity, was the first to warn his colleagues about the concrete risks of a blind triumphalism. This was a revolution haunted from the outset by its Thermidor. "I ask you not to take undue advantage," Combe urged his troops. Bakers had to learn to use the new freedom. Under the "arbitrary" regime of price controls, many artisans did not bother to pay close attention to business management. "You are now going to have to think carefully about all the factors that go into a cost price." (Later, Combe criticized René Monory, the centrist finance minister, for having offered the gift of freedom too abruptly, without leaving the associations time to prepare their members; this was a way of recalling that the border between dream and nightmare is a shifting one.)[16]

"No, I repeat, liberty is not license, that is, the ability to do just anything," Francis Combe exploded eight months later. He noted a "loss of control" that could only "discredit" the entire profession. "Certain [bakers] have gone too far," and he called on his departmental and regional federations to educate the bakers at the base so that they could make reliable cost calculations and learn to set prices. The problem lay in explaining the value of moderation to a baker and his wife who both worked sixteen hours a day and who wanted social and economic revenge at last. The only justification we can give clients for asking them to pay a higher price, Combe advised, is that ending price controls will be the way to "maintain and improve" the quality they seek.[17]

A few months later, the president modified his strategy, returning to a pugnacious corporatism. "We refuse the role of scapegoat," when the National Institute for Statistics and Economic Studies announced that the price of bread had gone up 22 percent in the past year, "an index forged," Combe declared, "in bureaucratic secrecy." Another of his arguments was much stronger: "I contest this assessment of freedom from price controls that is based on a percentage." He meant that it was necessary to contextualize and historicize, to make it clear that for generations "bread was not sold at its real price," thus to relativize the process of catching up that had been going on for a year. ("Why all this fuss around a necessary adjustment when it is impossible today to buy any daily newspaper for the price of a baguette?") Speaking to the press, Combe tried to explain the sacred vocation and the calvary of the neighborhood or village baker, worn down by work and fatigue, earning a mediocre living with the help of his wife, and so on. "If the trade were so easy and so lucrative, why would anyone leave it?" in an allusion to the recent reduction in the number of artisanal bakeries from 46,000 to 40,000.[18]

Still, Combe was a realist, and he was perfectly well aware that, even if "bread is not an expensive product," the press campaign over the 22 percent increase "has tarnished [the profession's] image." It was necessary to act by "making an impression on public opinion," that is, by making a solemn commitment to moderate prices (from then on). Masking a defeat as a master strategy, Combe called on all bakers to respect the lists of "recommended prices," for moderation was "the condition of [their] freedom."[19] A month later, "stupefied" and hurt, Combe denounced a "hard blow to the profession," the return to price controls, a diktat "prepared in secrecy and haste": the move was an implicit disavowal of the confederation president, who had been unable to impose his will on the bakery family. It was time for strikes and urban lobbying. Shortly before Christmas, the national association newspaper proclaimed: "The bakery business has been heard. Concerted action has begun." Instead of reimposing a system of classic price-setting, the government agreed to negotiate "commitments to moderation"; respecting these would be in the associations' interest.[20]

The popular press, the bête noire of the confederation, once again put the confederation president in an awkward situation, with its headlines in early July 1980 reading "Baguette Surprise." And in fact prices had jumped, here and there, starting in late June.[21] At the end of the year, "yet again," as Combe complained bitterly, "the media — newspapers, radio, and television — all lashed out at the bakery business." It was once more a matter of prices: Combe stressed once more that the symbolic and material value of bread could not be separated, even now that bread was no longer an "urgent necessity." M. Rodriguez, the baker in La Ciotat, was in the spotlight: his ephemeral glory had seriously embarrassed the baking establishment. Rodriguez sold his baguette for one franc ($0.22), and the press made him a hero.

The suspicion of conspiracy hovered, recalling the eighteenth-century famine plot and the Flour War. "As if an orchestra conductor were in the shadows guiding media eager to create an event, all the newspapers are talking about the bread war and declaring that yesterday bread was sold for one franc, today for 0.95 francs ($0.21), and tomorrow . . . why not give it away?" Apart from the "insults to our honesty, and even our honor" in the press, which the bakers "are not about to forget," Combe wanted above all to bring the public back to reality: "There is no bread war." The press had grossly exaggerated a local matter: "People are saying 'Bravo' to the La Ciotat baker who works twenty hours a day and makes a gift of his work to his clients!" But it turned out that M. Rodriguez was not actually an artisanal baker, "as he had deliberately been made out to be." Even "before the events," he was producing 3,000 baguettes a day, working on a quasi-industrial scale. When demand doubled rapidly and he could no longer cope, he made a discreet appeal to an industrial bakery in Marseille. ("The most serious issue was the lack of a qualitative reference," a disgusted Guy Boulet observed.) Finally, Rodriguez's baguette weighed 180 grams instead of 200 or 250, the common standard in other bakeries where baguettes were sold for 1.60 francs ($0.35) apiece; Rodriguez's price thus represented a 33 percent increase over 20 months, a period during which the average price rise was 35 percent. M. Rodriguez quickly dropped from public view, and according to Boulet the affair left "few traces in association reports, except for a reminder that each baker had to be responsible in calculating his selling prices."[22]

The confederation had hardly recovered from this melodrama when it was shaken once again, in fall 1981, by an "arbitrary" decision on the part of the state to reimpose price controls for a three-month period. "The first two weeks of October 1981 will be a black mark in the annals of the bakery business," the confederation newspaper lamented. "The price of ordinary bread is once again officially set in all departments." Speechless, hurt by the absence of any consultation, Combe protested vigorously. "I shall explain my deep disappointment to the Ministry, for the moderation agreement that had been negotiated with the Direction of Competition and Consumption and accepted by the Ministry seemed to me, with a few exceptions, to have been properly respected by the profession." "In a year," he declared, "the price of bread had risen 10.97%, whereas overall prices had gone up 13.61%." The government's move was an unjust, gratuitous slap in the face that would be "very badly received by the bakers, especially psychologically." Price controls weighed on the economy, calling planned investments back into question, investments that would have led to the creation of new jobs. Even while it was shamelessly increasing the fiscal charges that were putting a strain on the bakery business, the state was continuing—out of a demogogic reflex—to protect the traditional consumer population which, in the first place, no longer existed, and in the second place, no longer needed such benevolence ("everyone knows that the price of bread no longer had the impact it once had had on household budgets").[23]

This ideological and practical tension between the state and the baking business, crystallized by price controls, was not relieved until early 1987, when the 1945 bread rulings were abrogated and all controls on bread prices were lifted. The editorial in the confederation newspaper, this time signed by Combe's successor Jean Paquet, was prudently titled "An Opportunity and a Risk." The theme was once again the imperious necessity of moderation, not to please the state but because it was in the interest, well understood, of the artisanal bakers themselves. Moderation must no longer be viewed as a sort of capitulation, but as a powerful weapon against the enemy. The risk that loomed was the extension of deviations on the scale of a big box store: "anarchic competition that makes bread a loss leader by practicing reductions," price being the only argument that mass distribution was capable of advancing. Artisans had to promote quality above all else; this was an area where they were unbeatable, and quality is not sold at clearance rates. But on the eve of a major assault by the large and medium-size chain stores, "we have to postpone our legitimate repricing for a few months." With "the excellence of our quality-price ratio," Paquet argued, artisans could come out ahead. But "we must not rush anything if we want to keep this fragile equilibrium." We are far removed from dream freedom or utopia freedom. The best use of freedom requires that it be controlled. Under the circumstances, Paquet urged his colleagues "not to apply unjustified increases" and to develop promotional sales, which had been the virtual monopoly of the large and medium-size chain stores heretofore. The transition from *dirigisme* to liberty seemed hardly less difficult at the end of the twentieth century than during Turgot's era.[24]

The artisans on the ground did not seem very united in their reaction to this new exegesis of freedom and the new justification of moderation. Some reproached the president energetically for weakness, charging him with being "paralyzed by the threat of possible criticism" by the government. Others did not believe that the measure was an effective response to competition. Still others considered that prices, like politics, were essentially a local matter above all; they would go up if the local climate allowed. Freedom upset and disconcerted many bakers who wanted to use it intelligently but did not know how to do so. The departmental federations for the most part followed the national association. The Seine-Maritime association, for example, preached circumspection, without wanting to be killjoys, for liberty deserved to be celebrated! "It is not very easy anywhere," wrote the president in *Le levain syndical*, "but this freedom makes us entirely responsible for our own little businesses. . . . If we set our prices carefully in relation to products of good quality, we'll win back the ground that has been lost over the years."[25]

There was no ambivalence in the way Guy Boulet, the baker from rural Franche-Comté, reacted to the ultimate freeing of prices. His poetic dreamer side was not about to hide his character as an extremely serious professional and a rigorous manager, even if he had to take nonmaterial and nonquantifiable data into account. A social (and cultural) baker if there ever was one, Boulet is an enthusiastic free-market liberal as far as the relation between the state and the baking business in price-setting is concerned. From the time he set up his business, "the economic constraint represented by price controls" weighed heavily. It oriented his whole trajectory, obliging him "to accept the compromise of mechanization to the detriment of the pleasure of making [bread] and the satisfaction derived from the quality of the result." Boulet's itinerary is interesting in that he is deeply anchored in the history of the profession and in the continuing tension between Ancients and Moderns. "I shall have known domestic bread-making, kneading by hand, and the application of skill required by the flour-bread exchange with the farmers," he wrote, no doubt using a state-of-the-art computer. "I shall have participated in the technological evolutions of a profession whose practices had not changed for five thousand years, and I shall have observed its relation with industrial and capitalist society, a relation that will arouse its 'artisanal' awareness."

The artisanal and humanistic awakening of Guy Boulet and the articulation of his ideological and technological choices were delayed, even blocked, by the system of price controls that inexorably imposed, according to Boulet himself, "the choice of productivity" and an approach that gave baking rooms a frankly industrial aspect. The freeing of bread prices on January 1, 1987, constituted a psychological and technological liberation allowing Boulet to redefine his priorities "in relation to the pleasure of making [bread]." He continued to favor traditional, largely manual bread-making practices "while still searching for technological advances that [could] serve this end and could demonstrate its financial viability as well," with the help of appropriate marketing and management techniques. The baker from Franche-Comté radically reorganized his production; he gave up the western white bread in favor of a short, slow kneading method, with a prolonged first fermentation, more manual work (he suppressed even

184 BAKERIES AND THE STATE

the automated weighing of the *pâtons* and "all the forms of mechaniza-
tion that have replaced the Roman scales"), and diversification of the line.
This strategic (and affective) reorientation would not have been possible,
Boulet affirmed, without the freeing of prices.[26]

While the demand for freedom had always been the official dogma of
the bakery business, at the end of the twentieth century, as in the middle
of the nineteenth, many bakers preferred the predictable, reassuring shelter (with various compensations) of the *dirigiste* regime to the unpredictability ("anarchic competition") of the so-called free market regime. Jean
Cabut warned that freedom could prove to be an illusion, or even a trap,
an opportunity to be devoured by mass distribution, if it were not in some
way qualified or controlled. "The altar of freedom, like that of Moloch,"
the future confederation president wrote, in his concern over the hidden
cost of modernity, "demands the sacrifice of thousands of victims." In dramatic fashion he cited the words of Mme Rolland—an editorialist from
Lyon like himself—at the foot of the scaffold: "Oh, Liberty! How many
crimes are committed in your name!" A little later, Cabut railed against
the "savage" and "sneaky" competition that ended up "doing away with
the liberty of others." Two hundred years after the fact, he borrowed the
voice of Séguier, the advocate general of the Paris Parlement, to proclaim
that, "under cover of the famous freedom of trade there are people who
allow themselves everything. . . . It is no less logical that there be limits to
everything and that they be respected."[27]

This pessimism was echoed in the press and elsewhere. When the
Auchan store in Avignon offered baguettes for sale at one franc ($0.23)
apiece in 1979, a generalist newspaper commented: "The lifting of price
controls has stirred up a trade war between the artisans and the industrialists." The directors of *Toque Magazine* noted that the confederation had
had the choice between freedom and price controls in August 1978; Francis
Combe and company had opted for the latter, "certainly thinking that all
bakers were going to get rich quickly." And this anticonfederation newspaper took the association establishment, and freedom, to task: "It would
have been better, it seems to us, to keep price controls, even highly restrictive ones, for today [June 1995] baguettes would sell for around 4.50 francs
($0.92) apiece everywhere. The loss leader prices in supermarkets and big
box stores would not be possible. Everyone would sell at the same price
and the artisans would have no trouble standing out thanks to the quality

of their work." Those in opposition to the confederation were not the only ones who thought along these lines. During the same period, an energetic rural woman baker from Saône-et-Loire expressed a similar conviction: "Bakers had the bad idea to decide that the price of bread would be free from now on. The supermarkets were the ones who profited."[28]

At the beginning of the twenty-first century, price controls are only a bad memory; certain young bakers do not even know what the term means. But the association leaders are trying to maintain a "responsible" attitude about prices. With little inflation, it is difficult to justify significant increases, except by playing on the so-called specialty breads. Jacques Mabille, the president of the Paris federation, sketches out a different argument, it too based not only the quality of specific products but on an overall mastery of food safety in breadmaking during a period when consumers are experiencing doubts and fears in many other sectors. Thus, for example, against this background of confidence, in fall 2000, given a mediocre harvest, the increase in the price of flour, expenses connected with the shift to a thirty-five-hour work week, and other regulations, Mabille judged that a (reasonable?) increase in the price of bread was acceptable. However, believing that such an increase would be very badly received by the public, he hesitated to support a proposal advanced by several of the big mills that had outposts in the bakery business according to which the top-of-the-line baguette would be sold for one euro ($0.88) apiece starting in January 2002. Nevertheless, many bakers jumped the gun on the transition to the new currency by increasing prices in advance, despite association caution at all levels. The Rétrodor and Banette 1900 "breads in the French tradition," excellent products sold in bakeries on my street on the border between the thirteenth and the fourteenth arrondissements, made a considerable, even surprising leap (in the sense that the increase exceeded what I had thought would be the maximum).[29]

From Price Controls to (Re-)Classification:
The Bread Decree

Freed from permanent control by the state, the bakery business did not intend to remain a political orphan. In the great corporate (and, in a quite analogous fashion, capitalist) tradition, it wanted to be protected while retaining as much independence as possible. While it did not like cer-

tain regulations that it found stifling, it requested others that would reinforce its competitive position. Yes to (reasonable) freedom, no to (wholesale, fundamentalist) free-market liberalism. "If I militate in favor of a
very large-scale relaxation of administrative constraints and the resulting
charges that accrue to businesses," Jean Paquet proclaimed in 1987, "it
does not follow that I count myself among those who seek to preserve for
the state only its attributes of sovereignty: security, defense, justice, and
foreign relations." The state could not look the other way, either on the
economic level or on the social level. "For us, the state has to define the
rules of the economic and social game and make sure they are respected,"
Paquet explained. "The state has to remain the referee of the economic
game even if its role in the social realm has to be revised so that society
will be regulated by the individuals that make it up and by the groups and
organizations that they freely create." But the kind of refereeing that the
confederation sought implied an interventionist if not a *dirigiste* state, a
state that translated certain cultural and social choices into institutional
and practical terms. When he spoke out ten years later against an "over-
statized" France, Jean Cabut nevertheless asked for a heavy dose of activ-
ism on the part of the state: "Responsibilities have to be met, and laws
have to play the role of safety barriers; otherwise, as General de Gaulle
reminded us, all hell will break loose."[30]

Faced with the brutal and agonizing competition of the 1980s, questioning the moral if not the commercial legitimacy of that competition, the
bakery business asked the state for a helping hand. In a world in which public relations (is it a pleonasm to add the adjective "manipulative"?) weighed
more and more heavily and in which being and appearances were easily
confused, the confederation no longer believed that artisans could count
on their own merit alone to succeed. It wanted the state to create a sort
of national brand, making the French artisanal exception in breadmaking
official. It wanted the state to provide a strict definition of authentic work
in the timeless baking room and to guarantee the authenticity if not the
quality of the product made there. With clear new definitions and some
controls filtering access, the surveyor state and the taxonomer state were
supposed to restore their turf to the (despoiled) artisans and provide them
(again) with a legitimate preserve of their own. People would finally know
unequivocally who was who, and everything would be quite clear to consumers. While the primary objective was essentially related to marketing,

the confederation hoped to shore up the artisanal bakers' morale and reinforce their sense of identity and self-esteem by mobilizing the public and
ensuring its fidelity, once the choices open to it were made clear.

From the confederation's viewpoint, it was not asking the state for
either a crutch or a drug, but rather for the restitution of its original,
sacred, and inviolable rights, in particular the ownership of certain basic
appellations. There was no consensus about priorities, at the outset. Some
wanted to begin by defining the term "baker," an idea that was finally deferred. Others preferred to establish designations for products, labels that
would consecrate the specificity and originality of bread (regular or specialty loaves) made by artisans and that would perhaps announce a new
banner recipe designed to galvanize the entire profession and to reaffirm
in a concrete way the singular virtuosity of the true baker, that is, the traditional artisan. The confederation settled on the latter project. "My first
action on your behalf," Paquet announced to his troops, "will be to obtain
the publication of a decree on bread labeling. The client must be able to
clearly identify products made by a qualified man of the trade. The anonymous industrial product cannot be put on the same plane as artisanal bread
in the French tradition." If the desire to nourish or even to reestablish the
artisanal distinction was the prime impetus behind the project, the confederation also wanted to confront the liberalization of the use of additives in
breadmaking that was to take place in 1993 under pressure from Brussels,
another potential enemy of the French artisanal exception. The association leaders feared a sort of leveling from below if Brussels took the lead
in establishing a new system of bread classification. Thus they pressed the
state to impose new designations taking into account both the composition of the product and the method of fabrication, in the context of French
history and practice.[31]

The debate that would eventually lead to the bread decree began in the
mid-1980s, if not earlier. On one hand, acting consistently with its own historical practice, CNERNA, the great codifier and superego of the profession
since the 1950s, focused on updating certain aspects of the traditional procedures. In 1986–87, its cereals industry commission proposed a "definition
of bread products," a text quite close to several of the drafts composed by
a group of professional and academic experts convened by the DGCCRF.[32]

The first draft we have, developed in November 1985, distinguishes between two broad categories of products: the "traditional" breads and "the

other breads." Generic traditional bread corresponds to the product that results from preparing a kneaded dough composed exclusively of bread-making flour, drinking water, and kitchen salt, fermenting the dough with the help of alcoholic fermentation agents (so-called bakers' yeast and/or sourdough, the latter being defined in a separate article), and baking the dough in an oven. This bread "in the French tradition" may contain authorized "additives" and "adjuvants." For the other "traditional" breads, the text is quite laconic: bread made "of" rye must contain at least 65 percent rye flour; bread made "with" rye must contain more than 10 percent rye flour; bran bread must contain at least 25 percent bran, and so on. The often indefinable country loaf is an exception. Its criteria are listed in some detail, with the explicit injunction to avoid bleaching the dough (in other words, it requires a slow and relatively brief kneading, without a boost from fava flours); bakers are instructed to develop an acidulous taste (which implies fermenting with sourdough alone or in combination with yeast) and to prolong the bread's "freshness" (good keeping qualities being the fruit of technological choices and the selection of ingredients). In late 1985, then, the goal was not to create a new product that would be a resurrection of yesteryear in a practical synthesis, within reach of any artisan and endowed with significant marketing potential. Instead, we find a modest and scrupulous effort to rehabilitate the descriptor "traditional" in everyday breadmaking so that producers and consumers would be on the same wavelength.[33]

Some months later, a new version was prepared, in which the notion of the "traditional" no longer plays a structuring role. What formerly constituted a traditional bread now simply characterizes "breads for everyday consumption." The text has changed little, except where it specifies which additives may go into the composition of everyday bread ("only adjuvants authorized to compensate for diastatic and visco-elastic deficiencies of the wheat," in other words, to increase the fermenting capacity of the flour). The word "traditional" is reintroduced to designate breads that are called specialty breads today, such as rye bread (both "made of" and "made with"), whole-grain bread, fine-ground wheat bread, and so on, which are described here as "breads for everyday consumption" that include rye, bran, or type 150 flour (a very high rate of extraction). The constraints on making a traditional country bread are spelled out: no fermentation with yeast alone in the direct method (this does not produce an acidulous taste), no intensive kneading, no use of "flour from leguminous plants" (the famous fava flour).[34]

The version dated January 1986 returns almost exactly to the original text; the word "traditional" again has iconic if not conceptual primacy. The April 1986 version differs only in its third part, which deals for the first time with designations for Viennese pastry products. The February 3, 1987, draft recycles the previous text in large part, completing it with a new (broad but coherent) definition of the category of specialty breads and a much more specific definition of the term "sourdough" (it authorizes the addition of bakers' yeast up to 0.2 percent, and reserves the mention of sourdough to bread in which sourdough is the sole fermenting agent; the sourdough may be dehydrated or not, and it must fulfill precise criteria for its pH and its degree of acetic acid). The next document, undated, introduces a significant nuance. For the first time a "traditional French bread" is presented exclusively as a bread made from a type 55 flour (a rate of extraction around 75 percent). Previously, this product had been called "bread," with no further qualification. The author seems to be taking a step toward the crystallization of a product that is specifically rather than generically "traditional."[35]

The note that follows further clarifies this definition. Henceforth bread "made according to tradition" is bread made from dough baked in an oven according to the basic recipe, composed "of breadmaking flours, mixed or not," with no stipulation as to type. The fall 1989 draft goes back to the idea that the standard for traditional bread must be linked to a type of flour — or a range of flours — identified in highly technical terms: traditional bread is composed exclusively of flour from a breadmaking wheat containing no more than 0.75 percent ash (measuring the quantity of minerals present in the flour and thus its relative "purity") — in other words, types 45, 55, and 65. This text does not speak of additives or adjuvants but rather of "authorized substances." Finally, it suggests another way of verifying whether a loaf presented as "country" really is one, by articulating more "conditions" (for example, slow kneading, fermentation by an indirect process, a progressive mode of baking, the use of a sourdough alone or with yeast), but without obliging the artisan to satisfy them all in order to use the label.[36]

Presented as a decree in twelve articles, the August 21, 1990, draft tackles the definition of the traditional by introducing a new distinction, probably at the confederation's request. The recipe-plus-basic-procedure must still be respected, as had been the case all along, but a product is traditional "only when the breads contain no additives, with the exception of agents for treating flour that are authorized by the regulations in effect." Traditional bread is pure bread, uncorrupted by modernity, plausibly associated with the utopian yesteryear. But the definition is hardly transparent, since it fails to enumerate the "treatment agents" that were currently tolerated. The complementary section of the draft edict christens "house" bread (*pain de maison*) the simple or ordinary bread described in all the previous versions (basic recipe), with one crucial specification: the bread-making process—implicitly from A to Z—must take place on the business premises for direct sale to the consumer. In other words, the artisan makes his "house" bread in his own baking room. He follows the procedure indicated, like the traditionalists, but we have to suppose that he is free to add more additives—otherwise, what would distinguish his bread from any other? And he sells it directly to his clients, without any intermediary whatsoever.[37]

The confederation, which openly claimed paternity once the decree was promulgated, had plenty of time to orient the measure in the direction it preferred. At its request, in April 1991, five deputies asked the minister in charge of commerce, the artisanate, and crafts for a modification of Article 7 of the draft decree, which allowed the use of the term "traditional" for industrial, precooked, or deep-frozen bread. The association leaders wanted the law to specify that only breads containing no additives (except for the authorized agents for treating flour) and made entirely on the bakery premises for direct sale to consumers could be called "traditional." After "extensive consultation with all the partners in the [wheat-flour-bread] sector," who had all approved the draft as a basic text, moreover, the minister gave a rather vague response—for the time being—as to the possibility of the appropriation of the "traditional" label by industrial bakers, who would presumably be hampered by the "very restrictive" use of the recommended additives. At this stage, the text included the designation "house traditional bread"—implicitly leaving room for the industrialists—"with the goal of allowing businesses that make their bread themselves to set themselves apart from bake-off terminals and those who use premixed ingredients." Guy Boulet, one of the association leaders who was most closely involved in drafting the decree, represented the "elitist" pole of the confederation, which was itself divided over the requirements that it could impose on artisans; he points to the pressure coming from the mills in favor of using fava flour as an acceptable adjuvant and from the "Vitamin c lobby."[38]

The bread decree saw the light only three years later, under the ministry of Édouard Balladur, on September 3, 1993. An "authentic victory of the confederation," according to its in-house newspaper, the decree had been "pulled off despite the opposition encountered both on the national level and on the level of the European community."[39] Commenting on the results from Bercy (the complex in Paris where the Finance Ministry is located), a highly placed civil servant described the way "the artisans as a group crammed it through by the force of their influence." In any event, the final version proved to be much narrower than the many drafts. The bakers did not have the same ambitions as the regulators; the latter were seeking real taxonomic coherence and wanted to achieve an authentic renewal of the old CNERNA texts — which were largely "outdated," from the standpoint of the DGCCRF — that constituted the half-theoretical, half-practical paradigm of the bakery business. The association lobby succeeded in avoiding any consideration of the country loaf (*pain de campagne*), one of the most highly contested products, badly defined, the source of many frauds, and the emblem of a not very lucid bakery business that viewed the public with disdain. Unless a very well-informed and highly motivated inspector from the supervisory services came along, country bread was going to remain a treasure of manipulation for many artisans. All the other specialty breads also eluded the eye of the panoptic classifier; a certain number of officials and experts would have liked to define traditional rye and whole grain breads, and so on. Finally, the artisans were able to prevent the inclusion of Viennese pastries in the list subject to renewed scrutiny by the authorities.

A little more than one page long, the text of the bread decree consisted of six articles, four of which directly concerned the bakery business. The first created the designation "house bread" to confer a sacred character on artisanal work: the double redemption of the baker and his bread, a "noble product" degraded and sullied by imposters and profiteers. Only "breads entirely kneaded, shaped, and cooked on the site of the final sale to the consumer" could be sold under this label. The decree drew a line of demarcation between true breads and false, good breads and bad: its logic was frankly Manichean. Controlling the entire process, making everything himself or with the help of his workers, the artisan produces a bread that is necessarily exceptional: this was the implicit message. The Other is in some sense officially demonized, while the miraculous disappearance of bake-off terminals remains the unspoken utopia of the bakers. However, the designation "house bread" did absolutely nothing to improve bread quality; as one of the protagonists remarked during the preparation of the decree, "lousy bread remains lousy bread." Article one is more political than technical; the regulators would probably have been willing to distinguish between artisans and "dough cookers," but perhaps without recourse to the double play of apotheosis and anathema.

Article two opens up a new horizon at the end of the second millennium for artisanal baking, a profession besieged by its enemies, colonized by its friends, destabilized by a plethora of challenges to be confronted. The better to profit from the folkloric legacy known as yesteryear, this clause would allow those bakers who agree to adopt the protocol to appropriate "tradition" for themselves. In the eyes of the most optimistic members of the confederation, the "traditional" bread defined here was the bread of the future, the bread of recovery and vengeance, and the flagship product of the revived bakery business. In order to have access to tradition as a designation and thus as a marketing tool, artisans had to make bread from a mixture of breadmaking flour, drinking water, and kitchen salt, fermented with breadmakers' yeast and/or sourdough. This bread cannot be subjected to deep-freezing at any point: an obvious taboo, but another way of hammering home the difference between artisans and industrialists. Up to this stage, there is nothing very remarkable in the text. But what immediately distinguished this bread from the vast majority of breads made either in baking rooms or in factories was the absence of any "additive," meaning first of all ascorbic acid, which emblematizes the rejection of tradition and capitulation to facility in the modern breadmaking business and is a major source, in the eyes of certain reform-minded bakers, of the organoleptic degradation of the bread and its tendency to grow stale quickly. Here was a bold idea indeed — another frontier, this one at the heart of the artisanal corps itself, marking the separation between the bold and the fearful, between creative entrepreneurs and lethargic stockholders, between fans of quality and partisans of the ordinary, between holists and instrumentalists, between healthily nostalgic modernists and superficially modern nostalgics.

The story of the additives is a very complicated one. It was somewhat demagogic to celebrate their disappearance as a return to the sources and the purity of an earlier age, since the use of additives of all sorts — coloring, emulsifiers, stabilizers, preservatives, even taste enhancers — is a very old practice. Not all additives are equal, of course. It would be essentially unthinkable today to inject calcium proprionate — a classic preservative — into the artisanal kneading trough, or to add rising powders (although yeast, the most commonly used fermenting agent, comes out of an industrial culture and can be considered, according to Roland Guinet, as "one of the first corrective means of breadmaking"). Prohibiting vitamin c, which is used as an agent for treating flour by the miller as well as an additive by the baker in his baking room, is an extremely significant move. However, as if to right the balance, the bread decree explicitly allows bakers to add very limited quantities of certain "adjuvants," a word that does not appear in the vocabulary of the regulations. For example, traditional bread may contain up to 2 percent fava flour (an authorization acrimoniously contested by purists and a practice quickly disavowed by certain millers and bakers, which did not make them literally more "traditional," for the use of fava flour in breadmaking goes back at least as far as the eighteenth century); up to 0.5 percent soy flour; and 0.3 percent wheat malt flour. Fava and soy flours improve fermentation (the dough has greater tolerance and retains gas better); malt also helps fermentation by reinforcing amylasic activity. While the value of malt is rarely questioned, critical voices have been raised for thirty years or more against fava flour in particular as a source of whitening and degradation of taste.[40]

Almost half of the bread decree is devoted to sourdough, a traditional element in breadmaking par excellence, but hardly relevant for the vast majority of artisans, who do not use it and often would not even know how. An esoteric and extremely technical subject, the use of sourdough is of much greater interest to the experts than to artisans, and it concerns only the tiny fraction of the public that is intimately familiar with breadmaking techniques. For those who dream of a renewal of sourdough, the clause allowing the baker to boost his sourdough during the last phase of kneading with a dose of no more than 0.2 percent yeast (in relation to the weight of flour used) is an advance. But the use of a sourdough leaven that permits the designation "bread made with sourdough," as this text defines it, remains a hypothetical case, for the text does not take into account the constraints of the way the production process is organized or the way bread is sold. Even if bakers could find the time to prepare a classic sourdough, it is not at all certain that they could fulfill the technical conditions (for example, the pH level required, or the absolute criterion of acetic acid, which is too narrow; it would have been better to speak of organic acids instead, recognizing lactic as well as acetic fermentation). Rather than motivating and valorizing artisanal bakers, these clauses risk excluding them or inciting them to cheat.[41]

At the association level, both at the center and at the periphery, the decree and the "big media exposure" to which it led were celebrated for months on end. The associations focused much more on the "house bread" clause than on the "traditional French bread" section, because the former concerned everyone right away: it conveyed a message that was simple (probably too simple), transparent, and powerful, and required no supplementary effort whatsoever. The artisan was thus reconciled with himself via the state. As the confederation newspaper commented: "Today, the decree allows consumers to distinguish a true artisanal product, kneaded, shaped, and baked in the same place, from bread of mediocre quality made from deep-frozen *pâtons* and sold by bake-off terminals." "This decree will serve the artisanal bakeries and enable them to differentiate themselves from the bake-off terminals that receive frozen dough and bake it on site," the Hérault Federation reminded its members. "It was urgent to be able to identify a true professional who kneaded, shaped, and baked his own bread . . . it will now be up to the professionals to spread the word as widely as possible." Fairly quickly, however, once the initial enthusiasm faded, the association leaders began to wonder whether the awarding of the designation "house bread" constituted adequate protection, whether it was a sufficiently visible banner, a distinction that "communicated" enough. They soon remobilized to ask the state for one more try.[42]

Philippe Viron, a miller and a supporter of the bread renaissance, was one of the few players in the sector to give immediate priority to the other principal aspect of the decree, the one that instituted a bread identified as "in the French tradition." "Thanks to the bread decree prohibiting the use of ameliorants and other chemical products in breads in the French tradition, we have taken a step toward the rehabilitation of taste and quality," he wrote with fervor to Claude Willm, professor and researcher at the

École de meunerie. Guy Boulet regretted the political schizophrenia of the confederation, which implicitly invited bakers to choose between the two approaches, for the house bread option undermined "the progress of the 'bread in the French tradition.'" Bernard Ganachaud, an innovative and always thoughtful baker, criticized the bread decree as "a bit restrictive." He was sorry to see it limited to wheat bread, excluding a whole range of specialty breads and regional breads from a "traditional" treatment—and a corresponding designation. But bakers such as Ganachaud or Jean-Luc Poujauran did not need that "crutch" to experience success.[43]

Those who needed it objectively did not take to it with enthusiasm. We shall see in the next chapter that bread in the French tradition met with vigorous resistance on the part of artisanal bakers. The constraints of producing it were unacceptable to many artisans, who were dependent on ascorbic acid and reluctant to return to a long first fermentation. Other bakers did not believe that the product, necessarily more expensive, could attract the public. During the first years following publication of the decree, a small number of bakers—no more that 5 percent at most—adopted the designation, according to the DGCCRF. Of these, probably half did not have the right to use it (as they were not "too kosher" in their methods, especially where the use of additives was concerned).[44] One of the great ironies of this law, proudly "pulled off" by the confederation, is that its enemies were among its greatest beneficiaries. Certain of the big chain stores, sharing the optimistic analysis of the new product's marketing potential, were the first to turn to "traditional" breads and flours. Around 2000, up to 10 percent of the artisanal bakers seem to have committed themselves to the path of tradition, often pushed by their millers, who had hesitated for a long time themselves (Banette is the prime example). The number continues to rise slowly but sturdily, especially in the large cities. As of 2005, I estimate that over 75 percent of the 1,200 bakeries in Paris offer a bread in the French tradition.

Policing Bakers Today

The DGCCRF and the DDCCRFs do the bulk of the "policing" of bakers and their bread. To make sure the bread decree is respected, they act on three registers. First, to guarantee the rigor of the designation "house bread," their inspectors verify that the place where the bread is sold is not simply a depot or bake-off terminal, but a true baking room in which dough is kneaded, shaped, and cooked. Next, they audit the bakery's accounts so as to verify that the raw materials purchased correspond to the products sold, a type of surveillance that the law of September 13, 1993, did not envisage. Finally, they sample products at every stage in the manufacturing of traditional French bread and subject them to analysis in order to discover possible fraud. Beyond the 1993 decree, the greatest concern of the DGCCRF in the monitoring process probably arises from "the abusive and fraudulent use of positively-valued appellations for bread."[45]

The anarchy of appellations may be the DGCCRF's greatest worry, for it has few means for controlling them. Implicitly, judging from the arbitrage that led up to the bread decree, the government rejected the idea of providing a strict definition of ordinary bread (or of specialty breads, for that matter), although definitions had been proposed in several of the drafts prepared by the services of the DGCCRF. In the absence of precise definitions in the texts of the rulings, the bread police had to rely on texts of a very general nature having to do with food (dealing for example with deceitful advertising), or very outdated texts that were largely unknown to CNERNA, practices and customs that did not always constitute an argument capable of convincing the courts. What is more, these texts sometimes lent themselves to divergent interpretations that the DGCCRF's "own doctrine" was not in a position to sort out. Often sold without a label, bread sported "allegations" or "sales designations" that were not justified. Looking at a selection of breads that all bore the same name, one could find dozens of different recipes. Moreover, in order to set themselves apart from the competition, bakers had an increasing tendency to multiply the sales designations of their products and thus to confuse public perceptions. The politics of brand names practiced in the major lines sold by mills added to the confusion, since the brand names were used to designate breads ("according to the doctrine of the DGCCRF, brand names such as 'Banette,' 'Campaillette,' 'Rétrodor' . . . cannot be used, no matter how well known they are, in the place of the regulation sales name of the product").[46]

DGCCRF agents carried out 3,600 verifications throughout France in 1998–1999 and observed that certain positively valued designations were used "deceptively." As we have already seen, some house bread was not made entirely on site, and some breads in the French tradition were enhanced by additives. Under the bread decree, the use of the complementary term "with sourdough" was reserved "unambiguously"—one of the regulators' favorite formulas—to breads that fulfilled the conditions spelled out in detail in article three of this law. To control the use of the allegation "old-style bread," in the absence of regulations in the legal document, the DGCCRF fell back on its own doctrine, which in this case was extremely severe, if not draconian:

> The notion of "old-style" bread can be identified with the expression "of yesteryear" or "old-fashioned." Thus a bread may be sold under a designation including one of these terms when it is, in conformity with the faithful, long-standing practices of the profession, made solely with the help of sourdough leavening, when its dough is subjected to a slow and not very intense kneading (in order to limit its oxidation), and when it is baked over wood in a traditional stone oven. Moreover, the use of such a term is incompatible with the use of additives of any sort, as well as with the use of production procedures that no longer correspond to standard traditional breadmaking practices.

It is so difficult to fulfill these conditions that few bakers anywhere in France could boast of making "old-style" bread. The DGCCRF committed itself to being just as merciless with the bakers who, trying to free themselves from the constraints associated with this designation, hid behind a term such as "old-style flavor" or "the flavor of yesteryear."[47]

The same strict interpretation was applied to another positively valued term: "bread baked over wood," "bread baked in a wood fire," or "bread baked in an oven heated by wood." A well-established set of legal regulations allows this reference only for bread baked in an oven with a stone hearth heated *directly* by a wood fire. According to the doctrine, "such a definition clearly presupposes that the heat is discontinuous and that the baking takes place with 'decreasing heat,' favoring the formation of a thick crust and thus the preservation of the bread."[48]

In the final analysis, the effectiveness of the agencies that monitor bakers and bread today is limited less by the lack of legal texts supplying precise definitions and a well-articulated doctrine than by the lack of adequate staffing. In the eighteenth century, with the doctrine drawn from the *Traité de la police* by Nicolas Delamare, the great codifier of the science of government at the everyday level, the bread police carried out more and closer surveillance because at the time—something that is no longer the case today—the social stakes were enormous and the political will was strong. At the end of the twentieth century, over an eighteen-month period, the DGCCRF for the Paris region inspected 192 bakeries; in the eighteenth century, for intramural Paris, that many shops and market stalls were often visited in a single month. Only fourteen investigators carry out these inspections today, and their oversight is not limited to bakeries. In the domain that interests us, the agents of the DG or DDCCRF often have training either in the food processing sector (as does Gilles Morini, Mr. French Bread, head supervisor in the Office of Agriculture and Food Processing) or a legal background (as does Philippe Richard, the chief DDCCRF inspector in Paris); the two specializations complement one another advantageously.

In the capital, the DDCCRF shares inspection responsibility for inspections with the Office of Veterinary Services, which focuses above all on questions of hygiene and reports directly to the Prefecture of Police. More bakeries are subject to administrative closings by the latter agency than by the DDCCRF (which imposed only two closings from mid-2000 to mid-2001). The prefecture's policy seems to be influenced by the economic climate (it is easier to close a shop when the economy is flourishing than during a crisis) and probably also by the political climate (the standing of the associations from the government's viewpoint). In their unannounced inspections, the DDCCRF agents look at every aspect, technical and commercial, of the baking room and the shop. They undoubtedly place special emphasis on hygiene, a topic around which a great deal of public anxiety has crystallized as general awareness of the problem of food safety has risen. The agents look for the presence of potentially disease-causing parasites or rats, for example; they look for problems in the way ingredients are stored and for deficiencies in sanitation (dirt in the workshop, loose tiles, chipped paint, lack of hand-washing facilities, lack of a ventilation system, inadequate arrangements for garbage disposal, and so on).

Richard judges that bakeries in Paris have food safety more or less under control. His agents run into more problems concerning claims about quality, the famous positively valued designations. They make reports, prepare court cases, and inform the Procurer of the Republic. But the courts do not always follow up on these charges, especially, as Richard notes, on the subject of the term "old-style bread," the rampart of the house doctrine in the bakery business. Inspecting a bakery on Rue Saint-

Honoré in early 2001, the agents verified the quality and the authenticity of certain ingredients, including organic flour; they took five samples, probably pastry selections and sandwiches, for analysis in a search for contamination by listeria or other kinds of bacteria (the laboratory showed that all was in order); they looked closely at the sanitary conditions in the baking room and the shop; they verified the claims made in bread labeling (they found one illegitimate "old-style bread"), checked the use of obligatory terminology (an Eskimo signifies a frozen product), and monitored posted notices (additional forms of information for the consumer). A recent inspection of sourdough quality in four Paris baking rooms revealed that two were defective (too acid).[49]

Bakers Take to the Streets

For centuries, people have frequently revolted in France to protest against the state's exactions: the state as tax collector, ultracentralizer, army, enemy of freedom. But the French have also risen up to demand more from the state, or to remind the state of its duty, to incite it to accept its responsibilities and take action. When the consumer population felt threatened by hunger during the Old Regime, through a manifestation of real or symbolic violence it demanded that the king, *baker* of last resort, fulfill his contract with his subjects by supplying them with bread. Sometimes the convenient and immediate (but always metaphorical) targets of this violence were the bakeries, as during the period of serious scarcity in 1725 when the inhabitants of the Faubourg Saint-Antoine, the future revolutionary quarter par excellence, invaded and looted dozens of the shops they patronized every day. When the baker population went into the streets in 1995 to demand that the state, protector of last resort, do still more to help them keep—or rather reconquer—their shrinking consumer population, the role reversal was striking.

The campaign against the enemy was not going very well for the bakers, despite their efforts at mobilization, renewal, and propaganda. At bottom, the competition—of extremely dubious legitimacy and completely unfair in the artisans' eyes—seemed objectively stronger than they. It was David against Goliath: the metaphor caught on among association leaders. After having manifested a certain indifference—a kind of liberal agnosticism—with regard to the difficult trials the profession was undergoing, the state had recently proved to be more understanding. The bread edict of September 1993 was among the first fruits of this good will, but it had not had the immediate effect the associations had hoped for. Increasingly panicked—worried by their own partners, the increasingly aggressive millers, as well as by their avowed antagonists—the bakers turned importunately to the state. It was urgent to act because at stake was the future of France itself and not merely that of artisanal bakers. The confederation rehearsed a now familiar argument: saving the artisanal bakery meant saving a part of France herself to which French women and men were deeply attached.[50]

On December 7, 1994, the confederation organized a National Day of Dialogue "to inform the responsible public authorities about the bakers' worries concerning the future of artisanal breadmaking." To the extent that every departmental association was received by the prefect, the confederation declared the day "a great success." In this sort of "dialogue," the supplicant expects the state not only to respond, but to respond positively. The association leaders could not go home empty-handed: had they been repudiated by the state, they would have been immediately disavowed by the members—among whom there was already an undercurrent of internal opposition. "Despite the clarity of our demands, and contrary to the promises received [promises the state denied having made], there was no response whatsoever to our fair and reasonable claims." Confederation president Jean Cabut took up the same theme of betrayal: "The bakers were deceived by promises." On December 7, the artisans "firmly" invited "the leaders of the country to apply the elementary rules of fairness, in a spirit of objectivity and out of respect for the laws." The confederation sought neither "privilege" nor "favor": it was a civic and moral voice crying out for justice, not a corporatist voice. If the state considered the survival of artisanal bakers in cities and villages indispensable, as it claimed, its silence was illogical.

"We now have to react at a higher level and more strongly, all together," Cabut concluded. Before the growing impatience in their ranks, the associations could not remain passive. "Why do farmers, nurses, and taxi drivers strike and we never do?" they asked. "Convinced that it expressed the deep feelings of the 35,000 artisanal bakers," the confederation announced a national demonstration for May 29, 1995, in Paris "so that the men and women of the bakery business might express their demands still more strongly." The goal was virtually the same as on December 7: the institution of fair and transparent competition, without which the artisans could not survive. Above all, this meant a national text ensuring that every site where bread was sold would close one day a week. "Only such an arrangement will allow the artisans to benefit from a weekly day of rest like everyone else," something demanded universally by all the salaried employees in the trade; all the associations were unanimous. A law was necessary because the large and medium-size chains and the industrialists scoffed at the prefectoral decrees requiring the weekly closing. If the competition was not going to be fair and equitable, the association maintained that the artisans would not be in a position to produce the quality that was necessary for their renewal, an easy alibi for the critics, a strong argument for the sympathizers.[51]

The first point: a text providing for a weekly closing. The second point: the artisans wanted a measure that defined what a real baker was more clearly than the "house bread" clause of the bread decree had done. Where their identity was concerned, the bakers' demands took on an eminently commercial character: the industrialists were usurping the title of baker in order to valorize their standardized, additive-laden, deep-frozen, in no way artisanal products. The bake-off terminals, Cabut insisted, "must no longer be able to hide their industrial character behind the hypocrisy of their store or a misleading sign." The third point: it was not enough to deny the title of baker to people who simply "cooked" dough. In the spirit of the eighteenth-century corporations, which exercised a monopoly over recruitment in their trades, often with narrow filters allowing them to drive out "unqualified interlopers practicing the profession with no legitimacy," what the artisans wanted to prevent, in Cabut's formula, was a situation in which "anybody at all could set himself up from one day to the next as a baker and thus claim the right to the traditions of quality and service that have gone into [their] reputation; it is normal to react against cheating." The fourth point: in view of honest competition, the confederation spoke out violently against the discounting of bread "at a ridiculous price" that did not even take into account the production cost. It was a moral question as well as an economic one: "Respect for the trade and for the professionals who practice it is at stake." A final point: The bakers demanded that public incentives and subsidies "no longer" be reserved for the big companies, "while the small artisans have to settle for paying taxes and charges and listen to consoling speeches." *Les Nouvelles de la Boulangerie-Pâtisserie* went further, evoking corruption in a melodramatic scenario: "scandals, bribes to get permission to open the big box stores, after provoking the disappearance of hundreds of shops with family dramas."[52]

In 1995, at the end of May, more than 5,000 bakers (2,000 from Paris and the surrounding region) marched in the capital, dressed in their professional garb (according to the confederation newspaper there would have been 20,000 marching, but "out of respect for consumers" they did not want to close their bakeries). Their placards and their chants clearly betrayed their anger and their anxiety: "Down with the big box stores, their bread is disgusting"; "Bakers mean jobs; big box stores mean disaster"; "Bread is the business of bakers"; and "Frozen bread, cheated clients" (a denunciation to which not all artisans could subscribe!).[53]

The Bakers Find a Minister and Celebrate

This time the bakers were heard, thanks to the particularly sympathetic — and well-informed — ear of Jean-Pierre Raffarin, minister of commerce and artisanship, future prime minister, son of a radical with a strong social sensibility, the ex-leader of the Young Giscardians. Genuinely interested in bread, as somebody who appreciated good food, who recognized the primordial place of bread in French culture, and who excelled at public relations, Raffarin understood that several things were needed to save the traditional baking business: a new regulatory framework, a renewal in baking rooms themselves (a "return to quality," a lucid appreciation that would not paper over the mistakes of the past), and serious "work on the image" of the profession. As far as the first category was concerned, Raffarin began by promising that the weekly day of rest would be respected everywhere bread was sold. Next, he addressed the question of bread prices straightforwardly: "It is absolutely necessary that consumers cease to be drawn in by artificially low prices. Quality and work must not be discounted by way of loss leader prices that are in fact only unemployment prices." With the secretary of state for finance, he undertook a reform relating to competition similar to the 1986 order whose result, as we have already seen, was quite favorable to the artisanal bakers. The latter were delighted to hear their minister say without beating around the bush: "When consen-

sus proves impossible, or when it is not respected, we must also know how
to use coercion." The Galland law of July 1, 1996, on fairness and balance
in business relations, sought to prevent the sale of baguettes for one franc
apiece.

For the confederation, the most important measure, on both the practical and symbolic levels, concerned the identity of baker and the right to
claim it. "The artisanal baker must be better recognized, better defined,
in order to be better defended," Raffarin asserted. He sought on one hand
a definition taking into account all phases of artisanal breadmaking, the
famous A to Z, and on the other a distinction between artisanal bakeries
and bake-off terminals that would reinforce commercial transparency.[54]

The so-called Raffarin decree, issued on December 12, 1995, restricted
the use of the appellation *boulangerie* (on signs and elsewhere) to establishments "held by a professional [the only one entitled to call himself a
boulanger] who was personally responsible for the various phases of breadmaking from selected flours: kneading, shaping the dough, fermentation,
and cooking, on the site where the bread is sold to the final consumer."
The measure allowed "bakeries" of all sorts a year to bring themselves into
conformity with these provisions; some 5,000 were thought to be in viola-
tion. In early 1997, the DGCCRF noted thirty infractions. To give the decree
"more teeth" and make it more dissuasive, Raffarin drew up a proposed
law in March 1997 threatening "false bakers"—an eighteenth-century formula picked up by the associations—with fines as high as 10,000 francs
($1,750) for every day of continuing infraction.[55] The cultural role of the
artisanal baker was primordial; he was "the very symbol of the quality of
life," just as bread was the symbol of life itself. This minister was not going
to let the profession be stripped of "its identity, its place in French culture.
It's humiliating for real bakers to see people who sell bread manufactured
elsewhere passing themselves off as bakers. It's unacceptable to have warm
bread passed off as fresh, and a bread depot presented as a place where
bread is made."[56]

More concretely, Raffarin and confederation president Jean Cabut
signed a "national charter for the development of artisanal baking" in early
1996. This document was important symbolically and politically, for it pro-
claims urbi et orbi the state's implication in the future of the breadmaking
business and the return of bakeries to a certain relationship of dependence
on the formerly oppressive state, even if the agreement was presented

under the auspices of a kind of partnership. The concerned parties committed themselves to a number of measures: to promote as "brands of quality" the house bread and the bread in the French tradition created by the decree of September 13, 1993 — a missed opportunity to single out and celebrate artisanal production; to keep reminding the public of the qualitative gap between baking rooms and terminals (deep-frozen bread, additives, and so on); to struggle still more effectively against "unfair competition" (respect for the weekly closing, prohibition of "abnormally low prices"); to help artisans tune in to public opinion by establishing a tool for observing consumer tastes; to advise bakers on in-house marketing (for example, how to make the most of product presentation); to make it easier for artisanal bakeries to modernize (government-subsidized loans, support for taking over an existing bakery); to relaunch artisanal practices in rural areas (subsidies for the acquisition of a delivery vehicle); to increase the number of apprentices — a natural extension of the ministerial policy of encouraging apprenticeships and a way to confront the ongoing crisis in the workforce; to educate (on the civic and cultural register) and attract (on the sybaritic register) the public, and to inform people — young people in particular — who are searching for a career.[57]

On the level of "national public relations," a field in which Raffarin was a virtuoso performer, the charter announced that henceforth on May 16, the day of the patron saint of bakers, Saint Honoré, France would celebrate bread and honor its bakers. As Raffarin recalls it, the idea grew out of a convivial and cosmopolitan conspiracy: "This idea is also an act of sharing, born of a generous discussion around a warm table where I had brought together at the Ministère des Petites et Moyennes Entreprises the scholar Kaplan, the faithful Calvel, the famous Poilâne, the artist Robuchon, the talented Poujauran, and the bakers' president Jean Cabut." Above and beyond the goal of officially integrating bread into the French cultural and culinary patrimony ("the quality of the bread, the quality of the trade, the quality of life are part . . . of the heritage we leave our children"), the minister wanted to offer the profession a great annual moment in "prime time" in order to mobilize the public and put across his message of distinction in both senses of the word.

The first festival took place over a period of several days. On May 13, elementary school teachers, with the help of kits supplied by the confederation, taught classes on the wheat-flour-bread sector; hundreds of bakers went into schools to talk about their trade, and thousands of students went on field trips to baking rooms; a major colloquium in Paris brought Jean-Pierre Raffarin together with fourteen association leaders, a number of experts, and various bakers; Raffarin also attended the festival in Poitiers, where a Meilleur Ouvrier de France made him a loaf in the French tradition (still the great hope of the refounders). On May 16 bakers throughout France opened their doors, organized tastings and contests, and the associations, in collaboration with a large number of municipalities, put on public breadmaking demonstrations, gave talks, and distributed informational posters and brochures in order to "reinforce [their] ties with consumers."[58]

"The media have never had so much to say about the breadmaking business," rejoiced the Paris association's president, Gérard Delessard, on the occasion of this first bread festival. Without toning down the playful dimensions of the festival, the following year the minister and the confederation added a warlike note, as much to emphasize how serious this matter was for bakers as to defend bread. Beyond the unending fight for quality, three other "battlegrounds" were identified: pricing ("artisanal work deserves its fair price": watch out for the unhealthy and dangerous maneuvers of the discounters); competition (weekly closings, and so on); and cultural and social issues ("the artisanal baker fully satisfies the criteria of legitimacy and proximity ... he is an indispensable link in the policy of strengthening regional infrastructures"). The festival has become an institution, the high point of the bakers' year. In Paris, in particular, large crowds invade the square beside the City Hall where for years now the association has set up a giant baking room."[59]

The Raffarin Law Challenged, Revised, Still Controversial

The National Association of the Bread and Pastry Industries (Syndicat national des industries de la boulangerie et de la pâtisserie [SNIBP]) vigorously contested the December 1995 Raffarin decree, filing several appeals with the Conseil d'État. For the industrialists, the appellation *boulangerie* was a generic term that belonged just as much to mass-production bakers and bake-off terminals as to artisans. At the very moment when

the decree went into effect, *La Tribune Desfossés* published a paper showing that being denied the label was in no way hampering expansion by
the large and small industrialists—neither Neuhauser (whose headquarters are in Moselle), the French leader in deep-frozen raw dough with a
billion francs ($200,000,000) in annual sales, nor PaniFrance in Meurthe-
et-Moselle, which was planning to add twelve terminals to the twenty-five
already established in Lorraine. But it was not just a matter of principle for
the SNIBP; this association feared that the withdrawal of the appellation
might seriously penalize the industrialists who exported bread; the prestige of "French bakeries" abroad was a major commercial asset. Judging
that the text did not have a legal foundation that would allow the current minister, Raffarin, to control labeling and signage in the breadmaking
industry, the Conseil d'État annulled the decree on December 29, 1997.[60]

Furious, the association press reacted with headlines such as "Anyone
Can Be Called a Baker," "A Scandal," "Artisanal Bakers Orphaned." Today,
people complain that judges have too much power; at the time, the confederation denounced their "hands-off" approach: the state betrayed by
the state. But were the state and the enemies to blame? "The industrial lob-
bies have won a battle," confederation president Cabut insisted, "but they
have not won the war." The artisans were fighting "cheaters," "thieves of
[our] profession," "thieves of [our] image," and "identity thieves." Without
regulations—as the corporations warned on the eve of their abolition by
Turgot in 1776—false workers were going to replace true ones, false gold
would drive out the real thing, the suburbs ("false towns") would eclipse
cities. "The absence of regulations is synonymous with the loss of identity," said Paul Gilles, president of the Provençal Federation, to the prefect
of the region. "It is as if someone who sells frozen fish patties had the right
to call himself a fish-seller!" a woman baker in Orange said indignantly.
"What will we have to be called?" The profession responded collectively
with a national day of protest on March 2: meetings, speeches, delega-
tions sent to see prefects, a few street demonstrations. Ex-minister Raffarin
showed his solidarity by accompanying four association presidents from
Poitou-Charente to file a motion at the prefecture. "We are not backward
corporatists" demanding "arbitrary protections," Cabut insisted, but "we
demand a law affirming the identity of our profession on unchallengeable
legal grounds." Making fun of the industrialists' "recriminations" and of

the Conseil d'État's inability to make "the obvious distinction between these two professions," *Le Figaro* expressed hope that "this step backward [would] be short-lived."[61]

Marylise Lebranchu, Raffarin's socialist successor, quickly promised to submit a law to Parlement. Michel Crépeau, a former minister of the artisanate, sponsored the measure that the Assembly voted to approve on April 3. Astonished by the unprecedented rapidity, association leaders congratulated themselves on an "unquestionable victory." The law gave artisanal bakers the protection and the consecration they had been seeking:

> The appellation *boulanger* and the commercial sign *boulangerie* or any designation apt to bring confusion in the place where bread is sold to the final consumer or in advertisements except for commercial documents intended exclusively for business use [allowing the industrialists to refer to the French bakery industry in the export context] cannot be used by professionals who are not personally involved, using selected raw materials, in the kneading of the dough, its fermentation, and its shaping, as well as the baking of the bread on the site where it is to be sold to the final consumer; at no stage of production or sales may the products be deep-frozen or frozen.

Violators would be subject to severe penalties, up to two years in prison and/or a fine of 250,000 francs ($40,275). Almost at the same time, to emphasize and protect the specificity of artisanal baking even more securely, a decree spelled out the conditions for access to the trade. Henceforth, in order to "exercise the activity of baker," one would have to have a diploma (at least a CAP) or three years of experience in a baking room. This is the postmodern equivalent of the old corporatist *chef-d'oeuvre*.[62]

Some four years after this law was passed, the balance sheet remained mixed, to say the least. Two months after the Raffarin decree went into effect, *Pâtisserie-Boulangerie: Vie Pratique* expressed its skepticism. Identity and distinction come from quality, not from a label:

> The only worthwhile fight is the fight for quality and service. Never mind what it says on the sign. With the inflation of labels, *appellations contrôlées*, certificates of conformity and other charters, the consumer is a little more lost every day in the labyrinth. So new regulations are not going to change artisans' lives. . . . Flexible hours, a friendly wel-

come, fresh and tasty products: that is what makes for a good shop. Whether it is called a bakery or not.

This was also the way many industrialists analyzed the situation. After the initial symbolic and taxinomic shock, and the disagreeable aspect of a certain official ostracism, they observed that the stakes were fairly minor. They changed their names, and they played on the panoply of possible bread metaphors or imagery, cobbling together acceptable solutions. According to a note by the DGCCRF written in April 2000, they "proved more adaptable, especially in that they did not deem the question of labeling a fundamental one for their own activities."[63]

The DGCCRF conducted a national survey consisting of 3,600 in late 1998 and early 1999; one purpose was to see how the May 25, 1998, law was being applied. Artisans were the objects of more than 80 percent of the warnings and reminders (for the medium-size and very large chain stores, which were inspected far more often in proportion to their numbers, and the bake-off terminals, the respective figures were 4.6 percent and 11 percent) and about 70 percent of the fines (8.4 percent and 21.7 percent, respectively, for the big box stores and the terminals). Beyond the figures, the DGCCRF's note points out that "the chains and bake-off terminals seem to have been subject to stricter inspections than the artisanal branch, where the agents sometimes hesitated to write up violations" (does cultural solidarity win out over strict policing?). In some departments, the associations, informing their members about the provisions of the new law, "had failed to point out that the use of freezing and deep-freezing was incompatible with the use of the term *boulangerie* on signs and elsewhere," information that many artisanal bakers had no desire to hear. The inspectors "regularly" observed frozen or deep-frozen *pâtons* in storage in artisanal shops.[64] But the most common reason for the infraction in use of the designation, more often noted among artisans than the others, was the possession of several stores ("from two to ten, if not more") by an artisan who made bread in a central baking room to rationalize his production. According to the DGCCRF, these inspections gave rise to "energetic protests" on the part of artisans "who felt implicitly placed on the same level as bake-off terminals" in relation to their secondary stores. Ironically, they thought that this law, which was supposed to save and protect their identity and shelter them from unfair competition, "was only penalizing them, especially the most dynamic among them." Some announced their intention to inform their professional organizations with the goal of bringing about a modification in the law. This unexpected protest movement might explain in part the brutal fall of Jean Cabut, charged with "archaism," and his replacement by Jean-Pierre Crouzet, an artisan who had several stores and was viewed as "modern." The "victory" of 1998 was proving to be increasingly less "unchallengeable."[65]

From Protector to "False Friend":
The State and the Thirty-Five-Hour Work Week

At the dawn of the new century, anxiety and anger were fermenting in the baking rooms. Like overripe sourdough, the relations between the breadmaking business, in its association incarnation, and the state were turning sour. In the 1990s, thanks in large part to the intervention of Jean-Pierre Raffarin, the profession celebrated its renewed liaison with the state, which had historically been considered by the bakers more as an adversary (some would have said tormentor) than as a protector. After the honeymoon, a return to earth: with the imposition of the thirty-five-hour work week, the state showed its true colors. From the beginning of this affair, the confederation maintains, it sought a frank exchange with the government, the opportunity to explain why the thirty-five-hour principle could not be applied in the baking room as it was elsewhere. It claimed that the ministry, shilly-shallying, preferred "fog that submerges problems in a regrettable vagueness." With respect to the new regime, bakers were saying: "I don't know how to do it"; refusing to respond to their anguish and distress, the government was "destroying the organization of [their] work." The state acted as a friend to the bakery business when it granted the bread decree and the one limiting the "baker" designation to artisans. But it became a "false friend" when it refused the artisans' demand "for a decree recognizing clearly that in breadmaking one cannot brutally cut back on work time." Secretly enamored of the "industrial model," the state was in fact a traitorous friend, for if "[it] had set about industrializing the artisanal baker, it would not have acted any differently."[66]

The bakers' argument can be boiled down to the observation that, for their profession, the thirty-five-hour limit is "an ill-fitting rule." The confederation spokesman was caustic, but also serious and frank. His argument, in sum: The state has encouraged us to do quality work for a long time. Now that we are finally there, it is disavowing all this effort. Making good bread takes time; this is not simply a marketing slogan on the part of Banette or Campaillette. Bread in the French tradition, the ("tenacious and courageous") confederation's brain child, born with the state as midwife, requires time for a long *pointage* and work that is manual in part. Since the cost of the thirty-five-hour work week would destroy many shops ("an increase in staffing costs of around 15–20 percent"), because in any event labor is in short supply ("how can we manage to work less tomorrow when we already find fewer and fewer employees?"), the ultimatum of January 1, 2002, can only "destroy the profession." The clients—but not their political representatives—understand that "quality is not the spontaneous product of machines. They know that if the fermentation process is cut too short, the pleasure of the taste will be killed. They sense that the promise of good bread in a concentrated time period is like a politician's promise: a pretty lie that flutters away like a dead leaf."

Furious that the Union Professionnelle Artisanale (UPA), the national organization of artisans, had approved the modalities of the transition to a thirty-five-hour work week, association leaders insisted still more strongly on an exception for the bakery business. In forcing everyone to lie down on a procrustean bed, the state was showing its "disdain for manual labor." One cannot measure everything "by the same gauge." Even more ardently than it sought ephemeral financial aid, the profession demanded the abrogation of "the absolute obligation to give up overtime hours." In the confederation's logic, this obligation constituted an injustice, for it "denied reality."

When bakers feel "gravely wounded," they make themselves heard. Now, at the urging of their associations ("the hour of truth"), they took to the streets. The pendulum was swinging back: after having eagerly sought protection for a time, in late 2001 the bakers were insisting on freedom. According to Jean Fourchaud, an artisanal baker, an imaginary candidate for the presidency of the Republic, "the state's determination to control the totality of our lives is an attack on the principle of liberty." He said "no" to the state, and he urged his colleagues to join him on November 26, 2001, in Paris. On that day, several thousand bakers in professional attire came from all over France to join the march and demand "time to make good bread," "time to serve our clients well," "time to work freely." To shouts of "Jospin au pétrin [Jospin to the kneading trough]," the demonstrators threw a few eggs on the signs of industrial bakeries on the Boulevard du Montparnasse. The industrial sector had quickly obtained some exemptions concerning the right to work, "for its specificity." The artisans were impatiently waiting their turn.[67]

Whether or not the bakers' arguments in this debate were sound, the government did not choose a good moment to shift to a thirty-five-hour work week. For that same January 1, a day when every oven in France is lit to bake *galettes*, a day when the shops are very crowded, was the day the euro was inaugurated. From the bakers' standpoint, it was a double imposition, orchestrated with a touch of sadism. Even without taking the impact of the thirty-five hours into account, the euro alone "[was] going to cost bakers a lot." For forty-seven days, beginning January 1, they had to finance and manage two currencies. They had barely had time to train their staff when they had to inform their clients, who were very numerous during this season and somewhat destabilized by having to give up the franc. Changing coins and bills is normally the role of bankers, the bakers were saying loud and clear; they were less than thrilled "to be promoted [to the role of] teachers, and unpaid ones at that." From the bakers' point of view, the state was asking a great deal of them and offering very little in return.[68]

chapter six

Bound to Quarrel, Condemned to Get Along: Millers and Bakers

G IVEN THE PRIMACY OF BREAD ON THE POLITICAL and nutritional horizons of the Old Regime, mills were among the principal institutions of social life, on the same basis as churches, markets, courts, and taverns. Millers were once artisans, and sometimes tradesmen, rooted in the local economy and in everyday culture, not "small businesses" or big international companies completely removed from the public eye. A plethora of tales and aphorisms, collective memories, and rumors propagated in every corner of France depicted the miller and his mill in the darkest of hues. Just as "white bread" systematically evoked something good, the word "miller" inevitably suggested evil, corruption, infamy. Didn't the miller confiscate part of the merchandise that fell from his millstone by means of a "blind" trap? He substituted cheaper merchandise for high-quality flour or grain; he passed off mediocre or bad flour as excellent; he cheated on weight and volume. One man would accuse another of being "as thieving as a miller." "Millers' pigs grow fat fast," another adage maintained. In one story, a dying man urged his family to get the two local millers and place them at either side of his bed. "Now I can die in peace," he explained. "Like Christ, I'm dying between two thieves." The priest in Cucugnan heard villagers' confessions from Monday through Friday, and saved all of Saturday for the miller. As Rabelais saw it, millers were nothing but "ordinary robbers."

This negative image was not restricted to folklore and fiction. An intendant in Provence, just like the great liberal minister Turgot, echoed the representation of the miller as a liar and thief who defrauded the public. If he was not always dishonest, from the bakers' point of view the miller was fundamentally greedy: the amount he charged for crushing grain was usually excessive. Millers had such a poor reputation for trustworthiness that bakers—hardly above all suspicion themselves—could easily argue that they had to set up their own mills (a practice formally prohibited by law but widely tolerated) owing to their trade partners' "lack of integrity."

The miller's task was very delicate, for it involved not only redistributing the raw material used to make bread but also transforming it: the elements had to be decomposed before they could be recombined. This transformation of a substance that was to be assimilated by the human body implied an enormous and somewhat mysterious power, the power to alter nature (and consequently man), and even to *denature* nature. A dishonest miller was also an impious magician, conquering the spirit of rivers and streams and subjecting them to the torture of his mill wheel. If mills exploded sometimes, was it not the just vengeance of the water spirits, in league with the realm of fire? Did nature not rebel against the miller's tyranny by provoking droughts or floods that paralyzed the mill? Harnessing the wind, a primordial cosmic force, was yet another proof of the miller's power, his audacity, his deceitfulness. When Dante goes into the lowest circle of hell, in Canto 34 of his *Inferno*, he discovers the arms of a windmill whirling in the darkness like a threatening bird. The devil has turned himself into a mill in order to grind up sinners' souls. The miller of L'Étang de l'Olivette offered his soul to the devil in exchange for a promise to have his mill running again after it had been immobilized by a drought. The devil kept his word, but the flour produced by the mill was nothing but black coal dust.

In addition, the mill was a terrifying place. More or less set apart from the rest of the community, it was not a good place to go at night; it was a machine that always seemed on the verge of taking off, a spirit that emitted plaintive noises and threats. Inside, the building presented other dangers. The moaning of the millstones, the vibrations that shook the walls and floor, the flow of flour, the ambient heat, the fine dust, all that helped create an atmosphere of powerful, fluid, irresistible sensuality. The mill was at once a metaphor for lost virtue and its theater, even its cause, as attested by a vast corpus of bawdy tales, saucy stories, and horrible scandals with sexual overtones. Were the citizens of Bussières-en-Brie really surprised that the miller Louis Leroy set out one fine day to enjoy "criminal commerce" with the daughter of his deceased wife? Was it not logical that Louis XV, denounced by some as a king who starved his people, contracted the smallpox that was to cost him his life from a miller's daughter who had been recruited to devote herself to royal pleasures?

Given the millers' reputation, it was hardly surprising that their honesty was often doubted by their baker clients. Jean Cousin, a master baker, drinking with colleagues at an inn called La Corne, unleashed a string of invectives against Claude Mergery, an important miller from Paris, accusing him of having deceived a hundred bakers about the quality and the quantity of his merchandise. Mergery was "a thief, a scoundrel, a damned rascal," Cousin declared. Cut to the quick by this attack on "his reputation and his honesty" before men "with whom he might well have occasion to do business," Mergery went to the police to file a complaint against his slanderer. Jean Dumas and his wife, Porcheron bakers, brought public accusations against the miller Jean Devaux of Montmartre on the pretext that he had deceived them and stolen some of the wheat he had had sent to them. Years later, another baker noted in the margins of his account book that his miller, Devaux, quite probably the same one, "was a thief."[1]

However, the tensions between millers and bakers stemmed from deeper causes. The traditional division of labor made the miller an employee of the baker, in a sense. An artisan rather than a merchant, the miller transformed the grain that the baker sent him. During the eighteenth century, this passive practice of milling on command gradually gave way to a new form of trade: a speculative activity, commercial or "merchant" milling. Instead of waiting for the client, a robust, enterprising miller took the first step, buying grain—a practice formally prohibited earlier—and milling it when he could, then offering the flour to bakers, who were often aware of the advantage that the restructuring and rationalization of the supply system entailed. In a first phase, they continued to impose the rules of the game on the big "flour dealers," who competed to win their favor. The cleverest bakers were even able to make their growing indebtedness toward their suppliers an advantage rather than a handicap

Historic bakery site in the Marais. © Perrin.

Allegorical decorative detail on a bakery façade, Rue de Ménilmontant.
© Perrin.

Traditional bakery façade, Avenue Parmentier. © Perrin.

View into the interior of an old-fashioned bakery, Rue de la Roquette. © Perrin.

One of the "modern" shops in the Paul chain, whose leitmotif is the old-time bakery. © Perrin.

Shop in a working-class district emphasizing its artisanal character. © Perrin.

The warm, welcoming atmosphere of a bakery in the Paul group. © Perrin.

A new shop under the Baguépi label (Soufflet group). © Perrin.

The shop of an artisanal baker in the Banette group. © Perrin.

A bakery in the Ronde des Pains network (Grands Moulins de Paris). © Perrin.

The Grands Moulins de Paris, one of France's largest mills. © Perrin.

A Rétrodor bakery (Moulins Viron). © Perrin.

Festival, the brand emblem of Moulins de France. © Perrin.

A retrofitted "traditional" bakery façade, Rue de Montreuil. © Perrin.

in their exchanges, in which real power was at issue. However, from the beginning of the nineteenth century on, the millers were the unchallenged masters of the grain trade in the Paris region. This hegemony gave them the possibility of taking their revenge on the bakers; their erstwhile lords became their vassals. Sure of themselves, the millers established the terms of the exchange on their own authority, excluding bakers at will from the grain trade, advising them on breadmaking methods, taking control of certain shops. From then on, according to a contemporary observer, the baker was merely "the miller's man," a hired hand paid by the task. In 1859, an economist wrote: "The milling business runs the bakery business; it is absorbing and exhausting it."[2]

Beyond the threat of seizing bakers' property in payment for their debts, one of the principal means by which the millers ensured their domination over the bakers was the baking agreement [*marché de cuisson*], a contract guaranteeing a year's supply. In exchange for deliveries every two weeks, the baker would turn all his sales receipts over to the miller, less a fixed fee per sack. But this type of "servitude," to go back to the bakers' association's bitter epithet, served both parties: the baker, trapped in a dependent relationship, nevertheless benefited from credit from one two-week period to the next, and he was sheltered against fluctuations in the price of flour, while the millers profited from guaranteed outlets and regular revenues. The last third of the century was marked by a growing concentration of the milling business, technological modernization, and projects designed to industrialize breadmaking and integrate it under the aegis of the big millers.[3]

The miller once waited impatiently for the baker to arrive and made flour for him by crushing his wheat between two millstones that were about two meters in diameter; they were made from stone slabs of similar hardness and porosity, soldered together with plasterwork and encircled with iron. Since the physical characteristics of wheat grain made milling particularly difficult, the millstones had to be operated gently, with discernment, in order to avoid excessive pressure and overheating and to guarantee maximum yield both in quantity and in quality. What differentiated one miller from another was not the machinery itself, which was of a common, elegant, relatively simple design, but the source of energy drawn from the outside, wind or water. Windmills often worked in spurts; mills operated by water power were considered more regular, but they posed problems of channeling, supply (too much or too little water), and water use rights. While the milling business perceptibly improved its efficiency toward the end of the eighteenth century, two determining changes came along in the nineteenth century: first, artificial energy from steam replaced the natural forces of wind and water, and then metal cylinders were substituted for millstones.

Contemporary mills have taken over functions that once belonged to the baker, the grain merchant, or even the farmer. Millers today often organize wheat production, favoring varieties that have properties especially valued in breadmaking; they direct every harvest "campaign," collecting the wheat or overseeing the process and evaluating the quality of each variety in each region in terms of its suitability for breadmaking. Then they store, clean, and transform the wheat; purists maintain that the modern milling process (in which the grain is cut, separated, and crushed) deprives the flour of certain nutritional and organoleptic qualities. Millers are responsible for bolting and mixing, tasks that once belonged to bakers. Beyond technical laboratory tests, they make bread from the various wheat varieties to determine what difficulties bakers will confront and propose solutions. Today's miller can "correct," compensate, and supplement. On an entirely different scale and with a very different science, millers practice what would have been called a sort of alchemy under the Old Regime. "At this stage," according to a spokesperson for the Soufflet-Pantin mills, the largest in France, "we determine the qualities and optimal dosage of the glutens, flours of malted wheats, amylases, and ascorbic acid to be added, depending on the mill and on the intended use of the flour." Mills work with astonishing precision in highly automated settings, allowing the baker, whose competence in the historical sense is increasingly limited and whose freedom of action is increasingly restrained, to obtain greater volume or more pronounced slashes, to favor alveolage or the production of flavors, to eliminate blisters on the crust, and so on.[4]

An Ambiguous Partnership

Although the milling business has managed to shed its bad reputation in the late twentieth century, it is still in conflict with artisanal baking, which continues to fight for its autonomy in a difficult economic context. In the face of the ongoing decline in bread consumption, deemed catastrophic,

during the Thirty Glorious Years, and in the face of the bakers' agonized
paralysis, a number of millers have come up with various initiatives intended to boost bread consumption by an in-depth restructuring of the
bakers' practices and their relations with their flour suppliers. But these
efforts have been perceived by many artisans as power plays aimed at their
profession, a new stage, as they see it, in a long process of subordination.
These bold millers, driven as much by a lucid analysis as by the (normal)
lure of gain and the (historical) taste for domination, sought to win the
bakers' loyalty through a dense network of services (updated, extended,
enriched). They also sought to mobilize bakers collectively under labels
proposing the same quality breads to a public that was increasingly unhappy with the daily offerings from the artisanal bakeries in their neighborhoods.[5]

The millers' ambitions came with a set of rigorous requirements, for
their commitment was extremely risky. Given the crisis, it was not purely
hypocritical of them to construe their own commercial interest as a matter of general interest. The bakers, first of all those who were part of the
association establishment, saw things differently. For them, the millers'
proposals entailed intolerable linked presumptions. On one hand, these
big modern flour merchants were usurping some of the crucial functions
of the National Bakery Confederation, calling into question its very reason for being. On the other hand, they purported to teach bakers (again)
how to make bread, reducing them to the state of apprentices and robbing
them of their own trade culture (rather as the great chemist Parmentier
had done in the 1780s, "smelling overwhelmingly of the pharmacy," when
he created the École de la Boulangerie to free the crude artisans from
their "blind routines" and their "vulgar errors").[6] The gamut of offerings
proposed by the mills, although diversified and rationalized, did not constitute a real break with traditional practices of seduction, conquest, and
partnership (historically complex relationships in which a fictional reciprocity often masked a practice of domination). "The complete offerings"
of the Grands Moulins de Paris (GMP) represented the flour makers approach quite well: "from strategy to adjustments," advice on investments,
staffing, marketing, regular monitoring of the results, and so on. The Banette mills did the same thing, offering start-up assistance, logistical and
technical support, legal counsel, management tips, store layout, and, of
course, a whole array of marketing ploys. In theory, the millers were com-

mitted to making the bakers autonomous, but in practice not too much so, not too completely. The baker would have the keys—this is one of the recurring images in the millers' advertising—but not all of them. The GMP was prepared to send a technician at 4:00 A.M., if necessary. Which was a way of saying that the baker could really count on his miller. Without being alarmist, the Verdelot-Bourgeois mill reminded bakers that artisans "are constantly confronted with new forms of distribution and marketing" and that the mill was determined to "help the bakers defend themselves" with a multitude of "high-level" services.[7]

Ideally, millers want to win a baker's loyalty at the very beginning of the baker's professional career. They look for good candidates working in the baking rooms they supply or for graduates of a training program (in this respect, GMP has an advantage, in that it can identify good potential candidates coming out of its own school). The mills offer assistance in the search for a site. "Bakers and pastry-makers, are you looking for a business to buy?" asks Euromill Nord (formerly affiliated with Banette, now linked with the GMP). Its "targeted service" could find a solution quickly, but the mill is "more than a helper in buying or selling your business; we are your partner in development." Euromill would like to involve itself in the artisan's future, forever if possible. To seal the engagement, the mill offers to help in the acquisition and start-up process with "complementary financing" or surety for a bank loan, less often with a more significant direct loan. Turnabout is fair play; the baker who is "helped"—from now on a "partner"—has to take the bulk of his flour, if not all, from his godfather.[8]

To penetrate the artisanal mentality, a hybrid of fraternal collectivism and Darwinian individualism, the mill emphasizes "personalized" service based on a "personalized study" of the baker's needs (the Moulins de Cherisy from the Banette "stable" offer "personalized flours"). The bakers unquestionably appreciate this. It is not just the bottle of champagne for their birthdays; it is the idea of being able to count on their suppliers and not be just another client, according to a purely commercial logic. This is an atavism that works; it refers back to traditional practices that stabilized relations of exchange on the basis of not only mutual trust but also a certain affective rapport. A baker in the fifteenth arrondissement laid low by a sudden illness is visited by his miller every day for a week. A baker in the twelfth, victim of a serious fire in his baking room, has a place where he can bake in the first hours after the catastrophe, thanks to his miller.

A baker in the eighteenth was not abandoned by his miller when he was going through a long dry spell in the wake of a difficult divorce.[9]

Instinctively searching for this paraprofessional intimacy, certain bakers reject from the outset the very large mills that are thought to be impersonal.[10] But the talent of the best salesmen working for giants such as Soufflet-Pantin (Baguépi) or GMP (La Ronde des Pains/Campaillette) lies in being able to reestablish village-like ties despite considerations of distance and size. While some bakers, disillusioned by their experience, skeptical, or simply reticent, maintain rather cool relations with their suppliers, others feel very strongly about and boast of a quasi-sacred relationship in which loyalty is figured by a romantic language with chivalric overtones. One has the impression that they would deceive their wives rather than betray their millers. Like bread itself, the relation between miller and baker is at once material and symbolic, a matter of body and soul, profit and honor. Embedded in a dense complex of reciprocity, miller-baker exchanges can only rarely be reduced to business alone, just as the notion of interest is highly inflected by what could be called ideology. Thus, for example, before agreeing to supply a rising star among Paris bakeries, a prestigious mill that grinds with stones asks for the approval of its long-term clients. Similarly, a miller feels obliged to give up selling to a particular baker even though the latter does a big business and has a brilliant reputation, because one of his major clients does not want him to continue.

Yes to Help, No to Charity

As a consequence of persistent postwar penury, state commitment to a controlled cereal market, and the corporatist-*dirigiste* inclinations of the dominant millers, bakers could not freely choose their flour supplier. This was the major source of friction between the two professions. Other squabbles erupted in the mid-1950s, sketching out certain familiar themes of conflict. Bakers reacted very badly, for example, when the director of the *Petit Meunier* declared that their "bread [was] made in haste, [was] subject to overly rapid fermentation through the use of yeasts, and [was] characterized by excessive humidity." *La Boulangerie Française*, the newspaper of the Paris federation, recorded the baker's response: "It would be fairer to say that the flours that are currently being given to bakers for breadmaking do not allow [us] to make good bread." Starting in the 1980s, following initiatives deemed too aggressive by the representatives of artisanal baking, the relations between the milling and breadmaking businesses became acutely strained. Jean Paquet, the energetic president of the bakery confederation, made the nature of this tension clear: the millers had crossed a line. To each his own field of action and his own garden to cultivate. One had to consider not only the quality of the raw materials, but also "the quality of the relation" between bakers and their suppliers, "respect for everyone's work."

The observation of some particular cases might seem to suggest that certain important millers think it behooves them to help their baker clients to the extent of doing their work for them, whether this involves the work of breadmaking or that of management. Artisanal baking is too proud of its independence to encourage such projects, and the bakers who, for various reasons, might let themselves be led down that path would not fail to regret the loss of their freedom in short order.[11]

Less constrained by diplomatic imperatives, the president of the Seine-Maritime Federation expressed the bakers' complaint more crudely: "It is regrettable to have to remind our flour suppliers that it is no more their job to replace financial agencies than it is to teach us our trade, and it is especially not their job to turn us into 'independent workers' for their own benefit. Their role consists in supplying us with the best flour at the best price, period. And that is already a lot," especially because "it is often those that 'love' us the most that are the most generous with our competitors"; the big discount chains always get more favorable prices. Like the master bakers in the eighteenth century who made fun of the "doctors in bakery" who came to "enlighten [them] thanks to the torch of theory," the president from Normandy noted ironically that he had heard "those gentlemen talk about a trade that they had never practiced." "To each his own trade," Paquet said some years later, but this time more forcefully. He asked: "Has anyone ever seen bakers or bakers' associations concern themselves with the qualifications of their suppliers, millers, equipment manufacturers, bankers, or others?" Alongside solidarity, the association variety in particular, the artisan's supreme value, Paquet suggested, was "independence." He urged his troops never to let themselves "be kicked around by their suppliers, . . . never to let themselves be abused by self-appointed advisors who use what may be [their] lack of professional capacity 'the better to trap [them]' in promotional 'training' schemes that actually lead to the establishment of disguised franchises."[12]

The current confederation president, Jean-Pierre Crouzet, in economic terms the least corporatist of all the heads of the bakery business, has rejected the millers' usurpations just as energetically and with the same arguments. Millers are their "natural partners," but "everyone has his place in the realm of his competencies." The millers "are very present and very useful suppliers," Crouzet has insisted, "but we have to watch out: by piling up nice services they may threaten our independence." He recognizes with lucidity that artisanal baking, "incapable of navigating the turn toward modernization on its own" around 1980, needed a healthy boost from the mills.[13] The mills had some good ideas and the dynamism necessary to carry them out; at the time, what was good for them seemed to be good for the whole wheat-flour-bread sector. Consumers had to be brought back into the shops and bakers, somewhat disoriented by the competition and the apparent disaffection of the public, had to be remotivated. With their brand names, their clear and repeated messages, and their project of basing the renaissance of good bread on rigorous criteria of quality, the mills found a well-disposed audience. For the leaders of artisanal baking, nevertheless, things began to deteriorate as the renewal operation was imperceptibly transformed into the institutionalization of a new dependency, a sort of servitude, a modern analogue of the old baking agreements.

Fairly quickly, the price of entry began to seem too steep, and the way out was not clearly marked. "Yes to help, no to charity." From now on, at least in consumers' minds if not in the reality of power relations, the Banette-style operations were edging toward franchising systems, toward an anonymous standardization that detracts from the artisan's individuality and is not certain to satisfy increasingly attentive consumers. According to the confederation, it was time for the baker to rediscover his personal identity, to put his own name on his shingle, to take charge of the supply process, to advertise his own way of doing things. After all, Crouzet recalled, with Banette flour one can make good bread or bad. Without any illusions as to the millers' interest in modifying their terms, Crouzet warned his colleagues that nothing less than their survival was at stake. Just as Ulysses warned his companions, Crouzet in effect told his colleagues: "If you give in to the enchanting appeal of the Siren, you will die."

In his view, "if [bakers] are not capable of resisting, the next step is franchising and the loss of the profession." Elsewhere, he asserted that solid,
profitable businesses have to be developed: "Otherwise, the big millers' or
bankers' groups will gain control of our entire trade at very little cost."[14]

Irritated by the millers' general arrogance and appetite, the association leaders lashed out at the same time against quite specific practices.
The idea that the millers could find themselves at once on the side of the
artisans, almost like members of the family, and at the same time on the
side of the opposition seemed both illogical and fundamentally unfair to
these bakers. As early as 1961, confederation president Gringoire was ful-
minating against the mills that were betting on the industrialization of
the bakery business. In 1969, L'Express reported that the "big millers" had
given up on a marriage with industrial baking: "One cannot want something and its opposite at the same time: [one cannot] become the baker's
rival while serving as his supplier." Scarcely twenty years later, the GMP
came close to crossing the Rubicon when they were contemplating the
creation of a chain of "hot shops" — bake-off terminals — that would sell
hot bread all day long. "If the GMP implement their project, it will be open
warfare," warned Gérard Delessard, president of the association serving
the Paris region. He was deploring a double transgression: encroachment
on a trade — breadmaking — which was not their own, and degradation of
this noble profession by the endorsement of lowly dough warmers. The
base continued to echo this protest, in one way or another. For example,
a baker in Lutzelbourg spoke ironically about "our partners the millers"
who offered "anti-competition" prices to the bake-off terminals and big
discount stores: "rebates, discounts, etc."[15]

The confederation dreamed of the monopoly it once had over various
institutional services — legal councils, accounting, and so on — that kept
the bakers attached to it. "The profession will have to look into ways for
associations to offer personalized assistance to each bakery, in order to
tighten the bonds of a necessary unity," according to an editorial in the confederation newspaper. One of the projects dear to Crouzet's heart advocated the promotion of a savings plan based on salary deductions, in an
effort to regain control of the process by which young bakers set themselves up in business. For the current confederation president, the answer
to the millers' way of constructing their world lies in reconquering young
people. If young people espouse the primacy of the ethic of freedom in

business and in life, according to Crouzet, they will be able to avoid becoming "the drudges of the mill business."

Training, another area of intolerable encroachment, has also preoccupied Crouzet, partly because it concerns young people and partly because it touches on the historical prerogatives of the trade, where masters and masters alone used to take collective responsibility for renewing the ranks. Even if the state has been involved of necessity for more than a century in the education of future bakers, the profession plays a crucial and privileged role in the organization and delivery of diplomas. Hence the confederation president's anger at the Banette millers' group, which "conspired to acquire an officially sanctioned diploma authorizing Banette to say who can set himself up as a baker." For Banette to establish an on-site school to offer continuing education to experienced bakers was perfectly normal; for the miller to set up of his own accord and in the greatest discretion an accelerated training program—an intensive course—for future Banette makers (most of them "recycled") might also be tolerated. But "to create a diploma at a level equivalent to the one that exists for a selected public with private financing," noted Paul Gilles, who was responsible for professional training in the confederation, "is regrettable on the part of people who want to be seen as professional partners." The diploma is offensive not only because "it is arrogantly ignorant of the client profession," but also because "a baker taken in by the Banette group is a member lost to the organized bakers' movement."[16]

Outside the ranks of active association members, the bakers seem divided in their attitude toward the mills. Many artisans who have signed up under one of the mills' labels assure me that they can listen to the Siren's call without succumbing, that they are not fooled, that they are profiting from the notoriety of the trade name without losing their soul (that is, without completely fulfilling the set of requirements to which they are theoretically subject). A certain number of them are evolving from the clear-cut dependence of their careers toward a more balanced relationship—marked, for example, by diversification in their choice of supplier—once their sales figures start going up and they begin to have confidence in themselves and in their clients. Others find the mills more efficient and more discreet in their services than the confederation. The ambivalence of Pierre Demoncy, winner of the 2001 award for the best baguette in Paris, captured the prevailing attitude in the profession. While he criticized the mills for ensnaring the artisans in their insidious web, he could not deny that, "despite this loss of independence, the bakers who join the mill brand system seem satisfied. They feel much less alone when confronted with the new competition," notably the chains and the terminals.[17]

Brand Names

In France, if you buy your bread from an artisan in your neighborhood, there is a good chance that you are implicated, without knowing it, in this long, tense story between bakers and millers. For it is quite possible that your baker is affiliated with one of the trade names that are seen pretty much everywhere: Banette, probably the most famous, but also Baguépi, Festival des Pains, La Ronde des Pains (Campaillette), Copaline, Club Le Boulanger, and so on. You probably do not know that each of the partners in the trade name is a big mill or a group of mills. It is not at all a question of chains—a natural but completely erroneous supposition on the part of many consumers. Each of the bakers involved is an independent artisan (the millers, Banette in particular, insist on this point, trying to exorcise the defamatory specter of Jacobinism in the bread business, a "McDonald-ization" of this everyday patrimony). Bakers may be more or less involved in the association; those who run their "shop" under the mill's colors and according to its "concept" are much more committed than those who ad-vertise only some of the products developed by the flour supplier. Having visited hundreds of bakeries, I would say unhesitatingly that, without any other reference points, you considerably increase your chances of getting good bread if you patronize one of these establishments, although you must be warned at once that there are qualitative differences among labels and within a single label. Dough is a living thing; every dough marks out its own life cycle from batch to batch, and every baker has his own way of working; even if he uses the same brand of flour according to the same recipe, the bread coming out of the oven will never be exactly identical to the bread that came before or after.

The emergence and the affirmation of the trade name mark a real turning point in the trajectory of the postwar bakery. Distressed by the uninterrupted decline in bread consumption, upset by the increasingly brutal competition from industrial bakers and from the large and medium-size chains, unable to find a magic formula for "quality" that would adequately highlight artisanal virtuosity and the artisanal vocation, often insufficiently aware of the perverse effects of technological "progress," and sometimes ill-prepared to face the new freedom in pricing that was granted in an initial phase in the late 1970s and then "definitively" several years later, the bakers wallowed in a stagnation that was by turns anesthetizing and traumatizing and from which only a minority of strong-minded individuals managed to escape. If the millers were not knights coming to the rescue on their white horses, they nevertheless came along at the right time. Since everything was going badly for the bakers, everything was going badly for them. They brought in some new ideas, which the bakers sorely needed.

The contribution of trade names may have been almost as significant on the psychological level as on the technological and commercial levels. Here, finally, was a coherent, comprehensive, rather bold strategy. From now on, bakers who played the game need not pull their oars alone. With marketing tools and a public relations plan, the mill was going to help the baker where he knew himself to be most vulnerable: in sales and advertising techniques. Mounted on the façade of a shop, the trade name had the function of "reference and guarantee."[18] It distinguished the baker from the competition, linked him to others who shared the same methods and goals, and incorporated him into a circle of excellence whose merits would be well known to the public thanks to advertising campaigns in all the media, including television. The baker who opts for the "store concept" hopes for greatly increased visibility and wagers on a marketing aesthetic—a warm decor, often in wood, which conveys a "traditional" feeling—designed to calm and stimulate the consumer simultaneously. The store offers an arrangement of the selling space that organizes consumer traffic and the presentation of the products in order to encourage impulse buying.

The question of production methods was necessarily more delicate. The skilled miller had to pass the codification of the "new" procedures along to the baker and make them palatable—in fact, they entailed a rehearsal of old breadmaking methods (a slow and relatively brief kneading, a long first fermentation or *pointage*, hand shaping, and prohibition of the ameliorants on which the baker had depended the most, all this not as an implicit critique of the baker's mastery of his craft but as a common return to sources, a new start in partnership, a pact of quality for the future

Table 3. State of the Major Brand Names in 1998–99

Brand (and miller)	Date of creation	Type of association	Total number of members	Number of stores with the brand name
Banette (Cie Unimie)	1982	Brand name with or without a store	3,000	1,009
Rondes des Pains (GMP)	1986	Brand name with or without a store	990	50
Baguépi (Moulins Soufflet-Pantin)	1990	Brand name with or without a store	2,500	[?]
Festival des pains (Cie Meuniers de France)	1990	Brand name with or without a store	3,000/5,000	[?]
Copaline (Inter-Farine)	1988	Brand name	1,200/1,000	—
Rétrodor (Minoteries Viron)	1993	Brand name	350	—
Club le Boulanger (Générale des Farines France)	1996	Brand name	130	—

Sources: *Filière Gourmande* 61 (May 1999); *Enjeux* (November 1999)

based on age-old values. The character and intensity of the partnership varied from mill to mill. Some sought a fairly thoroughgoing integration, subjecting the baker to major constraints in exchange for multiple services in a context of contractual rigor. Others preferred more flexibility, requiring neither the exclusive right to supply flour nor a complete range of breads, and not granting commercial exclusiveness in a given consumer zone. If everything went well, the miller would say, the public, galvanized by the advertising and reassured by its own taste, would learn to associate good quality with the brand. According to the most favorable scenario, the customer would end up asking for a "Banette" instead of a baguette; the former would become a generic substitute for the latter. With this new notoriety would come a new triangular confidence that linked millers, bakers, and the public, and the sales figures of the first two groups would rise in consequence. If the Banette maker encroached on the business of his colleagues, the logic would no longer be that of bleak mercantilism, a zero-sum game. Thanks to the Banette maker and other bearers of brand names to come, there would be a larger and larger pie to share, for consumption would pick up again once the public noticed that good bread was back.

The Banette Story

Banette was the first to attempt to restructure the wheat-flour-bread network and to reinvigorate artisanal baking. Even its critics and rivals agree in praising the boldness and pioneer spirit of this group of independent mills, a dozen at first, some forty at the apogee. The product of a particular economic and cultural conjuncture and a series of parallel preoccupations in the early 1980s, Banette—the word evokes the name of a Provençal bread (baneto), the form of a sailor's hammock, and a *banneton*, a small basket without handles in which dough is placed to rise. Its success reminds us that that not all good ideas come from Paris. Alain Storione, a miller from Marseille, was behind the creation of the millers' consortium (Unimie). He was an entrepreneur and, according to his admirers, a "visionary" who understood ten years before anyone else that habits would have to change. He wanted to tackle several closely related problems. First, a technical imperative: better control of wheat varieties (1,000 in the world, 250 in France) and qualities in order to make better flour. Rather than carry out spasmodic experiments in breadmaking on the outside, Storione imagined a sort of federation of collegial competitors (the idea of a common brand was not part of the picture at the outset) who would collaborate systematically on the analysis of cereals and flours. A troubling if not fateful event accelerated the embryonic common project. France-Farine, a preeminent group, sold one of its mills in the Toulouse region to a behemoth, the GMP. Confronted with the rapacious appetite of the big mills, the medium-size mills were frightened. Storione thought it crucial to create a pole of resistance.

In order to remain independent, the regrouped mills would have to fight on the ground of quality. But to be conclusive, the search for quality would have to be pursued all the way through the breadmaking process. The reflections of Storione and his colleagues took place against a more generally alarmist if not defeatist background; how could one prosper, or even survive, in a world in which people ate less and less bread every year? Millers (especially those who did not have major outlets in industry or in the export trade) and bakers alike had the impression that they were living through the end of history. To explain this postmodern phenomenon, certain analysts often privileged exogenous factors outside the control of the network, such as the medical malediction. Without denying the weight of these factors, Storione conducted his own investigation and ended up putting the stress squarely on variables that might be modified by the concerted action of the network: if consumption continued to fall, it was because "people [did] not like the bread" they were expected to eat. Hence the determination to start a dialogue with the bakers of southwestern France, who had come together in 1980 in a Bread Quality Association to examine the changes that would be needed.

In a first phase, Unimie-Banette was still anchored in a physiochemical laboratory, carrying out sophisticated electrophoreses as well as more classic tests of the properties of flour, and in an experimental baking room, very quickly set up in Briare (Loiret), more or less at the center of a network of mills covering nearly all of metropolitan France. Starting in 1980, the Unimie center undertook an annual summer "quality survey," making 500 sample breads and serving as liaison for a rapid exchange of information between growers' cooperatives and the mills, for purchases remained totally decentralized. Briare became the superego and the customs office, inspecting each batch of wheat as it entered, accepting only those that corresponded to the required standards, and subsequently transforming the practice of rigor into a principle of ethics when technology was transmuted into deontology on the altar of marketing. The bags of flour that came from member mills bore the Unimie logo, standing for the promise of a better day in terms of taste, hygiene, and morale. The laboratory evaluated both the quality of each member's flour and that of their chief rivals. Later, Unimie was the first to win the "red label" for its flours: this attestation of superior quality, certified by an independent bureau, took into account the specifications that farmers had to respect and the conditions of sanitation, production, and storage in the mill. This was an important argument for the bakers that Banette was preparing to recruit.[19]

Storione created Banette with the help of other men of his caliber. Marcel Cocaud, a Parmentier steeped in baking room experience and trained by Raymond Calvel, the most famous bakery professor since the eighteenth century, ran the laboratory of analysis and quality control that generated a monthly sample group indicating the qualitative level of each member and his rivals, a methodical and meticulous task. At the opposite pole in the sense that his training had nothing whatsoever to do with bread, the future director general, Bernard Seller, a cultivated and inquisitive certified public accountant, quickly mastered both the basics and the fine points of the trade. Thanks to an impressive ability to listen and a subtly critical mind, he was able to impose himself in this exotic realm. Channeling Storione's enthusiasm, he built up the organization, managed its finances, and took charge of the implementation of the sales and advertising policies adopted by the mills. Coordinating a "federated" structure consisting of members who differed considerably in size and who were always somewhat suspicious was not an easy task. Even today, after more than twenty years of work in common, tensions persist among member mills that supply the same regions.[20]

The birth of the partnership with bakers was not without its painful aspects. The sector developed slowly, because the bakers, often delighted with the quality of the flour, were much less prepared psychologically and professionally to submit to all the explicit or tacit constraints involved in joining the organization, and they had trouble facing the implicit challenge to their professionalism: "Who are you to tell me how to make bread?" The fact that some Banette bakeries in Marseille met with success at the outset was not necessarily telling, since Storione himself set them up.[21] The start-up rites at the big professional Europain salon for professionals in February 1982 did not lead to a surge in membership. The tipping point came in 1983 with the first big marketing campaign, on television in particular, a campaign designed to get bakers to espouse the brand name. In a climate that was still rather inhospitable to the artisans, Banette was telling them that its strategy would work miracles, and the publicity impressed and gratified many bakers. The following year, 500 clients had signed up for the trade name, mostly from the southeast and the Rhône-Alpes region, with the beginning of a Paris presence. In 1986, Unimie introduced the concept of the Banette store, entailing a deeper commitment; it was accompanied by the definitive version of its signature product, called a Banette, distinguished by its pointed ends. The form attested to respect for hand shaping and served as the emblem of a dual contract signed by the artisan: first, vis-à-vis the public, to whom he promised a rediscovered quality, powerfully associated in the public imagination with an Edenic yesteryear, a tacitly expiatory gesture (the right way was being restored), and then vis-a-vis Banette, his new adoptive family, to whom he promised (through the local miller "uncle") that he would play the game in good faith.[22]

Building a project around a new flour supplied by a new structure inaugurated by a publicity campaign that had no precedent in the sector was already a challenge. The intent to oblige bakers to make their bread differently entailed still more risks. If they did not stand behind the bakers from start to finish, the people responsible for the Banette plan did not believe they could achieve their goal. Support for this deep conviction had already been provided by the apocalyptic statistics revealing the trend in bread consumption. Relying on the advice and prestige of Raymond Calvel, whose role as an expert baker employed by the École française de meunerie (millers' school) seemed to echo the new relationship between bakers and millers, Banette posited a radical break with the stigmatized "white-bread method" that had dominated the profession since 1960, engendering a bread that was lovely, voluminous, and ultrawhite, but without either taste or character. Banette's flour was of top quality owing to the choice and treatment of wheat (initially, mainly of the Capitole Hardi variety) and also owing to the prohibition on fava flour, an additive that had been used everywhere since the nineteenth century to promote fermentation and the resistance of the dough (Calvel himself extolled the virtues of this "precious food" in 1961), but that had since been denounced for its role in bleaching dough and, as Calvel said fourteen years later, in "altering the flavor of bread."[23] Banette did retain adjuvants, euphemistically called "technological auxiliaries," such as ascorbic acid; Banette flour was not going to complicate bakers' lives very much. But Banette was asking bakers to knead for a shorter time and more gently in order to guarantee the flavor and proper consistency of the crumb, to add a dose of prefermented dough to fortify the physical properties of the loaf and enrich its taste, and to shape the loaves by hand so as to retain the carbon dioxide needed for rising. All this was intended to reassure the public by giving an unmistakable sign of traditional — and thus better — work, and to remind the artisan himself that he should not take mechanization too far. (This message served as proof that, even though it sought a certain level of standardization, Banette wanted to highlight every baker's "personal touch.") Boasting of a soft, well-alveolated crumb, creamy in color with a hint of yellow, and a crunchy golden crust, easy to recognize, this everyday baguette, a little more expensive than ordinary baguettes elsewhere but decidedly more flavorful, met with real success, even if its quality varied from one Banette maker to another.

Although it focused primarily on its signature baguette, Banette quickly reinforced its offerings with a line of specialty breads that it has continued to expand and that sell more or less well in relation to the sociocultural and demographic criteria of the target clientele. While taste remains the universal leitmotif of the Banette line, bran bread and Banette fiber bread emphasize health and well-being. Whole grain bread blends "equilibrium" (a key word in the medico-nutritional rehabilitation of bread that accompanied and supported the Banette experiment) and tradition (the natural wisdom of a certain past). Then comes the country loaf (in a generic house version called "Briare" and a sourdough version whose acidulous taste is the madeleine of a timeless moment gone by) that identifies the constantly sought-after yesteryear with the rustic dream that marks Frenchness; made from dark flour combining wheat and rye, it is a far cry from the "floury transvestite" denounced years before by Raymond Calvel. The company also offers two rye breads; two multicereal, multigrain breads; a sports bread playing on the register of health slanted toward high energy — youth, success, and fun; breads containing fruit and/or chocolate; and even an organic Banette, embodying nature despite its reliance on yeast.

More important than these specialty breads, which are after all just optional complements in a panoply of extremely varied offerings, is the (belated) emergence of a "bread in the French tradition," the concrete realization of the 1993 bread decree, 1993 being henceforth the official date of the renaissance of artisanal breadmaking. While on one hand this move represented the cultural "Banettization" of the entire sector, on the other hand it signified in part the irreversible banalization of the Banette way;

this might account for a certain ambivalence on the part of the Briare leaders toward this so-called historic moment. They were reluctant to cast any shadow on their flagship product, the Banette, which would be inevitably be upstaged by a majestic loaf in the form of a baguette that better embodied the Banette philosophy and artisanal virtuosity, although the bread would lack the signature pointed ends. This innovation threatened not only to confuse the consumer, but to disturb the Banette maker, for whom the new bread imposed constraints that were manifestly more significant than anything that had constituted the special nature of the affiliation until then. The Banette millers were not unaware, either, of the degree to which the vast majority of French bakers were exhibiting resistance to this new product that prohibited ascorbic acid. (In Briare they used to call that additive "a bonus for the bad ones," because of the way it facilitated the breadmaking process and could make a tasteless bread look good.) Bakers would also have to go back to a long fermentation (*pointage*) and manual shaping that required, if not more work, at least a serious reorganization of the process. But Banette was forced to go that route by the competition, as much from the inside (potentially more dangerous) as from the outside. For at least one of the member mills—soon to secede from the consortium—had introduced its own brand of traditional bread—"Tradi," sold in a bag that did not give the name of the brand's owner and offered a brief for bread in the French tradition based exclusively on its nutritional properties—without highlighting in any way its organoleptic properties (that is, its taste and its aromas), although these constituted its true originality.

The "Banette 1900 Tradition" was introduced in March 2000 by a new television campaign that focused for the first time on the *product* instead of celebrating the baker; the very name seems to betray its producers' uncertainty.[24] Calling it a Banette rather than simply a traditional bread (like their country or rye breads) was already a crucial marketing decision. The new product was designed to embody the matrix concept at the dawn of the twenty-first century. The adjective "traditional" is normal, even necessary: it situates the product not only in the realm of the imagination but also in a specific legal and commercial context. But the decision to anchor the bread in a recent and specific yesteryear—1900—is more problematic. What can this mean to most consumers? Perhaps "la Belle Époque" in all its gaiety, a certain pleasure in life. The label plays on an idealization of

the past, but, like it or not, the moment singled out marks the beginning
of a period of aggressive modernism. While the idea of reckless pleasures
might be compatible with an emphasis on some vague tradition, the extraordinary development of science and technology is harder to reconcile.
1900 for Banette means a very long fermentation and the patient work
of a master, but 1900 in history evokes speed above all else: it signals the
dawn of everything "fast." It was a time of triumphant optimism but also of
great moral, social, and religious distress. While the paradox is too subtle
to bother the marketing department, we still have to wonder whether the
label's message is sufficiently readable to "optimize" the impact of the new
product.

    On the strength of their traditional flour (which they of course repre-
sent as the indispensable key to high quality), the developers of the Banette 1900 worked out a procedure in their test baking room in Briare that
was capable of producing an exceptional bread, distinctly superior to the
good standard Banette (although the latter would nevertheless continue
to lead in production and sales). By definition, a traditional bread boasts
of an archaeological recipe rather than a revolutionary one; Banette was
returning to a style of breadmaking not exactly like the one that prevailed
in 1900 (when most bakers were still kneading by hand and had not yet
given up the difficult and delicate practice of working with sourdough),
but anchored in premechanical experience even though it was compatible
with many stages of modern technology. The artisan kneads for ten minutes at low speed, an idea that had been virtually inconceivable for about
half a century. After a strong hydration (70 percent, 10 points above the
common practice), the dough undergoes a three-hour-long *pointage*; this
is followed by manual shaping, without knife-cuts—a single, "natural"
slash generated by the baking is supposed to mark the loaf distinctively
when it comes out of the oven (which has a refracting soleplate, needless
to say). When it is properly prepared (and Banette had to worry about
whether bakers would follow the instructions faithfully or not), this bread
has an astonishing "nose"; its rich aromas of wheat, spring flowers, and
dried fruit permeate the taste buds and linger on the palate, where a slight
salty note can be detected. The crumb is pearly in color, even a bit yellowish; with uneven holes but no gaping chasms, it has a supple, elastic
texture. It holds its body when chewed, but its mouthfeel is pleasant and
easy, sometimes even rather voluptuous. The crust is golden, not entirely

smooth when the slash is formed spontaneously; it adheres well to the crumb, giving off a slight toasty odor, and it has a nice crunchiness in the mouth. And this bread keeps remarkably well instead of succumbing to a dismal rigor mortis within three hours.

To come across this bread (one time out of three, in my own wanderings) is to be happy, reassured; even with the knowledge that the return to tried-and-true values is a phantasmagorical marketing phenomenon, there is no doubt about it: this bread is infinitely better than the norm, and its higher price is perfectly justified. One wants to shout "Bravo, Banette!" and offer a toast to its creativity and to its success. Its failures are disappointing, even infuriating, especially when the baker's wife enthusiastically sings the praises of the bread or seems to see her clients as dupes. But the 1900 bread is not easy to bring off, without hefty doses of both skill and desire; with enhanced motivation and the help of itinerant technicians, its quality will improve.

In 2002, there were 3,200 bakers in the Banette network, 800 of whom have shops set up in the standard Banette arrangement. The base of partner-clients continues to grow, although quite gradually, in an extremely competitive market. Many bakers leave the network, after "quality" controls, but they usually remain clients of their mill under other labels. Normally a baker becomes a Banette maker through the intermediary of a miller member with whom he has established ties. Given the federated structure, each member mill keeps its own habits and approaches; thus it is difficult to generalize about the behavior of the millers in the group. On the average, their sales force seems to spend 80 percent of its time maintaining client relations and 20 percent seeking new clients. The transition point — the initial installation in a shop or a change of shop — remains the privileged moment for switching suppliers. In principle, a future partner sets up on a trial basis with Banette for two or three months, a period Bernard Seller refers to as the "betrothal." The baker, given certain tools, is invited to test products, question his clients, and ask himself the ultimate question: "Is there something in it for me?" Depending on his response, he may join the network or not. Studies have convinced Banette that roughly 75 percent of the bakers in France are interested in quality and believe that quality, a virtue and a goal in itself, will above all else increase their sales figures. When a decision to consolidate the partnership is reached, the two parties sign an agreement spelling out their mutual obligations.

Several different itineraries lead to Banetteland. In the beginning, in order to put together a significant nucleus very quickly, Unimie drew on its own reserves, concluding partnerships with a certain number of bakers who had already been clients of one of the mills belonging to the federation. Another path, which ought to be even more satisfying than "internal" enrollments, entails the seduction of an experienced baker who is thus led to leave his customary miller to join the Banette group, a move producing a gain both for the base and at the center. Many of these conversions have had less to do with the relative quality of the flour or the relative merits of local millers than with the decisive commercial advantage the newcomers expect to get from the brand. We shall look below at two other routes toward Banettization targeting two markets that are crucial for the future of the brand: the recruitment of young people and the recycling of non-bakers into the breadmaking trade, an iconoclastic idea on Banette's part that remained for some time more or less its exclusive (and controversial) preserve.

If we look at the case of Tony Lebehot, for example, we have the sense that the choice was self-evident for him, notwithstanding the somewhat august staging with which Briare likes to surround the rites of passage for new members. A native of the Manche region, without any family connections to the bakery business, Lebehot had been fascinated by breadmaking since elementary school. At the end of ninth grade, under the wing of an excellent master, he completed a brilliant apprenticeship culminating in a first place award in the departmental competition for the best apprentice. Next came a professional diploma, followed by military service, two years as a bakery worker (under "a good boss"), and eighteen months as a pastry worker; the young Lebehot was now ready to set himself up and bold enough to try his luck in Paris, with the backing of his gracious, strong-minded, and highly intelligent wife, the ideal type of partner as defined by the Women's Commission of the Bakers' Confederation. He turned to a representative of the Moulin de Verdelot, a Banette member, who helped him find a shop in the thirteenth arrondissement and lent him some money. Lebehot seems to have signed on without any anxious moments. He feels a real allegiance to his miller, but he gets only 75 percent of his supplies from Banette. The French edition of this book concludes: "The Verdelot mill is associated with a young, hardworking, likeable and talented couple — Tony makes a superb 1900 and Florence sells it efficiently in a convivial environment — and it will surely do all it can to help them move to a larger shop in a better location, not necessarily set up according to the standard Banette layout." But there is no happy ending here for Banette, for Verdelot opted out of the consortium a few years ago, draining it of some of the best bakers in Paris.[25]

The story of Michel Philippe, formerly the regional head of sales for a large retail chain and converted quite late to the bakery business, is very different; he spent four months in the Banette school in Briare when he was forty-five years old, rather than two or three years in a training center for apprentices who start at age sixteen. Philippe was more mature and much less autonomous — but no less resolute — than Lebehot. Although his choices have an extremely rational cast, for Philippe the commitment to Banette had a truly solemn, even emotional aspect. Lucid and unpretentious, he knew he was entirely dependent on the mother mill that got him off to a good start. Whereas many bakers with whom he had spoken dreaded being subservient to Banette ("they have you, you are no longer free to make your own choices"), Philippe saw an association that was very flexible and mutually advantageous. His miller, his "godfather" and the sponsor of his schooling, found him a shop, and Briare suppplied the floor plan: a complete Banette layout. Scrupulously following the recipe for the Banette loaf that he had repeated dozens of times in Briare, he quickly drew a clientele, two-thirds of which preferred the baguette with pointed ends to the ordinary product, in a district overflowing with bakeries selling mediocre if not frankly bad baguettes.

Seven years later, he registered 3,500 kilos of flour transformed per month, a very satisfactory indicator of development; he found that the competition had improved and that his clients were more conscious of the wide choice of products and more demanding than ever as to quality. Michel Philippe listened to them constantly, all the more so in that he did not work in tandem with his wife (she pursued her own career), and like many of his colleagues he had difficulty finding reliable salespeople. Consumers wanted hot bread all day long, especially in early evening, so he had to cook until 7:30 P.M. But the task was lightened by his use of deferred fermentation overnight, which allowed him to wait until 5:00 A.M.

to begin his morning, assisted by two or three young bakery workers and a female pastry chef (women are gradually penetrating into baking rooms and laboratories). Philippe produced between 300 and 500 Banettes a day; a year after the Banette 1900 was introduced, he sold no more than 40 loaves of it a day, so he did not have to do too much delicate work. No one could be a more thoroughgoing Banette maker, but Michel Philippe retains a critical outlook and like other Banette loyalists he worries about a certain lack of coordination between the center and the periphery, Briare and the local mill.[26]

Although the recruitment of bakers is basically a local affair, Briare is concerned with all its baker partners to the extent that the credibility of the brand is at stake every day in every shop. Banette's good reputation is not simply the result of clever advertising. Born of a gamble on quality, if it is to prosper in the long run the group has to impose a certain rigor on the practice of its artisan clients and has to maintain a certain ideological consensus, without going as far as total conformity of outlook. Banette seeks to motivate bakers to respect the prescribed working procedures and their other obligations; it says it is prepared to sanction flagrant departures. It prefers to think in terms of holding people responsible rather than coercing them. Beyond exhortation, there is science, in particular the effort — still somewhat utopian, despite the brilliant experiments of Pavel Hyndrak, who heads the laboratory in Briare — to establish objective standards for quality in baking, to develop reliable criteria to measure (and thus to compare) bread quality. Banette begins by supplying its artisans with a quite detailed grid of the factors involved in breadmaking that derive from common sense in the trade, and then it provides meticulously refined organoleptic parameters. With these tools in hand, bakers can carry out their own self-evaluations, identify possible flaws, and correct them on their own. A technician from the mill carries out a second evaluation during a site visit, assessing all the steps in the breadmaking process. This evaluation leads to a plan for improvement; the baker is given opportunities to reinforce his mastery through internships and demonstrations.[27]

The third phase brings an "animator" from Briare, an experienced baker well versed in the house methods; his job is to verify the results of the first two evaluations, propose solutions to remaining problems, and sound out the intensity of the baker's motivation (for Banette, the baker's state of mind remains more crucial, in the last analysis, than his technical skill, which can be more easily remedied) and spur him to do even better work, if possible. If their notebooks are to be believed, animators take an exhaustive, penetrating look. Following the technical evaluation grid, they look at the type of flour used (Banette red label? used exclusively or not?), the type of oven (a soleplate oven is strongly encouraged), and above all else the degree of respect for the prescribed breadmaking procedure (is the kneading "moderate"? is prefermented dough added to the kneaded dough? is shaping done by hand? is the baking done in stages? and so on), and for the cleanliness of the baking room and the staff. On the sales end, the grid encompasses exterior and interior signage, the percentage of Banette products on display, the way the products are exhibited ("a fine presentation respecting Banette's recommendations"), the quality of client reception ("smiling, personalized; gives advice" as opposed to "impersonal, hands over the bread"), and a rubric that is fundamental for Briare: "involvement with the brand," going from "uninterested in or even hostile to the brand" to "highly involved, commercial dynamism"). Finally, a separate organoleptic grid stresses taste and smell above all, without neglecting visual appearances. In making recommendations to bakers who have earned relatively high ratings, an animator might note: "take more care with the form and presentation of the Banette" or "hydrate a little more" or "make shallower slashes."

The goal of the operation is to preserve and even increase Banette's collective capital, both material and symbolic. There is a risk of frightening off the artisans and of bringing grist for the mill of those who equate Banettitude with servitude. A Banette maker whose quality remains deficient is invited to "withdraw voluntarily." I cannot say how many are obliged to leave the network: one can imagine a complex negotiation during which the local miller does everything to save face for his client and to preserve his commercial loyalty. According to Bernard Seller, keeping the bar high is not a practice of enforced servitude; it serves the general interest of the brand. "We are not frightful totalitarians," he insists. The image of tyranny on the inside is as harmful as its corollary, the image of "franchising"—a highly pejorative term—on the outside.[28] It is probably true that Banette is more draconian in practice than in its discourse. It is proud of the partner-bakers' high degree of attachment to the brand. Those who want to leave of their own accord "are not prisoners"; they can end their affiliation without cost. Briare is realistic: a certain level of defection in relation to its flour and breads has to be tolerated. The chief executive officer recognizes the originality and specificity of each artisan; Banette strives to take these differences into account at the level of the evaluations, despite the seeming rigidity of the grids. Adopting the Girondin spirit when necessary, Briare also adapts to regional disparities. In the south, for example, good bread is much whiter, less well done, not crusty, with less resistance to chewing, than elsewhere; in the north, bread has less alveolage and thus a denser crumb good for spreading butter or jam.

Banette is not likely to experience revolts or stubborn resistance from the bakers' side. The principal danger comes chiefly from within the millers' group; whether stemming from defections or civil war, such confrontations would be devastating. As a federation whose structure is rather loose, Banette cannot impose strict discipline on its members. Their interests, as they understand them, do not always correspond to the ones articulated by Briare in their name. Thus competition between member mills could sabotage some of the center's objectives. The withdrawal of the Bourgeois family, owners of Verdelot, reflected internal tensions between rival associates. The surprising and contentious departure of Euromill, a powerful group in its own right, including interests of the Storione family, involved external encroachment and courtship, a proposition for collaboration with the leviathan GMP (recently rebaptized Nutrixo).[29] Banette denounced "the betrayal," and demanded that Euromill drop out of the new relationship or else stop using the Banette label, the loss of which would surely cost them dearly, at least in the short run. After turning to the courts in 2001, Banette and the Euromill-Nutrixo coalition subsequently reached a settlement that clearly reserves Banette trade dress for the exclusive use of the Briare consortium.

Reminding the wheat-flour-bread sector that Banette intended to remain a pioneer, the Briare consortium launched a new Banette baguette in 2004–2005. It is called "Fermentolyse," in testimony to the modified fabrication process, beginning with the protracted fusion of flour and water called autolysis that is intended to enhance flavor by predisposing the dough to an intensified first fermentation. Marked by a darker, more sensual crumb, with a more articulated architecture of uneven cavities, the Fermentolyse has a more complex aroma and a richer taste than the standard Banette. It will be interesting to see how client bakers react to this new product, which is not yet widely available.

Rétrodor

Alongside the Goliath Banette, Rétrodor in 2002 was a very modest David, with 400 shops concentrated in the Paris region. But in the campaign for the return of good bread, this brand from the Viron mills in Chartres, thanks to the energetic owner, has played a role that goes far beyond its weight in the market. The fifth patriarch in a long line of millers, Philippe Viron clearly wanted to sell more flour in a market that was less and less hospitable to small and medium-size mills. But his passion for good bread went beyond a strictly rational calculation about how to make the most of the company's commercial assets. His discourse, capable of offending just about everyone, had two aspects: a lyrical side that could be dismissed as outdated or hyperbolic, and a "home truth" side that was harder to disqualify. Restoring the quality of bread was a patriotic and aesthetic vocation as much as a commercial one. For Viron associated the deepest values of Frenchness, even of humanity, with the best bread in the world, seeing bread as consubstantial with the identity of France, a symbol and trope of its civilization, a guarantor of its continuity. If he thought of himself as a guardian of bread as patrimony, it was of a living patrimony, like the dough that reconstitutes bread every day, a heritage that ought to have a prosperous future in daily life rather than in museums.

Philippe Viron began to utter "cries of despair" for his country and for his mill in the mid-1980s.[30] His son and successor, Alexandre, acknowledges that the "wake-up call" came from Banette, provoking a double realization that one should speak openly about the deterioration in bread quality and that one could attach a brand name to bread by advertising it on a vast scale. Viron knew, on one hand, that his modest mill was not capable of exploiting advertising the way Banette did and, on the other hand, that communication about quality must not be allowed to obscure the real problem of quality in the practice of breadmaking. "I was born in 1930, and I had the opportunity to appreciate the taste of real bread as a child," the miller observed. While the war of course brought about terrible dislocations, the shake-ups of reconstruction were what really seemed to have sealed bread's fate: "The urgency [of the need] meant an emphasis on the quantitative aspect, to the detriment of quality," and the demands of modernity and democratization led to "industrialization carried to an extreme . . . in all areas of economic life." This resulted in "a sort of standardization of all aspects of [French] life," hence "the ultra-white, tasteless bread for which bakers today [1995] are being criticized."[31]

While Banette created a propitious climate for entry "into the war," it was a serendipitous contact with a baker who had a shop on Rue de l'Ourcq in Paris (nineteenth arrondissement) that galvanized Viron's energy and determination. Sporting the "predestined" family name of Meunier (= Miller), this former student of Raymond Calvel had worked in the experimental baking room of the Grands Moulins de Pantin and was a skilled artisanal baker. He was desperately looking for "a pure flour, without any additives whatsoever, unlike all the flours on the market today." Viron thought this would be a catastrophe, a recipe for the production of *galettes*—flatcakes—rather than bread. "As soon as you've delivered my flour," Gérard Meunier told the miller, "come see me and I'll show you my flatcakes." A fairy tale: Viron paid a visit and tasted Meunier's baguette. "It was true perfection! A well-done crust, just the right golden color, but also a creamy crumb, with wild, irregular alveolations, as I've gotten into the habit of saying. An incomparable taste and odor that made me dream." Which explains the baker's enormous success, transforming 8,300 kilos of flour a month—"it was miraculous," said Alexandre Viron—in a largely low-income neighborhood. Meunier did not make much of this virtuosity: he credited a prewar recipe passed down by "the old folks." Very open, he invited Patrice Tireau, a gifted young baker who had been trained at the Institut national de la boulangerie-pâtisserie in Rouen and who was in charge of the mill's breadmaking laboratory, to join him in his baking room and follow the breadmaking process by spending the night at his side. The recipe was very simple, even austere: the customary doses of yeast and salt were halved, the hydration level was 70 percent, and kneading was kept to a quite moderate level, barely ten minutes. The product was delicious, but not very attractive according to the canonical criteria. "Impossible to transmit," Alexandre Viron commented, even as he admired the bread's unparalleled taste.

But the foundations for the future Rétrodor were being laid. The Viron mill, among the top fifty in France despite its small size (thirty-seven employees), perfected its additive-free flour, the flour Gérard Meunier ordered, well ahead of the development of the flour "in the French tradition" that was to mark a turning point in the profession. Working the dough in the mill's baking room, Tireau perfected an artisanal baguette, initially called Fournée d'or before being definitively baptized Rétrodor. The Viron family saw an opportunity to compete with Banette. To be sure, they got off to a very slow start, repeating the Banette experience on a much more modest scale. In 1991, only five bakers were producing Rétrodor baguettes. Viron's good clients, like most of the other bakers, resisted instinctively, sometimes stubbornly: "I know how to make bread." In late 1992, the Viron family purchased the shop of a bankrupt client in Rue Ordener (eighteenth arrondissement) and became bakers themselves. (In fact, this was not their first experience: a Rétrodor bakery had been flourishing in Brussels for several years.) The gamble was typical of Viron, who was determined to force the issue: "Either it works or it crashes." In a neighborhood that was neither chic nor poor, the miller played the quality card, baking only Rétrodor baguettes and selling them in little bags that insistently proclaimed the identity-value of the product. An unqualified success (as much as 10,000 kilos transformed per month!) with significant fallout in the media: the professional grapevine went to work. Old clients shifted to Rétrodor, and new ones signed up.

The famous bread decree of September 13, 1993, defining traditional bread—legislation for which Philippe Viron had led a veritable lobbying effort for years on end—marked a second stage in Rétrodor's advance, for it was one of the few products on the market that already fulfilled the conditions of bread in the French tradition, and its recipe was simple. In a third stage, with his slogan "no additives, more taste" (a vaguely organic variant of the more generic "let's produce yesterday's quality today!"), Alexandre Viron believes that Rétrodor scored an important point with consumers, who were disturbed by the spread of mad cow disease (a matter of toxic flours of a different sort) and were distressed by the idea of not knowing what was being put in their food. It is hard to measure the impact of this argument on the public, for the Viron mills do not engage in Banette-style advertising. But many bakers, and in particular many who did not want to make Rétrodor baguettes, were interested in the Viron flour, which since 1987 has contained nothing but fine wheat from Beauce and malted wheat.

The key to the Rétrodor recipe is the long bulk *pointage*, after insemination with very little yeast and a gentle kneading, eight minutes at low speed. The Virons have maintained this method because it gives extremely positive and consistent results, good bread that is also beautiful. Patrice

Tireau has experimented with other approaches. He rejected the injection of fermented dough, in the first place probably because it was Banette's signature technique, but also to avoid problems for the baker, as improper use of the technique could produce too much acidity or compromise the formation of aromas. Attached as he was to the "old ways," Philippe Viron could not help thinking about sourdough. But he rejected it because it was better suited to round loaves than to baguettes, and because he was afraid it would not induce the public to increase its bread consumption — the primordial objective of this crusading miller — because of its acid taste.[32] Tireau experimented with liquid sourdough fermentation; the process was rather delicate and did not always give a reliable product. Even as he was reducing the risks and obstacles that bakers would have to face, Tireau was counting on their professional self-esteem. The process presupposes a rigorous, careful artisan: he must constantly take the temperature of his dough, his water, his oven; he has to weigh often, or he will make mistakes; he has to add his own personal touches so the bread will be his own.

Along with its baguette in the French tradition, the mill offers a gamut of other breads, in particular the round Mannedor loaf (a fine marriage of wheat and rye), a bread made with six cereals and four grains, and rustic breads made with sourdough. But the company relies most on Rétrodor, the traditional baguette (weighing 300 grams, a sign of authenticity for Philippe Viron, although the weight of baguettes used to vary a good deal, even in the 1930s). Jean-Noël Julien of Rue Saint-Honoré won the first competition for the best baguette in Paris with Rétrodor in 1995; Bernard Maeder of Boulevard Berthier did the same in 2000 (and his son Raoul in 2002!). After several recent tastings, I can attest that Bernard Maeder's Rétrodor is a masterpiece in its class: a splendid crust, with a beauty more proud than fragile, smooth but ripe, golden but not artificially so, well-structured, neither too thin nor cumbersome, engraved with well-positioned slashes, exhaling a pronounced odor of toast with a few caramel counterpoints. In Rétrodor baguettes, the crust often tends toward arrogance, dominating and eclipsing a crumb that does not dare show signs of life. But Maeder reconciles them perfectly, for his crust perfectly complements a sensual (but not passive) crumb that is agile and athletic, alveolated the way Philippe Viron likes it, pearly but not dull in color, giving off earthy perfumes. The combination produces a rich, engaging, convincing taste that is not too good to be true, a coherent taste; an advertising copy writer would call it authentic, while a romantic would deem it sincere. A bread with this flavor ought to incite the Virons to re-consider their own overly conservative advertising; they would do well to emphasize what the bread is rather than what it is not ("Rétrodor is neither insipid nor too salty nor acid . . ."). Of course, like those of other brands, Rétrodor baguettes vary considerably in quality from one baking room to another. But while I have identified few made with Maeder's mastery, I have rarely found any that are out-and-out failures.

Staking so much on the "authenticity" of his "Yesteryear," and obliged to counter Banette's attempt to monopolize "old times," Philippe Viron could not make many concessions that would privilege machinery over hand work. He could not forgive the equipment manufacturers for having obliged bakers to modify — he would have said mutilate — their recipe in-stead of modifying the machines to take into account the needs of the dough. His son Alexandre and his bakery advisor Patrice Tireau, from a new generation better equipped to deal with machinery, did not see things the same way, and their attitude won out in the Viron mills. They were younger, less involved in the company director's liturgico-polemical dis-course, and probably closer to the contemporary client base; they were less distrustful of machinery, and they did not believe that even the most enlightened artisans would subscribe to a future without machines, espe-cially the divider-shaper. Giving the dough a rest or rolling it after ma-chine division would reinvigorate it, they contended, and a loosely set me-chanical fashioner did not really harm the dough, although hand shaping retained carbon dioxide better. Having studied the question thoroughly, both in theory and in practice, Patrice Tireau was sure of his conclusions: (1) Machines work faster and are more consistent than human hands. (2) It is not the machine that destroys the dough but the baker who does not know how to control the machine. (3) The trade has a reputation for "grueling labor" that deters young people; intelligent use of machinery to save time and effort would be an asset for recruitment.

Alexandre Viron has changed the style of the company without reject-ing his father's goals. Like other millers, Alexandre Viron plays the role of big brother to his bakers, young and not so young alike ("as to a friend," their sales discourse insists). But he acknowledges that he pulls out his checkbook less often than his father did. Like his father, he will make a site visit very quickly to advise or reassure a client. He rails against the giant rivals who play unfair tricks with prices or otherwise distort the market, as he sees it, speaking with the same spleen and indignation as his father. With the energy of his predecessor, he "wages war" in a 250-kilometer radius around Paris to win clients. Like his father, he fights against the inertia of the sector. Allergic to self-analysis and locked into baleful old habits, bakers have too often rejected opportunities for renewal. Hence the historic reflex, the Banette reflex: the miller has to act on his own initiative (at the risk, as always, of infuriating the bakers' organizations, although the Virons have been more attentive than others to the associations).

Since immobility is reinforced by the bakery schools, whose teaching is essentially limited "to the modern method of breadmaking," the Viron diagnosis concludes that "it is imperative to reform teaching and to create, as needed, a new diploma." The Viron millers mention several projects, some of which are in the Banette spirit (recycling professionals), others in the spirit of Guy Boulet and Gérard Brochoire (stress the candidates' motivation and desire, seek to raise the level of recruitment, insist on rigor in instruction, and strive to refurbish the image of the trade by presenting an attractive picture so younger members of the profession in particular will be proud of it). Other projects bear the Viron signature: recuperate young people who have left the trade under bad conditions, "burned out at twenty-five"; train bakers' wives and saleswomen in a systematic and serious way; envisage a school that is state-certified but autonomous. Where the father dared to imagine "re-educating" the consumer, the son is content to follow the consumer's lead prudently ("the customer is king"), but he hopes to be able to influence consumer habits by multiplying storefront events (more than 200 a year) and by tirelessly reiterating the gospel of quality (for example, no additives).

Festival des Pains

While all milling companies were influenced by Banette starting in the mid-1980s, Meuniers de France (MF) was under its astro(techno)logical sign. MF is the largest group in France in terms of the numbers of its members, some fifty mills scattered throughout metropolitan France. Established in 1985 according to the same federation model, MF took two observations as its starting point: it would have to face up to the crisis in the breadmaking industry, and it would have to reckon with Banette's innovative competition. Its first goal was a rapid and efficient analysis of the wheat available, in order to offer good purchasing advice. A buyers' association was set up in 1990. The mastermind behind all this was Marcel Cocaud, the knowledgeable baker and head technician whom we met earlier in Briare. He was one of the driving forces behind the Banette project; his departure jolted the Unimie group.

Cocaud's knowledge of the entire sector was deep and wide, and his own calm strength inspired trust. He knew how to talk to bakers and millers alike, in his own baking room, in the laboratory, and at the decision-making table. As MF's general director, Cocaud imprinted on the group the personality that was to condition its trajectory. Installed in an ultramodern facility in Lamotte-Beuvron, not far from Briare, Festival's headquarters are a center for research and quality control and also a center for continuing education. The laboratory focuses on the quality of wheat for each harvest season (or campaign, in the jargon of the sector); for Cocaud, wheat quality is paramount. Technicians also examine the quality of flour and flour blends, both those of their member mills and those of their competitors. While they use a whole panoply of sophisticated machines to measure the quality of the raw materials in all their parameters, master baker Cocaud insists on the ultimate test: he directs from 4,500 to 6,500 breadmaking trials a year. Like his rivals, he is sensitive to consumer anxieties about food, and he is leading the group toward a practice of traceability whose practical modalities (list of specifications?) and ideological tenets (rational agriculture?) have not yet been articulated.

MF-Festival's two principal business mottos, addressed of course to their baker clients, highlight the historical tensions that have pervaded the wheat-flour-bread sector for two and a half centuries: "Flour is our business," and "Bread is your business." The first translates a total consensus: who but millers would get involved in the production and sale of flour? The second is politically and commercially correct, but it is not exempt from a certain casuistry. If breadmaking could be left entirely to bakers, the MF could justify its existence, but not the Festival des pains. A baker's baker, Cocaud has always been proud of his original profession. In public, with complete sincerity, he says: "You can sell flour, but then you have to let the artisan reveal himself as an artist, and not tell him exactly how he is supposed to make his bread." But by personal observation and statistical analysis, he knows that artists are not a dime a dozen, that bakeries are closing or going bankrupt, that for some decades now many bakers have had a hard time tracing out their paths to success. Historically, he locates the root of the problem in the experience of World War II, the memory of unspeakably bad dark bread, the association between liberation, freedom, and reconstruction and bread that was extremely white and excessively puffy, bread that satisfied some pressing psychological needs but (unconsciously) threw gustatory needs to the winds. Hence the persistent decline in consumption, the increasing space available for the emergence of industrial and mass-market competitors, the crisis in artisanal identity. Hence Banette, Festival, and their ilk.[33]

In the final analysis, although Cocaud does not completely avoid talking out of both sides of his mouth, he tries to avoid any hint of conscription or subjection. The situation was different in the eighteenth century, when journeymen solicited acceptance as masters in the corporation by producing masterpieces. Without denigrating or even naming the competition, Cocaud positions MF-Festival in relation to Banette. The Festival system is less restrictive. Artisans are asked—but not required—to take 50 percent of their flour in Festival products or in supplies provided by a mill that belongs to the group. They are asked to respect specific fabrication methods (they receive extremely detailed and clearly presented instructions), but they are not subjected to rigorous evaluations. Festival very rarely punishes a lapse in quality or in loyalty by withdrawing the right to use its name. Cocaud represents Festival as a flexible "system for recognition" that is capable of evolving, rather than as a network built around precise standards.

Cocaud conceived the Festival baguette as the flagship product of the line. Perhaps in order to set Festival apart more strikingly from Banette (which is made with a supplement of fermented dough), but especially because of the results and the implication of the baker's talent in the process, Cocaud advocates the use of poolish in its fabrication; this system of prefermentation produces a concentration of organic acids that will convey "an exceptional flavor." Normally composed of a mix of equal quantities of water and flour, activated by a modest dose of yeast, variable according to the season, Festival poolish is prepared the night before and left to develop over twelve to sixteen hours. Boosted by poolish, the dough requires bulk *pointage* of just an hour before it is divided. The recipe stresses in bold type that "manual shaping is strongly advised."

The product is an excellent everyday baguette, with a long, creamy crumb and a crackling crust, although I have never been able to detect the "subtle taste of hazelnuts" touted in the ads. More interesting, but much more difficult to find because much more complicated to achieve, is the "old-style" Festival *flûte*, a loaf with a more pearly center, rich in aromas, the product of an excellent recipe that allies a supplement of prefermented dough with a twenty-four-hour autolysis (water and flour mixed and then left to rest) and a long first fermentation.

The Payse, Festival's bread in the French tradition, is making its way rather slowly. I rarely find it in its immaculate version in Paris, where bakers tend to present a more or less generic loaf. The recipe is elegant and simple: "pure flour," salt, water, and yeast, without the adjuvants that have been specially created to increase the tolerance of the dough used for Festival baguettes. A first fermentation, the driving force behind the aromas, takes place in the kneading basin and then in tubs. Hand shaping follows; two knife strokes cross in the middle; the bread is baked in a hot soleplate oven. The Payse that I tasted in Lamotte was a pure marvel: Its dense flavor mesmerizes the nose and explodes on the taste buds. The rather thick crust consummated a perfect marriage of toast and caramel. The center, well alveolated and creamy with a slight yellowish tinge, was like a plump, full-bodied, well-rounded wine; it is satisfying in the mouth and agreeable to chew.

Probably the best Festival bread in the French tradition that I have encountered in Paris is a somewhat personalized version of the Payse made by Jean Hautecoeur in his baking room in the tenth arrondissement on the Canal Saint-Martin. Hautecoeur's output grew from 1,600 kilos of flour transformed per month in 1995 to 7,000 in 2001, with a fivefold increase in annual sales. Hautecoeur has recently joined the MF ranks and is quite satisfied with the Festival flours, but he does not see himself as "assisted," to use his own term, and he makes selective use of the suggestions that emanate from Lamotte-Beuvron. The son of a café owner who expected him to be a machine operator (*fraiseur*), he did his apprenticeship in the early 1970s with a boss who combined "old-style" techniques with the use of ascorbic acid — which the young man quickly learned to hate. After that, his experience was extremely varied; he learned speed and dynamism from a boss who transformed 40,000 kilos of flour a month in a more or less industrial fashion; he learned poolish from a small-scale baker, yeast from a demonstrator in another large baking room, and management, staffing, and "total responsibility" while working for Carrefour and Continental as department head, and later for Francis Holder/Paul in Créteil as head of breadmaking. Jean Hautecoeur is at once very sure of himself and ready to rethink his own practices. It is not surprising that he is modifying the Payse recipe, adding more water and increasing the *pointage* even more. The result is a well-structured baguette that looks sturdy rather than graceful; it is rather pugnacious but tamed by a convivial taste of caramelization. More rustic than the baguette from the Lamotte bakery, its creamy center, not overly alveolated, smells of harvest and appeals to the appetite.[34]

La Ronde des Pains/Campaillette

The giants of the milling industry also had to face the crisis in the breadmaking business. As it happened, the GMP was going through its own crisis at the same time; the firm passed from a great old mill family first to Bouygues (1989), a huge group specializing in construction and communication whose vocation for producing flour was not obvious, and then to a financial group headed by AXA (1998), also a novice in the sector. The GMP comprised thirteen mills holding 10 percent of the flour market in France and drawing 25 percent of its annual sales from artisanal bakeries. The two changes of ownership, ten years apart, did not enhance the company's capacity to react. After some hesitation, Bouygues invested in modernizing the mills' physical plants and equipment; before selling GMP, the parent company had completely refurbished all the factories. In the late 1960s, in the hope of stimulating renewed consumption, GMP had launched a whole series of specialty breads in mix form. But its leadership had understood that, one way or another, it would have to follow Banette's lead. At a time when things were starting to budge in Briare, GMP began to reconsider its lines of bread, privileging taste rather than appearance. The discovery of a strain of a natural leavening agent growing on the wall of a mill in Nancy—a mill protected by a statue of the Virgin, I have been told—led to the creation of a new product, the Campaillou, a yeast bread. The natural leavening was dried and incorporated into the flour, so bakers were exempted from the hard job of producing their own leaven. The Campaillette, another baguette fermented thanks to dehydrated sourdough, was created in 1988, and it quickly became GMP's flagship product and its most famous brand name (with a 92 percent satisfaction rating among consumers, as compared to 88 percent for the Banette, according to an in-house source). This dough was made from T 65 flour, which is slightly darker than the standard T 55. When perfectly executed, the combination of the leaven and a true *pointage* gave the Campaillette a palette of rich aromas and a robust flavor.

In another response to Banette, a new structure was developed for new products. In 1986, GMP had set up La Ronde des Pains, a brand name that rapidly attracted almost a thousand artisan subscribers. The organizational principles strongly resembled Banette's pioneering ideas: support and motivate bakers, ensure their loyalty, reinforce the qualitative image of the network, attract and win over the clientele, and dramatize the bread lines offered. Bakers could participate in a variety of ways tailored to their needs: "They can choose what they want," according to Michel Crignon, chief executive officer in 1995. In the so-called light formula, bakers were expected to get all their flours and mixes from GMP (though they rarely did so exclusively), and they sold their bread under GMP brand names (Campaillette, Campaillou, Campagrains). La Ronde des Pains invited these bakers to participate in all the promotional events staged both locally and nationally. Fully committed members (38 in 1990, even today just a small minority) transformed their shops according to a standard layout and adopted the entire line of breads in all its glory. Although the overall number of baker clients has continued to grow in recent years, La Ronde is becoming more selective. Network animators—bakers who serve as demonstrators—make site visits to reward the bakers' commitment but also to help them raise the level of quality. The weaker ones withdraw or are excluded, more or less gently; most of those who leave continue to buy GMP flour without using the brand names. In Paris, for example, the number of Rondes has fallen from 200 to 130 (of a total of 430 GMP shops throughout the capital).[35]

An agribusiness giant, with 2,200 employees and almost three billion francs in profits (over $410 million), 75 percent of which come from supplying flour to industry (Danone, Nestlé, industrial bakers) and to the big chain stores (Auchan), from frozen foods, and from exports, GMP has trouble conveying an image of proximity and intimacy with artisanal bakers. Its sales force tries to overcome or dispel the idea that a big company cannot maintain relations of conviviality and complicity as well as small mills located close to their clients can. It spends four times as much time on "maintenance" of client relations as on recruitment of new clients. GMP representatives are often the ones who spot promising workers in baking rooms, people who are eager to set themselves up on their own and need a hand. In 2000, GMP "set up" 430 bakers, supplying guarantees or loans, technical assistance, legal advice, and so on.

Another essential spot for encountering future clients is one that the small and middle-size mills cannot offer, the École de boulangerie et de pâtisserie de Paris, formerly the École de boulangerie des Grands Moulins de Paris. Established in 1929, this is the oldest and most prestigious bread-making school in France. It no longer offers virtually exclusive access to the sons of GMP clients, but it retains a privileged relation with GMP, which partially underwrites its operations and sends its specialized staff and its clients to the school for training. GMP is well situated to attract future artisans who are getting their diplomas and to place adults who are changing careers, following the Banette model. In 1999–2000, the school accepted 200 young people ("a bit of everything") and a handful of adults ("very motivated") in a variety of degree programs, with a success rate of 90 percent on the examinations and more than 80 percent on the score of "professional insertion," i.e., job placement; in addition, 800 professionals were admitted for continuing education.[36]

After considerable hesitation, GMP launched its version of the baguette in the French tradition, construed as a product "that breaks with the past" and heralds a new beginning, as much for the baker as for the consumer. Fabricated with T 65 flour ("containing nothing," the test baker insisted, by which he meant no additives beyond a bit of reinforcing gluten), this bread was very close in recipe to its Banette and Rétrodor counterparts: a small dose of yeast, 70 percent hydration, twelve to fifteen minutes of slow kneading, two to three hours of bulk *pointage*, mechanized division and shaping, and a spontaneous slash in place of the hand-wrought, canonical signature (no agonizing here over giving up hand work). The marketers baptized this "tradi" the Campaillette "Grand Siècle," a choice meant to convey to the consumer an odyssey back toward an unspecified yesteryear. As a historian, of course, I cannot help thinking of the age of Louis XIV connecting classicism, refined taste (vaguely alluded to in GMP's advertising), and the construction of the administrative state, but also rampant structural misery, famine and dearth, endless war, and so on. One wonders what image the Grand Siècle evokes for the general public: the Sun King? Molière? Versailles? Or a vague timelessness when things were more authentic, better, closer, slower ("it's better when one takes one's time making it" was one of the advertising slogans)? Without coming across as the promised reincarnation of "forgotten flavors," the Grand Siècle impressed me as a worthy baguette, well constructed, handsome in aspect, pleasant in the mouth, yet often bereft of crust and somewhat dull in crumb.

Under the guidance of Hubert François, a graduate of the elite Polytechnique school, formerly number two in the National Cereals Office, who engineered the leveraged buyout that put the company essentially in the hands of its executives and employees, GMP, now called Nutrixo, is determined to give a second wind to its artisanal baking campaign. Shrewdly emphasizing the organoleptic potential of wheat, a surprisingly neglected sphere of action, the company's scientists are exploring blends of old and new varieties and its test bakers are reworking various stages in the breadmaking process. A tasting in early 2005 left me enthusiastic: a yellowy plump crumb with a nervously uneven inscription of cavities, a crunchy yet aristocratic crust, and a rich flavor unlike anything the commercial Grand Siècle has ever achieved. The challenge now will be to translate these experiments into commercial reality, which means first of all remobilizing the baker clients and resensitizing them to the realm of aroma and taste.

Baguépi-Soufflet/Pantin

In the race to restructure relations with bakers launched by Banette, two of the major competitors were two of the largest mills in France, Pantin and Soufflet, Baguépi against Fleuriane. The Grands Moulins of Pantin and Corbeil introduced the Baguépi brand in 1990; they immediately recruited five hundred artisans who were attracted by the mills' eagerness to win public attention on a broad scale. In the same year, the agribusiness giant Soufflet (which had become the third largest milling conglomerate in France after acquiring its first mill only twelve years earlier) set out to mobilize artisans around its Fleuriane brand. Claiming to offer a "*true* partnership with artisans," implying that bakers would find as much support as elsewhere and more freedom than with others (i.e., Banette), Fleuriane too announced a flour made of the best wheat with no added soy or fava flour; the quality of the raw materials was the strong point of this company, which had grown out of the wheat trade. While it anticipated a significant expansion in sales owing to its techniques and support system (including Fleuriane shops that had sculpted wood façades embellished with scenes from the transformation of wheat into bread; the first of these opened in Troyes in late 1991), Soufflet exhorted its clients to "give [their] bread taste." Was this an implicit acknowledgment that taste had vanished? Promising "a true, authentic artisanal baguette" in the canonical linkage to ancestral gestures, the sole guarantees of true quality, Soufflet nevertheless assured its bakers that the Fleuriane baguette was "easy to make" — a claim that did not necessarily flatter the bakers' pride in their own competence.[37]

The Soufflet group, fully diversified and global in its reach, had a simple philosophy: "Keep on growing in order to have an impact on the market." In July 1994 it swallowed up Pantin, a larger mill and one of its most ferocious competitors, although Pantin initially put up strong resistance to the forced merger. Rational considerations outweighed sentimental ones, and Soufflet immediately sacrificed the Fleuriane brand name (200 clients, 2 specialized shops) in favor of Baguépi, which was better situated commercially (1,000 clients, 15 shops). To ensure the restructuring of the sales force and to develop the single brand, Soufflet-Pantin turned to none other than Banette, where it recruited its new regional sales director. Dominique Malézieux was a genuinely dynamic young man: impatient, sure of himself in his area of specialization, which was merchandising rather than breadmaking ("I have not been injected with knowledge; I don't know how to make bread"); he was later rewarded for his success with the title of director of sales and marketing. His itinerary is rather unusual: an agribusiness degree, leftist Catholic and Third-World tendencies, several years in Africa, a brief return to "hard" capitalism with Auchan. Thanks to an uncle with Champagne Céréales (a Unimie subsidiary), he then landed a position with Banette, serving as Paris sales director from 1991 to 1994.

For Soufflet, Malézieux managed to integrate the Baguépi and Fleuriane teams without too many setbacks; he made selective use of the Banette culture in order to give the mix of Baguépi and Fleuriane flours a new

254 MILLERS AND BAKERS

cohesion and identity. In baking rooms and in marketing, he placed his bets on quality. In his relations with bakers, he exploited the à la carte concept, promoting a panoply of choices that Banette (and others) presumably could not offer. Malézieux's form of *glasnost* was not an "all or nothing" approach. According to their means and their motivations, bakers could opt for "variable degrees of involvement." [38]

In Baguépi's clever wheat-based hierarchy, *un épi* — "one stalk" — signifies commitment without passion; the baker gets his flour from Soufflet/Pantin but does not mention the brand. Two stalks signal more enthusiasm, with a clear-cut reference to the brand and the articulation of reciprocal obligations. On the baker's part, these include the requirement to produce the basic Baguépi baguette following the official recipe and the purchase "of a minimum quantity [unspecified] of flour." On the company's part, the obligations include the right to use the name, a supply of paper baguette wrappers, and — free of charge — the services of a baking room demonstrator plus opportunities for internships focusing on the products of the line. Real commitment comes with the third stalk, celebrated by the installation of a Baguépi façade (astonishingly discreet, emphasizing the vocation of the artisan rather than the brand name). The baker signs a "partnership agreement" based on a "list of specifications" and undertakes to produce virtually the gamut of Baguépi products, while the mill provides all sorts of help, advice, and promotions and grants "a perimeter of exclusivity in the zone of retail activity," a genuine Baguépi monopoly in the neighborhood.

Four stalks announce a veritable wedding, a "concept shop" in which the baker produces only Baguépi products and the mill furnishes the expertise — and financial assistance, if necessary — to set up the shop according to the model; it also provides communication tools to boost sales. With five stalks, the marriage is ritually consummated with the total concept, store plus baking room (usually a laboratory visible to clients located on the same level as the shop). About 10 percent of Baguépi's clients settle for a single, barely ripe stalk. Like Philippe Gosselin in Rue Saint-Honoré, a gifted baker honored for the best baguette in Paris in 1996, "they operate under their own names." Malézieux's goal was to have 15 percent of the member bakers reach the fourth and fifth levels, with an exclusive commitment and a model shop. All categories included, in early 2001 he could boast of 2,500 official Baguépi artisan clients, plus a great number of others who did not use the brand name.[39]

The "good Baguépi," a solid ordinary bread "with a golden crust and a yellow center," is not likely to make it into the breadmaking pantheon. Alongside this everyday loaf, the Baguépi baker might offer a broad range of specialty breads, available to artisans in the form of mixes ("preparations ready to use"), for example, rustic loaves (all sorts of "country" breads), rye breads, "health and vitality" breads (bran, whole wheat, wheat germ, and so on), and "enriched" breads (seven cereals, twelve cereals and grains, honey bread). Under the Lauriou label, Baguépi sells organic and stone-ground flour, allowing bakers to reinforce their offerings in terms of health and old-style taste and to appease certain anxieties with a so-called natural product.

The proof that Soufflet-Pantin believes in the marketing value of the appeal to anxious clients who are hygienically and culturally allergic to bad food lies in the way it frames and presents its new flagship product, the traditional Baguépi. Vaunting rational agriculture (a list of specifications ensures quality control from the purchase of seeds through harvest and several stages of storage and transformation to the blending of flours, with certification at every stage by experts from an independent agency), Soufflet-Pantin guarantees that the Baguépi Tradition is completely "traceable." The recipe is very similar to those used for other breads in the French tradition: a gentle kneading (but at low and medium speeds, preceded by autolysis); a long first fermentation in a trough or basin, with two punching down phases, a small dose of yeast (1 percent), and significant hydration (70 percent); hand shaping, which is advocated, or the use of a loosely set mechanical fashioner; and a hot oven with a refracting sole-plate. The use of refrigeration requires certain modifications. According to my taste tests, the "traditional" Baguépi is quite variable in quality; the two poles consist of a very unappealing baguette in the fourteenth arrondissement in Paris and a solid baguette with the beginning of a "nose" and a tasty center in the sixth; the latter has a pleasing appearance, but it lacks the "pointed ends" that are supposed to allow the consumer to recognize the product.

Christian Hubert, who is responsible for the quality of Baguépi's artisanal bakeries, also comes from Banette, where he worked for Alain

Storione in the mid-1980s on the team in charge of opening new shops. Perhaps inspired by "that little revolution" in the relations between miller and baker, this Breton got his master's degree at the Institut national de la boulangerie-pâtisserie in Rouen under the tutelage of Jean-Claude Mislanghe, one of the legendary instructors, before joining Soufflet as a test baker in Sens. Like Malézieux, Hubert notes a slow evolution in the bakery business toward the new (retro) culture of quality, with the same lag between Paris and the provinces (in his native Brittany, "insipid" bread always gets the most acclaim) and between those who believe that traditional bread will succeed and those who do not. Hubert reasons with recalcitrant bakers by arguing that bread in the French tradition will bring them in a larger market share without requiring more work, merely some modifications in the way their work is organized. But he recognizes that working by hand is often an annoyance to the artisans and that the cost of "personalization"—for example, work with sourdough—is often prohibitive. Studying a Baguépi brochure (titled "Mélior plus"), I note that, despite the return to old-style methods, Soufflet proposes ameliorants (euphemistically called regulators, an image or notion that is much in vogue) of all sorts, to facilitate the use of refrigeration or the direct method, or else as an "enhancer of taste and color," a formula that marketers will not be in a hurry to adopt. As Philippe Viron feared, there is even a "breadmaking agent for breads in the French tradition" that promises "decidedly improved volume and a lovely crumb," even though the bread decree's prohibition on "additives" is respected. In practical terms, Hubert remarks that fewer and fewer ameliorants are sold, not owing to artisanal purism, but because they turn out not to be very profitable.[40]

The complete sector calls itself "wheat-flour-bread." However, flour is increasingly dominant. Far from being a new phenomenon, this ascendancy is inscribed in a long history studded with lively tensions and acrimonious disputes between millers and bakers in the framework of a necessary, ongoing collaboration. Facing a spectacular, uninterrupted decline in the consumption of bread, the bakery business has proved incapable of reacting. The millers could not remain indifferent to this paralysis. It was at this moment, in this context, that Banette was born. It is widely acknowledged that Banette has changed everything, or almost. It has reorganized the network, structured relations with bakers, created new tools or adopted methods borrowed from elsewhere. Banette was audacious enough to promise and produce better bread, resuscitate and renew skills and knowledge (to practice retroinnovation, Lionel Poilâne would say), and to elaborate the practice of conveying information. The other millers followed suit, although not right away (about half of them were probably waiting to see Banette fail). Starting in the early 1990s, a large segment of the large and middle-size milling businesses went the Banette route, in one sense or another. In 2005, some estimates indicate that nearly four of every five artisanal bakers are enrolled in a brand organization or some analogous commercial association. It is worth noting, however, that at the time of the major institutional shake-ups evoked in this chapter, certain bakers took up the challenge of renewal on their own, carving out highly personalized paths.

chapter seven

Rue Monge Rivals and Other Mavericks

ROUND THE MID-1700S, A NUMBER OF BAKERS HAD set up shop between the Place Maubert — a sinister spot in the sixteenth century, irrigated by the blood of supposed heretics, though it later became the site of one of the sturdiest of the twelve official bread markets in Paris — and the Gobelins, where Colbert had established the "Manufacture royale des meubles et des tapisseries de la Couronne" on the banks of the Bièvre, a river that has since been covered over. These bakers were dispersed along both sides of what was to become a major artery around 1860 under Haussmann, called Rue Monge in honor of the great mathematician who was a friend of Turgot's and a Revolutionary minister. The Maubert market drew large crowds on Wednesdays and Saturdays starting around 6:00 A.M. The bakers were compelled by law to set the price of their bread slightly below the regular rate, because as itinerants in the region as well as master bakers in the city, they did not have to bear the costs of a shop on the Place Maubert. They were also under pressure to "bargain" with their clients before agreeing on a price, which was almost always paid in cash. Master bakers in shops might also have stalls in the Maubert market or any other; these bakers regularly sold on credit, made home deliveries, and were allowed to remain open seven days a week.[1]

The World of Rue Monge before 1800

Bakers who lived in the same neighborhoods frequently clashed. Master baker Jean-Baptiste Beaumont lodged several complaints about the itinerant Josse, a "foreigner" who encroached on Beaumont's territory by selling bread in the street in front of Beaumont's shop on the way to the Maubert market, and he even had the effrontery to deliver to nearby houses. The widow Lecoq, a master baker herself, did not get along well with her master baker neighbor Fiacre Maillard; Maillard's wife was constantly trying to attract Lecoq's clients. This was a serious transgression, for every baker viewed his or her clientele as private property. Mme Lecoq's son, a baker in Rue Mouffetard, avenged his mother by spreading "the most atrocious calumnies" against the Maillards throughout the neighborhood. Impugning their most precious possession, their honor, he called the husband a "rogue," "bankrupt," and a cuckold; he called Mme Maillard a "whore" and a "rotten ass." In the tavern at the sign of the Bear on Rue des Boulangers, which was patronized by merchant millers, François Élouard, who had his shop right next door, proclaimed loud and long that his neighbor and rival, Fromentin, failed to pay for his flour and was disloyal to his suppliers. But when a fire obliged Master Antoine Robert to abandon his damaged baking room on Rue de la Clef for several days, his neighbor, colleague, and rival, Félivien, let him bake a half-dozen batches a day.

Among bakers, relations oscillated between the poles of solidarity and rivalry. The need to defend common interests against external agencies (suppliers, the public, the police) brought them together. Similar personal and professional trajectories, organized around similar rhythms of work, leisure, and responsibility, wove a multitude of bonds. At the same time, the existence of these bonds and this intimacy gave rise to tensions, jealousies, and misunderstandings. In addition to feuding over reputation and clients, bakers quarreled about access to raw materials, hired help, financial obligations, and the application of unwritten rules and standards of behavior.[2]

For a young baker who wanted to set himself up in the jurisdiction of the capital, obtaining the title of master was the surest, most prestigious, and best known of all the paths to professional ascension. It required a considerable investment of money, time, discipline, and energy, except for sons of master bakers, who benefited from preferential status. The aspirant had to complete three years of apprenticeship (for which he was often charged a fee), followed by a probationary period called *compagnonnage* that lasted three to six years, and then he had to produce a masterwork that was judged by a jury, which often subjected the candidate to a complementary oral examination. Finally, he had to pay a number of admission fees; some of these were fixed and legitimate, while others were illegal but customary. The latter were generally negotiable, depending on the candidate's relations with the guild oligarchy, and they might be paid in the form of gifts or more or less elaborate meals. The status of master was a necessary but not sufficient condition for setting up one's own shop. The baker needed a baking room and its equipment, a shop, clients, and a favorable business environment. And then the beginner also needed ready cash or a fair amount of credit to acquire raw materials (this was long before millers undertook to "install" young bakers).[3]

In the eighteenth century, it was very rare for a new master baker to start from scratch. The best sites in the city had been taken for years, and consumer habits were well entrenched; the corporation discouraged new installations that might increase competition and in so doing threaten the prosperity of the older bakers. Instead of creating their own businesses, young master bakers preferred to buy a business from older ones who were retiring or leaving for another location (the latter practice was far less common than it is today, when changing sites is almost standard practice). These "successions" resulted in remarkable continuity in the way in which shops were set up and exploited.

To locate and acquire a prosperous business, good contacts in the profession were needed, along with a comfortable nest egg. Information was shared by word of mouth (even today, this means of communication is crucial) and through the intermediary of guild leaders. A handful of bakers, often retirees, took care of property transfers in a quasi-professional manner, although they had little in common with the specialized brokerage offices that have structured the market since the early twentieth century. In 1750, for example, a succession could be had for 350 or 400 pounds, less than the annual salary of a baker's boy who had just finished his apprenticeship. At this price, though, the buyer might easily find a business in ruins, entirely without fixed capital and without clients, or else a lethargic enterprise in an out-of-the way spot. A prosperous business could sell for more than 6,000 pounds; the average price in the eighteenth century seemed to oscillate between 1,600 and 1,900 pounds.

Normally, the price of a business covered two elements. First, the tools, equipment, and all other objects connected with the breadmaking business, except for the stocks of flour and grain, which were always dealt with separately. The average price for all this was probably less than 1,000 pounds. The second component was what was called the *pot-de-vin*, a term that means "bribe" today; in the eighteenth century, however, this part of the price represented the commercial value of the business, apart from the capital assets. This amount was supposed to compensate for the years of assiduous work on the part of the baker couple, their good reputation, and their sales record. Put another way, according to the standard definition used in contracts, the *pot-de-vin* was "the price of the clients" that the seller turned over to the buyer. Structurally, an eighteenth-century sale did not differ very much from today's arrangements, in which the baker sells his clientele and his premises, including all the equipment in the baking room and the shop. The buyer pays close attention to the proportion of clients who buy their bread on site (full shop) as compared with those, presumably less reliable, to whom bread is delivered. The current price varies between 60 percent and 110 percent of the annual sales figure; in 1995, that meant an average price of 1,253,000 francs ($251,425).[4] Today's buyer pays the larger share of the agent's commission; this kind of intermediation was uncommon in the eighteenth century. Part of the price might have been paid under the table, but this was rare, certainly much less frequent than it is today.

In exchange for the *pot-de-vin*, a seller in 1750 made two crucial promises to the buyer. With the first one, he turned over his clientele. Most contracts represented this transfer as a real "sale" even while explicitly stipulating that it was made "without guarantees." In other words, as soon as he had introduced the buyer and his clients to one another, the seller had acquitted his obligations. It was then up to "the said buyer to find satisfaction at his own risk and with his own resources." There was no formal "trial period" before the nineteenth century, but the serious buyer studied the business carefully before making an offer; he periodically showed up in the shop to assess the level of transactions, and he queried neighbors about the preferences and habits of the people who lived nearby. A handful of bakers kept accounts with enough rigor and clarity to allow the buyer to determine the monthly value of his supplies. Bakers today speak in terms of *quintals* — one-hundred-kilo units — of flour used per month; this is an important measure of a business's prosperity, and bakers produce certified balance sheets that give a general (though not always completely accurate) idea of the real health of the enterprise.

The second promise, also tied to the *pot-de-vin*, completed the first. The seller committed himself not to hold back or try to recuperate any of his clients. He solemnly renounced the right to set up another bakery shop for a period that could be as long as six to ten years (or "forever," as one contract stipulated) in the vicinity of his old shop. The prohibited area varied considerably from one contract to another; by and large, its extent was inversely proportional to the buyer's confidence in the seller. One contract set the boundaries vaguely at the "neighboring streets"; another, with respect to a shop in Rue Dauphine, forbade any installation in the parishes of Saint-André, Saint-Sulpice, and Saint-Germain-l'Auxerrois; a third, referring to a shop on the Place Maubert, excluded the parishes of Saint-Étienne-du-Mont, Saint-Séverin, Saint-Nicolas-du-Chardonnet, Saint-Yves, Saint-Benoît, "and other adjacent parishes." When Jean-Luc Poujauran shocked the bakery world in 2004 by selling his celebrated shop on Rue Jean-Nicot, he had to sign a draconian noncompetition agreement that prohibited him from baking under his own name in Paris for several years.

For the youngest master bakers, acquiring a shop was a terribly trying and costly undertaking. Except for a handful of spoiled offspring, the initial investment was heavy, and the first years of independence were chaotic, to say the least. Jean Galland evoked a situation common to a number of his colleagues when he recalled "the losses that are the inevitable consequence of starting out" as a shop-owning baker. Louis-Martin Meusnier must have had painful memories of his early years. He got his start without family support and without a financial cushion. He experienced heavy losses because he had "begun [his] profession without any advance" and had "committed himself to a state about which [he] knew nothing [yet]." Some penniless young bakers were lucky enough to receive advances from their families. Others had to take out loans that they had trouble reimbursing. To set up his business, Master Nicolas Éloy had to borrow 540 pounds from a manservant. Master René Morin had to borrow 1,000 pounds for his *maîtrise*, and then had to seek another 1,000 "to make a shop, Rue de la Lingerie, and pot de vin also paid." Nor was the problem of setting up a business merely financial; paying for it was just the beginning. The young baker then had to take advantage of the agreement that came with his purchase. He had to convince clients to buy their bread from him, a complicated matter that had to do both with the production facility and the business, and he had to be prepared to face what Meusnier called "the misfortunes of the times."

Once his business was up and running, the baker had to face up to two serious, ongoing issues: the quality and regularity of delivery of his supplies and the recruitment and retention of his help (two hundred years later, these problems have taken on different forms, but at bottom they remain more or less the same). To get supplies, eighteenth-century bakers had, paradoxically, more choices, more autonomy, and more responsibility than bakers have today. A baker could buy wheat from the major port markets or in the central market called Les Halles, or he could scour the countryside, looking in farms or markets beyond a certain distance from the capital. Once he had selected and acquired his own wheat, he had to transport it or have it transported to the mill of his choice, a mill powered by wind or water. The eighteenth-century miller was in a sense the baker's client, and not the other way around. On the slow road to commercialization, the milling business itself was extremely fragmented and just as artisanal as the breadmaking business. But a certain number of millers turned themselves into flour merchants or merchant millers. They bought grain on speculation so they could make flour in anticipation of the demand. The baker wanted to simplify his life; if he wanted to trust his miller (not always easy to do), he could buy directly from this sort of merchant, who delivered to the baking room, or he could turn to an intermediary, a broker known as a *facteur* (as it happened, more often a *factrice*) based in Les Halles. Since he almost always needed credit, the baker tried to establish relationships of trust with a certain number of suppliers, so that he would never be left without what he needed. The play of reciprocity and (partial) fidelity between baker and supplier resulted from complex and continuous negotiations and ritualizations. In the delicate, tortuous pyramid of credit that went from the producer of wheat to the consumer of bread, passing through numerous intermediary stages, the baker "held" his creditor as much as the latter had power over him.[5]

Every master baker in the eighteenth century dreamed of training the

perfect apprentice or hiring the ideal journeyman (mentally alert, physically strong and agile, morally submissive, tireless, and not too ambitious)
and of keeping him in his baking room for life. In practice, training was
very uneven, staff turnover was relatively high, frictions between masters
and workers were chronic, and open insubordination was fairly common.
The master had all sorts of ploys at his disposal to attract and keep a good
journeyman, including advances, bonuses, or a salary level above what the
guild deemed correct. To keep a good worker from leaving, the master
sometimes behaved like a tyrant, refusing the certificate of leave without
which the employee in theory could not find work in another shop, or
threatening to denounce the worker for a crime he had not committed.
While the guild claimed to hold a monopoly on placement, obliging all
journeymen to register in its headquarters and to accept the assignment
proposed by the clerk, journeymen tried to find their own positions, by
mutual agreement or through the intermediary of a "placer" employed by
a clandestine association of workers, a brotherhood, or a specialized inn.
The clerks were often capricious, and journeymen detested them. On the
afternoon of Monday, May 28, 1742, Estienne Berton, a master baker and
the first clerk of the community, entered a wine merchant's shop to have
a drink with a colleague. He quickly spotted a certain number of journeymen bakers in the garden. As he needed a "head boy," or *geindre*, for
another colleague, he approached their table. According to several wit-
nesses, the bakers' boys suddenly lit into him, pummeling him and beating
him with sticks so violently that they broke his skull. Berton died the next
morning. After that, some clerks never went out without pistols. For their
part, determined and individualistic masters — as "rebellious" in the eyes
of the guild as the mutinous journeyman — did not hesitate to lure journeymen away from their own colleagues, or to take in a journeyman on
the run without papers, or to buy him by reimbursing his debts.[6]

Rue Monge Today

At first glance, everything seems to have changed since the Old Regime,
except perhaps the impulse to buy bread, even if the search for bread is
no longer *the* crucial question of daily life. The opening up of Rue Monge
and the successive revolutions in individual and collective transportation
have profoundly restructured everyday habits and exchanges. The bread

market that had served as an anchor on Place Maubert has disappeared. The neighborhood has been modernized.

The breadmaking business, too, has been transformed, but the invisible thread that binds it to its past remains unbroken. The search for the best location still has priority today, but it is easier to set up shop, and businesses change hands more rapidly than in the past. There is no longer a corporation to impose a costly *maîtrise* and a discipline that was often flouted, but we find more institutionalized mediators — commercial mills and banks, for example — that help bakers get their start. Obtaining supplies is no longer subject to the sometimes nerve-shattering uncertainties of the eighteenth century, but bakers must still have their wits about them when they negotiate with millers, all the more so because the global balance of power has shifted massively in favor of suppliers. The demand for workers rarely puts bakers in a given neighborhood in direct competition, but the availability of workers and the quality of their training remains a concern for everyone. Finally, in comparison with the often violent jealousies of their ancestors, relations among bakers today are essentially pacific and sometimes cooperative (they may coordinate closings and vacation periods), even if they are rarely warm.

In the early 1990s, on this modern Rue Monge, six or seven well-established bakeries were unevenly distributed along what is a major artery. The zones from which they drew their clients were not very well defined: there were shops almost opposite one another in two spots (street addresses 28/31 and 66/69). No one bakery dominated, either by reputation or coverage of the territory. The neighborhood was not particularly well known for its bread. In 1996, the arrival on the scene of a new young baker, Éric Kayser, abruptly woke up the community of bread producers and consumers and jarred them out of their somnolent tranquility. At the north end of the street, at number 8, just a short distance from Place Maubert, Kayser bought a business and opened his first bakery, after totally remodeling the shop in the retroinnovation style, to borrow Lionel Poilâne's formula. He offered an array of breads that had never been seen in the neighborhood and perhaps not anywhere in the country. The bread was delicious. The press raved. Kayser's shop drew crowds, people from the neighborhood and consumers from all over. As if one seismic shock did not suffice to reinvigorate the area, three years later, at the south end of the street (number 123), right at the intersection with the Avenue des Gobelins,

another young baker famous for his creativity arrived: Dominique Saibron. Theatrical and exceptionally welcoming, like Kayser's shop, this
new bakery attracted customers above all for the exceptional quality of its
breads.

From one day to the next, Rue Monge became the premiere street in
the capital for buying bread, but it also became a sort of OK Corral, if not
a battlefield. War inevitably broke out between Kayser and Saibron, although the protagonists both deny that there was any confrontation. The
Monge war was a struggle between giants: at stake were pride, virtuosity,
reputation, and sometimes nerves. It was a war of religion—that is, of
contradictory conceptual, technological, and aesthetic truths. In this war,
the principal weapons were aromas and flavors; it was a war in which both
the direct strikes and the collateral damages made bread eaters very happy.

To explain and illustrate this struggle that was decidedly salutary for
the profession and for the public, but not without personal costs, I shall
focus more intently on the two bakers' passions, their talents, and their
respective research than on the sociology and psychology of their trajectories. Still, it is important to note that these are two very different men with
very different temperaments and highly dissimilar itineraries, although
they have some common traits as well. Kayser belongs to a family that has
carried the breadmaking banner for five generations, and there are millers
among his ancestors; he started off with a very substantial cultural and
professional capital, even though he took his career in his own hands virtually from the start. He learned the trade following the most aristocratic—
and exigent—path. He also took risks that he could have avoided. And although he is an inheritor, he quickly showed that he is first and foremost a
creator. Dominique Saibron started with nothing, and he was an outsider
(thus doubly removed from the baking room, for his working-class family
had nothing to do with bread; he got his start by making pastry). He recycled himself as a breadmaker virtually on his own, outside of the canonical structures. He has shown an immense gift for breadmaking, a trade
that he continues to enrich. Both of these men are fiercely hard workers.
While Kayser is more sure of himself, and more cosmopolitan, Saibron,
obsessed by the need to make up for a late start, is probably more of a per-
fectionist. Both are remarkable teachers: Kayser has powerful charisma;
Saibron embodies calm strength. They share an acute sense of organization and order, and each seamlessly blends the entrepreneurial spirit with

the artisanal outlook. They both project a rather Jospinian air: "austere types having a good time."

The Maison Kayser

Born in 1964 in Haute-Saône into a dynasty of bakers, Éric Kayser knew from an early age that he did not want to leave the baking room, which already fascinated him.[7] Starting at age six, he would accompany his father to the bakery at 4:00 in the morning. After his family had moved south to Fréjus, he did his apprenticeship there, in a classic setting that confirmed the outlines of his vocation: an old oven, sourdough, a paddle for handling the loaves. He learned a lot, but the work was very hard, 16 hours a day, and the country boy was not used to city ways ("I got wised up"). With his CAP in hand, he did his military service and then (in 1984) moved to Paris, where he signed on as a worker in a baking room in Créteil. Soon after, he replied to an advertisement that offered something like the program Rousseau sketched out for Émile, an apprenticeship to life as well as to a trade. In the great tradition of artisanal youth, which goes back to the Middle Ages in some locales, Kayser plunged into a bakers' Tour de France, joining the work fraternity called the Compagnons du Devoir, "Journeymen of the Duty."

Until the middle third of the nineteenth century, *compagnonnages* were illegal secret associations, countercorporations, as it were, that provided workers with weapons to resist their masters' tyranny and paternalism and that schooled them in a highly ritualized ethic and mystique of solidarity, virtue, and good conduct (as the fraternities defined it), the independence and dignity of the worker, and pride in the trade. As heirs of antagonistic lineages (each one proposed its own version of the genesis of the movement), several *compagnonnages* fought over the territory; their members struggled violently for control over placement in cities or for symbolic domination. Jacques-Louis Ménétra, journeyman and son of a master glazier in the eighteenth century, relates their odyssey of technical refinement and politico-cultural affirmation, their fraternal rites and their acts of mutual assistance, their sexual exploits and their huge bloody brawls. Prisoners of their own institutions and their ideology, the compagnons had difficulty adapting to the new social, political, and economic needs of the nineteenth century. A number of *compagnonnages* still exist today; each cultivates its own identity, but they are mainly devoted to the formation of an artisanal and moral elite.[8]

Attracted by the Compagnons' ideal of fraternity and rigor and by their quest for excellence, Kayser spent more than four years crisscrossing metropolitan France, learning new and old methods, becoming acquainted with all the regional specialties, attentively observing all the gestures of practitioners in the field, maturing. He found the travel itself stimulating. He adored moving from place to place with everything he needed in his backpack. He was thrilled by the discipline, sociability, and mutual respect that he found in community life. He has tender memories of the old journeymen who welcomed him in one city after another.

As soon as he had his *brevet de maîtrise* (which he earned as an independent candidate in Nîmes), Kayser began to take an interest in the way the elite that he had just joined reproduced itself; this has been one of the leitmotifs of his career. The Compagnons asked him to come up with a new plan for training. Then, to put himself to the test, he became a trainer, first for the Compagnons, and later, on a part-time basis, with the National Bread and Pastry Institute (Institut national de la boulangerie-pâtisserie, INBP) in Rouen, the pinnacle of teaching in the trade. Then, taking up the pilgrim's staff on a full-time basis for the institute, he served for seven years as an itinerant trainer, again crisscrossing France, reconnecting with the regional practices that he had known during his journeyman years, and subsequently discovering the larger world. From Mexico to Dubai, from Stockholm to Toronto, in Africa and in China, in Lebanon during the war, he shared his skills and knowledge with artisanal and industrial bakers alike. His travels confirmed his sense of identity and the traditions in which it was anchored, but at the same time the experience helped him overcome certain ethnocentric reflexes and added to his store of mental and technical tools. He discovered unknown flour types and he became familiar with a wide variety of breadmaking methods. "I travel to learn for myself, as much as to train others," he has acknowledged.

At INBP, Kayser's teaching experience "nourished [his] head, mind, and hands"; he was constantly grappling with reality. Even as he was offering immediate solutions to his students in order to prepare them to do their jobs, Kayser had the distance and the pedagogical cast of mind that allowed him to undertake a critical analysis of French breadmaking, its historical itinerary, its current state, and its prospects for the future. His conclusions were harsh: He observed "a degradation," "a decadence" in the profession. In the race toward productivity, the breadmaking business had lost not only its mastery of certain techniques and rigorous execution, but also the pride of the independent, skilled artisan. Poorly trained and badly counseled, bakers languished in a sort of anomie, turning in desperation to millers, equipment salesmen, and purveyors of "improving" additives in the hope of finding a way out.

Kneading too long and too quickly, adding more and more yeast (which had become a relatively inexpensive product) in order to skip the first fermentation (*pointage*), bakers began to produce bread in which they could not ultimately take pride, bread that did nothing to restore the image of the artisanate, which had been destabilized by devastating competition. Refrigeration, a socially beneficial innovation, could also have contributed to a renaissance in quality, but many bakers used it inappropriately, stopping the proofing process at 0° c (32° f) and then abruptly raising the temperature to 25° c (77° f); the thermal shock inevitably damaged the bread. If "conservative fear on the part of the bakers who take no risks" was responsible for the decline of the profession in the first place, Kayser did not hesitate to point an accusing finger at the colonizing millers in particular; he saw them as vicious and greedy dei ex machina who helped bakers and at the same time made them "prisoners," "prevented them from thinking" by reducing them to the status of aid recipients.

This diagnosis required radical therapy; the profession would have to be "reinvented." Éric Kayser contributed significantly to the effort, first as a teacher, later by setting up an advising office and by starting his own shop. With his friend Patrick Castagna, another charismatic INBP teacher and crusader for innovation in the profession, he created the "Fermento-levain," a liquid leaven machine, in the early 1990s. In the past, the test of the baker's art was his ability to work with sourdough. This fermenting agent was also recognized as one of the greatest sources of organoleptic bounty in bread. Yet for the most part it had virtually disappeared, the two teachers believed, because the practitioners no longer wanted or were no longer able to master the complex, delicate, arduous process. Since bakers were no longer going to keep their sourdough under the bed and refresh it three or four times a day, Kayser and Castagna noted, why not turn to a machine that would be able to keep it indefinitely, with little oversight? After two years of experience and adjustment, the Fermento-levain was born, probably inspired by larger-scale German machines. It was introduced at the big Europain exhibit in 1994, and it was manufactured and sold by Électrolux (later taken over by Pavailler). Encouraged by winning the prize for innovation and by the positive response of users, the two inventors continued to proselytize for the machine, which found its place in many baking rooms throughout France (at a rate of three to four hundred sales per year).

With Castagna's collaboration, Kayser expanded the activities of his consulting business—felicitously named Panis Victor—both in France and abroad. But to bring about the real triumph of bread, the teacher had to act. Kayser says he had always dreamed of opening a bakery one day in New York, Tokyo, or Paris. For a long time, though, he felt he was not ready. The idea of being confined in a single baking room after fourteen years of constant travel was troubling. He learned one day from one of the giants in industrial baking—this artisan has all kinds of friends—that a bakery on Rue Monge was for sale. Although he did not really know Paris very well, his wife, a biologist who had gotten her degrees from a university located nearby (Paris VI, Jussieu), convinced him that the site was a good one.

Completely remodeled, the shop confirms the new trend toward reality bakeries: not all of the baking room is visible, but a refracting soleplate oven is set up near the entrance, just behind the counters, and the spectator consumer can see (and smell) the final stages of breadmaking, when the loaves are put in the oven and taken out. Symbolically, Kayser the elite baker confers a democratic right to observe on his consumers, promising them that he remains accountable for everything that is produced before their eyes. The shop is decorated in dark red brick and blond wood; the air is permeated by intoxicating aromas of warm bread; the whole space is bathed in soft light. The shop has become a sort of wide-open agora where clients can examine many varieties of bread displayed on shelves behind a glass pastry case featuring in particular a wide choice of tarts. The staff, which can be the weak link even in good bakeries, is well informed about the products (they know what sourdough is, here!), courteous, and efficient.

Bread constituted 50 percent of the bakery's sales in 2002; it accounted for 33,000 kilos of wheat per month, an impressive quantity. The Monge site produced between 3,000 and 4,000 baguettes a day. The flagship product is Monge bread, embodied not only in baguettes, where crustiness takes precedence, but also in *gâches*, *bâtards* (these are stockier than baguettes, with a more prominent crumb), large 1.2-kilo loaves, and small 50-gram rolls destined mainly for restaurants. The procedure for making Monge dough begins with a four-minute low-speed kneading of a flour and water mixture, which is then left to rest (this phase is called autolysis) for half an hour. Next, for each kilo of flour, the baker adds 22 grams of salt, 150 grams of liquid sourdough, a small dose (4 grams) of yeast, and 700 grams of water (depending on the liquidity of the sourdough, hydration may reach 74 percent). The spiral kneading machine goes back to work for four or five minutes at medium speed. Then comes the bulk *pointage*, in the kneading trough or in a basin, lasting a good hour. After the dough is divided by machine, the *pâtons* are left to relax for thirty minutes in order to regain strength and tolerance. They are then weighed, preshaped by machine, and finished by hand, with the pointed ends that signal the artisanal touch. They undergo slow proofing at 8° c (46.4° f) for eight to twenty hours in rolling refrigerated chambers that can hold up to 3,200 baguettes. Finally, they are baked for twenty-three minutes on the refracting brick hearth of a gas oven.

Each step—the product of thorough research, tested over and over—is in a sense primordial, or in any event indispensable for the success of the work plan. But Éric Kayser stresses the role of his Fermento-levain machine as catalyst and midwife, the cradle of aromas and flavors that in his view could be obtained in no other way. Into this machine that never stops, the baker puts t 65 flour, stone-ground and extracted at 80 percent, more or less; he adds water and sometimes a little honey to reinforce the perfume, or some rye if the sourdough is tired, or perhaps some malt syrup. By adjusting the temperature and periodically refreshing the mixture with additions of flour and water, one can enrich and maintain the fermentation. Kayser argues that fermentation triggered and nourished by liquid sourdough is much easier to control than fermentation started by a solid sourdough leaven; it keeps better and is easy to stock; even more importantly, it is "more regular" and makes it possible to work with softer doughs in order to obtain "bread of constant quality that is well alveolated."

Monge bread is delectable in all its forms; each loaf is well structured. The baguette highlights the toastiness of a crisp crust that is gloriously allied with a powerful sensation of country freshness given off by the crumb; the latter is not overly dense and is shot through with numerous unequal cavities. The pulpy flesh of the *bâtard* probably serves better to bring out the complex aromas of the crumb, which are hard to differentiate. One might well speak of a Monge "bouquet." In the mouth, one tastes a touch of butter, which triggers a symbiotic play of chiaroscuro with the toastiness of the crust. Sometimes the flavor seems to include a touch of hazelnut. The other breads in Kayser's palette are original in conception or elegant in their realization or both. Paline bread is a bold creation made of blended wheat flour and buckwheat flour (the latter is not very widely known and is inscribed in collective memory as a cereal associated with food shortages). This bread offers a somewhat rustic taste, with a hint of dried apricots and almonds. The *tourte*, made with hearty stone-ground flours irrigated with wheat germ, is a full-bodied bread that is surprisingly light. Kayser's rye bread, containing 90 percent rye flour, is without harshness, acetic or otherwise; on the contrary, it opens up onto a sweet array of spices punctuated by a hint of roasted chestnuts. For essentially logistical reasons, the organic breads are all currently made with solid sourdough, a process that Kayser has severely criticized but has nevertheless mastered; among these, the semi-whole-grain loaf is particularly pleasing, with large cavities giving off an ethereal sensation.

Born "next to the flour sacks," Éric Kayser does not neglect the stage that precedes breadmaking proper: the selection and mixing of flours. He works in close collaboration with his miller, Yvan Foricher, who has his own roots in the wheat-flour-bread sector and shares Kayser's passion. Here, however, the miller is the baker's client. Kayser's list of specifications spells out his requirements: the right wheat will give a solid balance of strength, structure, and organoleptic values (Camp Rémy wheat, prized by several of the great bakers in part because of the lovely yellowish cream color it imparts to bread, is one of his choices), and he rejects additives or adjuvants such as fava flour or ascorbic acid.

Owing to his experience as a teacher, Kayser is better positioned than most bakers to understand the problems of training and recruiting a workforce. He is concerned as much about motivation as about technical prowess. He is ready to entrust important responsibilities to dynamic young people; at one point, his head baker was only twenty-two years old. He looks for staff who "want to work hard." Alongside intelligence, the ultimate safeguard, he looks for a certain impertinence: he wants a worker baker who will speak up, challenge him, "rebel." Convinced that routines can be deadly, he leaves his workers some leeway. He does not expect them to follow established procedure to the letter every time. They have to be able to compensate or improvise, in relation to atmospheric or climatic conditions, the state of the flour, and so on.

Given Kayser's career path and the unquestionable quality of his breads, his resounding success on Rue Monge came as no surprise. But he could not stop there. Three years after opening his shop at number 8, he opened a second outlet at number 14, consolidating his conquest of the neighborhood. The new shop, an old bakery dating back to the nineteenth century, feels more like a salon than an agora, as the ordinary décor of yesteryear has acquired a cachet of elegance corresponding to contemporary nostalgia: large mirrors, doors with beveled mirrors, a ceiling with stucco motifs, and antique *boulangerie-pâtisserie* signs. Kayser set up his organic headquarters here, in the service of the theme that combines nature and health — flourishing values at a time of mounting unease about safety, at table as well as in the street. One of the most charming dimensions of the famous French paradox is that, alongside products that include breads once stigmatized as poor man's bread and today transformed into bourgeois-bohemian dietetic specialties (whole- and semi-whole-grain bread, bread made of mixed wheat and rye, chestnut bread) and alongside the health delicatessen department, we have the realm of *la France gourmande*, an array of the great regional pastries.

From here, Kayser has gone on to shake up the landscape in other neighborhoods where good bread was not necessarily easy to find. He has bakeries all over Paris: in the sixth, thirteenth, fifteenth, and sixteenth arrondissements. Several years ago he opened a shop on Boulevard Malesherbes with a concept reminiscent of Francis Holder's Paul paradigm, a bakery within a large café and restaurant space. A smaller, more Italianate version can now be found near the Odéon. With the most illustrious artist entrepreneur on the planet, Alain Ducasse, Kayser opened a "BE" on the Boulevard de Courcelles. With its existential consonance, the name translates a project that goes far beyond boulangerie plus épicerie: it is more like Fauchon reinvented and rejuvenated, an upscale New York-style delicatessen. In Paris on Rue Didot and also in Toulouse there are bakeries bearing the Kayser name but held by independent artisans; these are linked to the Maison Kayser by a type of franchising arrangement that is a likely model for future expansions. At the same time, Kayser is setting out to conquer the world. He runs shops in Tokyo, owned in association with Japanese entrepreneurs, and is expanding elsewhere in Japan. With other partners, Kayser opened a shop in Los Angeles in fall 2005, the beginning of what promises to be a very long American campaign.

This highly diversified development corresponds to Kayser's analysis of the future of the profession. First, it is necessary to rationalize both purchases and production. The necessary and possible economies of scale, according to this young entrepreneur, are out of reach for most artisans. Second, apart from economic constraints, bakers are seriously deficient in the will to innovate. They have difficulty doing anything but "sticking to what they know." The French bread that is made in Japan today, for example, goes back to the Calvel method, a pioneering one in its day — which was more than thirty years ago. According to the principles of the eminent professor himself, Kayser believes, "we have to go beyond Calvel," in France and abroad alike. Today "the profession remains to be created." The vertiginous changes in technology (bakers have to enter the information age) and lifestyles have to be reconciled with certain great traditions that the French — and their most thoughtful bakers — hold dear. Kayser dreams of a great research center that would bring together the entire wheat-flour-bread sector and also the equipment manufacturers, one that would be financed by the interested parties themselves rather than by the no-longer-nurturing state, in order to achieve a collective reevaluation of all aspects of the trade.

Third, training has to be reformed. Kayser's recommendations converge in large measure with the "radical" propositions of Guy Boulet, an ex-vice-president of the confederation (to which Kayser belongs "for reasons of solidarity" but surely not out of ideological allegiance). While striving to transform the public image of the trade that ought to be celebrated as "noble," Kayser imagines a vigorous campaign in the schools and among young people that would go beyond the usual boundaries.

Dominique Saibron, Boulanger de Monge

While Éric Kayser was born to the trade and inexorably invested with a vocation, Dominique Saibron, born in 1961, is a complete outsider.[9] He is the son of a worker in the boilermaking business in the Paris region;

nothing in his environment destined him to carve out a path toward the baking room. And yet cooking intrigued him from childhood on. He prepared meals for his parents, improvising or refining recipes, already seeking to create or intensify flavors and to understand how products work together and are transformed. He left school at age sixteen and was hired as a kitchen helper in a clinic. There he learned the difference between family-scale cooking and the economy of collective catering with its technical and managerial imperatives, the obligation to reconcile the general (a necessarily limited menu) and the particular (individual needs and tastes), and the discipline of constraining rhythms. Even more determining for his future, however, was his discovery of pastry; his chef's passion quickly became his own. With backing from his brother, Saibron bought a Kenwood dough mixer on credit; he was thus able to experiment at home, where he began to make brioches and then tarts and other more elaborate products.

Seeking wider horizons, he made frequent pilgrimages on his Mobylette from Blanc-Mesnil to the great Lenôtre pastry shops in Auteuil and on the Avenue Victor-Hugo. As a window-shopper, he studied forms and colors, guessed at ingredients, and stockpiled his imagination with a spellbinding array of tastes and aromas. The young man was as serious as he was passionate; there was a logic to his fascination. He bought one of the books of the master pastry chef Lenôtre, "the one with the orange cover": it became his "bible," a guide both practical and liturgical, a source of documentation and inspiration alike. He also paid visits to Mora, a big kitchen supply store where he fantasized about his ideal kitchen and bought a metal rolling pin so he could make *pâtes feuilletées* at home.

Saibron seemed inexorably headed toward a career in pastry. He was already interested in what he calls qualitative products, which require the finest raw materials and great care in preparation. He worked in top-of-the-line patisseries in Corsica and in Val d'Isère. Later, he went into the "gastronomic" restaurant business. He was part of the team that opened Divellec (which went on to earn two Michelin macaroons); he next worked for a year at Marius and Janette, Avenue Georges-V, before following his boss to his new restaurant, La Saffronnée, as head pastry chef. Increasingly recognized for his virtuosity, he came close to getting hired as the number two pastry chef at Fauchon, the *nec plus ultra* in luxury foodstuffs.

For some time, however, and especially during his two years at La Saffronnée, Saibron had turned his hand to breadmaking. The idea seemed perfectly natural: he experimented day after day in order to master all the stages of the process. As it happens, on the question of the relations between the bread and pastry trades—which very often join forces in the same shops throughout France—there are two schools: the purist segregationists, who insist that the two have nothing in common, and the hybridizing integrationists, who extol the kinship in gestures if not in sensibility. Some of the best bakers today are defectors from the pastry side, while others attribute the erosion in skill levels in the trade to the invasion of pastry chefs. In any event, Saibron yielded to this new passion, which was at the same time a challenge, for his entire training to this very day consists in a weeklong internship in the shop of Gaston Lenôtre, his boyhood hero; Lenôtre had given legitimacy to the shift by infiltrating (and conquering) the breadmaking business himself.

But Saibron is above all a self-educated and demanding enthusiast. He wants to learn everything, and he masters the basics very quickly; he has a ravenous curiosity, singularly acute powers of observation, and an enormous capacity for hard work. If the first phase of his improvised apprenticeship was marked by humility and imitation, the second phase hinged on his acute critical sense. A method mastered is a method ripe for revision, rethinking, improvement. Like Éric Kayser, Dominique Saibron is a born researcher. Optimistic and constructive by temperament, he is nevertheless perpetually unsatisfied. There is always a better way to do things; one just has to find it. Without bravado, he calls everything back into question practically every day, starting with the solutions he himself had come up with the day before. Even before opening his first shop, he had thought through the entire trade. What remained to be seen was what he could achieve concretely with his own—exceptionally skilled—hands.

In 1988, the place where he had been working changed ownership, and he decided to give himself a bit of time. He was thinking about setting up his own shop, as a pastry chef or baker (the balance between the two arts still has not been settled in his mind), but he could not afford to buy an existing business, so he sought a less costly option. He was already leaning toward a "creation" rather than a buyout. Walking around the fourteenth arrondissement one day, he discovered a space for rent on the Place Brancusi, a newly created square in a neighborhood undergoing full-scale renovation (next to the shop, on one side, there was already Gérard Allemandou's great fish restaurant, La Cagouille, and on the other side there was soon to be a tearoom and a sales outlet for the other Poilâne, Lionel's brother Max, also an illustrious baker). Saibron quickly signed a lease; with financial support from his ex-employer at La Saffronnée, he opened his boulangerie-pâtisserie, in which bread imperceptibly became the most important product, even though the baker continued to be passionate about pastry as well. He met with resounding success, a long line of clients at all hours, and flattering press coverage.

He was already beginning to experiment with a little organic bread and with a sourdough bread made from stone-ground flour. He made his ordinary baguette with a poolish containing 2 percent yeast, the standard recipe, with a moderate kneading of fifteen minutes at medium speed; in retrospect, this now seems to him too lengthy. But his flagship product was called a baguette *sur pâte*, made with a small amount of yeast and a long *pointage*. Dense, with a robust crumb and a crisp crust, the color of an autumn landscape, this bread already betrayed the feverish quest for aromas that was to mark this novice breadmaker's career. Because they are made with no additives, these baguettes can lay claim to the denomination "bread in the French tradition" before the fact. In 1990, Gault and Millau (authors of a well-known restaurant guide) ranked Saibron among the best bakers in Paris, and the following year they nominated him along with a handful of great bakers, including Lenôtre and Max Poilâne, for an international breadmaking competition.[10]

After seven years, he decided to leave, taking advantage of the appreciation of his business to get out of debt, with the intention of acquiring a new shop. He passed the baton to Paul L'Hermine, an experienced baker to whom we shall return. The very day of the sale, Gabriel Binetti, one of his clients and a director of the Carrefour discount chain (responsible for fresh food products, including bread), offered him a job. The idea, as one might imagine, did not appeal to him at the outset. After all, Saibron was first and foremost an artisan; his business had been on a quite modest scale, and like everyone in the trade he was highly suspicious of—if not actually repelled by—mass market ventures. After lengthy discussions with Carrefour's management, however, Saibron became convinced that they were serious in their intention to improve their breadmaking procedures throughout the chain, with a genuine commitment to quality. Reassured and tempted by the idea of acquiring a whole range of knowledge and skills that were necessarily out of reach for an artisan, he agreed to the venture. Just as, for Clausewitz, war was a way of pursuing politics by other means, for Saibron accepting a job with Carrefour was a way of pursuing artisanal baking by other means. These means would give him the opportunity to do research and experiments that he could never have imagined doing alone in a baking room attached to a shop.

As we saw in chapter 4, Saibron changed virtually everything. He introduced a new line of breads, including a baguette in the French tradition, and he improved the organic loaf. He drew up new specifications for all his suppliers. He had the company buy new equipment compatible with his techniques that privileged quality. Convinced that human capital took precedence over everything else ("it's the man who makes for quality," he repeats tirelessly), he instituted a system of internal training and continuing assessment. He undertook hundreds of trials, working with sourdough and yeast, with organic products and ordinary ones, with various methods of deferred and direct fermentation, with manual and mechanical techniques, and so on. Working with large volumes and repeating his experiments over and over, Saibron was able to study the way dough reacted to variations in temperature, hydration, fermentation, and mechanical and manual manipulation, in much more depth than he could ever have done in his own baking room, caught up in the daily grind. He wrote down all his procedures in detail in order to standardize practices, insisting on the need to measure and weigh scrupulously, to pay special attention to the temperature of the dough, to watch over sourdough, and to write everything down at every stage in the process. Thanks to his initiatives, many Carrefour products are better than those made by most artisans.[11]

After reorganizing and relaunching Carrefour's bread and pastry production, Saibron was ready to leave. An artisan to the depths of his soul, he preferred to regain his independence, become his own boss again, and set himself up as a freelance consultant. He finally left in mid-1999, but not entirely. Carrefour sought to keep him, rather the way master artisans in the eighteenth century did everything they could to prevent their best journeymen from leaving and setting themselves up on their own. Even as he opened up his own shop, this time at the end of Rue Monge, Saibron continued to be a consultant for Carrefour, both in France and abroad, especially in Switzerland and Turkey, until February 2002. In the consulting realm, moreover, new opportunities have opened up.

Dominique Saibron found his second shop the way he found his first: by chance. This time, he could consider buying an existing business, which increased his chances of finding a good site, the primordial criterion for any installation. A miller, hoping Saibron would become a faithful client, alerted him one day that a shop magnificently situated at the intersection of Rue Monge and Avenue des Gobelins was going to become available, but that it was crucial to act quickly, before the business went on the market. Saibron immediately signed the sales agreement in July 1999. Taking possession in early October, he gutted the premises in order to create a shop in harmony with his own ideas; he received his first clients in late November.

The space is wide open, with no break between the shop itself and the baking room. Virtually the entire breadmaking operation is on display, not only the culminating work around the oven (whose hearth is made not of refracting bricks but of stone from the Vosges mountains, a substance Saibron believed to be more favorable to the "explosion" of the *pâtons* and their proper baking). Customers can watch the kneading, part of the division and shaping, and they can of course see the loaves being put into the oven and taken out. Two or three bakers are kept busy most of the day around this baking room theater. The shop area is not centered around a panoptic cash register protecting loaves held more or less hostage and out of reach. Instead, Saibron opted for grander volume and more breathing space (he learned this, too, from Carrefour), completely open shelving— within the legal limits—that invites clients to examine the whole array of breads without any barrier, from the entrance all the way to the exit. Two or three salespersons intervene discreetly along the way. Decorated in black-and-white wooden bricks, an idea that came to Saibron during a trip to Indonesia, the shop is warm, an extension of the baking room, reminiscent of early fall, harvest time, and rural roots.

Calm, discreet, and modest by nature, Saibron has an intransigent side where raw materials are concerned. Having come relatively late to the breadmaking business, learning along the way, he has never used additives (or adjuvants or ameliorants or technological auxiliaries) in his baking because he understood right away on one hand that he did not need them and on the other that they were detrimental to flavor. (Let us not forget that today's legislation allows bakers to put up to fourteen additives or adjuvants in their bread!) Saibron is legendary among millers for his violent hostility not merely to fava flour and vitamin c, but even to fungal amylase, an enzyme frequently added to enhance fermentation but responsible, Saibron believes, for degrading taste. On another divisive issue, he also takes an unequivocal stance: he is convinced that organic wheat, especially stone-ground, bears organoleptic fruit, a postulate contested by a panoply of agronomists, millers, and bakers. Half of his total production is organic, and he injects a dose of his organic wheat into his baguette.

Saibron attaches great importance to raw materials, but their purity and transparency constitute only part of his bakery's "signature." Without his procedures and his dexterity, even the best, most immaculate flour would not guarantee the production of good bread. The baguette of the Boulanger de Monge, by definition a bread in the French tradition, is a pure marvel. The crust, fine but crispy, is beautifully gilded and without defects. The crumb is equal to and in perfect harmony with the crust. Pearly in color, the crumb is denser than in most other good baguettes, with a texture that is at once silky and resistant, round and fluffy in the mouth. The alveolage is well articulated, discreetly rather than blatantly irregular. The crust's aromas of toast and caramel go perfectly with the whiff of country freshness emanating from the crumb. The taste lingers in the mouth, revealing several layers, with touches of crushed cereal, dried fruits, and winter vegetables with edible roots. A brilliant creation, Saibron's baguette is made up of nine parts flour extracted at 75 percent or a bit more, and one part organic flour extracted at about 85 percent. It benefits from an ultrahybrid fermentation (neither simply poolish nor liquid sourdough): a mix of organic flour, water, and a little yeast is blended a few minutes in a mixer and placed in a container kept at 10° c (50° F) for twelve hours; the next day it is mixed with water, salt, solid (homemade) sourdough, and flour. All this is kneaded with a dash of additional yeast, very gently, for about ten minutes at low speed. Then there is a two-hour-long bulk *pointage*; after division, the *pâtons* spend another hour or so in a resting tray. Preshaped in a machine specially designed not to squeeze them too tightly, the *pâtons* are finished by hand, with extremely pointed ends to prove it. These baguettes can also be made by the deferred method. After a shorter kneading around 5 P.M. and a *pointage* lasting two and a half hours, they are sent to rest in a refrigerated chamber, held at about 4° c (39° F) through the night. The next day they are divided and shaped without rewarming.

Saibron's offerings include at least twenty other breads. Among those of which he is proudest is his 100 percent sourdough organic loaf. It is a sublime bread, a veritable geyser of subtle floral aromas against a background of subdued honey and oriental spices. The sourdough comes from a *levain chef* Saibron created in 2000 and totally reinvented at the end of 2004: flour and water completed by a bit of honey, in the first version; the second is seasoned with cinnamon, cloves, anise, and licorice. He refreshes the *chef* every day for use with flour extracted at 85 percent and kneaded for barely five minutes at low speed, an exemplary emblem of the revenge of "slow food" over the frenzied "fast." Master of the "hard" sourdough matrix, Saibron contests Kayser's preference for liquid leaven; he accuses the liquid form of generating a sour aftertaste on occasion and of rendering the crust flaccid.

The Clash

Rue Monge runs for nearly a mile, between the Place Maubert and the Avenue des Gobelins; it harbors numerous bakeries. Still, Dominique Saibron's arrival could not leave Éric Kayser indifferent. Kayser had rapidly become the best baker in the neighborhood, and he had the feeling that Saibron had come to poach on his territory. No one else would have bothered him, especially because the two bakeries are so far apart (roughly the distance between four métro stops) that the eighteenth-century threat of stealing the neighborhood clientele did not apply. But Saibron was a great baker like himself, and the great take up more space than the others; their aura shines brighter and farther. Sure of himself, Kayser did not fear Saibron, but he was as irritated by the latter's presence in the vicinity as if Saibron had set up shop across the street.

In fact, despite the major differences in their origins and trajectories, the two men were alike in their quest for excellence, their cult of quality, their temperament as researchers, their interest in the world beyond their own shops, and their thirst for recognition. The architect that Kayser engaged for his Rue Monge bakery was the same one who had designed Saibron's shop on Place Brancusi and who would remodel Saibron's new place on Rue Monge. What is more, the two artisans knew each other, and their contacts had led to some more or less acknowledged tensions. They met several times when Carrefour was considering the purchase of the machine Kayser had developed, the Fermento-levain, for use in each of its baking rooms. In the last analysis, Saibron judged that Carrefour's bakers would have trouble controlling the acidity of the dough, and the company did not adopt the system of liquid sourdough. This did not prevent the two great artisans at one point from contemplating the possibility of working together to produce organic bread.

The last straw was probably the name Saibron appropriated for his shop ("Le Boulanger de Monge") and for his leading baguette ("la baguette du Boulanger de Monge"). This was an innocent choice made with no intent to provoke or harm anyone, according to Saibron; his rival perceived it as a gesture of symbolic violence. Kayser's argument is simple: he was on Rue Monge before Saibron, and his own baguette had been called "the Monge" from the beginning. Even if Saibron is not legally violating his industrial and intellectual property, Kayser considers that his competitor is transgressing an unwritten code of conduct among colleagues, more or less in the style of the old eighteenth-century corporation. Insisting on his respect for Kayser's talent and his business, Saibron declares that he has done nothing wrong. When he took over the shop on Rue Monge, he wanted to call it simply "Le Boulanger" (The Baker). After researching prior uses of this term as a brand and company name, he discovered that it had already been registered in Marseille. He then fell back, in extremis, on the formula "Le Boulanger de Monge," which had not previously been registered. After that—all's fair in love and war—Kayser prevented his miller from supplying Saibron. For the rest of us, what counts is that the Monge baguette and the baguette du Boulanger de Monge are undoubtedly the two best baguettes not just on Rue Monge but in all of Paris.

For economic, social, cultural, and even political reasons, good bread is coming back. The phenomenon is far from universal. We have to be wary of any triumphalism, even though it seems clear to me that the profession has crossed a sort of emblematic Rubicon. It will take time, but good bread will drive out the bad. Beyond increasing awareness on the part of many artisans, marketing on the part of the major mills, exhortations from the associations, and legislative measures, consumers are becoming increasingly sensitized, in the face of a growing range of choices, and they are the ones who will make the difference. Even if they are sure to be satisfied there, lovers of good bread do not have to go to Rue Monge. Throughout

Paris and throughout France there are good bakers who take their trade very seriously, who reject the trivialization of bread, and who stand out clearly from the competition, artisanal and mass-market alike. Let us not forget the cluster of bakers of rare talent who did not wait for the acute phase of the crisis and the last-minute rebirth to make bread of exceptional quality. The unchallenged head of the group, completely sui generis in the profession, was Lionel Poilâne; I can also mention Jean-Luc Poujauran, Bernard Ganachaud, and Basil Kamir, all great bakers who need no introduction here. In the remaining pages, I propose to tell the stories of several bakers who are for the time being less famous, most of them young, all rising stars in the profession.

Thierry Rabineau

The owner of four shops on the Right Bank in Paris, the principal figure in a consulting office, and a pragmatic dreamer who imagines a new bakery landscape in France, Thierry Rabineau is cut from the same cloth as the Mongistes.[12] A karting champion, he is a dynamic sort who likes to take risks and welcomes the challenge to surpass himself more than to outdo others. Born in Mayenne to a family with no bakery connections, he has nevertheless been fascinated by flour since childhood. He made pastry at home, and every Wednesday when there was no school he made bread with a friend whose father had a bakery. Many — too many — young people look for bakery jobs because they are not doing well in school. Rabineau was not a good student, either, but he had a real vocation for the baker's trade: he got his CAP first, then his *maîtrise*, in two years at the INBP. He held a series of jobs, including a year with Francis Holder, whom he admires enormously for the artisanal quality of his bread production, although he wonders how his empire, caught up in a spiral of costly investments, can hold up financially. But the decisive phase in his itinerary came under the enthusiastic and demanding tutelage of Basil Kamir, a pioneer in organic bread who has set up his Moulin de la Vierge in four Paris shops. "Bread is not merely a business," his mentor warned him, "it is an obsession" — a creative pathology that he transmitted to his young disciple.[13] Kamir indoctrinated Rabineau in his approach to breadmaking and made him his right-hand man.

Enriched on the technical, managerial, and human levels by this experience, Rabineau set up his own shop on Rue de Turenne in 1994, also "by chance." In six years, his sales multiplied sixfold. He launched a second shop in 1996 on Avenue Parmentier, doubling his profits in two years. Soon afterward he started a third enterprise, in a lovely shop with old-style décor, ornamental moldings in the form of a frieze, and ceramic tiles. Recently, he opened yet another shop in Montmartre. Drawing half of his receipts from bread, Rabineau makes two doughs to support a simple range of breads with attractive variations. For what he calls white bread, though it actually has a somewhat creamy color, the mark of beauty these days in the breadmaking business, he uses little yeast, kneads for ten minutes at medium speed, with thirty minutes of autolysis, and then gives the dough a bulk *pointage* for an hour and a half. After division and shaping, the *pâtons* go into slow proofing at 10° c (50° f). Rabineau's "country" dough undergoes almost three hours of *pointage* (with a punching down that interrupts the process in order to incorporate air into the dough and give it renewed strength). Made with yeast, it is hydrated at 80 percent, a fairly spectacular level, and it is shaped by hand to emphasize its rustic character. These breads are all out of the ordinary. Of noble appearance in the country squire style, armed with a nicely caramelized and crispy crust, the country baguette has a fairly dense crumb, resisting a certain trend toward anorexia. Soft and tender, hinting of the farm but without any bitterness, the crumb, long-lasting in the mouth, finds the perfect complement to its full-bodied aromas in the slightly sweet flavor of the crust.

Thierry Rabineau is a man who says what he thinks, and he judges the profession he loves rather harshly. The general level of the trade is "catastrophic." Most bakers, "navel-gazers," think they are "the best"; they make no effort whatsoever to "call themselves into question." This is why they have kept on making a bread Rabineau calls "steak with hormones" for so long: swollen, bleached, and tasteless. On one hand, "they don't hesitate to cheat" by using excessive amounts of ameliorants and frozen products and on the other they seek scapegoats—especially among the mass marketers—for the erosion of their profits. But Rabineau excuses them to some extent. If they are not able to break free of their reassuring inertia and their consoling routines, it is in part because they are marked by the original sin of the breadmaking business, the terribly traumatizing memory of their entry into the trade: "You're worthless, go work in a bakery." They never manage to fully transcend this inaugural negativity.

While the trade requires a certain thoughtfulness and a willingness to take new data into account and adapt to them, according to Rabineau it is basically "very simple." Certain technical gestures have to be mastered, but "there's nothing mysterious" about it. Bakers have to be motivated and clear-sighted; after that, all they need are "good eyes" and a "good feel" for bread. With that practical intelligence and an even slightly analytical mind, one can do good work. The golden rule is to know how to spot an error and then never to make it again.

Thierry Rabineau savages the good as well as the mediocre members of his profession. Kayser is skewered for his "brutality" (his unchained ambition) and Saibron for his "extremism" (his flour mania). For Banette and company, he reserves contempt: they created vassal-bakers unable to deal with the craft on their own. Rabineau no longer takes apprentices; like many of his colleagues, he is deeply disappointed in their moral temperament and technical competence. He begins training the workers he recruits by "unteaching" them virtually everything they had learned before. He dreams of launching capable young practitioners in a franchising system and of founding baking schools, in particular abroad, where the demand for good bread is burgeoning.

Hervé Malineau

It seems easy to move from Thierry Rabineau to Hervé Malineau, both mavericks in the breadmaking business. Their names even rhyme. They are both based in the Marais district of Paris, they both admire Jean-Luc Poujauran, they both recognize the qualities of Francis Holder, and they both make among the best breads in Paris. But their resemblance stops here. Hervé Malineau's career path is extremely atypical in the world of artisans.[14] He got a master's in biology, then a DEA (a third-cycle degree preparatory for a doctorate) in nutrition with the idea of working in agribusiness. Answering an ad in 1974, he got a job with Jacquet, a big industrial breadmaker, and stayed eighteen years. He started out as a production engineer on the assembly line, later became a team director and then head of the *biscotte* (toasted bread) division. After serving as associate director of the Blanc-Mesnil factory (not far from Saibron's family home), he was appointed to head a research laboratory. He undertook in-depth studies of the microbiology of breadmaking, especially the fermentation of leavening agents. He was intrigued by one of the great mysteries of the bread business, the relation between bacterial cultures and the production of taste. He was particularly interested in the development and maintenance of taste in deep-frozen dough, which could not take advantage of a rest period. While the results of this type of research are widely applied today, Malineau recalls with regret that in his day management neglected them, seeing the laboratory only as a sign of prestige. When he later proposed a system of quality control, he ran into the same lack of comprehension; where he was concerned with positive results, his superiors thought only in terms of image and marketing.

Although he left Jacquet in frustration, even in anger, especially at a superior whom he found intolerable, Hervé Malineau defends the industrial approach, which is too often belittled and dismissed by the artisanal lobby. Overall, Jacquet made products of good quality, with appropriate and sometimes imaginative techniques. Whether or not it really counts as a bread, the Jacquet Hamburger "bread" was a good product, according to the ex-employee.

Wanting to be his own boss, Malineau left Jacquet in 1992 and set himself up as a consultant, thanks in part to the connections he had made during his industrial years. In Greece, Italy, Holland, and elsewhere, he worked on quality control, but also on the manufacturing of products such as brioches and various breads. Never far from biochemistry, he continued to reflect on the breadmaking process and was not content simply with a good result on the shelves: "If my bakers make good baguettes, I try to understand why." Since consulting work is fundamentally precarious, and since Malineau was attracted by the challenging of managing a business, he decided to buy a bakery with a friend who had just left the Holder Group, a great seedbed of artisanal creativity provided that one leaves it behind.

Malineau's religion is flavor, which can only be achieved by good fermentation. In particular, this means giving the dough time, the only strategy for optimal development of the taste of wheat. His procedure for his beacon product, *pain Paulette*, is simple, nonetheless: clean flour, with no additives (when I spoke to him, he swore by the Viron mill, where the Rétrodor concept was developed), only a small amount of yeast, gentle kneading that does not oxidize the dough, and an astonishingly protracted *pointage* lasting twelve hours. The baker's rejection of deferred fermentation — a far more convenient method — is not grounded in any philosophical aversion to mechanization; Malineau simply found that his Paulette did not perform well in cold gestation, thus the need to keep the baking room going twenty-four hours a day. A great sourdough specialist, Malineau nevertheless decided against using it widely, given consumer dissatisfaction with the touch of acidity it imparts to bread. To get the walnut taste he was seeking, he thinks he has found a good method. At Saint-Paul, he goes through 30,000 kilos of flour a month, making nine batches a day. He employs six ("rather mature") bakers who are willing to work at night as well as during the day. (For the entrepreneur in the bakery business, social progress is not measured by the prohibition of night work, the burning social question in the trade for more than a century and a half, but by the — so-called — freedom of the worker to choose his working hours.)

Bread accounts for 50 percent of Malineau's profits, with 75 percent ensured by the Paulette loaf. Offering unequaled voluptuousness, it is one of the best baguettes in Paris. Classic in appearance, it has a crisp, well-gilded crust, with cheerful, even exuberant slashes. Once the loaf is broken or cut open, its aromatic genius emerges. Its crumb, fleshy and alveolated with irregular and often quite large cavities, explodes with flavor. There is a whiff of fresh air against a floral background, with a suggestion of dried fruit. Overly dusted, the country baguette is not crisp enough. Its crumb has a dense texture and a slightly darkish cream color. Its flesh is tasty. The round sourdough loaf is pleasant in the mouth, without acidity. Well structured and astonishingly aerated given its density, its crumb does not generate well-articulated aromas, but they make a pleasing impression; its taste is generous and engaging.

Frédéric Lalos

Born in Normandy in 1970, with no family connections to the breadmaking business, Frédéric Lalos was seemingly destined to earn his baccalaureate degree with a concentration in science.[15] Without any immediate stimulation in his environment, he was nevertheless drawn to breadmaking. Instead of finishing the equivalent of eleventh grade, he went to a private breadmaking school in Caen and got his CAP in 1990. His professor, a Meilleur Ouvrier de France (MOF), transmitted the passion for excellence in his work that still seems to be the *primum mobilum* of his existence. He easily mastered the theoretical dimension of the training; as for the practical aspect, where the measure of success is harder to specify in objective terms, he worked tirelessly, spending even his days off in the baking room. Then he spent three years working for Lenôtre, whose shop was another seedbed for young talent; there he was influenced by another baker who would soon join the MOF ranks.

After a year of military service in Paris as a pastry chef at Matignon (the official residence of the French prime minister—"where I learned to weigh," Lalos explains), he wanted to develop his skills in a new arena; he was hired by the research division of the Grands Moulins de Paris (GMP), where he spent two years doing hundreds of experiments for his employer and thousands for himself. In this propitious atmosphere he was steeped in the idea that it was crucial to know flour. ("How many bakers know what their millers are sending them?") By seeing, touching, and smelling flour every day, he learned the properties of flour completed by various additives—fava flour, ascorbic acid, and so on. He observed their impact on dough and experimented with dozens of varieties of wheat.

This young man was both curious and competitive. He understood that knowledge was power; by learning, he sought to conquer. During all his vacations and free time, Lalos studied for the competitive MOF examination. Created in 1969, the title Meilleur Ouvrier de France en boulangerie has been awarded to some sixty bakers, of whom ten were still active in 2002. The competition takes place only three times a decade. It includes an oral examination before a jury half of whose members are MOF award winners and half professors; this is followed by twelve hours of practical tests the next day. Lalos passed all the preliminaries on the first try and made it to the end. At age 26, he became the youngest MOF in France: "the greatest joy of [his] life." Then he went back to Lenôtre, serving this time as head of production overseeing a team of some twenty workers.

At the GMP, Lalos had met Pierre-Marie Gagneux, who was ten years older, a graduate of a business school in Lyon who had worked in export and then abroad, before joining the GMP as head of sales, and then of sales and marketing. He had been wanting to be his own boss for some time. Lalos too was dreaming of starting his own business one day. By combining their complementary skills, they put together a strike force that was rare in the profession. The artisan brought a prestige and a virtuosity that allowed them to compete with the major players from the outset.

The salesman, intimately familiar with the milling business and with the world of the bakers whom he had courted and supplied for years, came not only with a wealth of management competence, a sphere in which few bakers are particularly gifted, but also with long experience in marketing, a sphere in which most bakers are completely incompetent. Having decided to go into artisanal breadmaking together, Lalos and Gagneux first opened a shop in Levallois-Perret, then another brand new one on Rue Saint-Charles, in the fifteenth arrondissement in Paris. Lalos confesses that he felt "the second most memorable shiver" of his life on May 1, 2001, when forty people lined up for the opening of their new business.

Decorated in light-colored wood, the luminous shop was baptized the "Quartier du pain" to mark it as a site of convivial gathering and to emphasize that bread bestows identity upon a neighborhood and thus weaves the social fabric that binds people together. The gap between producer and consumer is diminished, symbolically and pragmatically, by the open baking room that showcases the work process. Lalos and Gagneux seek an even closer proximity with their clients by means of their policy of transparency and traceability of raw materials, guaranteed by an Auvergne-based network called "de la Graine au Pain" (From the Grain to the Loaf); the network itself is vetted for its ecological and hygienic rigor by an independent, state-licensed agency.

Lalos makes two particularly sumptuous breads, a baguette in the French tradition and an old-style loaf (à l'ancienne). The first is made with poolish, with only a small amount of yeast, left to develop for twelve hours; this encourages a lactic fermentation. The dough for the traditional bread benefits from twelve hours of bulk *pointage* at 8–12 ° C (46.4–53.6 ° F). The process for making the old-style loaf is less constraining: it is based on pre-fermented dough, ideally separated out the evening before and developed for twelve hours, favoring an acetic fermentation.

Both breads are lovely to look at. Slightly dusted with flour, with large, sturdy slashes that are inscribed rather than sculpted, the old-style bread has a more bucolic air than the other. It is surely one of those breads that sings coming out of the oven, its music produced by the cracks formed as the bread cools. Inscribed in the crust, they create an image that evokes the volcanic earth of Limagne. The texture of the crumb is quite elastic, with highly irregular alveoli. Autumnal aromas emanate from the crumb, which lingers very long in the mouth. The taste is pleasantly acidic, opening onto a palette of secondary flavors that recall a thick vegetable soup. It is an interesting taste, one that speaks to the taster; it enters into a dialogue with the taste buds. The overall flavor is refined, George Dandin transformed into Philinte.

The bread in the French tradition is undoubtedly better looking, according to the classic criteria. Its golden crust is thin but crisp. When chewed, this bread has resistance, yet it is tender; the crumb, silky and aerated, is nevertheless round. This bread has flesh. It asserts its personality in the mouth, betraying a hint of hazelnut as proof of its charisma. Its aromas announce spring, giving a foretaste of the harvest. It is a bouquet of flowers from the meadows, punctuated by a slight citrus presence, the odor of Sicilian orange trees before the fruit is picked. The flavor is intense, complex, and persistent. Nevertheless, at the end of the tasting, the quality that strikes the most in this out-of-the-ordinary bread is its harmony. It is deliciously balanced.

Frédéric Lalos manifests the contradictions that seem inherent in all gifted young people: he is sure of himself, and at the same time, quite sincerely, he asserts the almost hygienic necessity to "rethink what he is doing every morning." He undertakes his self-examinations by working with his fifteen bakers and pastrymakers to evaluate the results of every batch. To avoid stagnation, he continues to create: ten new products since the beginning of 2002 and as many since. With his accomplice Pierre-Marie Gagneux, he has opened a third bakery in the sixteenth arrondissement and a sandwich shop in the sixth. It is easy to imagine that this highly symbiotic team will join the increasingly crowded ranks of consultants.

Philippe Gosselin

In the 1740s, Louis Germain, son of Jean-Baptiste (a master baker in Rue Saint-Denis who was himself the son of a master baker from Caen), married Françoise Lapareillé, daughter, granddaughter, and sister of a many-branched clan of bakers in Paris proper, the Faubourg Saint-Antoine, and Gonesse. Thanks to the network of the two dynasties, the couple set up their business in a shop belonging to a maternal uncle who was ready to retire, just steps away from the bakery run today by Philippe Gosselin, at 125 Rue Saint-Honoré.[16] Of Norman origin himself, Gosselin is no less anchored in the professional tribe. He is a fourth-generation baker, and his wife is a baker's daughter. Endogamy has always been one of the most powerful instruments of artisanal reproduction and expansion.

"Bread comes naturally for me," Gosselin asserts, "dough is putty in my hands." In fact, although he served his apprenticeship with his father, he earned his CAP in pastry, yet another transplant from cakes and creams who has become an exceptional baker. It is like a mantra: all the ex-pastry chefs insist that they acquired a certain rigor from their background in pastry, in particular the habit of weighing everything meticulously. This is an oblique criticism of bakers, who are often more casual and prepared to settle for approximations. "Bakers have a tendency not to respect the recipe," Gosselin observes. This can lead to missteps and especially to a lack of consistency in quality. For Gosselin, the artisanal bakery has miraculously come back from the brink of total catastrophe, where it had been trapped by its own postwar success, shaken by consumer disaffection, destabilized by the terminals. Devoid of taste, bread had become "cotton." Gosselin has a precise recollection of a consciousness-raising moment in the early 1990s, in the face of the apocalypse: the miller Philippe Viron, "a grand figure," called for renewal, and "the loud voice" of Jean-Pierre Coffe rose up "against shit" in the name of all self-respecting French people who cared about their patrimony; the bread decree, a psychological turning point, and—an extremely interesting factor—some of his own clients convinced Gosselin that they wanted better quality and were prepared to pay for it.

It was around this time that Gosselin began to make his bread differently, getting a head start on the procedures for making the baguette in the French tradition. He kneads for twelve minutes at low speed, then lets the flour and water mixture rest in autolysis for up to two hours so the dough will be smooth ("This way the water gets along well with the flour," which is hydrated at 75 percent).[17] He adds salt and a moderate amount of yeast, then shifts to medium speed for four or five minutes. At the end of kneading, the dough snaps, he says: "The baker recognizes a good batch by ear." It is fascinating to observe that every artisan has his own way of evaluating the result of each stage in the process, but privileging one of the senses at each point: hearing and even smell come into play as well as touch and sight. Gosselin leaves the dough in the vat for half an hour, then weighs it and allows it to rise for up to three hours. He shapes by hand and bakes within an hour, in an oven heated to 240° C (464° F), when he uses the direct method. In comparison to Rétrodor, for example, the bread he is looking for has a less dominant crust and a less radically alveolated crumb; it should have "the consistency of a crepe."

In my view, his traditional bread is a real triumph. Its crust to crumb relationship is a complete success. The crust is attractive but quite discreet: its lightly inscribed slashes do not assert themselves aggressively. The crust stands like the prince consort behind the queen, the crumb, which is sensual; consumed warm, it might even seem a little licentious. Gently off-white in color, it is creamily voluptuous in texture, extremely pleasant and long in the mouth. Its aromas give the impression of being embodied in an unctuous taste crowned by a hint of walnut.

Maintaining a monthly rhythm of 4,200 kilos of flour transformed in 1990, Gosselin increased his production to 9,000 in 1995 and 16,000 in 2001, a considerable expansion. The notoriety he earned in 1996 when he won the contest for the best baguette in Paris gave him a boost. Consumption of his bread in the French tradition, the product of which he is proudest, continues to rise, although it has not yet eclipsed his ordinary baguette. A growing share of his profits comes from a delicatessen department that is expanding fast, with offerings that go well beyond sandwiches. For the entrepreneur, this is a good thing. But is it a good commitment for the artisanal baker? The debate goes on, but more and more colleagues are following in Gosselin's footsteps. Finally, Gosselin has just marked another success as an entrepreneur by taking over a second shop on Boulevard Saint-Germain. Few good bakers today are not considering expansion. Commercial ambition? Thirst for greater celebrity? Economies of scale? These are undoubtedly some of the factors in play.

Jean-Noël Julien: The Saint-Honoré
War Will Not Take Place

One does not decide lightly to set up shop on Rue Saint-Honoré if one is a baker. For St. Honoré, a baker himself before he became a prelate, is the patron saint of the profession. He replaced St. Peter in Chains, the first patron, whose feast day fell on what was traditionally considered the first day of the harvests. He also eclipsed the profession's second patron, St. Lazarus, who was believed to protect bakers from the leprosy to which their trade exposed them—or so they feared—owing to their constant contact with heat and fire. In the eighteenth century, Parisian bakers continued to belong to two brotherhoods, one devoted to St. Lazarus and the other to St. Honoré. But most of their religious activities took place in the church that housed the brotherhood of St. Lazarus, and this brotherhood also was in charge of activities of mutual aid. It organized funerals for members and their spouses, supplied the silver platter and the stove, and arranged later on for the celebration of commemorative masses. But the brotherhood of St. Honoré also looked after the living, distributing alms to old, indigent, or ailing masters, and exhorting all its members to live in peace, fraternally, in a professional milieu known for turbulence and riven with jealousies.[18] War was thus not supposed to break out between two bakers installed on Rue Saint-Honoré, under the sign of such a pacific patron.

Jean-Noël Julien's shop is just a stone's throw away from Philippe Gosselin's.[19] They are rivals; they compete "fairly and squarely" every day, but they remain friends; they see competition as a challenge rather than as a threat or an obstacle. Their differing approaches to breadmaking do not keep them from having country houses close together or from expressing both their friendship and their competitive spirit in the practice of karting, following the example of Thierry Rabineau.

Although less deeply rooted in the bakery business than his buddy Gosselin—but just as much a Norman!—Julien nevertheless began to spend time in his sister's bakery in Dieppe starting at 4:00 A.M. when he was only eight years old. Two of his brothers also became bakers, although one of them has left the trade because he is allergic to flour. The young Jean-Noël was not yet thirteen when he began a pre-apprenticeship in Trouville; he went from there to the Center for Apprenticeship Training in Caen, where he earned his CAP in two years, working three weeks straight and attending classes the fourth week. Later, he had to forget much of what he had learned as an adolescent, because he worked with a rotating rack oven, using "outrageous" amounts of yeast and all sorts of ameliorants. When he got out of the army (where he had been assigned to the kitchen and had learned to oversee stocks), he worked on two occasions in a puff pastry factory, leaving a job as head of manufacturing to become production head in the baking room of a store in the Leclerc chain in Lisieux, yet another opportunity to master the demands of management. There he made white bread in the conventional way: "It was at least as good as artisanal bread." This assessment explains the panic felt by many bakers confronted by the mighty mastodons that had marketing power and the ability to undercut prices.

With the help of one of his brothers, Julien set up shop in Paris in the twentieth arrondissement in 1985. He was married (still a condition sine qua non for most bakeries); he was only twenty-one, and the prospects of the capital excited him. He still made white bread ("slightly pearly"), but not very developed, with a gentler kneading at medium speed; like almost everyone at the time, he used additives, but he experimented with the organoleptic possibilities of fermentation based on poolish. In 1989, with a (commemoratively) revolutionary flair, he bought a shop on Rue Saint-Honoré "just like that," and he is still there. The site was good, but he completely rebuilt the shop ("it was all rotten"). In just a few years he went from transforming 10,000 kilos a month to 25,000, and from a staff of nine at the outset to thirty-two today. Although bread represents 40 percent of his proceeds and remains his passion (he has five bakers and two apprentices working with him), like Philippe Gosselin, he counts heavily on his line of sandwiches and delicatessen food (three chefs) and on pastries and sweets (five pastry chefs).

Full of projects and ideas, Julien is nevertheless a pragmatic man. The method is respected, with consistency as the goal: the reproduction of the optimal result as precisely as possible with each batch. Working entirely with the direct method, Julien uses a modest dose of yeast. He kneads only at low speed, he lets the dough proof for three hours, and he bakes in a hot oven (preferably gas-fired). He stresses, even before anyone asks, that he does not shape by hand. For two reasons: first, because hand shaping crushes the alveoli, those precious pockets of carbon dioxide, to excess; this is just the opposite of the argument made by other good bakers, who blame the machine for damaging the unbaked loaves, even when it is programmed not to press too hard. He says, too, that if all his bakers shaped dough in their own way, he would be sacrificing the consistency that is the cornerstone of his philosophy. When he is asked to what factor in particular he attributes the good quality of his bread, he vehemently refuses to privilege one phase over another. "Everything counts," he says again and again. He watches over everything vigilantly: the smallest breach in the system could completely compromise the outcome. Where Dominique

Saibron could be described as a deconstructionist breadmaker, Jean-Noël Julien remains a true structuralist. As early as 1990, his bread was practically in the French "traditional" mode that was formally consecrated in 1993. His own virtuosity was formally consecrated in 1995 when, a year before his neighbor Philippe Gosselin, he received the prize for the best baguette in Paris (he came in second in 1997). Today his baguette in the French tradition is his lead product; he hopes gradually to phase out the old white baguette. A baker has to respect his clients, but our laureate would like to persuade them to eat well-done bread, the only kind that offers the full range of its charms. Julien says that the only baker in Paris who dares impose well-done bread on his customers is René Saint-Ouen, a forceful talker who cannot be stopped on the subject of good bread and who has twice won the award for the best baguette in Paris.[20]

If the two masters on Rue Saint-Honoré get along so well, might this be because their breads, exceptional in both cases, are so different? Julien's baguette in the French tradition has a more masculine beauty: it is more athletic, seductive as much in its strength as in its flesh. Here the crust wins out. Well structured, even muscular, it has a deep and persistent crispness. The crust is not only there as an accompaniment; it plays a primordial role. Highly caramelized, it generates on its own a powerful flavor that blends a rich, sugary taste with a bouquet of buttery aromas. The crumb does not submit to the tyranny of the crust; it meets the challenge by displaying a proud alveolage, highly articulated but randomly distributed, quite irregular. It exhales great freshness marked by a touch of hazelnut that nourishes and caresses the crust. Crumb and crust are united, at least in the poetry of tasting, by a kind of exchange of aromas that biochemists can identify in a laboratory; in the mouth, they reach an unforgettable crescendo.

Julien is sanguine about the artisanal future, but in Darwinian terms: only the best adapted will survive. Apart from technical skills, he has in mind those who "know how to respect their personnel": those who can motivate and train apprentices attentively rather than demoralize them with drudge work; those capable of inculcating "team spirit" via staff discussions, logos on t-shirts worn by everyone, and so on; and those willing to pay decent wages to all the personnel, including saleswomen, who are habitually relegated to marginal status ("without good saleswomen, a good bread is worth nothing"). A mark of Julien's confidence: he recently inaugurated a superb open–baking-room shop just up the street from Poujauran's Mecca in the seventh arrondissement. (Julien may also be charmed or oracular: Poujauran sold his bakery not long afterward, abruptly putting an end to his legendary hegemony.)

Paul L'Hermine: Brittany-Paris-Brittany

The story of Paul L'Hermine recapitulates the classic itinerary of the ambitious young man from the provinces who goes up to Paris and achieves professional success several times over.[21] With one difference: at the height of his conquest, this Breton, born in Côtes-d'Armor, goes back to Brittany. "Drenched in flour" by his father, who worked in the milling industry, he was twelve when he began to help his brother-in-law, a baker in Saint-Brieuc who became his master during his apprenticeship. Working fifteen to sixteen hours a day, seven days a week, making deliveries to rural customers after he finished in the baking room, he learned the trade from the bottom up during the six years he spent there, earning his CAP in bread, pastry, and cooking along the way. His demanding brother-in-law taught him the old methods rather than the emerging "western" version of breadmaking. He worked on solid sourdough (but already with just one phase of "refreshment" with additional flour and water), he did a long bulk *pointage*, he shaped by hand, and he used a paddle mainly to put big long four-pound loaves in an old wood oven. The young man never produced "super-white, hyper-fluffy" bread.

During his military service, he returned to Saint-Brieuc on weekends to make bread. When he got out, he spent two seasons in various shops to perfect his skills; his tour of France was strictly local. But he learned that not everyone made bread the way his brother-in-law did: he discovered bakeries "that looked like pharmacies," relying on heavy doses of ascorbic acid and other ameliorants. L'Hermine's attachment to his home town was confirmed by his marriage to Chantal Lebellegard. The attraction of place was doubled by a precious professional endogamy, for Chantal was the daughter and sister of bakers, and she knew her way around the baking room as well as the shop. She became Paul's business associate as well as his life partner; he relied enormously on her at every stage of what was to become *their* career. Endowed with an effervescent personality and an acute business sense, she knew how to enliven and manage a shop like no other baker's wife I have ever seen at work. Having often made bread herself, she is capable of talking about it. Her explanations are simple but concrete; as she guides her clients, she also charms them. She is attentive and listens as much as she speaks. Everyone who chats with her for a moment at the cash register has the impression that he or she is her only client.

In 1969, the couple occupied their first bakery as managers (which usually means a payment of 7–10 percent of the proceeds to the owner) in Saint-Brieuc; they had just gotten married and Paul was twenty-three years old. After three years, having more than doubled their annual proceeds and having had a son, they left.

Ready to take on the challenge of the Paris region, they took over the management of two more bakeries, first in La Courneuve (1972–1974), and then in Grigny, in the southern suburbs (1974–1980). In the latter shop, L'Hermine developed a poolish leaven, kneaded less and less ("to avoid massacring the dough"), skimped on the first fermentation but compensated with an addition of fermented dough, and reached astronomical levels of production (25,000 kilos a month, with eight bakers working in shifts around the clock). In 1980 the L'Hermines bought their first shop, chosen for its location on Rue du Poteau in the eighteenth arrondissement. They stayed there seven years, going from 5,000 to 9,000 kilos a month. Their method was the same as in Grigny, but L'Hermine was struck by a change in "the mentality of the staff." The employees seemed less invested in the work; they displayed less pride in work well done. Was this a matter of Parisian cynicism or alienation? In any event, "the business had run its course," and the family was too far away; the L'Hermines packed their bags and went back to Brittany to test the waters once again in *la France profonde* (deep France). After two years at the head of a "great house," La Duchesse de Bretagne, a luxurious *salon de thé* in the fanciest street in Rennes, they acknowledged that "they had made a wrong turn" and headed back to Paris.

On the advice of their miller, they bought the shop that Dominique Saibron was leaving on the Place Brancusi in the fourteenth arrondissement. Making his own the mixed leaven-yeast baguette *sur pâte* developed by his predecessor, L'Hermine changed his way of working. He started adding 10 percent *brute de blé*, a stone-ground wheat flour, to the standard flour. He used very little yeast, adjusted the temperature of the dough, and kneaded only at low speed; his *pointage* was very long this time, last-ing up to seven or eight hours. From beginning to end, he needed ten to twelve hours to make a batch — more than twice as much as it used to take him. To manage this, he prepared two batches the night before, allowing the dough to rise slowly in a refrigerated chamber all night long at 4–5 ° c (39–41 ° f). The following morning, without reheating the dough, he di-vided and shaped it, and an hour later his baguettes *sur pâte* were ready, exploding with flavor. He doubled his consumption of flour, introduced an enhanced line of delicatessen products, and opened a terrace; the business was a big commercial success.

Paul L'Hermine made a nice profit on the sale of this shop and, after a pause, took over another celebrated business, Moisan's bakery in the thir-teenth arrondissement. He kept the organic line, and he introduced his baguette *sur pâte*, an immediate triumph. But with 26,000 kilos a month and seventeen employees to manage, having to be in the baking room or in the shop from 5:00 in the morning to 8:30 at night, open six days a week but baking seven out of seven, he was beginning to lose the pleasure that he had always felt in working. For Chantal the pace was horrendous. In mid-2000, they found serenity again in Brittany, this time for good, they say. They bought a lovely, spacious, modern shop, with an enormous baking room, in a blue-collar area in south Rennes, next to a parking lot with a lot of pedestrian traffic and near a new métro station. The rhythm was much more relaxed and the scale relatively modest: two bakers, one pas-try chef, and three saleswomen. But the habits of consumers in the pro-vincial capital have not evolved much; bread in the French tradition was barely known, and the white baguette remained the dominant product. L'Hermine radically improved the quality of this standard bread by inject-ing prefermented dough to enhance the taste, eliminating additives, and slowing the kneading.

He made his old-style baguette with the same mastery as in Paris, but he only sold 60 to 80 a day, which was at once a failure and a small victory. This bread, much denser than any other baguette on the market, has a mother-of-pearl crumb, generously alveolated but compact, covered with a well-structured crust. The bread compensates for its unimpressive ap-pearance with monumental flavor. Thanks to a fermentation that is both lactic and acetic, the crumb has a pronounced taste of hazelnut against a background of dried apricots, heightened by the sweetish aromas of the subtly caramelized crust.

For Paul L'Hermine, these rediscoveries were extremely satisfying on the familial level and healthy on the level of stress reduction. But professionally, he has been hurt, first by the regression in quality, and then by the cold reception he has gotten from his colleagues in the city. He was identified pejoratively as "the Parisian," even though he was surely more Breton than most of them. "This is a very sleepy place," I was told by an old baker in Rennes. Will the artisan be able to hold on in a region where large-scale industrial breadmaking continues to flourish?

Guy Boulet and Rural Franche-Comté

The story of Guy Boulet is at once the adventure of an exceptional man and the story of rural bakeries' resistance to "denaturing" if not disappearance.[22] To meet Guy Boulet is to understand that his rural roots, his ties to the land, to a physical and affective space, a place and values, are what make him who he is. If he is still "deeply a peasant," as he insists, he is also authentically a philosopher, even though this label would make him uncomfortable. He is at once simple and complex, a manual worker and an intellectual, a particularist and a universalist, artlessly straightforward and an acute strategist, grave and replete with humor. The son and grandson of bakers, he is a canonical old-school artisan and a hypermodern entrepreneur, a militant bakers' association member (including a brief flirtation with the neo-Poujadists), and president of the Departmental Bakery Federation of Jura. He has an advanced degree in social practices (through a program organized by the Université de Franche-Comté in Besançon); he founded a baker's cooperative, served as vice-president of the National Bakery Confederation and as president of the Association of Cooperatives in France. He is the only baker with whom I have maintained an international e-mail correspondence for years and the only one who has written a book containing not recipes for making bread and pastry but recipes for life.

"Born in Asnans in the family bakery in 1943," he writes, "as much an ideological matrix as a birthplace, my childhood was perfumed with the odors of the baking room, flour, and bread. The most powerful images that remain with me are those of the huge flames licking the floor and the vault of the oven, the lovely golden color of the bread, and the repetitive gestures of my father or his worker, all this in the warmth of a happy family life that was inseparable from professional life. Touching dough, pretending to shape it was still a game for me."[23] Inexorably attracted by the trade and by the way of life that it demanded and made possible, he did his apprenticeship with his father (1957–1959), a difficult period of social and cultural rupture: no more sports or leisure time. Then he worked for two years as chief assistant in various artisanal enterprises, enriching his know-how and imbibing the values "of this community of familial work . . . as the natural situation for [the baker's] activity."[24]

At the beginning of the period of heavy mechanization and productivism, he was already caught up in a dilemma that would obsess him all his life. On one hand, there was the vivid recent memory of his training, essentially manual, "playing with dough," weighing and shaping it, putting it into a wood-fired oven with a paddle. On the other hand, there was the new fondness for white bread, voluminous and promising, a psychological imperative for consumers in search of an everyday material embodiment of freedom after the bleak wartime years. "For me," he observed later on, "the 'pleasure of doing' corresponded to the quality of the work, which depended on the 'know-how,' all this being in contradiction with the obligation to produce that was imposed by the constraints of the market."[25] Rejecting factory life, which was the alternative for certain rural bakers seeking to earn a decent living with less difficulty, Boulet had to get himself a two-speed kneader, the emblem and announcement of the race to modernize. Married at twenty-one, set up in a shop where he shared the responsibilities with his young wife, he was very successful among his clientele with his white bread method (about which his elders said, "That's not bread you're making"). He quickly acquired a divider, a shaper, a resting tray, a controlled fermentation chamber, and a steam oven with a conveyor belt loading system.

Although Boulet sided with the future against the past, he was an anxious modern, an artisan more and more removed from his roots. He attributes this to the impact of the market, very visible under the circumstances, and to the even more manifest intervention of the state (the politics of price controls: "Controls settled the matter and obliged me to adopt the same policy as industry, productivity; all I had left to do was carry it out as carefully as possible"). But at bottom he knew he was choosing to go along, and he was riven by a feeling of guilt, even betrayal. As if to do penance, he earned his *brevet de maîtrise* in 1970; he redecorated his shop in Asnans; in 1977 he opened a new bakery in Chaussin, doubling his turnover (going from 5,000 to 10,000 kilos of flour transformed per month) in less than five years, "with the same equipment as in Asnans, but by pressing hard on productivity." However, things started to deteriorate with the opening of a local Cora hypermarket and a very active Banette shop. His profits sank noticeably in 1984.[26] All this aroused a crisis of consciousness, the return of the repressed: Boulet lay the blame on his shift to mechanized production in the late 1970s when business was going well. What had happened to "the pleasure of the work itself, that is, of a traditional, largely manual breadmaking, accompanied by a quest for all the technological progress that could serve it?" Boulet saw only one solution: a return, ideologically, to the "nuclear economic couple"—the baker and his wife—as the motor of the enterprise, and, methodologically, to slow kneading, long bulk *pointage*, manual division and shaping, giving primacy to quality at every stage.

This deep and personal self-questioning led to a bold proposition: that the Jura bakers get together "voluntarily" with a collective brand christened Monpain. Paying implicit homage to Banette, the idea was to do better than the model, from the bakers' standpoint. For the bakers themselves would be taking the initiative and thus preserving their collective independence; they and not the millers would be calling the shots. This way they would obtain flour of guaranteed quality—a product that Boulet insisted be as pure as possible, wheat flour without additives.[27] Since the absence of adjuvants determined the manufacturing technique (*pointage* was made obligatory, mechanization would be minimized to avoid damaging the gluten, and so on), the Monpain protocol would impose a return to the classic skills and knowledge, to a traditional method of breadmaking.

At first only twelve or thirteen bakers responded to Boulet's appeal (out of about a hundred brought together by the association), but they were enthusiastic and determined. They hired a trainer who went from one baking room to another to instruct, encourage, and correct. "Where we were expecting requests for help with sales," the somewhat astonished founder noted, "we found a demand for help with techniques." Building on a basic agreement about procedures, each baker was free to personalize his bread by deciding on his own fermentation method. Boulet worked with poolish, which gave him a lactic fermentation, a matrix for interesting tastes and aromas.

Rejecting the "deviations" and "disenchantment" of modernization and industrialization, Monpain represented a double commitment to quality: quality of work and quality of life, a strategy meant to serve both consumers and producers. For Boulet, Monpain was the triumph of what might be called baker humanism, stressing the primacy of human beings at every stage without sacrificing the needs of business. It was also a permanent festival of taste. On a modest scale, Monpain was a response to the specter of globalization (and the bad food — *malbouffe* — that came in its wake) that anguished so many French women and men, perhaps a more effective response than José Bové's ritualized destruction of the McDonald's in Millau in southern France.

At the same time, Monpain was an incessant struggle. The millers tried to sabotage it because they did not want to lose control of the market (a million kilos a year). Then there was "the strain of democracy": when membership swelled at one point to over sixty, Boulet lamented "the philosophical dilution that came with the increase in size." Nor were wheat and flour supply problems ever fully resolved. In the end, Boulet had to abandon his dream of creating a national brand. Becoming a sort of "club," the cooperative went through a period of uncertainty. Boulet believes "that new suggestions will come out of this," perhaps precisely because Monpain is less "fundamentalist" and more "open."

In November 1998, Boulet and his wife decided to sell their business. For various familial, political, and professional reasons, it was time to turn the page (his ex-bakery remains in the Monpain orbit and he continues to buy a "delicious" bread there). One of the pillars of the Monpain project is training. As vice president of the National Bakery Confederation, Boulet continued to be involved in this endeavor, aiming particularly at young people. He militated in this realm for what he calls "quality," for a more demanding and enriching training program, and for consideration of a national diploma. Accused of elitism (his zeal for the bread in the French tradition already worried some of his colleagues in leadership positions), he ran into resistance and achieved only part of his program. He gave up his national position in 2001.

Even if Guy Boulet has experienced some failures, few twentieth-century bakers have accomplished as much on the ground or have done as much to oblige their colleagues — at the summit as well as at the base — to reflect with a critical eye on the presuppositions and practices of their profession. Far from being burnt out, his passion for French bread ("a worldwide standard") and for a certain conception of his trade has induced him to develop training programs abroad, particularly in Poland; this will surely not be the last stage in his continuing campaign to "prioritize the human dimension."[28]

Conclusion

ODAY, THE FRENCH ARE BOUND TO BREAD BY PAS-cal's "cords of imagination," not by "cords of necessity." Far from being a staple food absolutely required for survival, bread has been reduced to an accompaniment. Still, thanks to the persistence of its symbolic charge, it is valued at more than its (true or false) weight. Even if consumers eat much less bread than in the past, they see themselves in bread, which continues to contribute to their identity as French people. In public opinion, bread remains deeply bound up with the basic values of sociability and well-being, with sacred and secular communion. A powerful metaphor, a transmitter of memory, a marker of transformation and continuity, tradition and transcendence, unity and multiplicity, nature and culture, bread seems to sum up human experience. For years on end, through their associations, artisanal bakers turned their backs on this symbolic bread that was used by the state to dictate their collective behavior and especially to impose prices. The artisans have come to understand fairly recently that this symbolic straitjacket could become a real commercial and cultural refuge, an effective weapon in their struggle to survive.

Thanks to technological and social progress, baking rooms are no longer "gloomy cells," and bakers' work no longer resembles "the last scene of a murder" or "nocturnal slavery." But breadmaking remains a particularly difficult profession. Bread is no longer a matter of life and death; still, paradoxically, the rhythms of production remain "hellish." Consumers have been liberated from total dependency on bread, but they are nevertheless making new demands, in a climate of increased competition. Breadmaking techniques have evolved; the insistence with which many contemporary artisans speak of *returning* to the practices of yesteryear points up a certain distancing from the traditional canon according to which fermentation is "the soul of fabrication." While bread remains a living thing for modern bakers who have to ensure its new birth every day, these professionals have found ways to boost its growth and bring it to maturity much faster than before.

Requiring multiple refreshments with flour and water and almost round-the-clock work, sourdough fermentation was the traditional, noble method for making bread. The intrinsically delicate working procedures made each batch dependent on the success of the previous one. In the face of these constraints, artisans increasingly abandoned sourdough in favor of the so-called direct method, in which a dose of industrial or baker's yeast replaced the wild fermenting agents of sourdough, and each batch was autonomous. Easier, faster, more "social" (less night work), more consistent in its results, breadmaking with yeast led bakers to devote less and less time to the first fermentation, the source of flavors and aromas, and to rely on various additives, especially ascorbic acid (vitamin c), which made their work easier by giving the dough better tenacity, resistance, and tolerance. On the organoleptic (sensory) level, the lengthening of the second fermentation (*apprêt*) did not compensate for the shortening of the first one. The replacement of sourdough by yeast caused less of a stir than the introduction of deferred fermentation with refrigeration, a method that is almost universally used today but that seemed at first to betray basic artisanal principles. Like the recipe itself, almost all the major stages of breadmaking have been modernized, in particular by mechanization: first kneading, quite belatedly, owing to widespread resistance — it took off at the time of World War I; then, more recently, division and weighing, shaping, and the process of moving loaves in and out of the oven.

White bread, always the most prized, embodied dreams of social ascension (and revenge) and concretized the gradual process of democratization; this came about rapidly in cities, much more slowly in rural areas. Although it was vigorously criticized, first by moralists, then by certain scientists, and later by part of the medical establishment, white bread for a very long time commanded the absolute loyalty of the vast majority of consumers (and continues to have great appeal even today). Practically and psychologically, World War II, associating dark bread with the loss of freedom, could only reinforce this deep attachment to whiteness. In the decade that followed the Liberation, a certain number of artisans from western France developed a way of making white bread whiter than ever, voluminous and beautiful—exactly what the public seemed to be demanding. Based on the practice of intensive and prolonged kneading, typically with wheat flour "enriched" by fava flour (an additive that had been in use for two centuries) and "corrected" and reinforced by ascorbic acid (a miracle pill created by twentieth-century biochemistry), the white bread method rapidly conquered most of the country; it was preferred by many millers, equipment manufacturers, yeast merchants, and suppliers of ameliorants. A profession that had often been criticized for its inertia (it had taken more than a century to mechanize kneading!) managed to bring about a monumental metamorphosis in less than ten years. The conversion was usually translated by a remodeling of the often quite dilapidated baking room; this change was encouraged by the associations, who saw it as much as a token of the profession's durability as a response to the burgeoning industrial competition. The transformation harmonized perfectly, in spirit and technology, with the productivist and consumerist modernization brought by the Thirty Glorious Years.

The picture quickly grew darker, however. In the increasingly mechanized baking rooms, quantity took precedence over quality, yield over the excellence of the product. The prospect of improved working conditions and a rise in productivity coupled with heightened demand could only be seductive. No one foresaw the erosion of skills and artisanal autonomy that the onset of mechanization threatened to bring about. The new two-speed kneading machines "wore out" the dough, whose overoxygenation and excessive whitening were intensified by the presence of fava flour and ascorbic acid. Superwhite and excessively fluffy, bread produced this way had either no taste or an unpleasant taste. To compensate for its insipidity, bakers would add even more salt; to facilitate its passage into the dividing and shaping machines, they would practically do away with *pointage* and would increase the amount of yeast (which allowed them to proceed even faster by shortening the *apprêt*). Although the experts were fairly well disposed toward this white bread at first, they turned against it during the 1960s, accusing it of "denaturing" French bread. However, as in the eighteenth century, there was a gap between the academic culture of the experts and the popular culture of those who worked in baking rooms every day. Heavily invested both materially and psychologically in the new system, the bakers in the field saw only the bright side of white bread. They could not believe that this modernization was just a matter of smoke and mirrors.

If the western tale of white bread had led to a lasting comeback in the rate of per-person consumption, there would have been a happy Hollywood ending to celebrate, for the drama of the bakery business in the twentieth century, the source of its slow but profound destabilization, was the uninterrupted decline in the number of bread eaters. Far from influencing the trend, the white-bread triumph only succeeded in congealing breadmaking in a model that led to the production and reproduction of mediocrity. At the very moment when the revolutionaries of the land of counterrevolution were preparing the revenge of white bread, scholars and experts of all sorts, under the aegis of the state and in response to pleading from the associations, were meeting in a commission set up by the National Center for Coordination of Studies and Research on Food and Nutrition (CNERNA). Charged with a dual mission that was necessarily somewhat contradictory, the commission was to conduct a rigorous scientific investigation whose results were unpredictable, *and* it was to reassure the 50,000 artisans and their world, along with the millions of consumers—a political, social, and moral imperative. Its conclusions did not disappoint the profession in the least. Published under the strategic title *La qualité du pain* (Bread Quality), they maintained that artisanal bakers and their associates in the wheat-flour-bread sector (farmers and millers), taking into account all the aspects of their modernization (including certain excesses), produced bread of very good quality, in no way inferior to the sacred bread of yesteryear. (CNERNA did not even hesitate to debunk sourdough; yeast was not only technologically and socially preferable, but it produced nutritionally superior and better-tasting bread!) What is more, yeast-based bread was perfectly healthy and even hygienically necessary to a balanced diet, and it was free from any chemical or other contamination, this in response to the negative judgments pronounced by large numbers of doctors, amplified by certain proto-ecologists, and deemed at least partly responsible for the decline in consumption. The rest—the bulk of the decline—betrayed nothing other than the forward march of history, according to CNERNA, the social and economic progress experienced by France and many other countries.

The double "whitewashing" of bread, by CNERNA (twice) and by the western bakers, had contrary effects. The profession lost on one hand what it gained on the other. The scientific establishment ruled the bakers innocent and reassured them, while the bakers' own troops plunged them back into gloom and doom. For fear of demoralizing its own members, the National Bakery Confederation was slow to articulate a (self-)critical discourse. Cautiously, confederation president Combe warned against excessive mechanization and pleaded in favor of the (rational) religion of respect for time in breadmaking. Admitting that the associations had underestimated the "quality factor," his successor, Jean Paquet, led the profession toward a (nonviolent) self-questioning with the goal of reconquering artisanal values. The call to arms took concrete form in the Estates General of the profession, a meeting that constituted an opportunity to mobilize not only the entire sector but also public opinion and the state. If the message to bakers was still ambiguous, thanks to the corporatist spirit (one cannot reject "progress wholesale," one cannot take on everything while sparing the unfair competition, profiting from state support, and so on), the confederation expressed its determination to take a serious inventory and even to break with the past. Beyond some interesting technological and ideological propositions (the confederation denounced the western method but refused to restore sourdough to its regal position), the profession developed two sociopolitical and cultural arguments, defending artisanal baking as a "public service" (an old refrain, but still sung with ambivalence by a profession jealous of its independence) and as an implicit choice on society's part (the rejection of mass production, the value of sociability on the village scale, the neighborhood bakery and the social bond).

The quality of the product could not lead to a rise in consumption unless it contributed directly to the customer's quality of life. By demonizing bread for half a century, the medical establishment had strongly aggravated the decline in "normal" consumption. During the annual Bichat medical meeting in 1990, it more or less officially lifted the ban by calling bread a complete, healthy, digestible food, and by formally discrediting the myth according to which bread is fattening. The bakery business today is ready to go on the offensive on the health front, exploiting consumer anxiety about food safety and healthfulness (mad cows, hormone-fed beef, genetically modified crops, the fast food menace, and so on), the imperative of a balanced, healthy diet (very low in lipids), and the idea of increased "nutritional density."

In what they are saying and to a certain extent in what they are doing, a number of bakers seeking renewal are turning to ancestral practices. According to that logic (which is not without its advantages for marketing), quality is not invented but restored. The so highly valued yesteryear is fixed in time and space on the one hand, atemporal and utopic on the other. For a long time, this affective or instrumental nostalgia exasperated association leaders, who rejected the idea that the Ancients necessarily had to triumph over the Moderns. The new line — already brilliantly sketched out in part by Lionel Poilâne — entailed a marriage between innovation and tradition. The launching of the new "bread in the French tradition" with a new/old recipe, made official by state decree in 1993, embodied this synthesis of past and future. Intended to be the flagship product of artisanal breadmaking, "traditional" bread got off to a very slow start, in part because of the constraints inherent in the fabrication process ("yesteryear" was, after all, more demanding), and in part because the confederation hesitated, fearing it would get too far ahead of its members (or destabilize them).

At bottom, however, the association leaders knew that the Rubicon had been crossed. Consumers, more "aware" and more discriminating, were not going to return if bread quality did not improve considerably. Moreover, breadmaking was no longer a neighborhood phenomenon. Marketing and the quest for pleasure led prospective clients to look for their bread beyond the nearest street corner, perhaps even in the big supermarkets, where the in-house baking rooms were just as good as those in many artisanal shops and the bread was less expensive. Mediocre bakers threatened to drive out the good ones, especially as clamorous denunciations began to reach the public at large, thanks to the critiques of Alain Schifres and Jean-Pierre Coffe among others. Finally, the profession understood that it had to take a hard look at the way it reproduced itself if it was to ensure the quality of the goods it produced. Instead of passively deploring the low skill levels and poor attitudes of apprentices, the confederation began to contemplate a thoroughgoing reform of the training and recruitment systems.

It is hard to thwart the competition without modifying some of one's own standard operating procedures. Historically little inclined to change direction, and all the less so after the white bread revolution of the 1960s, artisanal breadmaking did not want to acknowledge at first that the nascent industrial bakeries and mass distribution were serious threats. Even when the competition proved quite tough, taking away large market shares in an overall context of lessening demand, instead of questioning their own approach the artisans preferred to challenge the moral quality of their competititors—they were as indignant as they were disconcerted. In their eyes, the competition was "unfair" in its practices (it refused to respect the weekly closing rule, posted ruinous loss leader prices, usurped the traditional trade designations—in other words, it "flouted all the rules"); it was illegitimate (and tragic) in its very essence. Given their numbers, their historical mission (public service at the local level), their social inscription (constituting the bond among citizens), their cultural role (bread was more than a simple market product), and their political weight (disproportionate, like that of the peasants, another anachronistic and emblematically protected group), the artisans believed that they should be sheltered from all competition. Buttressing their claims with their ontological and symbolic priority, artisanal bakers as a group demanded protection. Why confront the enemy on the ground when one could demonize him from a distance? Later, as the artisans began to understand that competition was not going to disappear, they got together and initiated a lengthy process of renewal, without ever being able to completely relinquish the idea that their right to survive was engraved in the social compact.

At the dawn of the third millennium, the supporters of the moral economy at the heart of artisanal breadmaking yielded to the realists, who focused on the trade as a business. Without renouncing the cult of the artisan, they implicitly abandoned the reductive Manicheanism that opposed them to their rivals. Artisanal breadmaking was going to win out, not owing to an exclusive hereditary privilege, but owing to the superiority of its products, its services, and its public relations. Jean-Pierre Crouzet, the current confederation president and advocate of this deliberate, lucid policy, hoped to reestablish the bakers' association movement, which had been badly damaged by the prevailing atmosphere of doom and gloom, on this new basis. Without totally repudiating protectionism, he explicitly gave up the old dream of prohibiting competition. The profession had been panic-stricken in the 1980s and 1990s by the powerful influx of bake-off terminals more or less everywhere and by the spread of chain and big box stores; it has much more confidence today in its capacity to resist on the grounds of quality and committed proximity. When the fusion of two industry giants was announced in March 2002, the confederation journal noted that "artisanal bakers are remaining calm" and explained that the situation they were facing could not be compared to the long, bitter struggle they had waged against these adversaries.[1]

The first-generation industrialists, who had come from the artisanate themselves, at first took their excommunication from the profession very badly. Organized in a well-run association, they looked more for common ground with the artisanate than for confrontation. Far from wanting to crush the artisans, the industrialists recognized that they needed them for the success of their own strategy, for the artisans were the ones inciting the French to love their own bread. They too were committed to the path of quality, especially from the early 1990s on; they thought they could provide taste in a diversified gamut of frozen, prebaked, or unbaked products, thanks to some extremely important technological advances. Without needing to advertise (ironically, the artisans were unwittingly doing it for them), the industrialists could devote all their available resources to heavy investments and the concentrations that would enable them to continue to make progress in the marketplace both at home and abroad.

Francis Holder's saga illustrates all the dangers of viewing industrialists and artisans as utterly irreconcilable. The son of a baker in Lille, he started off with little material or sociocultural capital. His story is almost too good to be true, the stuff of soap opera: relentless work in the baking room after his father's sudden, early death, an intuitive sense of what his customers wanted, determination to expand and conquer (at the local, regional, national, and finally international levels), a policy of technological and commercial innovation, a genius for marketing, lively curiosity, cultural ambition, social recognition and ascension. Under Holder's flagship brand name, Paul, several hundred shops offer a wide range of excellent breads, probably better than those of many artisans.

From the outset, bread was a natural target for mass marketing and distribution via chains of big box stores; this development, a result of social, economic, and cultural evolution, was marked by the entry of large numbers of women into the labor market, widespread mobility, and fundamental changes in the art of everyday life. At first only fresh industrial food products were involved (Holder being one of the suppliers); bake-off terminals were added later, and finally authentic baking rooms were integrated into big box stores. Since the early 1990s, these baking rooms have been more and more "artisanalized." Alongside giant rotating rack ovens (or rather, in front, to hide them), they come with refracting sole-plate ovens for making bread of high quality (and higher added value), including bread in the French tradition (well before the vast majority of artisans began to offer this) and "specialty" breads, especially organic products. The hypercentralized Carrefour chain and Auchan, which allows each of its stores much more autonomy, provide contrasting images of the breadmaking strategies of the big box enterprises. Calling on an exceptionally gifted artisan, Dominique Saibron, Carrefour introduced creative recipes and a rigorous production system in each of its sites, with an elaborate monitoring apparatus. While quality inevitably varied from store to store, Carrefour was nonetheless able to compete with high-level artisans throughout France. Auchan evolved more slowly, moving astutely toward production methods inspired by "old-style" quality. Extremely threatening to local bakers, especially in rural areas, the big chains can no longer be written off as interlopers or producers of second-rate bread.

In the minds of many bakers, the state ought to have protected them from all these dangers. However, the profession's attitude toward the state has always been profoundly ambivalent. From the time of the provider-prince to the Third Republic or even beyond, bread was not so much a commercial product as a matter of state policy. An indispensable staple, bread was the key to social and political stability. The state, whether embodied in the king or depersonalized, remained the baker of last resort; the French Revolution brought no change in the social contract governing subsistence which bound the consumer population to public authority. The state guaranteed the bread supply through its "policing" (in which prophylactic regulations predominated over repressive measures). Bakery policies had three principal objectives: the supply of a *sufficient quantity* of bread of *good quality* sold at a *fair price*. To achieve these aims, the authorities often relied on price controls, either through an extremely elaborate and rigid price schedule, or by means of a maximum price often established through negotiation (this was the typical method followed in Paris).

While bakers chafed under this oversight (inspections, confiscations, and fines for fraud involving weight, quality, and price; penalties could include demolishing the oven, closing down the shop, or imposing prison sentences), they also profited from it. Their guild, or corporation, accredited by state power, held a monopoly (at least in theory), controlled its own affairs (finances, recruitment, internal discipline), and participated directly in the oversight of its members, often managing to obtain reduced sanctions. Even though they always suspected bakers of "greed" and of "scheming," the authorities limited competition from outside the corporation and protected bakers against consumer anger during periods of high prices and scarcity.

As public welfare had precedence over free trade, the bakers' corporation was one of the few to be exempted from abolition and emancipation in the wake of the Revolution. In Paris and in other large cities, the reconstituted corporation had to maintain emergency stocks and had to fulfill other obligations that amounted to a sort of public service. In the twentieth century, having become an association of self-employed artisans, the corporation provided itself with a mythic past based on the image of a fierce and heroic resistance to a pitiless and tentacular state. However, despite its feisty rhetoric, the corporation benefited from various forms of "compensation" in exchange for submitting to price controls, for agreeing to maintain flour reserves, and for accepting other constraints in the public interest. The utopian situation of complete freedom was warmly acclaimed and studiously avoided by bakers. Like many other players on the economic scene, including the largest, bakers wanted to have their bread and eat it too, as it were: they sought freedom and protection alike, according to circumstances and in variable doses.

Nothing aroused bakers to action during the twentieth century more than the struggle against price controls—the scapegoat for virtually all that ailed the profession, according to the associations' overwrought discourse. The stakes were more complex than the noisy denunciations suggested. While some bakers attributed the technological stagnation of their trade to price controls, others insisted, on the contrary, that these controls had forced bakers to modernize and adopt solutions that increased production. Although in an earlier era—a long one—the associations had demanded that bread be treated like any other product, seeking the end of the "bread taboo" that justified price controls, the same associations later pleaded in favor of making a "cultural exception" for bread, since bread after all was not just a commercial product like any other. When the state did consent to grant autonomy, first in the late 1970s and then in the early 1980s, some bakers rejoiced because they would now be able to focus on quality, while a certain number of others quickly succumbed to nostalgia for price controls and an era in which everything was comfortably programmed in advance.

The bakery business had scarcely achieved emancipation and "adulthood" when it turned again to the state to ask for emergency assistance. After encouraging the development and establishment of mass chain-store distribution as well as industrial breadmaking, the government revised its policy. Implicitly admitting that modernization was neither socially neutral nor culturally innocent, the state agreed to reconsider the idea of the general interest insofar as the role of artisanal baking was concerned. Starting in the 1990s, it sketched out a new relation with the bakery business; the partnership reached a peak of affinity during Jean-Pierre Raffarin's mandate at the Ministry of Commerce and the Artisanate following the election to the presidency of another great friend of the profession, Jacques Chirac.

No longer believing that artisans could rely on their own merits alone to win on the battlefield, the confederation sought national brand definitions that would make the French artisanal exception official. The government complied by promulgating the "bread decree" in September 1993. The new policy had two aspects. The first underscored the sacred character of artisanal work. The label "Pain Maison," bread made in house, was intended to be both prestigious and didactic; it was reserved to bakers who carried out the entire process of breadmaking in their own baking rooms. While this did nothing at all to improve bread quality, the confederation hoped it would boost bakers' morale and increase public awareness. The second aspect, the fruit of dozens of successive versions, was much more audacious and controversial: it defined a new product to be known as "bread in the French tradition." Required to be made without additives such as ascorbic acid, it signaled a return to the sources. This was translated by the resurrection of an old method that included a long *pointage*, the seedbed of flavors and aromas. Its partisans wanted traditional French bread to be the beacon product of the resuscitated artisanal baking business. But this somewhat schizophrenic legislation seems to have offered bakers a tacit choice between the made-in-house option, which reconciled the baker with himself without requiring the slightest change in the way he

did things, and the "traditional" option, requiring a profound modification in the recipe and working procedures. Triggering an active although
quiet resistance, bread in the French tradition had conquered only a tenth
of the artisans by the dawn of the new century.

In the face of the extremely limited moral and commercial impact of the
bread decree, the confederation intervened once again to extract yet another effort from the state that would make it possible to struggle against
a still devastating competition. To preserve artisanal breadmaking, the
newly appointed minister (whom the bakers affectionately call Raf-*farine*,
playing on the French word for flour) advocated a triple strategy: a new
set of regulations (protection against the enemy), a renewal at the level of
the baking room (quality, quality, and more quality), and recrafting of the
brand image (more and better public relations). Raffarin was committed to
enforcing the obligatory weekly closing, a commercial and symbolic issue
for the artisans, and to prohibiting the sale of bread at loss leader prices. He
signed a national charter for the development of artisanal breadmaking, a
sign of the return of the bakery business to a degree of dependence on the
once-oppressive state. Among other measures, the charter created an annual bread festival to be held on May 16, the feast day of the patron saint of
the profession, St. Honoré. This amounted to the consecration of bread as
part of the patrimony, its inscription in France's social and cultural excep-
tionality. Henceforth, at least once a year, the bakery business would be
in the spotlight, taking over national prime time to put across its message
of pleasure, health, safety, sociability, and folkloric history.

In a decree issued on December 12, 1995, Raffarin responded to one
of the confederation's principal requests by giving recognition and distinction to deserving artisans of particular value to the profession. As of
that date, only bakers who personally oversaw the various stages of breadmaking on the premises where the bread would be sold to the ultimate
consumer were entitled to call themselves bakers and put up a "bakery"
sign. Vigorously contested by industrial bakers, the decree was overturned
by the Conseil d'État in late 1997 for want of a legal foundation. The National Assembly quickly passed a law incorporating the main points of the
Raffarin decree but allowing industrial bakers to use the labels for selling
products abroad. Ironically, the law does not seem to have done the artisans much good. Those who supplied their own cold shops no longer had
the right to call these sites bakeries, nor could those who resorted to freez-

ing, a rather common practice during some seasons and in some parts of the country, legally call themselves bakers. Industrial breadmaking gradually adapted, by choosing euphemistic labels such as "so-and-so's baking room" (*fournil*) or "baker's boy" (*mitron*).

A double crisis was anticipated on January 1, 2002, owing to the implausible folly of the administrative calendar. First of all, bakers feared the introduction of the euro, a cumbersome and anxiety-producing measure in itself, aggravated by the fact that it was to happen during the holiday period, the busiest time of the year. In fact, aside from certain pricing irregularities (a combination of increases and upward roundings) and some unusually long lines, everything went remarkably smoothly. But the shift to a thirty-five-hour work week was another story. Lacking enough help and compelled by the nature of the work to keep quite particular hours, artisanal bakers could only contemplate the thirty-five-hour week with horror. Rebuffed in their demand for postponement or modification of the application of the ruling, bakers took to the streets once more to demand "time to make good bread." (An ironic good sign: preparation time was valued again!) After having done so much to shorten the breadmaking process, especially at the height of the "white bread" craze, the bakers were pleading that time was the key to making quality products. Several of the major millers' groups used respect for time as the theme and token of the quality of the breads made under their names. In the eighteenth century, one could have imagined the mills under the bakers' control, but not the reverse. Around 1700, virtually all millers were artisans, not merchants; they worked for bakers, on demand. The milling business gradually became commercial, speculative, and dynamic. The flour trade outstripped the grain trade, and starting in the early nineteenth century millers took their revenge, getting involved in the bakery business, financing many bakery purchases (already!), reducing countless bakers to the status of quasi-employees. The bakers took their subordination very badly; the strongest among them rejected it by playing off one mill against another, while others tried to resist via the corporation. In other words, powerful tensions going way back were built into the history of miller-baker relations. Their "partnership," often built on significant bonds of affection and (asymmetrical) reciprocity, was nevertheless charged with ambiguities and latent tensions.

Of all the factors explaining the return of good bread, the intervention of the mills is no doubt the most significant. Deeply concerned about the constant decline in bread consumption and convinced that the bakers were not collectively in a position to meet the challenge, for want of clear (self-) analysis, imagination, determination, and suitable tools, certain millers concluded that they had to take the initiative themselves. The major risk they faced was the possibility of angering or even losing clients, stirring up the associations, which were hypersensitive in this climate of prolonged crisis, and also terribly territorial (it was their calling, after all), and possibly upsetting the public by blurring its familiar reference points. But for those who were doing the risk-benefit calculations, the danger of doing nothing seemed more serious in the long run. The reasoning of the interventionist miller was very simple, perhaps too simple: if it works, the whole sector will benefit. Depending on one's viewpoint, the millers' strategy could be described as friendly, focused therapy or as a thinly disguised power play. Carried out in full, the millers' most ambitious plans implied a profound transformation in breadmaking practices, in the shop as well as the baking room, in advertising and marketing as well as production. The most astute bakers were well aware that they needed to "know how to sell" and how to inform the public. Getting them to rethink their way of educating their clientele was the more delicate task of the two by far.

The first millers who dared to get involved in breadmaking under their own brand names came together under the Unimie label, which later became Banette. This group consisted of a good number of independent mills, some small and some quite large. The millers' initial objective was modest: they wanted to achieve certain economies of scale, to do better at buying wheat and selling flour, to do more experimenting with these materials, and to reinforce their reliability. Spurred by Alain Storione, an influential miller from Marseille preoccupied with the disaffection of bread eaters, which he attributed to a deficiency in taste, the group moved toward a real brand-name bread, in collaboration with bakers who were all independent artisans and usually owners of their own businesses, and were often already clients of one of the member mills. Established in Briare, not far from the canal that constituted one of Paris's major emergency supply lines in the eighteenth century, the mother house developed a line of breads with the baguette known as Banette bearing the torch. The chief argument in favor of the Banette was the pleasure its tastes and aromas afforded; these were produced by work said to be done the old-fashioned way, a method adopted both for fabrication (Banette touted the artisanal hand) and for advertising purposes. The millers' group asked its bakers to follow the prescribed recipe and procedures rigorously; they supplied technical assistance and sent monitors out to evaluate the quality and fidelity of the work, especially in baking rooms but also in shops. The group orchestrated national publicity campaigns, including televised spots, in order to familiarize the public with the brand (so that people would start to ask for a Banette rather than a generic baguette, the way one asks for a Kleenex and not a tissue), and—almost as important—in order to motivate and reassure their baker members by showing them the power of their marketing.

The Banette project was audacious, imaginative, and carefully implemented. Although it got off to a slow start, it ended up registering 10 on the Richter scale; it had a seismic effect on the sector. Almost all professionals, including those who detest the Banette phenomenon, agree that this was the turning point, the wake-up call for all the players. The very large mills, several millers' groups, and some others all followed suit very quickly. Probably 75 percent of all the bakers in France have been touched more or less directly by the Banette movement, if not by way of Briare, then through the intermediary of Viron (Rétrodor), Baguépi (Soufflet-Pantin), Campaillette/Ronde des Pains (Grands Moulins de Paris), Festival (Meuniers de France), Club Le Boulanger (Générale des Farines France), Copaline (Inter-Farine), and other brands, structures, or associations. The others have felt indirect effects: an inducement to reconsider their product line; a new impetus toward quality in order to respond to the intensified internal competition—a new experience for most bakers; an increased sense of solitude leading bakers to consider joining a brand name group, getting more involved in a baker's association, or even deciding to shut down the shop.

For some, Banettization was above all a public relations story: the creation of a brand, the manipulation of opinion. For others, it was an integrated concept that transformed the way they made bread. The associations reacted with varying degrees of hostility, seeing the trend as a subtle subversion of the trade, the eviction of competence, the enforced servitude of the artisans. The association leaders sensed the end of autonomy on the horizon, owing to a sort of imperceptible franchising, a gilded proletarianization. And they glimpsed something almost worse, because more humiliating: the transformation of bakers into an inferior race in need of "assistance."

Even so, without Banette the rethinking that had been advocated and piloted by the confederation would have been delayed and diluted, if not rejected in advance. Without Banette, the confederation would not have raised certain questions about its own practices and its ideological and technological presuppositions. By usurping certain of its canonical functions, especially training, Banette led the confederation to reflect in depth and to evolve toward a desire for partial *perestroika*. Without Banette, it is quite unlikely that the national association would have considered introducing a new product; this was an unprecedented gesture, an astute response designed to regain the initiative, an undertaking that put Banette temporarily on the defensive. Banette imposed the paradigm: all its rivals positioned themselves in relation to the company in Briare.

Banettization revitalized the entire sector. Few consumers had a clear understanding of what this was all about. Some suspected that it entailed a sort of industrialization of breadmaking or a gigantic franchising scheme —developments that might be frightening, if the quality of the products were not so obvious in a very large number of bakeries (and the advertising so emphatic). Banette was first to set forth the challenge: quality and a diversified product line, rigorous old-style procedures, and ultramodern public relations. Without Banette's emergence and the shock waves it generated, the message of quality (not only in words but in deeds) would have been slow to make itself heard by bakers and consumers alike. And if Banettization saved a good number of mediocre or lazy bakers, at least provisionally, and made others dependent for life, it nevertheless stimulated sincere and useful self-questioning among many perfectly autonomous artisans, and it spurred vocations among many young people who saw it as a means to ensure real freedom rather than asphyxiating "support."

Nevertheless, it is clear that Banettization, no matter what its form, has not been the sole path to salvation for the profession, not the only way out of the crisis. Let us recall first of all the handful of great bakers who have never stopped making good bread—bread with taste and aromas, bread that lasts. Next, let us turn to all the young mavericks who have made themselves known over the past decade or two. Inspired bakers governed by their passion for their trade, they have sought innovative solutions according to the rules of the art. They have succeeded in making a

Poilânesque synthesis between past and present. Passionate about bread themselves, they have won over the public with a range of exceptionally well-made products. The Rue Monge "war" shows us two of them right now, confronting each other by way of aromas and flavors. Both artists, though with very different histories, Kayser and Saibron manage to create breads so good and so interesting that they make us think and dream. Other bakers bear witness to the same spirit of independence, originality, and rigor. The same message is coming from many directions: good bread is back.

The question of bread quality no longer leads to riots or even to vigorous protests, as was the case in the eighteenth century, especially in the capital. Parisian consumers of those days seem to have imperceptibly and tacitly forced a consensus as to what constituted quality: wheat bread, white in color, or at worst a middling, not-too-dark gray. The stubbornness of the ordinary Parisian in demanding white bread was striking to contemporary observers. A fervent liberal, critical of paternalism where bread was concerned, Abbot Nicolas Baudeau deplored the fact that, in the capital, "the people [had] the bad habit of judging bread by its looks; they only considered its color; they had to have white bread." César Bucquet, a miller bent on reform, regretted that the Parisians had been allowed to "grow accustomed to eating white bread, too white." It is hardly surprising that a group of Paris workers, attracted to Lyon by significantly higher salaries around mid-century, came back a few years later, disgusted, "saying that they absolutely could not get used to the overly dark bread that was generally made there." Edme Béguillet, one of Bucquet's collaborators, observed that "the bakers almost have trouble making bread white enough to satisfy the false delicacy of the lowest category of Citizens." These included prisoners. Demanding "white bread," whiteness being the only sure sign that it would be "good bread," prisoners in Fort-l'Évêque, led by a woman, revolted in December 1751 and rejected the hard black bread they had been getting.[2]

We find it a lot harder today to reach a consensus as to what constitutes good (or bad) bread. We think, rightly, that quality is a subjective matter, especially where taste is concerned. We do not want anyone, not even a specialist, to tell us what is better or worse (as restaurant and movie critics do), and even if the expert purports to invoke certain objective sensory criteria of excellence (as oenologists do). To help move the discussion along, to encourage thoughtful tasting, and to help us understand one another better when we talk about bread quality, I suggest that we adopt a flexible protocol for evaluation. Within each analytic category, the taster may choose a very simple approach or a more elaborate one. The criteria are the following: appearance (3 points), crust (3), crumb (3), mouthfeel (1), odors and aromas (5), tastes and flavors (5), and then, as a bonus, harmony (1) and "bread intuition" (1). As tasters we need to experiment methodically, but we should also be able to let ourselves go a bit, take risks, inform ourselves, and have fun. And if, while they are deepening their knowledge of bread, tasters should develop more confidence in themselves, should become more autonomous and more demanding, should even find more pleasure, I will have won my wager.

The grid I am proposing remains very open. But in discussing the elements of each category, I do not hide my preferences; they remain my own predilections and my personal recommendations. Nor do I hide my desire to get the silent majority of consumers to examine their bread-eating habits, or, as dynamic bakers put it, to rethink their priorities. It is enough to ask some simple, straightforward questions. Why eat bread? What are its functions in my meals? Am I knowingly looking for pleasure in my bread? Do I buy my bread without thinking about it? Why do I go to bakery x rather than bakery y? The awareness triggered by these questions ought to lead consumers to make authentic choices and to try to do so in an informed manner, after reflection and comparison.

We cannot keep from wondering about the very large number of French people who cling to white bread as their ancestors did in the eighteenth century — a historically prestigious, reassuring product, often fine-looking, but impoverished today in terms of taste, if not completely without flavor or aroma. Taste is a very complicated matter, as we have seen: it is hard to explain, since it is at once biochemical in origin and constructed both socially and psychologically. Many people are not aware of the absence of taste. In this they are in the company of a good many bakers, moreover: bakers who do not taste their own bread critically, bakers who presume, as an instructor at the National Bread and Pastry Institute put it, that because they make bread they necessarily make good bread. Those who see their bread merely as a supporting element in the context of their daily diet may well find the absence of taste normal.

Social class and culture undoubtedly play a significant role in the use of bread, as they do in all dietary habits. The demand for good bread comes in the first place from those whose means are in line with their curiosity. But the search for taste is not narrowly rationed in monetary terms. The price difference between a very good bread (let us say a bread in the French tradition) and an ordinary baguette may be discouraging, even if it is not necessarily prohibitive. But within the realm of basic prices, one can still exercise one's taste. Dominique Saibron's ordinary baguette, at Le Boulanger de Monge, costs €0.75 ($0.93); it is far superior to the baguette made by most white-bread bakers, which often costs as much as €0.80 ($1.00). It would be sad, and impoverishing, to look at the question of good bread as a matter of snobbery, the privilege of an elite seeking to set itself apart. All the more so since, historically, ordinary French people have always seen quality as a feature virtually consubstantial with their status as simple consumers.

The most interesting bread on the bakery scene today is certainly the bread in the French tradition, which is found under different names according to the baker or label. This bread has a pearly and irregularly alveolated crumb; it is made with brief (and slow) kneading and a long *pointage* according to highly variable fermentation methods. When it is made well, this bread is impressive in the intensity and variety of its aromas and tastes. It got off to a slow start in the 1990s, but it has experienced a regular, though modest, growth curve. We have to hope that the National Bakery Confederation will do everything possible to promote its spread both in major cities throughout France and in the countryside, and that millers will encourage bakers using their brand names to make it both the flagship product and the standard one (following the Rétrodor example). Realistically, it is probably the supply — well presented — that will attract and convert the demand, and not the other way around, in the white bread world.[3]

Another way of promoting awareness of taste and discernment in the choice of bread is to make an effort to arouse interest in the question and to educate people involved in institutional food preparation. The culture of bread ought to be introduced in school cafeterias and dining halls (is price the suppliers' only criterion?), and in company restaurants. Children offered tasteless bread today will form an aversion that will translate into lower per capita consumption tomorrow. More generally, we must all demand good bread in all the ordinary and extraordinary restaurants that are capable of attracting us with exquisite dishes but settle for offering bread that the prisoners of Fort-l'Évêque would have rejected. It is time to draw the line!

In the short run, the bread market will probably continue to be segmented within the most inventive and vigorous shops and among bakeries of varying ambition, in differing socioeconomic contexts, and so on. Rural areas are threatened with the loss of bakers, as much for demographic reasons as because of competition from the big chain stores or from industry. Frozen products will penetrate urban as well as rural bakeries increasingly, especially Viennese pastries and specialty breads. Bold solutions like that of the Franche-Comté cooperative Monpain have little hope of seeing the light of day. In cities, we shall see accelerated concentration; artisan entrepreneurs will follow the international capitalist model on a modest scale. The most dynamic bakers will open their second, third, or tenth shop, baking room, or cold shop; these may be new creations, or they may involve swallowing up bakers on the point of failure. Some bakers will continue to diversify within their own shops; fast food will continue to proliferate.

While quality always has to come first, marketing will necessarily play a major role. Bakers can no longer wall themselves off within a logic of production; they have to know how to sell, and marketing begins behind the counter. For INBP director Gérard Brochoire, women may well be the future of breadmaking. Historically, the committed baker's wife or female baker has been endowed with a higher cultural level than her husband or male counterpart; she was often responsible for client and customer relations as well as bookkeeping in the eighteenth century. She has the means to make a difference in the brutal arena of contemporary marketing, so long as she is intimately acquainted with the products and the way they are made. Finally, will millers' brands be as important in the future as they have been in the past? Will the public perceive them as reassuring brand names or as standardizing chains? Will the bakers who have been trained, retrained, or polished by the mother houses be tempted to reclaim their freedom? I anticipate major adaptations and new modes of collaboration rather than wholesale de-Banettization.

The liberal and ultramodern minister Jean-Pierre Raffarin never stopped repeating, while he was in office, that the bakery business needed strong associations in a complex world. For a half-century or more, the association movement has been absorbing some hard blows. Today, scarcely half of all French bakers belong to a professional association. A counter-association is currently developing at the national level. Although it is still very modest in size and speaks in reductive, even extremist terms, this group raises questions and expresses anxieties that the established national association will have to confront. Confederation president Jean-Pierre Crouzet is inclined to forge ahead with a modern and liberal vision of the trade. But how can one surmount its difficulties and still take them into account? Stop whining, get a grip, be better than the competition, he tells his troops, most of whom are still dreaming of a protective barrier around their shops. Crouzet would like to build the profession's future around enterprising, innovative young bakers. But his base, while it has grown much smaller, is far from homogeneous. He has to offer varied forms of moral and technological support, come to terms with an association movement that is as segmented as the market, and reconcile regional, ideological, and cultural differences.

Training is probably the area in which the confederation could exercise its greatest influence. Put the precious resources of the INBP to better use, create other institutions that will teach, experiment, and spread knowledge, especially in the provinces: these are obvious strategies. Yet to ensure the future, the most important task is to attract talented young people, especially those with baccalaureate degrees.[4] It has never been enough to be big, strong, and stupid to be a baker; the cliché is even less plausible today. A survey indicates that bakers are second only to emergency personnel and firemen in their public image. But this image has not yet led to gains in recruitment. It is worth recalling, in the end, that good bread depends above all on the quality of the men and women who make it.

Acknowledgments

For his warm welcome, his many suggestions, and his stimulating conversation, I am grateful to Gérard Brochoire, director of the Institut national de la boulangerie-pâtisserie. Many librarians, at the INBP as well as at the Bibliothèque nationale de France and at Cornell University, have helped me find texts and sources. Raphaëlle Sauvé, a student navigating between Paris and Ithaca, was very effective in opening up bibliographical avenues. The late Lionel Poilâne kindly opened his magnificent personal library to me and enriched my work with his ideas and experience. Maurice Aymard once again offered his generous hospitality at the Maison des Sciences de l'homme. I want to express my gratitude to Gilles Morini, *contrôleur* at the Bureau des Industries agricoles et alimentaires de la Direction générale de la concurrence, de la consommation et de la répression des fraudes, for the invaluable information he gave me. With his characteristic blend of modesty and passion, Guy Boulet was willing to share his philosophy and his adventures. Michael G. McBride, a serious gourmet, constantly reminded me that tasting had as much to do with pleasure as with rigor. I owe a debt of gratitude to Caroline Delabroy, Olivier Delabroy, and Martin Bruegel for the documents that they were kind enough to supply. The critical reading done by Renée Kaplan enabled me to tighten up my narrative in many places.

The book could not have been written without the interviews that I was generously granted by bakers, millers, association leaders, government employees, company heads, managers, and other actors in the bread saga. May they excuse me for expressing my gratitude collectively by simply listing their names: Jean-Paul Barré, Patrick Castagna, Marcel Cocaud, Marie-Georges Colombe, Bernard Comboroure, Jean-Pierre Crouzet, Yvan Fouricher, Jean-Marie Gagneux, Jocelyne Gantois,

326 ACKNOWLEDGMENTS

Philippe Goisneau, Philippe Gosselin, Jean Hautecoeur, Francis Holder, Christian Hubert, Frédéric Lalos, Florence Lebehot, Paul L'Hermine, Jean-Noël Julien, Éric Kayser, Laurence Kayser, Jacques Mabille, Dominique Malézieux, Hervé Malineau, Jean-Claude Mislanghe, Mireille Peyrac, Michel Philippe, Maryse Portier, Thierry Rabineau, Philippe Richard, Dominique Saibron, Bernard Seller, Patrice Tireau, Alexandre Viron, Philippe Viron, Nicole Watelet.

Catherine Porter has gifted me with a masterful translation for which I am deeply obliged. Sporadically, I have used the occasion of vetting the English text to update or revise certain passages, introducing modifications resulting from my recent investigation of Paris bakeries (*Cherchez le pain: le guide des meilleures boulangeries de Paris* [Paris: Plon, 2004]) and from my study of the national wheat-flour-bread sector from the Liberation to the ascension of De Gaulle (to appear in a book titled *Le pain maudit*).

To say that Marie-Christine Fabiani Kaplan was involved in every stage of this odyssey hardly sums up her innumerable contributions. I dedicate this book to her as a sign of my deepest gratitude.

Notes

Introduction

1 Only recently have women, in very small numbers, in the face of persistent cultural resistance, begun to enter the baking world as bakers rather than as spouses or salespersons. Historically, the work was considered far too onerous for women (since it required lifting sacks weighing 100–150 kilos, kneading up to 50 kilos by hand, working at night, and so on); in more diffuse terms, breadbaking has been traditionally viewed as a male profession in France. In the guild tradition, widows were the only women allowed to accede to ownership of a bakery, and they were explicitly discouraged from entering the baking room. Women were not apprenticed in the trade until the second half of the twentieth century, and their numbers remain excessively small. Given this context, the text occasionally uses masculine pronouns to refer to the stereotypical baker, the baker one encounters almost always in real life.

2 France officially adopted the metric system in 1795. The preexisting term *livre*, designating a variable quantity roughly equivalent to the English pound, remained — and remains — in use in France with the meaning "approximately 500 grams," or half a kilo. The term *pound* is used in this sense throughout the book.

3 Meg Bortin, "Give Us Our Daily Bread," *Paris Métro*, October 26, 1977.

4 Raymond Calvel, "L'évolution de la qualité du pain," *Actualités Agricoles*, April 30 and May 7, 1976; interview with Calvel in *Michel Montignac Magazine*, no. 1 (May–June 1993); Jean-Pierre Coffe, *Au secours le goût* (Paris: Le Pré aux Clercs, 1992). We shall come back to these two authors (especially Calvel) and examine their analyses in much greater depth later.

5 See Steven L. Kaplan, *Le pain, le peuple, et le roi: la bataille du libéralisme sous Louis XV* (Paris: Perrin, 1986); Kaplan, *Les ventres de Paris: pouvoir et approvisionnement dans la France d'Ancien Régime* (Paris: Fayard, 1988); Kaplan, *Le meilleur pain du monde: les boulangers de Paris au XVIIIe siècle* (Paris: Fayard, 1996).

6 Kaplan, *Le meilleur pain du monde*, 9–10.

7 "Jurisprudence, police et municipalités," *Encyclopédie méthodique* (Paris, 1789), vol. 10, 168.

8 Kaplan, *Le meilleur pain du monde*, 48.

9 Ibid., 49–50.

10 Interview with Lionel Poilâne, May 2001. Paul Rambali cites the paraphrase from Baudelaire's "Alchimie de la douleur" without indicating its source in *Boulangerie: The Craft and Culture of Baking in France* (New York: Macmillan, 1994), 106.

11 On the problems of identifying and utilizing sources of information about bread consumption, see Kaplan, *Le meilleur pain du monde*, chap. 16.

Chapter 1   Good Bread: Practices and Discourses

1 George Sand, *Questions [politiques et sociales]* (Paris: Calmann-Lévy, 1879), 30, 34; Antoine-Augustin Parmentier, *Le parfait boulanger, ou Traité complet sur la fabrication et le commerce du pain* (Paris: Imprimerie royale, 1778), 378, 634; Paul-Jacques Malouin, *Description des arts du meunier, du vermicelier, et du boulanger* (Paris, 1761), 113; *La misère des garçons boulangers de la ville et faubourgs de Paris* (Troyes: Veuve Garnier, 1715); Joseph Barbaret, *Le travail en France: monographies professionnelles* (Paris: Berger-Levrault, 1886–1890), vol. 1, 412–14; Philibert Patissier, *Traité des maladies des artisans et celles qui résultent des diverses professions, d'après Ramazzini* (Paris: J.-B. Baillière, 1827); Archives nationales, series Y 15238, May 1, 1751; Y 18672, July 30, 1770; Y 12596, March 29, 1752; Y 18670, July 10 and September 30, 1769; Y 15093, June 5, 1785; Y 14953, May 15, 1738; Y 12729, March 1, 1735; Minutier central des notaires, Archives nationales, VII-329, November 4, 1760; CIX-412, November 14, 1712, and VII-287, May 17, 1753.

2 A skilled artisan in 1730 earned between 20 and 30 *sous* a day — in other words, between one and two pounds.

3 Louis-Sébastien Mercier, *Tableau de Paris*, vol. 12 (Amsterdam, 1788), 146; Baltasar-Georges Sage, *Analyse des blés* (Paris: Imprimerie royale, 1776), 46; Steven L. Kaplan, *Le meilleur pain du monde: les boulangers de Paris au XVIIIe siècle* (Paris: Fayard, 1996), 248–49.

4 Parmentier, *Le parfait boulanger*, 273–75; Kaplan, *Le meilleur pain du monde*, 85–87.

5 Kaplan, *Le meilleur pain du monde*, 75–77; Parmentier, *Le parfait boulanger*, xvi-xx, xlii–xliii, 209–11, 441, 536–37; César Bucquet, *Observations intéressantes et amusantes*, ed. Edme Béguillet (Paris: Les Marchands de Nouveautés, 1783), 7, 15, 18–21, 68, 96n, 121; Bucquet, *Traité pratique de la conservation des grains, des farines et des étuves domestiques* (Paris: Onfroy, 1783), 42, 52; Mercier, *Tableau de Paris*, vol. 8 (1783), 135–37; Cadet de Vaux, cited by Nicolas-Toussaint Des Essarts, *Dictionnaire universel de police* (Paris: Moutard, 1786–1790), vol. 7, 473. Malouin had already sketched out the same scientistic position as Parmentier in *Description des arts du meunier*, 115–16. Mercier was well aware that peremptory assertions from the outside and on high had no chance whatsoever of convincing "all the baker's boys, all the servant girls, and even their mistresses, who proclaimed with one voice

that bread as they make it is perfect, there is nothing to add, and that it's just the way their grandfathers ate it" (*Tableau de Paris*, vol. 7, 137).

6 CNERNA, *La qualité du pain*, Les Journées Scientifiques, November 1954–April 1960 (Paris: Centre national de la recherche scientifique, 1962), vol. 2, 552–65.

7 Jean Buré, ed., *Le pain*, proceedings of the CNERNA colloquium, Paris, November 1977, followed by *Recueil des usages concernant les pains de France* (Paris: Centre national de la recherche scientifique, 1979), 13–14, 245–47.

8 Michel Perrier (a baker, son, and grandson of bakers, from Mussidan in the Dordogne), interview in *Michel Montignac Magazine*, no. 1 (May–June 1993): 23; Parmentier, *Le parfait boulanger*, xxx, 278–80, 293; René Augé, ed., *Le pain* (Paris: Delachaux Niestlé Spes, 1977), 2.

9 Augé, *Le pain*, 2–6; Jean-Yves Guinard and Pierre Lesjean, *Le livre du boulanger* (Cachan: LT Éditions J. Lanore, 2001), 84–88, 91, 103–4; Roland Guinet, *Technologie du pain français* (Paris: Éditions B.P.I., 1992), 47–48, 50–53, 89–91; Gérard Brochoire, ed., *Devenir boulanger* (Paris: Éditions Sotal, 1998), 90–92; Raymond Calvel, *Le pain* (Paris: Presses Universitaires de France, coll. Que-Sais-je?, 1964), 55–58; Calvel, in *Le Boulanger-Pâtissier*, February 1983; Calvel, *Le goût du pain: comment le préserver, comment le retrouver* (Paris: Jérôme Villette, 1990), 26–28, 38–39; Buré, *Le pain*, 263, 287; Roger Drapron et al., *Notre pain quotidien* (Paris: Antenne générale de publication, 1999), 139. See also Centre de perfectionnement des cadres des industries agricoles et alimentaires (Jean Buré and F. Delmer), *Fermentation panaire* (Paris: Apria Diffusion, 1983).

10 Buré, *Recueil des usages concernant les pains de France*, 300.

11 Brochoire, *Devenir boulanger*, 96–97; Guinet, *Technologie du pain français*, 92; Guinard and Lesjean, *Le livre du boulanger*, 109–10; Raymond Calvel, *Le goût du pain: comment le préserver, comment le retrouver* (Paris: Jérôme Villette, 1990) 29, 33–37.

12 Malouin, *Description des arts du meunier*, 135–48, 152; Parmentier, *Le parfait boulanger*, 281–82, 329–30; Nicolas Baudeau, *Avis au peuple sur son premier besoin, ou petits traités économiques par l'auteur des "Éphémérides du Citoyen"* (Paris: Hochereau jeune, 1768), third treatise, 47.

13 Malouin, *Description des arts du meunier*, 155–56.

14 Parmentier, *Le parfait boulanger*, xxx–xxxi, 317–29, 406–8.

15 Émile Dufour, *Traité pratique de panification française et parisienne* (Château-Thierry: Imprimerie moderne, 1937), xxi.

16 Raymond Geoffroy, "De l'emploi des levains en panification et de son influence sur la qualité du pain," *Bulletin des Anciens Élèves de l'École Française de Meunerie*, no. 82 (September–December 1939): 236. Cf. Geoffroy, "Pain d'hier, pain d'aujourd'hui," *Techniques des Industries Céréalières*, no. 154 (April–May 1976): 4.

17 Raymond Calvel, "Pain, progrès technique et qualité," *Bulletin des Anciens Élèves de l'École Française de Meunerie*, no. 181 (January–February 1961), and *Le Boulanger-Pâtissier*, July–August 1933; interview with Lionel Poilâne, June 2001; Hubert

Chiron, "Cinquante années de progrès en technologie boulangère," *Industries des Céréales*, no. 116 (January–March 2000); Lesaffre advertisement, *Les Nouvelles de la Boulangerie-Pâtisserie*, January 1, 2002. Cf. Sara Mansfield Taber, *Bread of Three Rivers: The Story of a French Loaf* (Boston: Beacon Press, 2001), 191–210 (a non-historicized and thus extremely simplified representation).

18   Interviews with Éric Kayser and Patrick Castagna, spring 2001; Brochoire, *Devenir boulanger*, 98–99.

19   Dufour, *Traité pratique de panification française et parisienne*, 25; Brochoire, *Devenir boulanger*, 94; Guinet, *Technologie du pain français*, 93–94; Calvel, *Le pain*, 65–66; Guinard and Lesjean, *Le livre du boulanger*, 107–8; Richard-Molard, "Goût du pain," 468; Bernard Ganachaud, interview in *Michel Montignac Magazine*, no. 1 (May–June 1993): 28.

20   A. Savoie, *Meunerie, boulangerie, pâtisserie* (Paris: G. Doin, 1922), 80.

21   *Bulletin de l'Association des Anciens Élèves de l'École de Boulangerie des Grands Moulins de Paris* (April–May 1936). Cf. Paul Nottin, *Le blé, la farine, le pain* (Paris: Hachette, 1940), 59.

22   Dufour, *Traité pratique de panification française et parisienne*, 18, 21–22. Cf. A. Chargelegue et al. in Roland Guinet and Bernard Godon, *La panification française* (Paris: Tec et Doc, 1994), 297.

23   Brochoire, *Devenir boulanger*, 92–93; Guinet, *Technologie du pain français*, 94; Calvel, *Le pain*, 66–67; Guinard and Lesjean, *Le livre du boulanger*, 106; A. Brosson (an associate in the laboratory of the Grands Moulins de Paris, and—let us note in passing the quasi-institutional incest—a former vice president of the Paris Baker's Association), "Notice sur le travail 'direct' en boulangerie," in Roland Guinet, "Évolution de la qualité du pain: incidence de l'équipement et des méthodes de fabrication," in Buré, *Le pain*, 113.

24   Raymond Calvel, "L'évolution et la qualité du pain français," *Bulletin des Anciens Élèves de l'École Française de Meunerie*, no. 254 (March–April 1973), 60; Calvel, "L'évolution de la qualité du pain et le problème de son contrôle," *Bulletin des Anciens Élèves de l'École Française de Meunerie*, no. 268 (July–August 1975), 200; Calvel, *Le pain*, 66.

25   Léon Boutroux, *Le pain et la panification* (Paris: J.-B. Baillière et fils, 1897), 222–23; Georges Barbarin, *Le scandale du pain* (Paris: Nizet, 1956), 38–39; survey by the Laboratoire coopératif d'analyses et de recherches, *Le Pain Français*, no. 11 (September–October 1962): 149.

26   Steven L. Kaplan, *Les ventres de Paris: pouvoir et approvisionnement dans la France d'Ancien Régime*, trans. Sabine Boulongne (Paris: Fayard, 1988); Hubert Chiron, "L'évolution technologique en boulangerie française," *Industries Alimentaires et Agricoles* 3 (January–February 1994): 36; *France-Soir*, November 23, 1969.

27   CNERNA, *La qualité du pain*, vol. 1, 527–33, 552.

28   Ibid., 534–35.

29   Guinet, *Technologie du pain français*, 33, 36; Brochoire, *Devenir boulanger*, 29, 36.

30   *Les Nouvelles de la Boulangerie*, July 1, 1997.

31   Ibid., September 15, 1991; Raymond Calvel to Philippe Viron, March 30, 1980, and September 6, 1992, Viron correspondence; Raymond Calvel, "Maîtrise du pétrissage et de la fermentation pour l'élaboration d'un pain de qualité," *Industries des Céréales* (April–June 1994): 18–19.

32   Kaplan, *Le meilleur pain du monde*; Brochoire, *Devenir boulanger*, 102.

33   Brochoire, *Devenir boulanger*, 102; Guinard and Lesjean, *Le livre du boulanger*, 123–25; Guinet, *Technologie du pain français*, 95.

34   *Bulletin de l'Association des Anciens Élèves de l'École de Boulangerie des Grands Moulins de Paris*, June–July 1937; Hubert Chiron, "Un survol de l'apport de la boulangerie de l'ouest à la panification française," *Fidèles au Bon Pain*, no. 9 (1993): 17; Hubert Chiron and Bernard Godon, "Chronique," in Guinet and Godon, *La panification française*, 77.

35   *Le Boulanger-Pâtissier*, January 1939.

36   Chiron, "Un survol de l'apport de la boulangerie de l'ouest à la panification française," 17; Hubert Chiron and Bernard Godon, "Historique de la panification," in Guinet and Godon, *La panification française*, 77; Hubert Chiron, "1949/1993: incidences des mutations technologiques sur les caractéristiques du pain français," *Industrie des Céréales* (April–June 1994): 7.

37   *Pâtisserie-Boulangerie: Vie Pratique*, June 17, 1990, and September 18, 1991; *La Filière Gourmande*, August–September 2000.

38   Brochoire, *Devenir boulanger*, 60–62; Roland Guinet, "Conditions générales de la panification," in Guinet and Godon, *La panification française*, 223; P. Feillet et al., "La pâte," in Guinot and Godon, *La panification française*, 236; CNERNA, *La qualité du pain*, vol. 2, 577–85; Philippe Gosselin, cited in *Les Nouvelles de la Boulangerie-Pâtisserie*, March 1, 1996; Dufour, *Traité pratique de panification française et parisienne*, xi. Cf. M. Arpin, *Historique de la meunerie et de la boulangerie, depuis les temps préhistoriques jusqu'à l'année 1914* (Paris: Le Chancelier, 1948), vol. 2, 143, on the difficulty and the delicacy of kneading, before and after mechanization.

39   Alfred Carlier, *Histoire du pain* (Cannes: Imprimerie à l'école [Aegitna], 1938), 1; Barbaret, *Le travail en France*, vol. 1, 481; Calvel, in Augé, *Le pain*, 28–29; Sylvie Anne, *Victorine, ou le pain d'une vie* (Paris: Presses de la Renaissance, 1985), 236; *Les Nouvelles de la Boulangerie*, November 15, 1991; Roland Guinet, "Technologies de panification," *Bulletin des Anciens Élèves de l'École de Meunerie*-ENSMIC, no. 287 (September–October 1978): 227; Feillet et al., "La pâte," 239; Brochoire, *Devenir boulanger*, 62–64; Buré, *Le pain*, 272–73; Raymond Calvel, in *Le Boulanger-Pâtissier*, March 1987; Calvel, cited in *Le Levain Syndical*, May 1986.

40   Archives nationales, Y 11449, November 4, 1727, and Y 11673, September 30, 1749; "Mémoire des boulangers de Chaalons-sur-Marne [*sic*]," 1785, Bibliothèque nationale, cabinet des manuscrits, fonds Joly de Fleury 1742, fol. 43; "Mémoire pour

les boulangers de Troyes," 1789, in ibid., Joly 1743, fol. 134; Malouin, *Description des arts du meunier*, 206–12, 266; Nicolas Baudeau, *Avis au peuple sur son premier besoin* (Amsterdam: F.-A. Didot aîné, 1774), third treatise, 70–73; Parmentier, *Le parfait boulanger*, 426–44, 621–22; Polycarpe Poncelet, *Histoire naturelle du froment* (Paris: G. Desprez, 1779), 200–206. The four-pound long loaf measured between 60 and 65 centimeters in length (*Journal de Physique* [February 1782]: 90).

41   Brochoire, *Devenir boulanger*, 116–17; Guinard and Lesjean, *Le livre du boulanger*, 92–96; Guinet, "Conditions générales de la panification," 223–34; Raymond Calvel, in *Fidèles au Bon Pain*, no. 1 (January–June 1987): 24–25.

42   E. Favrais, *Manuel du boulanger et de pâtisserie-boulangerie* (Paris: B. Tignol, 1904), 105; Guinard and Lesjean, *Le livre du boulanger*, 96–101; Brochoire, *Devenir boulanger*, 118.

43   Brochoire, *Devenir boulanger*, 118; Jean-Claude Mislanghe, cited in *Les Nouvelles de la Boulangerie*, November 15, 1991.

44   Guinard and Lesjean, *Le livre du boulanger*, 101–4; Brochoire, *Devenir boulanger*, 119.

45   Guinard and Lesjean, *Le livre du boulanger*, 115–17; Brochoire, *Devenir boulanger*, 140–41; Raymond Calvel, in *Boulanger-Pâtissier*, February 1986. Cf. the more technical description in Drapron et al., *Notre pain quotidien*, 130.

46   Parmentier, *Le parfait boulanger*, xxxviii, 484–90.

47   Archives nationales, Y 11673, September 30, 1749; October 2, 1733; Y 15114, October 26, 1780; Y 11385, August 9, 1771; Y 14961, April 8, 1745; Y 13494, 1729; Y 15355, November 12, 1755; Y 14948, October 2, 1733; Y 15354, February 6, 1755; Parmentier, *Le parfait boulanger*, 454–78; Baudeau, *Avis au peuple sur son premier besoin*, 74–75; Malouin, *Description des arts du meunier*, 242–46; Denis Diderot, ed., *Encyclopédie, ou, Dictionnaire raisonné des sciences, des arts et des métiers, par une Sociéte de gens de letters* (Paris: Briasson, David, Le Breton et Durand, 1751–65), vol. 7, 222; Bibliothèque nationale, ms. Joly de Fleury 1743, fol. 134 (1786).

48   Kaplan, *Le meilleur pain du monde*, 100–101.

49   Parmentier, *Le parfait boulanger*, 482–503; Malouin, *Description des arts du meunier*, 246–54; Baudeau, *Avis au peuple sur son premier besoin*, 79–80.

50   Parmentier, *Le parfait boulanger*, 539–40; Paul-Jacques Malouin, *Description des arts du meunier, du vermicellier, et du boulanger* (new edition), ed. Jean-Élie Bertrand (Neufchâtel: La Société typographique, 1771), 392; Noël Chomel, *Dictionnaire encyclopédique* (Paris: Ganeau, 1767), vol. 2, 799.

51   *Recueil des usages concernant les pains de France*, 277–78; *Encyclopédie Roret* (Paris: L. Mulo, 1913), 428–90. See also "Du nouveau dans la panification," *Le Pain Français*, no. 11 (March–April 1958): 8–10; Jean Cabut, "Le pain et sa filière," report to the Conseil économique et social, November 1988, 20; and Bernadette Angleraud, *Les boulangers lyonnais aux XIXe et XXe siècles* (Paris: Christian, 1998), 143.

52   *Recueil des usages concernant les pains de France*, 278; J.-P. Barret, "J'ai retrouvé le goût du pain," *Bulletin des Anciens Élèves de l'École de Meunerie-*ENSMIC, no. 276

(November–December 1976): 304; Guinet, "Technologies de panification," 236; Raymond Calvel, *Fidèles au Bon Pain*, no. 1 (January–June 1987): 25.

53 Guinard and Lesjean, *Le livre du boulanger*, 120; Brochoire, *Devenir boulanger*, 148, 154.

54 Guinard and Lesjean, *Le livre du boulanger*, 118; Brochoire, *Devenir boulanger*, 142.

55 Brochoire, *Devenir boulanger*, 143; Guinard and Lesjean, *Le livre du boulanger*, 114.

56 Brochoire, *Devenir boulanger*, 144–46; Guinard and Lesjean, *Le livre du boulanger*, 119; Richard-Molard, "Goût du pain"; Guinet, "Conditions générales de la panification," 224; Drapron et al., *Notre pain quotidien*, 131.

57 Brochoire, *Devenir boulanger*, 156–57; Guinard and Lesjean, *Le livre du boulanger*, 120–21.

58 See *Actes de la Recherche en Sciences Sociales*, special issue, *Anatomie du Goût*, no. 5 (October 1976), and Pierre Bourdieu, *La distinction* (Paris: Minuit, 1979). Cf. Jean Buré on the tension between the consumer's subjectivity (values, memories, family traditions) and the propensity of science to impose truths that are supposed to be empirically demonstrable (CNERNA, *La qualité du pain*, vol. 2, 571). Before very discreetly suggesting certain time-honored criteria for good bread, the INBP manual adopts a nondictatorial stance: "Le pain idéal: à chacun le sien" (Brochoire, *Devenir boulanger*, 164).

59 Félix Depledt, "Qu'est-ce que le pain, comment et pourquoi est-il consommé?" in Buré, *Le pain*, 221. See also the interview with Roland Guinet in *Les Nouvelles de la Boulangerie*, September 15, 1991.

60 *Enquête sur la boulangerie du département de la Seine* (Paris: Imprimerie impériale, 1859), 56. And Bethmont, an attorney, adds: "The taste for good bread in France is being established not only in cities but even in rural areas. I am told that in the Paris region workers no longer accept the bread they used to be given" (ibid., 57).

61 Boutroux, *Le pain et la panification*, 306; François Malepeyre and J.-S.-E. Julia de Fontenelle, *Nouveau manuel complet du boulanger*, ed. Schield-Treherne (Paris: L. Mulo, 1914), 411; Dufour, *Traité pratique de panification française et parisienne*, 24. On the role of the artisan in the "evolution of consumers' tastes" and the social significance of changes in preference (for example, on the part of many consumers for crust, considered vastly less noble than the crumb), see Daniel Bertaux, *Transformations et permanence de l'artisanat boulanger en France* (Paris: CORDES, 1980), vol. 1, 348–49.

62 Drapron et al., *Notre pain quotidien*, 155.

63 Richard-Molard, "Goût du pain," 455.

64 Buré, *Recueil des usages concernant les pains de France*, 280; Jean-Claude Mislanghe, cited in *Les Nouvelles de la Boulangerie-Pâtisserie*, December 1, 1998.

65 Bernard Ganachaud, cited in *Les Nouvelles de la Boulangerie*, February 15, 1990; *La Filière Gourmande*, June–July 2000; Barret, "J'ai retrouvé le goût du pain," 302; Calvel, "L'évolution et la qualité du pain français," 71.

66   *Le Pain Français*, no. 10 (July–August 1962), 118; CNERNA, "La qualité du pain," vol. 2, 553; *Recueil des usages concernant les pains de France*, 281. See Viron, letter to Calvel, May 30, 1996 (Viron correspondence).

67   Philippe Viron, cited in *Pâtisserie-Boulangerie: Vie Pratique*, July 5, 1990; Cabut, "Le pain et sa filière," 72; Drapron et al., *Notre pain quotidien*, 132, 159–60.

68   Calvel, *Le goût du pain*, 49.

69   Paul Nottin, *Le blé, la farine, le pain* (Paris: Hachette, 1940), 87; *Pâtisserie-Boulangerie: Vie Pratique*, July 5, 1990; Jean-Claude Mislanghe, cited in *Les Nouvelles de la Boulangerie*, November 15, 1991; *Recueil des usages concernant les pains de France*, 282; B. Launay and Jean Buré, "Apport des méthodes rhéologiques à l'étude de la qualité des produits de panification," in Buré, *Le pain*, 163–78; CNERNA, "La qualité du pain," vol. 2, 571; Calvel, *Le goût du pain*, 52–53; Calvel, in *Le Boulanger-Pâtissier*, November 1985 and February 1988.

70   Daniel Richard-Molard and Roger Drapron, "L'arôme du pain," *Techniques des industries céréalières*, no. 166 (June–July 1978); Richard-Molard, "Goût du pain," 454, 460; Calvel, "L'évolution et la qualité du pain français," 67; Calvel, in *Le Boulanger-Pâtissier*, November and December 1985; B. Launay et al., "Flaveur de la mie," *Bulletin des Anciens Élèves de l'École Française de Meunerie-ENSMIC*, no. 288 (November–December 1978): 295–99.

71   Richard-Molard, "Goût du pain," 455; Drapron et al., *Notre pain quotidien*, 156–57. D. R. Bauer, A. G. Santi, and Virginia Utermohlen, "How Individual Differences in Taste Input Impact Smell and Flavor Perceptions: An Example of a Complex Process," *InterJournal Complex Systems*, GA letter CX.32, manuscript 364; Utermohlen, "Was Proust a Taster? Taste Sensitivity to 6-n-Propylthiouracil and the Relationships among Memory, Imagination, Synesthesia, and Emotional Response to Visual Experience," *Food and Foodways* 10 (2002): 99–109; "How We Smell," *Harvard Health Letter*, September 2001, 5; Dana Small et al., "Human Cortical Gustatory Areas, *Neuroreport* 10 (1999): 7–14.

72   Richard-Molard and Drapron, "L'arôme du pain," 3–5; Richard-Molard, "Goût du pain," 454–56; Roger Drapron and Daniel Richard-Molard, "Influence de diverse procédés technologiques sur la formation de l'arôme du pain," in Buré, *Le pain*, 143–61; Guinet, *Technologie du pain français*, 155; interview with Raymond Guinet, *Les Nouvelles de la Boulangerie*, September 15, 1991. For a summary of the work of Richard-Molard, Drapron, and others addressed to a popular audience, see Maurice Meyer, *100 questions sur le pain* (Geneva: Liber, 1997), 59.

73   See Calvel, *The Taste of Bread*, trans. Ronald L. Wirtz (Gaithersburg, Md.: Aspen, 2001). The works of the specialists of the French school on which Raymond Calvel relies were themselves less ambitious than Calvel realizes, as I noted above. One can find some of the premises of *The Taste of Bread* in Calvel's first book, *La boulangerie moderne*, first published in 1952. I have used the seventh edition (Paris: Eyrolles, 1975).

74 Pierre Anglade, ed., *Vins et vignobles de France* (Paris: Larousse-Le Savour Club, 1987), 611. See also the fine article on tasting by Jean-Claude Ribaut in *Le Monde*, October 27, 2001.

75 As a historian, I would be tempted to write that there is no such thing as a fact that is a raw "given" in reality; a fact is always more or less constructed, bearing the mark of the person who "observed" it.

76 The actual process of baking [*cuisson*], a classic category but hard for the consumer to evaluate, will be addressed under the other analytical headings.

77 See Bernard Ganachaud's campaign to put the accent back on taste in the major bakery competitions, a campaign that seems to have aroused some resistance: "I got them to add a grade for taste in the Coupe d'Europe de boulangerie [the European Bakery Cup]. The same thing for the competition for the title of Meilleur Ouvrier de France. I'll do the same for the World Cup project with which I am involved. Not everyone appreciates my enthusiasm, but that doesn't bother me!" (cited in *Michel Montignac Magazine* 1 (May–June 1993): 28.

78 Kaplan, *Le meilleur pain du monde*; Malepeyre and Fontenelle, *Nouveau manuel complet du boulanger*, 601; Barbarin, *Le scandale du pain*, 99; J. de Brévans, *Le pain et la viande* (Paris: J.-B. Baillière et fils, 1892), 119.

79 Dufour, *Traité pratique de panification française et parisienne*, xix, xxii, xxii; *Le Boulanger-Pâtissier*, October 1954; Roland Guinet, "La conservation du pain par le froid," *Technique Meunière*, no. 79 (November 1960); *Les Nouvelles de la Boulangerie*, February 1, 1990; *La Boulangerie Française*, May 15, 1990; Richard-Molard, "Goût du pain," 474.

80 Boulangerie Éric Kayser, press release, 2002, 5.

81 Lionel Poilâne cited in *Le Figaro*, February 17, 1999; Bernard Ganachaud cited in *Les Nouvelles de la Boulangerie*, February 15, 1990; Raymond Calvel, in *Le Boulanger-Pâtissier*, February 1998; Calvel, *Fidèles au Bon Pain*, no. 1 (January–June 1987); Henri Nuret, "La vérité sort du four," *Bulletin de l'École Française de Meunerie*, no. 216 (December 1966): 268.

82 Malouin, *Description et détails des arts du meunier, du vermicelier et du boulenger* [sic], *avec une histoire abrégée de la boulengerie et un dictionnaire de ces arts* (1779 ed.), 18–19, 81–82, 93–94); Parmentier, *Le parfait boulanger*, xxvii–xxviii, 119–29, 137–38; Poncelet, *Histoire naturelle*, 154–55, 173–78; Edme Béguillet, *Traité des subsistances et des grains qui servent à la nourriture de l'homme* (Paris: Prault fils, 1780), 74–76, 148–55, 161, 331–32, 423; Kaplan, *Les ventres de Paris*, 37–53; Raymond Calvel, in *Fidèles au Bon Pain*, no. 1 (January–June 1987): 26; Calvel, in *Le Boulanger-Pâtissier*, February 1986; Calvel, *Le Levain Syndical*, March 1986; Boulangerie Éric Kayser, press release, 2002, 5; interview with Dominique Saibron, January 17, 2002; interview with Patrick Castagna, June 2001.

83 Raymond Geoffroy, "Pain hier et pain aujourd'hui," *Techniques des Industries Céréalières*, no. 154 (April–May 1976): 6; B. Launay and M. Hourne, "Flaveur de

la mie des pains: apport de l'analyse sensorielle à la mise en évidence de diffé-rences de flaveur," *Bulletin des Anciens Élèves de l'École de Meunerie-ENSMIC*, no. 288 (November–December 1978): 293–99; *La Filière Gourmande*, June–July 2000 (a rather confused article that reflects neither on the conceptual problems of this future world nor on the tensions that threaten to destroy the sector). Along the same lines as Launay and Hourne, see Roger Drapron, "Le goût du pain," *Bulletin des Anciens Élèves de l'École Française de Meunerie*, no. 244 (July–August 1971): 127.

Chapter 2   Bread: The Double Crisis

1   Meeting held November 26, 1954; see CNERNA, *La qualité du pain*, Les journées scientifiques, November 1954–April 1960 (Paris: Centre national de la recherche scientifique, 1962), vol. 1, 55–58; *La Boulangerie Française*, May 16–31, 1958; Ray-mond Calvel, *La boulangerie moderne*, 7th ed. (Paris: Eyrolles, 1975), 449–50; M.-F. Rolland et al., "Pourquoi la consommation de pain diminue-t-elle?" *Annales de la Nutrition et de l'Alimentation* 31 (1977): 365–80. "People are striking for a slice of flank steak," the February 1995 *Boulanger-Pâtissier* noted. "People no longer say 'earn my bread,' they say 'my steak.' " One member of the CNERNA commission put it with similar succinctness: "People are eating less bread because it's poor man's food" (Jacquot, session of November 28, 1954, CNERNA, *La qualité du pain*, vol. 1, 59). In the same session: "Bread symbolizes the lower classes and meat the upper classes" (64). Or, as André Baril, a baker from Gironde, remarked: "As the layer of butter gets thicker, the slice of bread gets thinner" (*Les Nouvelles de la Bou-langerie*, June 1, 1985). "For some people, eating less bread proves that their place in society is higher" (*Ami de la Boulangerie*, February 15, 1957). Cf. more recent echoes of this problematic in the proceedings of the fifth "Belley" meetings devoted to food issues, in *Pâtisserie-Boulangerie: Vie Pratique*, October 17, 1991. Let us note that toward the end of the Old Regime, during noncrisis periods, a journeyman or an urban worker spent 50 percent of his budget on bread alone. According to Engel's law, as one's income goes up one spends a continually declining portion of one's budget on food. In 1960, one-third of a family budget in France, everything included, went for food. In 1999, the proportion had dropped to 18 percent.

2   *Le Petit Meunier*, January 31, 1957 (the article also asks "whether the policy of our governors is to continue to want to make France a country of wheat production in which no more bread will be consumed"); *La Boulangerie Française*, May 15–31, 1958; Paul Marquenne, "Le goût du pain," *Bulletin des Anciens Élèves de l'École Française de Meunerie*, no. 159 (May–June 1957): 137; *Plaisirs Gastronomie Magazine*, January–February 1989; interview with Philippe Viron, *Pâtisserie-Boulangerie: Vie Pratique*, July 5, 1990.

3   *Le Boulanger-Pâtissier*, June, August, September, and October 1954; July 1955 (com-

mentary by Jean Buré, an agricultural engineer and laboratory director at the École française de meunerie who was to preside over the CNERNA colloquium), and March 1956; *La Boulangerie Française*, February 1–15, 1955, and May 16–31, 1958; Marquenne, "Le goût du pain," 132–33, 136; *Le Petit Meunier*, December 12, 1957; Georges Barberin, *Le scandale du pain* (Paris: Nizet, 1956), 12, 47–48, 85. See also Raymond Calvel in *Le Boulanger-Pâtissier*, November 1983; H. Martin, "Le problème du pain," *Bulletin des Anciens Élèves de l'École Française de Meunerie*, no. 212 (March–April 1966): 85–86.

4 *Michel Montignac Magazine*, no. 1 (May–June 1993): 21.

5 E. Guillée, preface to Émile Dufour, *Traité pratique de la panification française et parisienne* (Château-Thierry: Imprimerie moderne, 1937), xxxi; Hélène Gozard, "La boulangerie à Paris pendant l'Occupation," Université de Paris-I, master's thesis, 1994–95, 10.

6 CNERNA, *La qualité du pain*, sessions held in November 1954, vol. 1, 23–55, 64. Cf. the long account in *L'Ami de la Boulangerie*, February 1, 1961.

7 Jean Buré, "Introduction," in Jean Buré, ed., *Le pain*, proceedings of the CNERNA colloquium, Paris, November 1977, followed by *Recueil des usages concernant les pains de France* (Paris: Centre national de la recherche scientifique, 1979), 13; J. Girault, "Si le pain ne meurt," *Le Pain Français*, no. 6 (May 1957): 4.

8 Raymond Calvel, "Notre pain quotidien," *Bulletin des Anciens Élèves de l'École Française de Meunerie*, no. 171 (May–June 1959).

9 *Le Boulanger-Pâtissier*, March 1954 and July 1956; *L'Ami de la Boulangerie*, February 15, 1957.

10 *L'Ami de la Boulangerie*, February 1, 1961.

11 CNERNA, *La qualité du pain*, vol. 2, session held July 8, 1958, 553–55.

12 Ibid., session held May 30, 1958, vol. 1, 71–98.

13 See Buré, *Le pain*, 225–312.

14 Raymond Calvel, "L'évolution et la qualité du pain français," *Bulletin des Anciens Élèves de l'École Française de Meunerie*, no. 254 (March–April 1973): 62–63, 67, and no. 268 (July–August 1975): 204; A. Verger, cited in *Le Boulanger-Pâtissier* (January 1983).

15 *Les Nouvelles de la Boulangerie*, September 1, 1976, April 1 and October 15, 1980.

16 Ibid., March 1 and April 15, 1983; October 1, 1984.

17 Ibid., June 16 and October 15, 1985; *Le Boulanger-Pâtissier*, November 1985, 8.

18 *Les Nouvelles de la Boulangerie*, October 1, 1983.

19 Ibid., April 1, 1984, and June 1, 1985; *Nice-Matin*, June 24, 1983; *La Montagne-Centre France*, June 24, 1983; *Le Républicain Lorrain*, June 24, 1983; *Ouest France*, June 24, 1983; *Le Figaro*, June 24, 1983; *Le Boulanger-Pâtissier*, June 1983; Guy Boulet, *Boulangers, artisans de demain: l'hypothétique mariage de la tradition et du progrès* (Rouen: L'Harmattan, 1991), 122; *États généraux de la boulangerie*, Paris, 1983, press release, part 3, 11–13.

20 *États généraux de la boulangerie*, press release, III, 11, 12 and 13; *Les Nouvelles de la Boulangerie*, May 15 and October 15, 1983.

21 Boulet, *Boulangers, artisans de demain*, 144; Raymond Calvel in *Le Boulanger-Pâtissier*, October 1983.

22 *Les Nouvelles de la Boulangerie*, November 1, 1986, February 15, October 15, and November 15, 1987; *Pâtisserie-Boulangerie: Vie Pratique*, September 6, 1990.

23 Raymond Calvel, "Le pain de campagne ou le travesti fariné," *Bulletin des Anciens Élèves de l'Ecole Française de Meunerie*, no. 218, March–April 1967, 85 (see also *Industries des Céréales*, November–December 1994, 35–36); Hubert Chiron, "Cinquante ans de progrès en technologie boulangère," *Industries des Céréales*, no. 116 (January–March 2000): 11, 13; Henri Chiron and Bernard Godon, "Historique de la panification," in *La panification française*, ed. Roland Guinet and Bernard Godon (Paris: Tec et Doc-Lavoisier, 1994), 39; *Le Monde*, August 31, 1993; *Nouvelles de la Boulangerie*, June 1, 1985, and February 15, 1990; *Nouvelles de la Boulangerie-Pâtisserie*, March 15, 2001. During the Old Regime, many bakers in the city offered a great variety of specialty breads, the most famous being the light and tender *pains mollets (à la Reine, de Ségovie*, and so on; see Kaplan, *Le meilleur pain du monde*). The rivalry among Lyon bakers in the late nineteenth century led the latter "to deploy treasures of the imagination to produce all sorts of 'specialty' breads that would appeal to a bourgeois clientele" (Bernadette Angleraud, *Les boulangers lyonnais aux XIXe et XXe siècles* [Paris: Christian, 1998], 29). See also J. de la Guérivière, "Les pains spéciaux: destinations, compositions et technologies," in Buré, *Le pain*, 131–42.

24 *Michel Montignac Magazine*, no. 1 (May–June 1993): 33; *La Boulangerie Française*, November 2000.

25 *Le Canard Enchaîné*, June 10, 2001; *LSA*, no. 1728 (June 10, 2001).

26 Gozard, "Boulangerie à Paris," 9; *Le Petit Meunier*, August 8, 1957; *La Boulangerie Française*, May 16–31, 1958, and May 16–31, 1960; H. Gounelle de Pontanel and D. Prandini-Jarre, "Valeur nutritive des pains," in Buré, *Le pain*, 179–200, and *Recueil des usages concernant les pains de France*, in ibid., 284–86.

27 *Les Nouvelles de la Boulangerie*, May 2, June 1, and November 1, 1983; January 1, April 15, May 2, October 1, and December 15, 1984.

28 *Nouvelle République du Centre-Ouest*, November 30, 1985; *Le Boulanger-Pâtissier*, November 1985; *Les Nouvelles de la Boulangerie*, April 1 and October 15, 1986.

29 *Les Nouvelles de la Boulangerie-Pâtisserie*, November 15, 1996; *Le Pâtissier-Boulanger*, February 1992; *Les Nouvelles de la Boulangerie*, February 1 and November 1, 1990; *La Boulangerie Française*, December 1996.

30 *Le Figaro*, February 17, 1999; *Télérama*, no. 2679, February 16, 2001; *Les Nouvelles de la Boulangerie-Pâtisserie*, January 1, 2001. Cf. the action of the Association Pain Qualité Santé created at the initiative of the Nord-Pas-de-Calais regional council

under the presidency of a physician specializing in nutrition (*Filière Gourmande*, March 2001).

31 H. W. Lopez, A. Adam, F. Leenhard, F. Batifoulier, and C. Rémésy, "Quelle évolution nutritionnelle pour le pain?" in *Aliments et boissons, densité nutritionnelle, choix alimentaires, santé* (Clermont-Ferrand: Université d'été de nutrition, 2001). These authors call on bakers to reduce "noticeably" the dosage of salt, while at the same time urging them to "improve the organoleptic qualities of the bread and diversify the taste of the products offered."

32 *Les Nouvelles de la Boulangerie*, October 16, 1986; *Les Nouvelles de la Boulangerie-Pâtisserie*, January 15 and November 1, 1997, June 1, 1999, December 15, 2000, and January 1, 2001.

33 Dufour, *Traité pratique de panification française et parisienne*, xxii.

34 The accusation of "elitism" hurt, flattered, and troubled Guy Boulet, who sought a path for himself in the confederation for a long time before resigning from it in 2001. He had genuine intellectual ambition (and gifts: he began his university studies late but performed brilliantly) and high moral standards, but he is above all a baker, the son of a baker, a master artisan with apprentices. His "elitism" has nothing in common with the elitism for which his colleague Christian Vabre is reproached; Vabre, a Meilleur Ouvrier de France and, like Boulet, passionately interested in training, once remarked: "They say we're the best, so let's show it" (*Filière Gourmande*, December 1995).

35 Boulet, *Boulangers, artisans de demain*; *Filière Gourmande*, June–July 1997.

36 *La Boulangerie Française*, January 1 and January 15, 1989, November 1996; *Les Nouvelles de la Boulangerie-Pâtisserie*, October 1, 1995, November 1 and November 15, 1998; *Le Levain Syndical*, January 1990.

37 Boulet, *Boulangers, artisans de demain*, 145; *Les Nouvelles de la Boulangerie-Pâtisserie*, December 15, 1993, October 15, 1995, July 1, 1996, July 1, 1997, and May 15, 2001; *La Boulangerie Française*, August 1997 and September 1998; advertisement for "Le Club," *Pâtisserie-Boulangerie: Vie Pratique*, May 2000. Cf. a research project spurred by the emergence of bread in the French tradition: Philippe Wirsta et al., "La pousse contrôlée dans la fabrication du pain de tradition française," *Industrie des Céréales*, April–June 1994, 22–27.

38 Steven Kaplan, "La lutte pour le contrôle du marché du travail à Paris au XVIIIe siècle," *Revue d'Histoire Moderne et Contemporaine* 36 (July–September 1989): 361–412.

39 A. Savoie, *Meunerie, boulangerie, pâtisserie* (Paris: G. Doin, 1922), 238. Cf. the ditty on 249: "Every baker's boy, when night falls, goes off in pain / Toward his baking room, as to his grave, stumbling / For people die from this 'dough,' as they live from it." In a well-known investigation of the bakery business in the mid-nineteenth century, the economist P. Gosset, exaggerating in the manner of the

police, testified that "journeymen, an indomitable race, lord it over their bosses and are the masters of the baking room" (in Frédéric Le Play, ed., *Enquête sur la boulangerie du département de la Seine* [Paris: Imprimerie impériale, 1859], 72). On the politicization of the social issue and of the baking room in the Lyon region, see Angleraud, *Les boulangers lyonnais aux XIXe et XXe siècles*, 101.

40 Kaplan, *Le meilleur pain du monde*; Kaplan, "L'apprentissage au XVIIIe siècle: le cas de Paris," *Revue d'Histoire Moderne et Contemporaine* 90 (July–September 1993): 436–79.

41 Isabelle Bertaux-Wiaume, *Transformations et permanences de l'artisanat: l'apprentissage en boulangerie* (Paris: CORDES, 1978), vol. 2, 31, 50, 53, 55, 67, 71, 81, 98, 104, 107, 109, 115–16.

42 *Les Nouvelles de la Boulangerie*, May 2 and December 15, 1976, July 1, 1986; Jean Cabut, "Le pain et sa filière," report to the Conseil économique et social, November 1988, 47, 78.

43 Interviews with Guy Boulet, Thierry Rabineau, and Jean-Claude Mislanghe, spring 2001.

44 *Les Nouvelles de la Boulangerie-Pâtisserie*, December 1, 1993, and February 1, 1995; *Le Monde*, September 24, 1997; *Les Nouvelles de la Boulangerie*, June 1, 1991; Syndicat Patronal de la Boulangerie et de la Boulangerie-Pâtisserie (Paris region), *Annuaire 2000, Guide Pratique*, 415–19; interview with Guy Boulet, May 2001.

45 *Les Nouvelles de la Boulangerie-Pâtisserie*, July 1, 2000; *Le Fournil Atlantique*, June–July 2000.

46 Interviews with Gérard Brochoire, May–June 2001.

47 *Boulangerie-Pâtisserie: Vie Pratique*, October 1986; interviews with Bernard Seller and with Alexandre Viron, spring 2001.

48 *La Boulangerie-Pâtisserie*, October 1955 and August 1956.

49 *Les Nouvelles de la Boulangerie*, July 17, 1991; *Les Échos*, November 1999; *Pâtisserie-Boulangerie: Vie Pratique*, February 1992 and April 1995; *Le Boulanger-Pâtissier*, January 1985; M. Drillech in *Le Monde*, April 21, 2001.

50 Alain Schifres, "Laissez-nous notre pain quotidien," *Le Nouvel Observateur*, December 25–31, 1987.

51 *Fidèles au Bon Pain*, no. 8, 1992. Instead of attacking Coffe, Clavel should have recruited him for his association. On television, too, Coffe made mistakes, got the rate of extraction of a т 55 flour wrong, and mixed up Joseph and the Pharaoh in the biblical story of the lean cows. It hardly matters: he played his role superbly.

52 *Le Figaro*, February 17, 1999.

53 *Médecine et Nutrition* 37, no. 3 (2001): 105. On the famous (and perfectly banal) formula attributed to Marie Antoinette (a formula that had already been articulated by Rousseau in his *Confessions* and, with numerous variants, by dozens of others going back at least to the sixteenth century, see the excellent study by Véronique Campion-Vincent and Christine Shojaei Kawan, "Marie-Antoinette and Her Fa-

mous Saying: Three Levels of Communication, Three Modes of Accusation, and Two Troubled Centuries," *Fabula, Revue d'Études sur le Conte Populaire* 41 (2000): 13–41.

Chapter 3 White Bread: A Western Story

1 Dr. Despaux, *Du pain blanc et du pain bis* (Meaux: Destouches, 1886); Roger Drapron et al., *Notre pain quotidien* (Paris: Antenne générale de publication, 1999), 150–52 (Drapron also provides a sort of scientific update concerning bread made from wheat at a high level of extraction); A. Gausset, text in *Annales des falsifications et de l'expertise chimique*, cited in *Le Pain Français* (Revue de l'Association des anciens élèves de l'École de boulangerie des Grands Moulins de Paris), no. 7 (January–February 1962); Bernadette Angleraud, *Les boulangers lyonnais aux XIXe et XXe siècles* (Paris: Christian, 1998), 52; Émile Fleurent, *Le pain de froment* (Paris: Gouthier-Villars, 1911), preface, 5–7; Marcel Arpin (former director of the Scientific Division of the Paris Bakers' Association), *Historique de la meunerie et de la boulangerie* (Paris: Le Chancelier, 1948), vol. 2, 312; Fédération de Provence des Commissions d'Études et de Propagande du Bon Pain, introduction to Dr. J. Romanet, *Le bon pain: les possibilités actuelles de l'amélioration du pain* (Marseilles: Imprimerie nouvelle, 1937), reprinted in part in *Bulletin des Anciens Élèves de l'École de Boulangerie des Grands Moulins de Paris*, May–June 1937; Dr. Henri Thiébaut, *Notre pain quotidien*, published by the author (1953), 9, 24–25.

2 Georges Barberin, *Le scandale du pain* (Paris: Nizet, 1956), 12, 14, 19–20, 29–37, 104.

3 CNERNA, *La qualité du pain*, Journées scientifiques du CNERNA, November 1954–April 1960, vol. 2 (Paris: Centre national de la recherche scientifique, 1964), 427–32, 436; *L'Ami de la Boulangerie*, June 1, 1959, and April 15, 1960. Cf. Jean Buré in *Le Pain Français*, no. 3 (November 1956): 20.

4 Claude Thouvenot, *Le pain d'autrefois, chroniques alimentaires d'un monde qui s'en va* (Paris: A. Leson, 1977), 32–33.

5 E. Guillée, preface to Émile Dufour, *Traité pratique de panification française et parisienne* (Château-Thierry: Imprimerie moderne, 1937), viii; *Le Boulanger-Pâtissier*, February 1939; Hubert Chiron, "L'évolution technologique en boulangerie française: méthodes, équipements, adjuvants," *Industries Alimentaires et Agricoles* 3 (January–February 1994): 37. On the very poor quality of bread (gray in color, made with substitute ingredients, rationing) during the war of 1914–1918, see the liberal, antistatist text by Alfred Beaucourt, *La politique du pain pendant la guerre (1914–19)* (Paris: Rousseau et Cie, 1919).

6 Raymond Geoffroy, "Le problème du pain," *Bulletin des Anciens Élèves de l'École Française de Meunerie*, no. 103 (January–February 1948): 4.

7 Hélène Gozard, "La boulangerie à Paris pendant l'Occupation," masters thesis, Université de Paris-I, 1994–95, 116, 118, 121; Raymond Calvel, *La boulangerie mo-*

derne, 7th edition (Paris: Eyrolles, 1975), 450–51; Calvel, "L'évolution de la qualité du pain et le problème de son contrôle," *Bulletin des Anciens Élèves de l'École Française de Meunerie*, no. 268 (July–August 1975): 200–201; Roland Guinet, "Évolution de la qualité du pain: incidence de l'équipement et des méthodes de fabrication," in Jean Buré, ed., *Le pain*, proceedings of the CNERNA colloquium, Paris, November 1977, followed by *Recueil des usages concernant les pains de France* (Paris: Centre national de la recherche scientifique, 1979), 121.

8 For this chronicle, see Hubert Chiron, "Un survol de l'apport de la boulangerie de l'ouest à la panification française," *Fidèles au Bon Pain*, no. 9 (1993): 12–13; as always, Chiron relies on Raymond Calvel, "Incidences de l'accentuation du pétrissage sur la panification," *Bulletin des Anciens Élèves de l'École Française de Meunerie*, no. 162 (November–December 1957): 281–82. According to Calvel, Albert might well have acquired his secret method from an old worker who used prolonged kneading to produce bread that was very white but that did not rise well. Even if Albert codified and popularized this approach, it is likely that the technique "[had been] known for a long time in the northwestern Deux-Sèvres region." Moreover, Chiron's summary description according to which breadmaking technology "remained frozen" (after the war until the late 1950s) is less a historiographic evaluation than a moral judgment. See Hubert Chiron, "1949/1993: incidences des mutations technologiques sur les caractéristiques du pain français," *Industries des Céréales*, April–June 1994, 6.

9 Calvel, "Incidences de l'accentuation du pétrissage sur la panification," 277–88.

10 R. Bousquet, "La fabrication du pain par pétrissage accentué en Charente-Maritime," *Bulletin des Anciens Élèves de l'École Française de Meunerie*, no. 171 (May–June 1959): 133–38.

11 "The bread we obtain without adding any improving agents is as good as—if not better than—when we use them. The production of good-quality white bread is thus in no way dependent on the use of such agents" (ibid., 16). Today's most gifted and conscientious bakers would say the same thing.

12 Raymond Geoffroy in *Le Petit Meunier*, August 15, 1957; Geoffroy, *La Boulangerie Française*, September 1–15, 1957; Geoffroy, "Bilan du pétrissage accéléré en France et à l'étranger," *Techniques des Industries Céréalières*, no. 135 (January–February 1972): 5–6. In 1961, Raymond Calvel applauded the often "spectacular" effect of fava flour as a whitening agent in the breadmaking process, one that also "contributes to a sharp improvement in the appearance of the loaves, [which are] rounder and a bit more fully developed." He sees fava flour, used in a dosage of 1 to 1.5 percent, as "a precious ameliorant" in the process based on intensive kneading. Moreover, he asserts that ascorbic acid, which had been authorized relatively recently (1953), "also plays a non-trivial role" (Raymond Calvel, "Pain, progrès technique, et qualité," *Bulletin des Anciens Élèves de l'École Française de Meunerie*, no. 181 [January–February 1961]: 21).

13 J.-S.-E. Julia de Fontenelle and François Malepeyre, *Nouveau manuel complet du boulanger*, ed. Schield-Treherne (Paris: L. Mulo, 1914), 312–81.

14 Paul Nottin, *Le blé, la farine, le pain* (Paris: Hachette, 1940), 68–69; Arpin, *Historique de la meunerie et de la boulangerie*, vol. 2, 173; L. Lindet (an agronomist), preface to *Pétrissage mécanique et pétrissage à bras: études comparatives* (Paris: Syndicat de la boulangerie, 1909), 5–6; Isabelle Bertaux-Wiaume, *Transformations et permanences de l'artisanat: l'apprentissage en boulangerie* (Paris; CORDES, 1978), vol. 2, 99; Fleurent, *Le pain de froment*, 200–205; Fontenelle and Malepeyre, *Nouveau manuel* (1914), 336–37; François Malepeyre and J.-S.-E. Julia de Fontenelle, *Nouveau manuel complet du boulanger*, ed. François Malepeyre (Paris: Roret, 1871), 355–60; J.-S.-E. Julia de Fontenelle and P.-M.-N. Benoit, *Nouveau manuel complet du boulanger* (Paris: Roret, 1846), 276; A. Savoie, *Meunerie, boulangerie, pâtisserie* (Paris: G. Doin, 1922), 215; CNERNA, *La qualité du pain*, vol. 2, 582–83.

15 E. Favrais, *Manuel du boulanger et de pâtisserie-boulangerie* (Paris: B. Tignol, 1904), 148; *Pétrissage mécanique et pétrissage à bras*, Syndicat de la boulangerie, 37ff, 131–36; Jean Cabut, "Le pain et sa filière," report to the Conseil économique et social, November 1988, 20; *Le Boulanger-Pâtissier*, December 1955 and April 1985 (editorial by Raymond Calvel); Guy Boulet, *Boulangers, artisans de demain: l'hypothétique mariage de la tradition et du progrès* (Rouen: INBP, L'Harmattan, 1991), 36–37.

16 Geoffroy, "Bilan du pétrissage accéléré en France et à l'étranger," 6; Roland Guinet, "Plus blanc que blanc," *Le Pain Français*, no. 1 (March–April 1961): 5; Chiron, "1949/1993," 6.

17 Boulet, *Boulangers, artisans de demain*, 104–5 (emphasis added; I wonder to what extent that tastelessness was apparent in the 1960s).

18 Roland Guinet, "Plus blanc que blanc," *Le Pain Français*, no. 3 (March–April 1961): 3–5; Guinet, "La qualité d'un bon pain de France," October 1964, cited by Hubert Chiron, "Cinquante années de progrès en technologie boulangère," *Industrie des Céréales*, no. 116 (January–March 2000): 12; J. Girault, "Les miracles n'existent pas," *Le Pain Français*, no. 7 (January–February 1962) (an exhortation mined with contradictions).

19 Calvel, "Pain, progrès technique, et qualité," 19–21

20 Ibid., 21; Calvel, "L'évolution et la qualité du pain français," *Bulletin des Anciens Élèves de l'École Française de Meunerie*, no. 254 (March–April 1973): 200–202; Calvel, "L'évolution et qualité," 64; Calvel, cited in *Les Nouvelles de la Boulangerie*, September 15, 1991; Calvel, in *Fidèles au Bon Pain*, no. 8 (1992); Raymond Geoffroy, "Effets de la farine de fève en boulangerie," *Technique Meunière*, no. 76 (March–April 1960): 5–7; Favrais, *Manuel du boulanger et de pâtisserie-boulangerie*, 27; Chiron, "L'évolution technologique en boulangerie française," 34. An attempt made in 1967 to launch an alternative to the western white bread, a "high art" bread made without fava flour according to the attenuated ("improved") method of kneading (although "the posters declare that this bread is made according to the traditional

method without artificial oxygenation of the dough"), seems to have failed, in part because this method exacted too high a cost in terms of the "machinability" of the dough and the volume of the bread. See the laconic allusion in Chiron, "1949/1993," 9-10, and in Chiron and Bernard Godon, "Historique de la panification," in Roland Guinet and Bernard Godon, *La panification française* (Paris: Tec et Doc, 1994), 38.

21 Geoffroy, "Bilan du pétrissage accéléré en France et à l'étranger," 8-9; Geoffroy, "Pain d'hier et d'aujourd'hui," *Techniques des Industries Céréalières*, no. 154 (April–May 1976): 6.

22 Calvel, "L'évolution et la qualité," 63.

23 Roland Guinet, "Évolution de la qualité du pain," 122; Chiron, "Cinquante années de progrès," 3-7; Chiron and Godon, "Historique," 37; Chiron, "Un survol de l'apport de la boulangerie de l'ouest à la panification française," 15-16; Boulet, *Boulangers, artisans de demain,*118-19.

24 Chiron, "Un survol de l'apport de la boulangerie de l'ouest à la panification française," 15-16; Chiron, "1949-1993," 12; Boulet, *Boulangers, artisans de demain,* 40-41; Roger Drapron, "Le goût du pain," *Bulletin des Anciens Élèves de l'École Française de Meunerie,* no. 244 (July–August 1971): 127-32; *Nouvelles de la Boulangerie,* January 15, 1980, and January 1, 1984.

Chapter 4   The Enemy

1 Steven L. Kaplan, *Le meilleur pain du monde: les boulangers de Paris au XVIIIe siècle* (Paris: Fayard, 1996); André Join-Lambert, *L'organisation de la boulangerie en France* (Paris: A. Rousseau, 1900), 144; P. W. Fouassier, *Pour le boulanger* (Paris: Dunod, 1939), 170-71; *La Boulangerie Française,* April 1 and April 15, 1950.

2 Jean Cabut, "Le pain et sa filière," report to the Conseil économique et social, November 1988, 7, 49; *Les Nouvelles de la Boulangerie,* June 1, 1988; *Pâtisserie-Boulangerie: Vie Pratique,* February 1996; *La Filière Gourmande,* April 1995; M. Hy, B. Lassaut, and F. Nicolas, "Concurrence entre les formes industrielles et artisanales de production-distribution des biens alimentaires: exemples de la boulangerie et de la boucherie," unpublished, INRA, 1989, 6, 8, 18-22. Daniel Bertaux evokes "the beginning of a violent struggle" around 1978 in *Transformations et permanence de l'artisanat boulanger en France* (Paris: CORDES, 1980), vol. 2, 367.

3 *Le Boulanger-Pâtissier,* May 1983, January 1984 (testimony by Ch. Risacher), and November 1985; *Les Nouvelles de la Boulangerie,* June 1, 1985, December 15, 1988, November 1, 1990 (noting that there were only 332 bakeries in Sweden and 900 in England around 1990), and July 15, 1991; Cabut, "Le pain et sa filière," 7, 40, 46; *Les Nouvelles de la Boulangerie-Pâtisserie,* November 15, 1996, and February 15, 1998; *Fournil Atlantique,* June–July 2000; *Toque Magazine,* no. 105 (January 2001); Bertaux, *Transformations et permanence de l'artisanat boulanger en France,* vol. 1, 28-

33; figures for the 1990s reported by the confederation, the Association nationale de la meunerie française, and *Les Nouvelles de la Boulangerie*, January 15, 1997. At the end of the 1980s, artisanal baking included nearly 175,000 persons: 43 percent were owners and their spouses, 20 percent baking room workers, 10 percent apprentices, 6 percent pastry workers, 21 percent sales and delivery personnel, and others (Cabut, "Le pain et sa filière," 47). Cf. *Les Nouvelles de la Boulangerie*, October 15, 1985, mentioning 106,672 salaried workers.

4 *Le Boulanger-Pâtissier*, February 1939 and March 1954; *Les Nouvelles de la Boulangerie*, July 15, 1988, September 1, 1988, and June 1, 1992.

5 *Toque Magazine*, no. 23 (July 1993); *Les Nouvelles de la Boulangerie-Pâtisserie*, January 15, 1995.

6 *Toque Magazine*, no. 23 (July 1993), and no. 39, January 1995; *Les Nouvelles de la Boulangerie-Pâtisserie*, January 15, 1995; *Pâtisserie-Boulangerie: Vie Pratique*, October 1996. See also Guy Boulet, *Boulangers, artisans de demain: l'hypothétique mariage de la tradition et du progrès* (Rouen: L'Harmattan, 1991), 80–81, on the catastrophic impact of industrial competition on rural bakers (to whom the industry presented itself as the only hope of salvation).

7 *La Boulangerie Française*, no. 212 (March 2000), and no. 216 (July 2000); *Les Nouvelles de la Boulangerie*, June 1, 1986, and July 1, 1990.

8 *Les Nouvelles de la Boulangerie*, April 1, 1977, June 15 and October 1, 1985.

9 Ibid., March 1, 1976, January 1, June 15, and December 15, 1985.

10 Ibid., November 1, 1986, July 15, 1990; *Les Nouvelles de la Boulangerie-Pâtisserie*, January 15, 1992, December 15, 1995, and December 15, 1999.

11 *L'Épi de la Profession*, March–April 2000.

12 *Les Nouvelles de la Boulangerie*, May 15, 1978, January 1, January 15, and February 15, 1980, January 1, 1987, June 15, 1988, January 15, 1989, and May 15, 1990. The word "enemy" turns up more or less everywhere in the bakers' discourse, both at the base and in the associations: see, for example, a text adopted by several associations in Boulet, *Boulangers, artisans de demain*, 81–82.

13 Ibid., February 15, 1980; June 15, August 1, August 15, and October 1, 1988.

14 Ibid., April 1, 1980, January 1, 1988.

15 Ibid., August 1, 1976, May 15, 1987; *Les Nouvelles de la Boulangerie-Pâtisserie*, April 15, 1988.

16 *Le Boulanger-Pâtissier*, November 1985; *Les Nouvelles de la Boulangerie*, February 15, 1991, and March 15, 1993. On the relation between the return of the manual trades and the cult of the artisan, see *Les Nouvelles de la Boulangerie*, September 15, 1998.

17 *Toque Magazine*, no. 47 (October 1995), and no. 95 (February 2000); *Les Nouvelles de la Boulangerie-Pâtisserie*, June 1, 1998; Philippe Viron, letter to Claude Willm, July 11, 1996, Viron correspondence.

18 Annick Colonna-Césari in *Le Monde*, January 22, 1985; *Le Boulanger-Pâtissier*, March 1985. Eighty-five percent of the respondents in a 1995 IFOP survey think that "the

artisanal trades are threatened." The bakery business is the third of the trades most commonly identified as artisanal, after carpentry and masonry (*Les Nouvelles de la Boulangerie-Pâtisserie*, October 1995).

19 Letter from Philippe Viron to Claude Willm, July 22, 1996, Viron correspondence; *La Filière Gourmande*, April–May 1994, March 1995, June–July and August–September 2000.

20 *Les Nouvelles de la Boulangerie-Pâtisserie*, November 15, 1998, July 1, 1999, March 1, 2000, July 1, 2000, January 1, 2001; *Fournil Atlantique*, June–July 2000; *Les Nouvelles de la Boulangerie*, April 15, 1988; interview with Jean-Pierre Crouzet, June 2001.

21 *La Boulangerie Française*, February 15, 1988, May 15, 1990, and March 1, 1995; *Les Nouvelles de la Boulangerie-Pâtisserie*, November 15, 1998, July 1, 1999.

22 Kaplan, *Le meilleur pain du monde*, 167–69, 345–47.

23 Ibid., 455–59.

24 Valérie Archenault, "L'idéal du pain," mémoire, Université de Toulouse le Mirail, 1996, 114–16; *Les Nouvelles de la Boulangerie*, January 1 and June 1, 1985. Jean Cabut takes up the same theme: "It's you, madame, it's the baker's wife, who represents—how much? 70%, at least. That figure isn't too high, I believe" (ibid., January 15, 1985). Cf. Isabelle Bertaux-Wiaume, "L'installation dans la boulangerie artisanale," *Sociologie du Travail*, no. 1 (1982): 8–23. On "the productivity of bakers' wives," see Bertaux, *Transformations et permanence de l'artisanat boulanger en France*, vol. 2, 194ff.

25 *Le Boulanger-Pâtissier*, July 1954; *Les Nouvelles de la Boulangerie-Pâtisserie*, July 1, 1996, January 1, 1998, January 15, 1999, January 1, 2001; *La Filière Gourmande*, December 1996; *Les Nouvelles de la Boulangerie*, April 15, 1988, January 1, 1989, May 15, 1990; *La Boulangerie Française*, September 1999. In the 1950s, there was a frankness in the instructions for welcoming customers that has not survived. In 1955, salespeople were warned to watch out for "differences in the way people were greeted according to their social standing" (*Le Boulanger-Pâtissier*, February 1955).

26 *La Boulangerie Française*, December 2000; *La Filière Gourmande*, May 1995 and March 2001; interviews with M. Portier and F. Lebehot, April and June 2001.

27 M. Lorin in *Toque Magazine*, no. 41 (March 1995); *Les Nouvelles de la Boulangerie*, November 1, 1983; *Recueil des usages concernant les pains de France*, in Jean Buré, *Le pain*, proceedings of the CNERNA colloquium, Paris, November 1977, (Paris: Centre national de la recherche scientifique, 1979), 274–75, 283; Raymond Calvel, "Panification, progrès social et qualité," *Bulletin des Anciens Élèves de l'École de Meunerie*, no. 249 (May–June 1972): 139; Calvel, "Pain, progrès technique et qualité," *Bulletin des Anciens Élèves de l'École de Meunerie*, no. 181 (January–February 1961): 23; session of the Assemblée nationale, published in *Les Nouvelles de la Boulangerie-Pâtisserie*, April 15, 1998.

28 *Les Nouvelles de la Boulangerie*, April 1, 1980; *La Filière Gourmande*, April 1997.

29 *Paris Match*, June 30, 1973.

30 *Toque Magazine*, no. 40 (February 1995), no. 44 (May 1995), no. 96 (March 2000), and no. 97 (April 2000).

31 Kaplan, *Le meilleur pain du monde*; *L'Express*, December 9, 1968; *Les Nouvelles de la Boulangerie*, September 15, 1979; *Le Monde*, September 9, 1979; Bernard Dupaigne, *Le pain* (Paris: La Courtille, 1979), 190, 197.

32 *Les Nouvelles de la Boulangerie*, December 15, 1993; information kindly communicated by Gérard Brochoire of the INBP; *Pâtisserie-Boulangerie: Vie Pratique*, February 1996; session of the Assemblée nationale, April 3, 1998, cited in *Les Nouvelles de la Boulangerie-Pâtisserie*, April 15, 1998.

33 *Les Nouvelles de la Boulangerie-Pâtisserie*, February 1, 1997.

34 Brochure, Syndicat des industries de boulangerie et pâtisserie (SNIBP) and Forbopain, c. 2000.

35 Much of the discussion of industrial breadmaking that follows is based on an interview with Nicole Watelet conducted in June 2001.

36 Direction générale de la concurrence, de la consommation et de la répression des fraudes (DGCCRF), note no. 2000–52, April 2000.

37 See the lyrical attack published in an artisanal newspaper against "Terminocui," an industrial baking apparatus depicted as a robotic cartoon figure: "It claimed to have discovered a new god: money. 'To earn more,' it said, 'I'll work even more. I won't close even one day a week.' A law had just imposed a 35-hour limit. [Terminocui] thumbed its nose at it and worked twice as much" (*Les Nouvelles de la Boulangerie-Pâtisserie*, June 15, 1999). The reproach could be made just as well against many artisans, especially some of the most enterprising.

38 *Le Figaro*, January 3, 1997.

39 *La Filière Gourmande*, January–February 2000; brochure, SNIBP and Forbopain, c. 2000.

40 Hubert Chiron, "Cinquante années de progrès dans la technologie boulangère," *Industries des Céréales*, no. 116 (January–March 2000): 11; Cabut, "Le pain et sa filière," 76; *Les Nouvelles de la Boulangerie*, March 1 and March 15, 1988; *Les Nouvelles de la Boulangerie-Pâtisserie*, January 15, 1995.

41 Interview with Hervé Malineau, May 2001.

42 *Le Monde*, September 24, 1997.

43 *Le Boulanger-Pâtissier*, October 1987; interview with Raymond Calvel, *Michel Montignac Magazine*, no. 1 (May–June 1993): 35.

44 Jérôme Assire, *Le livre du pain* (Paris: Flammarion, 1996), 180; *Le Monde*, September 11, 1998; *La Filière Gourmande*, October 6, 1995.

45 *La Filière Gourmande*, November 2000; interview with Marie-Georges Colombe, on whose account I draw heavily in what follows.

46 *La Filière Gourmande*, November 2000.

47 In the following section, I draw on numerous interviews with Francis Holder

and shorter discussions with his son David and with Arnaud Vignon, Holder's former marketing director; I also benefited from guided visits around the Holder Group's headquarters and from impromptu visits to sites in Paris, Rouen, Dijon, Lyon, and Aix-en-Provence. In addition, I combed published documents, press releases, and advertising brochures (generally of very high quality) directed at consumers and a number of newspaper articles.

48 Mylène Sultan, "Paul, une recette qui croustille," *Le Point*, June 29, 2001.

49 Holder's departure for the army and its impact on his way of conceptualizing the profession recall the case of Guy Boulet, another ambitious and ingenious baker, but at the opposite pole from Holder philosophically; see Boulet, *Boulangers, artisans de demain*.

50 Fully capable of recognizing and taking responsibility for his mistakes, Francis Holder deeply regrets having "demolished" the first Paul, the bakery taken over by his family, instead of keeping it as he found it except for some embellishments and improvements.

51 *Le Carnet de Paul*, no. 2 (April 2001), a handsome and instructive little advertising brochure which would benefit from adding a page about the history of the sector in order to contextualize and highlight the Holder/Paul enterprise.

52 Sultan, "Paul, une recette qui croustille."

53 In 1972, within the Paul enterprise, Holder had already given the name "Saint-Preux" to the first store he opened with a visible baking room. The return of the repressed?

54 See the introductory brochure published in March 2001 titled "Saint-Preux: A New Concept from the Holder Group."

Chapter 5   Bakeries and the State

1 Given that the Maréchal was the son of a baker (in Courcy-la-Tour, Pas-de-Calais), in some sense all bakers were folklorically Pétainist. See *Le Boulanger-Pâtissier*, March 1939. Some bakers betrayed a certain sympathy for "the Poujadist Movement" in the early years; see *La Boulangerie Française*, February 16–28, 1955. But it would be a mistake to stereotype the entire profession, politically or culturally.

2 On these themes, see Steven L. Kaplan, *Le pain, le peuple et le roi: la bataille du libéralisme sous Louis XV* (Paris: Perrin, 1986; this is an abridged version of *Bread, Politics and Political Economy in the Reign of Louis XV*, 2 vols. [The Hague: Martinus Hijhoff, 1976]); Kaplan, *Les ventres de Paris: pouvoir et approvisionnement dans la France d'Ancien Régime* (Paris: Fayard, 1988); Kaplan, *Le meilleur pain du monde: les boulangers de Paris au XVIIIe siècle* (Paris: Fayard, 1996).

3 Necker, letter to Sartine, February 14, 1778, Archives nationales, F11* 1, fol. 258; Nicolas Delamare, *Traité de la police* (Paris: 1705–1738), vol. 2, 566; *Journal de l'Agriculture, du Commerce, des Arts et des Finances* (January 1772), 48; Jacques

Necker, *Sur la législation et le commerce des grains* (Paris: 1775); Bertier de Sauvigny, "Observations sur le commerce des grains," Bibliothèque nationale, French ms. 11347, fol. 228.

4 Archives nationales, Y 10589, May 4 and May 9, 1775; Journal de Hardy, Bibliothèque nationale, French ms. 6682, 64 (May 6, 1775); George Rudé, "The Bread Riot of May 1775 in Paris and the Paris Region," in Jeffry Kaplow, ed., *New Perspectives on the French Revolution* (New York: Wiley, 1965), 198.

5 Kaplan, *Le Pain*, 263–90.

6 Comte de Saint-Priest, *Mémoires, la Révolution et l'émigration*, ed. Baron de Barante (Paris: Calmann-Lévy, 1929), vol. 2, 15; Voltaire, *Diatribe à l'auteur des "Éphémérides,"* May 1775, in *Œuvres complètes de Voltaire*, ed. L. Moland (Paris: Garnier Frères, 1878), vol. 29, 368.

7 "Manœuvre faite par les Srs Leleu et Cie," fall 1789, Archives nationales, Y 10506. Commenting on the well-known prayer "Give us this day our daily bread," Luther remarked that the coat of arms of a pious sovereign ought to display a loaf of bread rather than a lion or a crown. The Catholics did not have a monopoly on the social contract. See Jean Delumeau, *La peur en Occident, XIVe–XVIIIe* (Paris: Fayard, 1924), 123–30.

8 For the preceding discussion, see Kaplan, *Le meilleur pain du monde*, 490–507.

9 For the treatment of price controls, see ibid., 521–31.

10 See the insightful and well-written master's thesis by Nicolas Martin, "Les boulangers parisiens de 1801 à 1830: étude sur la condition sociale d'une profession 'non commerçante,'" Université de Paris-I, June 2001. See also the liberal reading in François Malepeyre and J.-S.-E. Julia de Fontenelle, *Nouveau manuel complet du boulanger*, ed. Schield-Treherne (Paris: L. Mulo, 1914), 11–16; Ambroise Morel, *Histoire abrégée de la boulangerie en France* (Paris: Syndicat patronal de la boulangerie de Paris, 1924), 112–33; André Join-Lambert, *L'organisation de la boulangerie en France* (Paris: A. Rousseau, 1900), 42–130; Marcel Arpin, *Historique de la meunerie et de la boulangerie, depuis les temps préhistoriques jusqu'à l'année 1914*, 2 vols. (Paris: Le Chancelier, 1948), vol. 2, 123–30.

11 Morel, *Histoire abrégée de la boulangerie en France*, 137; Martin, "Les boulangers parisiens de 1801 à 1830," chap. 2.

12 *L'ami de la boulangerie*, January 15, 1957.

13 *Enquête sur la boulangerie du département de la Seine*, 1859, 532; Gringoire, session held April 22, 1958, in CNERNA, *La qualité du pain*, Journées scientifiques du CNERNA, November 1954–April 1960 (Paris: Centre national de la recherche scientifique, 1962); Guy Boulet, *Boulangers, artisans de demain: l'hypothétique mariage de la tradition et du progrès* (Rouen: L'Harmattan, 1991), 111; *Les Nouvelles de la Boulangerie*, April 1, 1980.

14 Boulet, *Boulangers, artisans de demain*, 116; *Les Nouvelles de la Boulangerie*, August 1 and August 15, 1976.

15 Hubert Chiron, "1949/1993: incidences des mutations technologiques sur les caractéristiques du pain français," *Industries des Céréales*, April–June 1994, 9; *Les Nouvelles de la Boulangerie*, January 1 and February 1, 1984. See also the editorial by Jacques Mabille, president of the Paris area Chamber of Bakers, in *La Boulangerie Française*, December 2000.

16 *Les Nouvelles de la Boulangerie*, August 12, 1978; *Le Boulanger-Pâtissier*, September 1978.

17 *Les Nouvelles de la Boulangerie*, March 15 and 1 September, 1979.

18 Ibid., September 1, 1979.

19 Ibid., October 15 and November 1, 1979.

20 Ibid., November 15, 1979, December 1, 1979, and January 1, 1980.

21 Ibid., July 15, 1980.

22 *Les Nouvelles de la Boulangerie*, January 1 and January 15, 1981; Boulet, *Boulangers, artisans de demain*, 120. From then on, the confederation newspaper regularly published a "cost price calculation" in its technical dossiers, as part of the effort to reeducate bakers in free market practices.

23 *Les Nouvelles de la Boulangerie*, October 15, 1981.

24 Ibid., January 1, 1987; see also Jean Cabut, "Le pain et sa filière," report to the Conseil économique et social, November 1988, 48.

25 *Les Nouvelles de la Boulangerie*, March 15, 1987; *Le Levain Syndical*, September 1987.

26 Boulet, *Boulangers, artisans de demain*, 111–13, 142–43.

27 *Les Nouvelles de la Boulangerie*, July 15, 1976, September 1, 1976, and May 2, 1977.

28 *La Vie Française*, December 10, 1979; *Toque Magazine*, no. 44 (June 1995); Isabelle Azais, interviewed in *Pâtissier-Boulanger: Vie Pratique*, October 1996.

29 Between two Banette makers in the thirteenth arrondissement in Paris, each producing a good-quality bread in the French tradition, prices differed in early October 2001 by 20 percent.

30 *Les Nouvelles de la Boulangerie*, October 15, 1987; *Les Nouvelles de la Boulangerie-Pâtisserie*, July 1, 1996.

31 *Les Nouvelles de la Boulangerie*, July 1, 1988, January 1, 1990, July 1, 1990, and January 1, 1991; *Pâtissier-Boulanger: Vie Pratique*, March 21, 1991.

32 *Pâtissier-Boulanger: Vie Pratique*, March 21, 1991; Bernard Godon et al., "Définitions des produits de panification," *Industries Agricoles et Alimentaires*, September 1987, 817–18.

33 Working document, project dating from November 1985, DGCCRF.

34 Working document, project dating from late 1985 to early 1986, DGCCRF.

35 Working documents, projects dating from January 1986, April 1986, February 3, 1987, and undated (between February 1987 and July 1988), DGCCRF.

36 Working documents, projects dating from summer 1988 and fall 1989, DGCCRF.

37 Working document, project dating from August 21, 1990, DGCCRF.

38 *Journal Officiel*, May 27, 1991; interview with Guy Boulet, May 2001.

39 *Nouvelles de la Boulangerie-Pâtisserie*, March 1, 1995.

40 Roland Guinet, *Technologie du pain français* (Paris: Éditions B.P.I., 1992), 33–38.

41 See the internal analysis of a major field study undertaken by the DGCCRF in 1999–2000: "In practice, there seems to be virtually no 'sourdough house bread' or 'sourdough bread in the French tradition'; this is because the criterion for endogenous acetic acidity is a demanding criterion corresponding more to textbook conditions for breadmaking (a very long fermentation period) than to the actual conditions of production" (DGCCRF, note no. 2000–52, April 5, 2000).

42 *Les Nouvelles de la Boulangerie*, December 15, 1993, January 1, 1994.

43 Philippe Viron, letter to Raymond Calvel, May 20, 1996, and Calvel, letter to Claude Willm, July 22, 1996 (Viron correspondence); interview with Guy Boulet, May 2001; *Le parisien*, August 24, 1993; *La Boulangerie Française*, October 1, 1993.

44 DGCCRF, note no. 2000–52, April 25, 2000.

45 *Les Nouvelles de la Boulangerie*, December 1, 1993.

46 DGCCRF, note no. 2000–52, April 25, 2000.

47 Ibid.

48 Ibid.

49 Interview with Philippe Richard, June 2001. Richard kindly put me in touch with Gilles Morini of the DGCCRF, a discreet but extremely welcoming individual to whom I owe much valuable information.

50 "Les aspects sociaux et humains dans le cadre de l'aménagement du territoire," *Les Nouvelles de la Boulangerie-Pâtisserie*, June 15, 1995.

51 On the reasoning according to which quality requires fair competition, see, for example, *La Boulangerie Française*, June 15, 1995.

52 *Les Nouvelles de la Boulangerie-Pâtisserie*, May 15 and June 15, 1995; *La Boulangerie Française*, May 15, 1995.

53 *La Boulangerie Française*, June 15, 1995; *La Filière Gourmande*, August–September 1995; *Les Nouvelles de la Boulangerie-Pâtisserie*, June 15, 1995.

54 *Le Figaro*, September 27, 1995; *Les Nouvelles de la Boulangerie-Pâtisserie*, October 1, 1995, October 15, 1995, and April 15, 1998 (with reference to the parliamentary session evoking the Galland law).

55 *Le Monde*, January 3 and May 16, 1997; *Le Parisien*, January 31, 1997; *Les Nouvelles de la Boulangerie-Pâtisserie*, December 15, 1995, February 15, 1998.

56 *Les Nouvelles de la Boulangerie-Pâtisserie*, October 1 and October 15, 1995, May 2 and July 1, 1996, and June 1, 1998; *La Boulangerie Française*, May 1996; *Le Figaro*, September 27, 1995.

57 *Les Nouvelles de la Boulangerie-Pâtisserie*, March 15 and May 2, 1996; *La Boulangerie Française*, May 1996.

58 *Les Nouvelles de la Boulangerie-Pâtisserie*, May 2, 1996, June 1, 1998; *La Boulangerie Française*, May 1996.

59 *Les Nouvelles de la Boulangerie-Pâtisserie*, May 2, 1997; *La Boulangerie Française*, June 1996, May 1998, May and June 1999.

60 *Pâtisserie-Boulangerie: Vie Pratique*, February 1997; *La Tribune Desfossés*, January 22, 1997; *Les Nouvelles de la Boulangerie-Pâtisserie*, February 15, 1998 (citing the Conseil d'État: "Considering that no legislative disposition nor any regulatory disposition established in application of a law . . . has authorized the said minister to regulate, as he has done, the conditions under which the baking trade operates, and in particular the label 'bakery' and its use on signs . . .").

61 *Les Nouvelles de la Boulangerie-Pâtisserie*, February 1, February 15, March 1, March 15, and April 15, 1998; *La Boulangerie Française*, March and April 1998; *Le Figaro*, February 7, 1998.

62 *Les Nouvelles de la Boulangerie-Pâtisserie*, March 15, April 15, and June 1, 1998; *La Boulangerie Française*, March, April, May, June, and July 1998. The fate of laws is often quite curious. Concerning the regulation of entrance into the profession (and the purging of aspirants "without quality," as one category was characterized in the eighteenth century), a February 1988 decree had already required a diploma or proof of six years, not just three, of professional experience "for any matriculation into the repertory of trades." This measure, praised by Jean Paquet, obviously did not have the impact Paquet was counting on. See *Les Nouvelles de la Boulangerie*, February 15, 1988.

63 Session of the Assemblée nationale held April 3, 1998, reported in *Les Nouvelles de la Boulangerie-Pâtisserie*, April 15, 1998.

64 *Pâtisserie-Boulangerie: Vie Pratique*, February 1997; DGCCRF, note no. 2000–52, April 5, 2000.

65 On this point, the DGCCRF doctrine is intransigeant: "Thus, as soon as an establishment has a single frozen loaf or bread, it cannot keep either the label 'baker' or the commercial designation 'bakery,' or any name capable of leading to confusion" (DGCCRF, note no. 2000–52, April 5, 2000).

66 Ibid.

67 *Les Nouvelles de la Boulangerie-Pâtisserie*, October 15 and November 15, 2001; see also the fine text by Caroline Delabroy in *Le Nouvel Observateur: Le Journal Permanent* (online), November 27, 2001.

68 *Les Nouvelles de la Boulangerie-Pâtisserie*, April 1 and May 15, 2001; *Toque Magazine*, no. 111 (September 2001).

Chapter 6   Millers and Bakers

1 Steven L. Kaplan, *Les ventres de Paris: pouvoir et approvisionnement dans la France d'Ancien Régime* (Paris: Fayard, 1988), 232–39.

2 Ibid., 218–32, 239–45; *Enquête sur la boulangerie du département de la Seine* (Paris: Imprimerie impériale, 1859), 33, 35, 70, 140, 154, 156, 265–66, 544, 641, 789. Cf.

the suggestion that, by focusing too much on merchandising and finance, the miller forgot to concentrate on quality: "The master miller is too much the great lord; he devotes all his time to his purchases and his sales, to his speculations and his stakes; he is rarely at the mill. He knows that he will be able to impose his products, whatever they may be" (*Enquête sur la boulangerie du département de la Seine*, 71).

3 André Join-Lambert, *L'organisation de la boulangerie en France* (Paris: A. Rousseau, 1990), 114–16; Bernadette Angeraud, *Les boulangers lyonnais aux XIXe et XXe siècles* (Paris: Éditions Christian, 1998), 49–54.

4 Kaplan, *Les ventres de Paris*, 181–96; Moulins Soufflet-Pantin, "Enquête qualité, récolte 2000" (this is an in-house publication for technical and commercial use).

5 On the subject of the millers' anxiety, see the remarks of J. Mouchard, president of the French national miller's association, about the imperative of giving the bakery trade, especially its artisanal branch, "the possibility of making a good bread" (*Nouvelles de la Boulangerie*, January 1, 1984).

6 On the cultural and technological confrontation between science and skill, learned culture and popular culture, see Steven L. Kaplan, *Le meilleur pain du monde: les boulangers de Paris au XVIIIe siècle* (Paris: Fayard, 1996), 77–82.

7 *La Boulangerie Française*, no. 213 (April 2000) and no. 221 (December 2000): 13; *La Filière Gourmande*, August–September 2000.

8 *La Boulangerie Française*, no. 221 (December 2000).

9 F. Maurey (Chars-Banette) in *Le Boulanger-Pâtissier*, January 1986; *La Filière Gourmande*, August–September 2000.

10 To profit from their "proximity" to the artisans ("in most cases they do not use salesmen, there is a direct relationship . . . Human relations, based on mutual trust"), the small and medium-size mills have resurrected a "national committee" charged with promoting its special interests, which "generally coincide with those of the artisanal bakers" (*Les Nouvelles de la Boulangerie-Pâtisserie*, February 15, 2001).

11 *La Boulangerie Française*, February 16–28, 1955; *Les Nouvelles de la Boulangerie*, October 15, 1985.

12 *Le Levain Syndical*, March 1987; *Les Nouvelles de la Boulangerie*, December 15, 1992.

13 *La Boulangerie Française*, no. 198 (January 1999); *Les Nouvelles de la Boulangerie-Pâtisserie*, November 1, 1998, and March 1, 2001. Cf. the testimony of J.-P. Loques, a baker from the fifteenth arrondissement in Paris: "As for him, while it is good to cultivate excellent relationships with the miller-suppliers, he insists that these are allies and not masters." Like Crouzet, he fears an irreversible seizure of control: "If the millers control the bakers, the profession risks becoming a disguised franchise, and the selling price of shops will suffer" (*Les Nouvelles de la Boulangerie-Pâtisserie*, November 1, 1997).

14 Interview with Jean-Pierre Crouzet, June 2001; *Les Nouvelles de la Boulangerie-Pâtisserie*, January 1, 1998. Jacques Mabille, as president of the Paris area chamber

of bakers, rightly notes that the franchise image is turning against Banette. The group "has done such a good public relations job that the consumers in general forget that they are dealing with independent artisans" (interview, March 2001). With its growth slowing down, Banette will be compelled to move in the direction of franchising, according to Crouzet (interview, June 2001).

15 *L'Ami de la Boulangerie*, February 1, 1961; *L'Express*, March 24, 1969; *La Tribune de l'Économie*, February 25, 1986; *Toque Magazine*, no. 27 (December 1993).

16 *Les Nouvelles de la Boulangerie-Pâtisserie*, September 15 and November 15, 1998, May 15 and December 15, 2000.

17 *Les Échos*, November 1999.

18 *La Filière Gourmande*, September 1, 1999, and August–September 2000; *Les Échos*, November 1999.

19 Interview with Bernard Seller, April 2001; *Le Boulanger-Pâtissier*, June 1983 and October 1988.

20 Interview with Bernard Seller, April 2001; *Le Boulanger-Pâtissier*, October 1988.

21 On Storione's very tight control over his bakeries and the emergence of competition launched by the Grands Moulins Maurel, see *La Filière Gourmande*, March 1993.

22 The advertising offered in multiple forms, including fliers available to customers in the shop, reads as follows: "The Banette will appeal to lovers of real bread who want to rediscover the natural aroma of the bread of yesteryear. Banette: to find happiness again every day."

23 Raymond Calvel, "Pain, progrès technique et qualité," *Bulletin des Anciens Élèves de l'École Française de Meunerie*, no. 181 (January–February 1961): 21; Calvel, "L'évolution de la qualité du pain," *Bulletin des Anciens Élèves de l'École Française de Meunerie*, no. 268 (July–August 1975): 202 (here Calvel includes himself among those who had been emphasizing the harmful effects of fava flour "for a long time" without ignoring its positive aspects). While fava flour made the baker's task easier by making the dough more elastic, for a long time its use was viewed as fraudulent, a falsification. See E. Favrais, *Manuel du boulanger et de pâtisserie-boulangerie* (Paris: B. Tignol, 1904), 27. On the Banette method, see also *Le Boulanger-Pâtissier*, October 1988.

24 Banette counted on television to present the "1900" to fifteen million potential consumers simultaneously (*La Boulangerie Française*, no. 220 [November 2000]).

25 Interview with Tony and Florence Lebehot, June 2001.

26 Kaplan, *Le meilleur pain du monde*, 17–18, based on an interview with Michel Philippe in 1995 and another in April 2001.

27 The Banette school receives more than 750 bakers a year for a number of different types of internships, including "stores" and "sales" for their spouses. See, for example, *Pâtisserie-Boulangerie: Vie Pratique*, December 7, 1990.

28 On the "franchise" label that has stuck to the Banette system, see *La Tribune*

de l'Économie, February 25, 1986, and *Pâtisserie-Boulangerie: Vie Pratique*, February 1992.

29 See the exquisitely obscure announcement of this realignment in a press release of April 5, 2001, and the discussion in *Toque Magazine*, no. 109 (October 1002).

30 The expression comes from Jean Dutourd, one of the forty "immortals" in the French Academy, in his preface to Philippe Viron, *Vive la baguette* (Le Chesnay: L'Épi gourmand, 1995), 6.

31 Ibid., 7.

32 See *L'Impatient*, no. 185 (April 1993).

33 Interview with Marcel Cocaud and Mireille Peyrac, the very effective secretary general of the Meuniers de France, April 2001; *La Filière Gourmande*, October 1994; *La Boulangerie Française*, no. 221 (December 2000); *Pâtisserie-Boulangerie: Vie Pratique*, November 21–December 4, 1991. On Cocaud as a scientist, see "Caractéristiques d'une bonne pâte, d'un bon pain, défauts des pâtes et des pains," *Techniques des Industries Céréalières*, no. 163 (January 1978).

34 Interview with Jean Hautecoeur, March 2001.

35 Interview with Jean-Paul Barré; interview with B. Chatillon, *Pâtisserie-Boulangerie: Vie Pratique*, July 20, 1989; *Pâtisserie-Boulangerie: Vie Pratique*, May 17, 1990; interview with M. Crignon, *Pâtisserie-Boulangerie: Vie Pratique*, April 1995.

36 Interview with J. Gantois, April 2001.

37 *Pâtisserie-Boulangerie: Vie Pratique*, November 2–15, 1989, November 3, 1991, February 1992; *Les Nouvelles de la Boulangerie*, June 15, 1990, October 15, 1992; *Toque Magazine*, no. 5 (November 1991); *La Boulangerie Française*, December 1, 1992; *1900–2000: l'histoire du groupe Soufflet* (Paris: Groupe Soufflet et Cliomédi, 2000), 60–61.

38 Interview with Dominique Malézieux, June 2001; *1900–2000*, 62–63.

39 Interview with Dominique Malézieux, June 2001; interview with J.-M. Soufflot, *La Filière Gourmande*, August–September 2000; interview with B. Chatillon, *Les Nouvelles de la Boulangerie-Pâtisserie*, October 10, 1996; *La Boulangerie Française*, March and December 1997; "Baguépi, une gamme, un concept, des services," Baguépi advertising brochure.

40 Interview with Christian Hubert, June 2001; "Sur les traces de la Baguépi tradition," Baguépi brochure; "Régulateurs de panification," "Mélior plus brochure"; *Le Baguépi*, newsletter for the artisanal baker–clients of Moulins Soufflet Pantin.

Chapter 7   Rue Monge Rivals and Other Mavericks

1 See Jacques Hillairet, *Dictionnaire historique des rues de Paris*, 7th ed. (Paris: Minuit, 1963), vol. 1, 107–8, 353–55, and vol. 2, 134–35; Steven L. Kaplan, *Le meilleur pain du monde: les boulangers de Paris au XVIIIe siècle* (Paris: Fayard, 1996).

2 Kaplan, *Le meilleur pain du monde*, 455.

3 For this paragraph and those that follow, see ibid., 305–10.

4 *Un livre, un métier: la boulangerie* (La Ferté-Saint-Aubin: L'Archer, 1998), 40. Here are some before-tax prices for equipping a baking room in 1995: kneading machine, 56,000 francs ($11,237); divider, 30,000 francs ($6,020); shaper, 25,000 francs ($5,017); fermenting chamber, 50,000 francs ($10,033) (ibid., 88).

5 Steven L. Kaplan, *Les ventres de Paris: pouvoir et approvisionnement dans la France d'Ancien Régime* (Paris: Fayard, 1988).

6 Kaplan, *Le meilleur pain du monde*, 224–27, 236–38.

7 What follows is derived from a number of interviews that Éric Kayser kindly granted me.

8 Jacques-Louis Ménétra, *Journal de ma vie*, ed. Daniel Roche (Paris: Montalba, 1982). On the journeymen's associations, see Cynthia M. Truant, *The Rites of Labor: Brotherhoods of Compagnonnage in Old and New Regime France* (Ithaca: Cornell University Press, 1994).

9 What follows comes from a number of interviews that Dominique Saibron kindly granted me.

10 See *Pâtisserie-Boulangerie: Vie Pratique*, no. 31 (March 21–April 3, 1991).

11 On Saibron's role as creator and instructor with Carrefour, in pastry as well as bread, see Carrefour's internal newsletter, *Positif*, no. 63 (December 1998).

12 I owe what follows to the interview that Thierry Rabineau kindly granted me in April 2001.

13 Kamir's remark is cited in Paul Rambali, *Boulangerie: The Craft and Culture of Baking* (New York: Macmillan, 1994), 107–8; Rambali's mass-market book is full of charm but also full of rudimentary errors about French breadmaking.

14 I owe what follows to the interview that Hervé Malineau kindly granted me in May 2001.

15 I thank Frédéric Lalos and Pierre-Marie Gagneux for the interview they kindly granted me in May 2001 and on which I rely for what follows.

16 I owe what follows to the interview that Philippe Gosselin kindly granted me in May 2001.

17 Peter Reinhart, one of the leaders of the artisanal baking movement in the United States (yes, there is one!), asserts that Gosselin's baguette is the best he has ever tasted (previously, his Oscar for the best bread had gone to Raymond Calvel, whom he describes as "the chemist" of the process of dough fermentation). Gosselin's secret, according to Reinhart (but about which the artisan has never said a word to me) is the use of ice water during autolysis, which takes place in the refrigerator overnight (see Peter Reinhart, *The Bread Baker's Apprentice: Mastering the Art of Extraordinary Bread* [Berkeley, Calif.: Ten Speed Press, 2001], 20–21; see also page 192, where the author contradicts himself concerning the recipe, here adding yeast and salt in the autolysis during the nocturnal rest period).

18 Kaplan, *Le meilleur pain du monde*, 188–90.

19 The information that follows was provided during the cordial interview I had with Jean-Noël Julien.

20 On this legendary figure of Parisian breadmaking, see *Les Nouvelles de la Boulangerie-Pâtisserie*, December 1, 1996; *La Boulangerie Française*, February 1997; *Pâtisserie-Boulangerie: Vie Pratique*, February 1997.

21 I thank Paul and Chantal L'Hermine for their willingness to share their stories with me during several interviews in Paris and in Rennes.

22 For this discussion, I rely as much on several fascinating interviews I had with Guy Boulet as on his book.

23 Guy Boulet, *Boulangers, artisans de demain: l'hypothétique mariage de la tradition et du progrès* (Rouen: INBP, L'Harmattan, 1991), 100.

24 Ibid., 102.

25 Ibid., 103.

26 Ibid., 109, 113; see also 104–5.

27 Boulet, *Boulangers, artisans de demain*, 126.

28 Ibid., 147; see also 134.

Conclusion

1 *Les Nouvelles de la Boulangerie-Pâtisserie*, March 15, 2002.

2 Nicolas Baudeau, *Avis au peuple sur son premier besoin* (Amsterdam: F.-A. Didot aîné, 1774), third treatise, 134–136; César Bucquet, *Mémoire*, March 2, 1769, Archives départementales de l'Isère, series C47; Bucquet, *Observations intéressantes et amusantes du Sieur César Bucquet* (Paris, 1783), 64; "Réponse au Sieur Bucquet," c. 1768, Bibliothèque de l'Arsenal, ms. 7458; Edme Béguillet, *Traité de la connoissance générale des grains et de la mouture par économie* (Dijon: L.-N. Frantin, 1775–1778), 71; Antoine-Augustin Parmentier, *Mémoire sur les avantages que la province de Languedoc peut retirer de ses grains* (Paris, 1787), 400; Archives nationales, X 2B 1307, December 7, 1751.

3 For bread in the French tradition to succeed, it will have to expand its market. Thus we need to encourage bakers to maintain reasonable prices. Those who ask more than €1.00 ($1.25) (and some go as high as €1.40 [$1.75]) must not be surprised to be shunned by consumers.

4 On the INBP's recruitment of candidates with the baccalaureate degree, see "Ces CAP qui valent de l'or," *Le Nouvel Observateur*, March 7–13, 2002.

Glossary

adjuvant: A euphemism for additive, referring to any natural or synthetic substance (coloring, emulsifier, stabilizer, preservative, taste enhancer, vitamin, etc.) added to the ingredients during breadmaking in order to facilitate the work, to reinforce or preserve certain physiochemical or organoleptic attributes of the bread, and/or to improve its presentation or keeping quality. Cf. "ameliorant" and "technological auxiliary."

alveolated, alveoli: During baking, the gluten in dough coagulates, trapping air and carbonic dioxide, while grains of starch are swelling, bursting, and hardening, forming the crumb. By rising at the same time as it takes on solid form, the dough transmuted into bread definitively retains the alveolated structure — marked by uneven cavities engraved in the crumb, visible traces of the fermentation process — that it has been given by the pressure of carbon dioxide.

ameliorant: An additive intended to improve bread quality (see "adjuvant").

apprêt: The second fermentation before the dough is baked; it gives the bread its volume. The time needed for the *apprêt* depends on the temperature, the amount of yeast used, the kneading method, and the length of the *pointage*, or first fermentation.

autolysis: The mixing of water and flour, following by a more or less prolonged rest period, during which the glutenic structure of the dough is formed and the plastic qualities of the dough take shape. Many bakers believe that the aromas that will condition the bread's flavor begin to develop during this process.

baguette: The "classic" French loaf, elongated, slender and quintessentially crusty.

baking room (*fournil*): The place where the baker does his work; literally, the place where the oven is located.

bâtard: A loaf shorter and stockier than a *baguette*, with a more pronounced crumb, made from medium-density dough.

CAP: The *Certificat d'aptitude professionelle* (Certificate of Professional Aptitude) is the basic diploma in the breadbaking trade. Students are trained for the competitive examination in a specialized school or in a *Centre de formation d'apprentis* (Training Center for Apprentices) where they alternate between classroom study and internships with a master baker. Independent candidates may also take the examination. In order to set up one's own bakery, one must have earned the CAP or an equivalent or higher degree, or have three years of experience working in the profession.

CNERNA: The *Centre national de coordination des études et des recherches sur la nutrition et l'alimentation* (National Center for Coordination of Studies and Research on Food and Nutrition) is a board of experts established by the French government shortly after World War II to carry out an in-depth study of the state of the wheat-flour-bread network, which had been severely stressed starting in 1940 and was still in crisis ten years later. The scientific goal was to come up with objective measures of quality — a rather diffuse notion — in all the sectors and all the phases of bread production. The political goal was above all to reassure the French about the quality of the food — bread — that the government defined at the time as the nutritional staple for the overall population.

crumb (*mie*) : The center of a loaf of bread, covered and protected by the crust, is known as the crumb.

DGCCRF: The *Direction générale de la concurrence, de la consommation et de la répression des fraudes* (General Office Governing Competition, Consumption, and the Repression of Fraud) is a government agency best known at the departmental level for its efforts to eliminate fraudulent or illegal sales practices in the realms of hygiene and sanitation, product labeling, and pricing. At the national level, the agency (a branch of the Ministry of the Economy and Finance) plays an important role in the articulation of professional standards.

GMP: The *Grands Moulins de Paris* (Great Mills of Paris), once a family enterprise and currently owned by in-house investors, is one of the largest milling establishments in France.

INBP: The *Institut national de la Boulangerie-Pâtisserie* (National Bread and Pastry Institute) was created and established in Rouen by the *Confédération nationale de la Boulangerie et Boulangerie-Pâtisserie française* (French National Bakers' and Pastry-Makers' Confederation). It supports research, development, and training at all levels; its activities include preparing pedagogical materials, training in commercial establishments, testing raw materials and equipment, and publishing research results and other information related to the industry.

journeyman (*compagnon*): Under the Old Regime, someone who had completed a three-year apprenticeship under a master baker could be hired as a journeyman, or salaried worker, in a baking room. A journeyman had to work three to six years before he could be a candidate for certification as a master baker.

leaven (*levain*): Leaven is a culture made of flour, water, and wild yeasts and bacteria present in the raw materials themselves or in the air in the baking room. In ultra-traditional breadmaking, which relies solely on leaven (also known as sourdough), a certain amount of leaven from one batch of dough is set aside and "refreshed" — its yeasts and bacteria are revitalized through the addition of flour and water — for use as the starter for the subsequent batch.

leavening, leavening agent: Initially reserved for leaven in the strict sense (see "leaven"), the term can refer to any mixture including a form of yeast that causes the dough to ferment.

MOF: The designation "Meilleur Ouvrier de France" (MOF) is a prestigious title awarded through a competitive national examination that requires several years of preparation.

organoleptic: The term "organoleptic" refers to the sensory qualities that the consumer is in theory capable of perceiving directly through sight, hearing, touch, smell, and taste.

pâton: A *pâton* is an unbaked loaf that has been shaped and is ready to be put in the oven.

pointage: The *pointage*, or first fermentation, is generally begun in bulk after the dough has been kneaded. It is *the* crucial stage for the physical and sensorial development of the dough. It imparts strength to the dough and generates the aromas and the tastes that will permeate the bread. The quasi-suppression of *pointage* during the twentieth century by many French bakers seriously compromised the quality of their product.

poolish: The breadmaking method known as *poolish* was probably developed by Polish bakers and improved by Viennese bakers in the nineteenth century; it was commonly used in France before World War I. It is based on a culture consisting of equal parts flour and water seeded with a dose of baker's yeast and left to ferment for three to eight hours.

sourdough: Sometimes used as a synonym for leaven, the term also refers to the finished product, i.e., a loaf of bread made from leaven.

starter: The leaven that is reserved from one batch and refreshed to become the leavening agent of the next is called a starter.

terminal, bake-off terminal: A terminal or bake-off terminal is an industrial outlet that sells bread made elsewhere and shipped in the form of frozen or partially baked loaves for heating up or finishing on the premises.

type of flour (55, 75, etc.) : Flour types are technically classified in terms of ash content, but the numbers also correlate roughly with the percentage of flour extracted from a given quantity of wheat. Thus type 55 (T 55) flour is relatively white, with a rate of extraction between 75 and 80 percent; T 65 is darker, with a rate of 80 to 85 percent.

white bread: Historically, the white loaf signifies purity, goodness, and social distinction, and is the bread that the vast majority of French society dreams of consuming on a daily basis. During World War II the only bread available to the ordinary citizen in France was a heavy, coarse, and sticky dark bread (*pain bis*) of dubious quality and thoroughly unappetizing. The resultant nostalgia for white wheat bread led to the development, after the war, of a new method that produced a voluminous and very white bread, light and attractive but "washed out," "denatured," and essentially tasteless. This is for all practical purposes the bread that most French people continue to eat today.

Index

Steven Laurence Kaplan is the Goldwin Smith Professor of
European History at Cornell University. He is the author of
several books, including *The Bakers of Paris and the Bread
Question, 1700–1775* (Duke, 1996); *Farewell, Revolution: France,
1789–1989* (1995); *Provisioning France: Merchants and Millers in the
Grain and Flour Trade during the Eighteenth Century* (1984); and
Bread, Politics, and Political Economy in the Reign of Louis XV
(1976). He is coeditor (with Cynthia J. Koepp) of *Work in
France: Representations, Meaning, Organization, and Practice*
(1986) and (with Dominick LaCapra) of *Modern European
Intellectual History: Reappraisals and New Perspectives* (1982),
and the editor of *Understanding Popular Culture: Europe from
the Middle Ages to the Nineteenth Century* (1984).

Library of Congress Cataloging-in-Publication Data
Kaplan, Steven L.
[Retour du Bon Pain. English]
Good bread is back : a contemporary history of French
bread, the way it is made, and the people who make it /
Steven Laurence Kaplan ; Translated by Catherine Porter.
p. cm.
Includes bibliographical references and index.
ISBN-13: 978-0-8223-3833-8 (cloth : alk. paper)
ISBN-10: 0-8223-3833-5 (cloth : alk. paper)
1. Bread—France. I. Title.
TX769.K28713 2006
641.8'150944—dc22   2006012769